THE CROSSOVER NOVEL

THE CROSSOVER NOVEL

Contemporary Children's Fiction and Its Adult Readership

RACHEL FALCONER

Routledge
Taylor & Francis Group
NEW YORK AND LONDON

First published 2009
by Routledge
270 Madison Ave, New York, NY 10016

Simultaneously published in the UK
by Routledge
2 Park Square, Milton Park, Abingdon, Oxon OX14 4RN

Routledge is an imprint of the Taylor & Francis Group, an informa business

© 2009 Taylor & Francis

Typeset in Minion by IBT Global.
Printed and bound in the United States of America on acid-free paper by IBT Global.

Library of Congress Cataloging in Publication Data
Falconer, Rachel.
   The crossover novel : contemporary children's fiction and its adult readership / by
Rachel Falconer.
      p. cm.—(Children's literature and culture ; 57)
   Includes bibliographical references and index.
   1. Children's stories, English—History and criticism.   2. English fiction—21st
century—History and criticism.   3. Children—Books and reading—Great Britain—History—21st century.   4. Books and reading—Great Britain—History—
21st century.   5. Reading interests—Great Britain.   I. Title.
   PR481.F35 2008
   823'.914099282—dc22
   2008009225

ISBN10: 0-415-97888-2 (hbk)
ISBN10: 0-203-89217-8 (ebk)

ISBN13: 978-0-415-97888-0 (hbk)
ISBN13: 978-0-203-89217-6 (ebk)

For my mother
Charlotte Elisabeth Ann Falconer

With a tale forsooth he cometh unto you, with a tale which holdeth children from play, and old men from the chimney corner.

(Sir Philip Sidney, *A Defence of Poetry*, 1595)

Contents

Series Editor's Foreword

Dedicated to furthering original research in children's literature and culture, the Children's Literature and Culture series includes monographs on individual authors and illustrators, historical examinations of different periods, literary analyses of genres, and comparative studies on literature and the mass media. The series is international in scope and is intended to encourage innovative research in children's literature with a focus on interdisciplinary methodology.

Children's literature and culture are understood in the broadest sense of the term 'children' to encompass the period of childhood up through adolescence. Owing to the fact that the notion of childhood has changed so much since the origination of children's literature, this Routledge series is particularly concerned with transformations in children's culture and how they have affected the representation and socialization of children. While the emphasis of the series is on children's literature, all types of studies that deal with children's radio, film, television, and art are included in an endeavor to grasp the aesthetics and values of children's culture. Not only have there been momentous changes in children's culture in the last fifty years, but there have been radical shifts in the scholarship that deals with these changes. In this regard, the goal of the Children's Literature and Culture series is to enhance research in this field and, at the same time, point to new directions that bring together the best scholarly work throughout the world.

Jack Zipes

Acknowledgments

In writing this book, I had the help and advice of many kind and generous people. Special thanks are due to the following:

The helpful team at Routledge who steered the manuscript through to publication, especially the editor of this series, Jack Zipes.

The University of Sheffield which awarded me a grant to develop the Kiddult Fiction project in 2002, in collaboration with local schools. I would particularly like to thank Steve Collier, Paul Wigfield, Gabi Diercks-O'Brien and Claire Allam of the Learning Development and Media Unit, for their help in developing the project. Results of the project can be viewed at http://www.shef.ac.uk/english/modules/lit210/kiddult/

The M. C. Escher Company—Holland, for permission to reproduce M. C. Escher's 'Three Worlds' on the cover of this study. All rights reserved. *www.mcescher.com*

Springer Education for permission to reuse material from an article on Geraldine McCaughrean's *The White Darkness*, first published in *Children's Literature in Education* 38:1, March 2007: 35–44.

For kind permission to quote from unpublished interviews about crossover fiction: Colin Brabazon of North Lincolnshire Libraries and Chair of Judges for the 2003 Carnegie Medal Award; David Fickling and his assistant, Tiffany Burgess, of Fickling Books; Liz Cross of Oxford University Press; Rebecca McNally of Puffin Books; and Richard Welsh of *Rhyme and Reason Children's Books*, Sheffield.

Richard Knight of Nielsen BookScan, for voluntarily providing sales figures for a selection of the editions of texts discussed in this study.

Martin Hill for granting me access to the excellent *Kids' Review* [http://www.kidsreview.org.uk], which features 'book reviews by children for children.'

The learned contributors to the children's-literature-UK discussion board, with special thanks to Philip Pullman for giving me permission to quote from his postings about 'sprite narration.'

For discussions of, and help with, library collections: Julie Mills (Learning Resources Centre, Roehampton University), Helen Kenward (Social and

Community Services, Oxfordshire), Karen Batchelor (Cowley Library), Anna Cotsell (Abingdon Library).

The fellow academics who in different ways have generously supported my research, especially Steven Barfield, Sandra Beckett, Peter Bramwell, Charlie Butler, Dan Cook, Lucy Cuthew, Carolyn Daniels, Marie Denley, Geoff Fox, Nick Freeman, John Haffenden, Stuart Hannabus, Peter Harding, Peter Hunt, Pamela Knights, Joanny Moulin, Marek Oziewicz, Dulcie Pettigrew, Pat Pinsent, Diane Purkiss, Kimberley Reynolds, Neil Roberts, David Rudd, Sébastien Salbayre, Claire Squires, Susan Stern, Celeste Stroll, Michael Szollosy, Nicholas Tucker, Sabine Ulrich and Jack Zipes.

The children and teachers who participated in the Kiddult Fiction workshops which were run by Sheffield University undergraduates, especially the pupils of William Rhodes Primary School in Chesterfield, Derbyshire and their Head Teacher, Mrs Sharon Stone; Parson Cross Primary School, Sheffield; Longley Park Sixth Form College, Sheffield; Farringtons and Stratford House, London; and Rosethorn Junior School, Etobicoke, Canada.

The adult readers of children's fiction whom I have been privileged to teach as undergraduates at Sheffield University (some of whom are now teachers and scholars in their own right), including Abi Dean, Aileen O'Sullivan, Alex Holyoake, Amy Wilkerson, Andrew Fowley, Angela Boctor, Anneka Shah, Benjamin Hazel, Bethany Smith, Bethany Whittingham, Briony Chalk, Briony Checketts, Ceri Tallett, Charlotte Madge, Clare Webber, Daniel Baird, Emma Gepp, Estelle Hall, Fin Daly, Fraser Wilson. Gareth Shrubsole, Gemma Price, Grace Bennett, Joanna Clark, Katherine Jeffrey, Katy Garrett, Kirsten Kearney, Krissy Mallett, Laura Baker, Liana Koehler, Lucy Gaffney, Lucy Neale, Mike Cresswell, Pamela Balsdon, Phillipa Milne, Rachel Brierley, Rachel Fryirs, Rebecca Gowling, Rebecca Humphris, Rebecca Shackleton, Richard Elphick, Ruth Carrington, Sinead Gray, Siobhan Johnson, Thomas Prince and Victoria Richards.

My two PhD students, Mervat Al Jomaa and Yi-yin Laurie Lee, for their excellent work on young adult fiction.

For ideas, conversations, distractions, and everything else one needs to write a book: Paul Nordstrom August; Penny Brown; Cordelia and Hermione Dawson; Julia Falconer; Robert and Corinne Falconer; Shirley Foster; Nell Gray; Gillian and Gaston Hall; Sebastian Knowles; Michèle Lowrie; Tomáš Míka; Alison Mitchell; Pablo, Tom, Jenny and Sara Schneidermann; Polly Shulman; Sue Vice; and the members of the Sheffield University Women's Network Book Group.

For reading through drafts, and being the indispensable interlocutors in a dialogue of which this book is a product: Graham Falconer and Annabel Mills, who patiently and generously read through the whole, and Jenni Adams, Catherine Annabel, Mervat Al Jomaa, Yi-yin Laurie Lee, Pat Pinsent, Kiera Vaclavik, and Jack Zipes, who kindly commented on individual chapters. Any remaining errors are my own.

This book is dedicated to my dear mother, Charlotte Elisabeth Ann Falconer, for bringing me up surrounded by books, for reading to me and sharing her fascinations and taking a warm interest in mine, and for making it impossible that I should escape loving books as much as she does.

Introduction
A Decade of Border Crossing

Nine years ago, my sister handed me a paperback she had picked up in an airport shop on her way to India. It was a gloomy-looking book, with a black and white photo of a steam train approaching through fog on the cover. Cutting across the top of the photo was a lurid strip of orange backing a half-legible title, and in the middle, an author's name I didn't know: J.K. Rowling. I began to read the novel and by page three, I was hooked. I had become the child-reader I once was: voracious, oblivious to time, suspended by words in an attic room of excitement, fun, friendship and bravery. It was 1998, and my sister had handed me a copy of the first adult edition of *Harry Potter and the Philosopher's Stone*, which came out a year after its publication for children. Across the globe other readers, children and adults, were discovering Harry Potter and becoming hooked in their own ways. In Britain and elsewhere, there followed an extraordinary period in which children's literature exploded into the mainstream of popular and literary culture. Suddenly everyone was talking about children's books, and not just Harry Potter, not just fantasy, but children's fiction in all its variety and invention.

Now that the world has been saturated with Harry Potter hype, it is worth emphasising the individual reader's moment of discovery because, however aggressive the marketing of children's fiction has become, reading by definition is still an individual experience. Publicity can bring a book to a potential reader's attention and it can induce the reader to buy the book, but no amount of publicity can make a book speak to individual hearts and minds. And yet, quite evidently, the Harry Potter series and many other children's books do speak to adult readers, and this is happening on a scale that has not been seen in Britain before. The present study sets out to address the question: Why did so many adult readers turn to fiction for children over the decade or so spanning the new millennium? 1997 to 2007 is the ten-year span which saw the publication of the Harry Potter series. But exceptional as it is, Rowling's success with

1

adult readers is only one example of the way new and classic children's fiction shifted into the literary mainstream during this decade. In 2001, Philip Pullman's *The Amber Spyglass* won the Children's Book category of the Whitbread (now Costa) Award, then went on to win the overall prize of Book of the Year. Other writers of children's and young adult fantasy, including Eoin Colfer, Anthony Horowitz, Garth Nix, G.P. Taylor, and the pseudonymous Lemony Snicket and Lian Hearn, became bestsellers in both children's and adult fiction markets. Classic children's fantasy such as Lewis's *Chronicles of Narnia* reappeared in new editions, some of which were tailor-made for adult readers. And throughout the decade, children's fiction reached bigger audiences than ever before through the medium of film adaptation.

After the popular and critical successes of Rowling and Pullman, many commentators concluded that children's fantasy fiction alone had the magic ingredient to appeal to dual-aged audiences. In 2003, however, Mark Haddon's novel about a boy with Asperger's syndrome proved that the appetite for crossover fiction could also cross literary genres. Haddon's *The Curious Incident of the Dog in the Night-time*, a postmodern blend of realist autopathography, coming-of-age story and detective novel, was published simultaneously in two different editions, one for children and one for adults. It won the Best Novel (rather than Best Children's) category of the Whitbread Award, as well as the Book of the Year Award, a win which in the eyes of many people consolidated the status of children's literature as serious, literary fiction. But whether counted as high or popular art, realist children's fiction continued to reach adult audiences throughout the decade, with realist novels including Sonya Hartnett's *Thursday's Child* and Lionel Shriver's *We Need to Talk About Kevin* receiving critical attention in the national media. Generically hybrid and experimental narratives, such as Malorie Blackman's *Noughts and Crosses* (realism and dystopia), Meg Rosoff's *How I Live Now* (realism and futuristic war fantasy) and the American Louis Sachar's *Holes* (realism and fairy tale) all attracted mass adult readerships in addition to their primary young adult audience. *Holes* was selected by Liverpool City Council to be read and discussed throughout the city in 2004.[1]

The question as to why children's literature became so popular amongst adults was aired periodically throughout the decade on national radio and television, in newspapers, book clubs, and specialist academic journals. The very insistence of its articulation points to some major cultural anxiety at the heart of the phenomenon. In *The Independent*, Jonathan Myerson took a low view of 'Harry Potter and the sad grown-ups' (14 November 2001), while Philip Hensher predicted dire consequences 'when adults want to become children again'. (16 July 2002) Jasper Rees asked more uncertainly in *The Daily Telegraph*, 'are we yearning for old-fashioned stories, seeking spiritual solace, or merely dumbing down?' (15 November 2003). As these articles demonstrate, crossover novels emerged into the public arena amid a cacophonous mixture of outrage, disgust, defensiveness, and conspiratorial solidarity. The hostility to cross-reading expressed by these and other journalists suggests a broader anxiety about the blurring of boundaries between child or youth culture and adult culture in the millennial years. In Bakhtinian terms, we might see crossover fiction as a new genre emerging as a response to a particular moment of cultural crisis and change.[2] If nothing else, the success of crossover fiction made people acutely aware of the lack of consensus about what constituted appropriate reading for children as opposed to adults, and by extension, about the difficulty of maintaining traditional distinctions between childhood and adulthood. Just as the mixed reception of the eighteenth-century novel reflected anxieties about the then emerging literate and affluent middle class, so the charge of illegitimacy, so often lodged against 'kidult' or 'kiddult' fiction in the early twenty-first century reveals discomfort over the way child and adult cultures are clashing, intersecting and hybridising in our own time.

While many writers and publishers have been keen to claim that their books are suitable for readers of all ages, I would argue that cross-readers, like other cultural migrants, are often highly conscious of having crossed a border. Adults who declared themselves 'kiddults' were aware of transgressing the bounds of social respectability. They were often defiantly asserting a right to find delight in childish things. Perhaps, too, there was amongst adults a dialogic interaction developing with children's culture, such as already exists amongst children in relation to adult culture. David Rudd describes children's culture as 'an intertextual refashioning of the adult world', and now adults may be engaged in the same process in reverse.[3] In any case, as the label 'kidult' gave way to the soberer though fuzzier term, 'crossover', more ambitious claims were made for children's fiction. In praising Pullman's *His Dark Materials*, adult readers could be confident that their reading tastes were serious and sophisticated. By 2007, children's literature had 'come of age' and consequently could be 'legitimately' read by adults.[4]

Various explanations have been put forward as to why adults began reading children's literature in their millions over the millennial decade, but thus far, none has addressed the full complexity of the issue. The most frequently expressed opinion is that cross-reading children's literature is a sign of adult 'infantilisation'.[5] Harry Potter is invariably the first example of fiction to be cited, and it almost always appears in a composite reference to 'kiddult' accessories (roller blades, PlayStations, etc.) deemed unworthy of thinking adults. For example, David Aaronovitch writes, 'I don't like to see adults reading Harry Potter when they haven't read Nabokov, or men on shiny scooters when they should be on foot.'[6]

But given that such commentators almost never engage with the substance of Rowling's novels, nor indeed any other children's book, one can only assume they are indulging in what Pierre Bayard refers to in *Comment parler des livres que l'on n'a pas lus?*[7] Howard Jacobson acerbically remarked on the radio programme, *Lebrecht Live*, that people are choosing 'the lowest common denominator, which is the children's book', but his comments did not suggest an intimate acquaintance with any of the books he so forcefully decried.[8] The decade saw the phenomenally popular success of many works of fiction which possessed very little obvious literary merit, but this was as true of adult popular fiction as it was of children's. Readers of Dan Brown's *The Da Vinci Code* could be as easily accused of 'dumbing down' as readers of Christopher Paolini's Tolkien-derivative *Eragon*. But for critics of the crossover phenomenon, it was not just fiction that was the problem; it was the extension of youth culture into middle age in general. Thus one *Times Literary Supplement* contributor, in a fit of anticrossover pique, railed against 'the juvenilization of everything'.[9]

This oft heard criticism will be considered in greater detail in the two chapters following. But there are two general responses to the charge of adult infantilisation that need to be made at the outset. Aside from the fact that adult fiction has no greater a monopoly on seriousness than children's fiction, we should credit the fact that children's literature is being absorbed into popular culture more deeply than ever before. As Jack Zipes has argued, books that appeal to a mass number of people are likely to appeal to more homogenous tastes.[10] On the other hand, when there are so many kinds of entertainment to choose from in the twenty-first century, maybe we should be celebrating the deepening and broadening of interest in books and reading? The other point is that while there is plenty of rubbish in circulation (in adult fiction markets as well as children's), there are today many complex, beautifully written, thought provoking children's novels crossing to adult readerships. The practice of cross-reading also demonstrates how our attitudes to childhood, adulthood, and the in-between state of adolescence are all shifting, becoming more flexible and porous, as we adapt to changing social conditions in the developed world.

An offshoot of the infantilisation argument is that our reading tastes, like everything else in popular culture, are increasingly being determined by clever marketing. According to this line of argument, Rowling triggered a fad with Harry Potter, and since then, publishing companies have been working hard to spin a profit out of the popularity of children's literature while it lasts. The implication of this argument is that the trend is fleeting and superficial, little more than a marketing ploy to reap twice the profits from a fixed number of products. To this argument it might be countered that publishers changed their practices to meet a new demand amongst adult readers, but they were not responsible for creating the demand out of nowhere. It was the new readership that triggered the changes in marketing strategies, rather than the other way around.

Viewing the expansion of children's literature in a positive light, children's authors and publishers, critics and educationalists have all argued that adults began paying attention to contemporary children's fiction when they discovered that these novels were addressing some of the major issues of our time:

the war of religions, the relativity of good and evil, the fragility of the natural world, and so on. And in contrast to serious 'literary' novelists, they were doing so in straightforward, well-crafted but accessible prose. In recent years, Philip Pullman has been one of the most outspoken apologists for children's literature, and in typically polemical vein, he has declared, 'there are some themes, some subjects, too large for adult fiction; they can only be dealt with adequately in a children's book'.[11]

His argument is not only based on thematic content. For Pullman, children's literature is also often stylistically superior to contemporary adult fiction because it returns us to the roots of narrative: the pure, undiluted drive of storytelling and listening.[12] In *The Telegraph*, Pullman is quoted as saying,

> Stories are vital . . . There is more wisdom in a story than in volumes of philosophy, and there is a hunger for stories in all of us. Children know they need them, and go for them with a passion, but all of us adults need them too. All of us, that is, except those limp and jaded people who think they are too grown up to need them.[13]

Indeed, while the atheist Pullman himself would probably resist this view, there are children's writers and critics for whom 'story' comes to represent a quasi-religious force, as will be explored in Chapter 6. Whether or not one accepts the quasi-religious explanations often advanced for strong stories and 'pure narrative', there do seem to be compelling psychological reasons for readers, both adults and children, to engage with chronologically ordered, accessible narrative. As Robert Musil writes in *The Man Without Qualities*,

> when one is overburdened and dreams of simplifying one's life, the basic law of this life, the law one yearns for, is nothing other than that of narrative order, the simple order that allows one to say: 'First this happened and then that happened . . . ' It is the simple sequence of events in which the overwhelmingly manifold nature of things is represented, in a unidimensional order, as a mathematician would say, stringing all that has occurred in space and time on a single thread, which calms us; that celebrated 'thread of story,' which is, it seems, the thread of life itself.[14]

For Pullman, children's literature seems to provide, more specifically, a chance to go beyond modernist and postmodern writing. Whereas postmodern writers become trapped in the self-absorbed art of demonstrating their artistry, the children's writer must put the interests of his reader first:

> In a book for children you can't put the plot on hold while you posture artistically for the amusement of your sophisticated readers because, thank God, your readers are not sophisticated. They have got more important things in mind than your dazzling skill.[15]

The story is what keeps the children's writer grounded and savingly unself-conscious. Whereas,

> in adult literary fiction, stories are there on sufferance . . . Other things are felt to be more important: technique, style, literary knowingness . . . The present-day George Eliots take up their stories as if with a pair of tongs. They are embarrassed by them.[16]

It is important to note, however, that Pullman elsewhere reluctantly concedes that self-consciousness is an inescapable part of contemporary life and hence, of its literature: 'We can't go back and regain the same innocence . . . The only way is forward; the only way is to . . . try to deal as best we can with our own self-consciousness, in life as well as in literature.'[17] Indeed the very fact that storytelling was so highly prized in the early years of the new millennium as a 'pure, unadulterated and spontaneous' art should be taken as a measure of our distance from this idealised spontaneity. If we had not become self-conscious about stories, we would not have been discussing their vital importance; we would just have been practicing the art.

In any case, the worship of story was, in some critics' eyes, a thing to be condemned rather than celebrated. Decrying the media-machine's ceaseless productivity, Howard Jacobson declared, 'We have stories crammed into us from morning till night; the last thing we need is more stories'.[18] While there is undoubtedly truth in this remark, it does not follow, as he implies, that children's literature automatically constitutes escapist or comfort storytelling for adult readers.[19] Nothing could be less comforting than Lian Hearn's *Tales of the Otori*, which recounts medieval atrocities of war, or Meg Rosoff's *How I Live Now*, which depicts modern war scenes, including one in which a child's face is blown off by gunshot at close range.

Quite apart from its hard-hitting content, contemporary children's fiction can also be formally challenging. Anthony Browne, Aidan Chambers and Alan Garner, to name only a few, have written experimental or postmodern fiction for child readers. In Karen Coats's view, the hybridity, playfulness, and indeterminacy of postmodern writing are naturally suited to children's literature. She argues that 'the child's perceived delight in and celebration of the multivalence of the world his imagination presents to him makes him a perfect viewer for the postmodern aesthetic.'[20] Maria Nikolajeva goes so far as to claim that 'children's literature today is catching up with mainstream literature in its . . . postmodern phase.'[21] Whether or not one classes all of its formal innovations as postmodern, some contemporary children's fiction is becoming much harder to distinguish from fiction for adult readers. Julia Eccleshare suggests that this group of novels—which she refers to as 'crossover fiction'—have had a stimulating effect on the production of contemporary children's literature in general, 'edging it ever upwards'.[22]

But clearly, it was not only (and not even primarily) postmodern or formally innovative children's fiction that crossed to adult readerships in the late nineties and early years of the new millennium. J.K. Rowling, Eoin Colfer, Anthony Horowitz, Philip Reeve, Jonathan Stroud and G.P. Taylor are, at least *prima facie*, more easily described as traditional storytellers rather than postmodern novelists. It should be stressed from the outset, then, that crossover fiction includes both conventional and avant-garde, sophisticated and straightforward, clear-cut and morally ambivalent novels. Any consideration of the question of why children's fiction crossed in such volume to adult readers during this decade must take account of the range and diversity of material crossing that particular threshold. One reason for the crossover which this study explores is that our reading tastes are shifting to reflect changing views of childhood, adulthood and the ambiguous spaces in between. In Britain, one must also take into account the change of political climate from Thatcherite conservatism to a youth-conscious New Labour. Blair's reign as Prime Minister spanned exactly the same decade as Rowling's, 1997 to 2007. Even if the shared dates are fortuitous, the promotion of youth culture under Blair can have done nothing to damage the popularity of children's authors. Children's literature publishing is also becoming an increasingly globalised industry. Some of the reasons for adult engagement with children's cultures, including book reading, must therefore be addressed at an international level.[23]

The aspect of the 'crossover phenomenon' which is the focus of the present study is that of the adult reader choosing to read children's fiction, not (or not only) for a child's sake, but for her- or himself. But there are, of course, many other forms of cross-reading, not least of which is children reading adult literature. From the early years of the new millennium children had unprecedented access to adult reading material, and the subject matter deemed appropriate to younger readers expanded in the late twentieth century to include many topics which earlier writers, publishers and adult book buyers would have regarded as off-limits. Sex, drug abuse, torture, depression, mental illness, death, the Holocaust and genocide are all subjects treated in contemporary children's literature, so whether or not they are consciously reading a novel 'for adults', today's children are arguably cross-reading more than they have in previous generations. While this development is part of the larger story of the increasing hybridisation of child and adult cultures from the mid-nineties to the early years of the new millennium, the present study focuses on the phenomenon of adults cross-reading children's literature, an area that raises related but different questions about our society's changing attitudes both to reading, and to the idea of childhood. The central question addressed here is why so many adults are reading children's fiction and discovering value in books which are not, or at least not primarily, addressed to us as adults. The answer lies partly in the texts themselves and partly in the changing tastes and habits of contemporary readers. Hence the double-barrelled focus of this study on crossover fiction *and* cross-reading, because in my view, one cannot be accounted for without reference to the other. Even if my focus is on adults cross-reading, however, it would be neither desirable nor possible to exclude child readers from the discussion altogether, since adult engagement with this category of fiction is always mediated through children's reading tastes and habits as well as our own memories of past childhood reading.

The first chapter of this study provides a wide-angle view of crossover fiction and cross-reading as it developed in Britain over a roughly ten-year span, 1997 to 2007. While this first chapter addresses a range of immediate and material causes for cross-reading, some of the deeper issues at stake are explored in the chapters that follow, with each focusing on a particular text and a different aspect of contemporary cross-reading. Within this period, three texts (or series) had a particularly important impact on the development of cross-reading in Britain, so each of these three—Rowling's Harry Potter series, Pullman's *His Dark Materials*, and Haddon's *The Curious Incident of the Dog in the Night-time*–receives a chapter-length analysis of text and immediate context of publication and reception. With Rowling, Pullman and Haddon, I also explore three different preoccupations that are characteristically found in crossover fiction: a sense of lightness and, conversely, of mortal limit; a sense that the process of coming of age means something new and different in our time; and a sense that the child's eye view can reinvigorate, transform and even redeem adult lives. Chapters 5 and 6 focus on two outstanding novels published in 2005, Geraldine McCaughrean's *The White Darkness* and David Almond's *Clay*; both were published for children but were also described by reviewers as fiction for adults. In these two novels, as I hope to demonstrate, children's fiction becomes a medium through which child and adult readers (re)fashion a sense of subjectivity in relation to the extreme edges of human experience—death in *The White Darkness,* and birth in *Clay.* The final chapter focuses on adults rereading the books they first read as children, because this is an aspect of millennial cross-reading that has expanded alongside the reading of contemporary children's fiction. Indeed the market for new children's fiction has expanded in a symbiotic relationship with the expansion of the market for re-edited or reissued classics, the one market stimulating the other, and both being partly fuelled by adult nostalgia for their own childhood books. Rereading is a major theme of C.S. Lewis's *The Silver Chair,* so this text is chosen as a means to explore adults' relation to their childhood books, in the broader context of the millennial expansion of children's fiction to adult audiences.

While particular focus is given to an individual text in chapters two to seven, my aim with this close analysis is to illuminate different aspects of crossover fiction and cross-reading in general. Therefore I have included many lateral connections to other texts, as well as fairly extensive discussion of the broader issues and ideas at stake in the reception of individual texts. Some readers may find these lateral connections distracting, but in our age of narrow specialisms, I think it is important to bear in mind Primo Levi's idea that reading (and living) should be about building bridges and making connections.[24] One of the bridges I am trying to build here is between children's and other fiction (and thankfully, there are and have been other scholars doing the same). While I argue that the crossover novel came into its own over the past decade or so in Britain, it is also important to see that its insights are retrospective. Contemporary cross-reading highlights how children's literature has never existed in a truly separate sphere. I have also avoided constructing any hard-edged definitions of what does and does not constitute 'crossover fiction' because an essential feature of this category of fiction is that its boundaries are unfixed. Not only are the texts themselves often generically hybrid, but readers are hybridising different readerly identities when they 'cross over' to reading a book that was intended, at least ostensibly, for someone other and elsewhere. Cross-reading is another of the ways in which we become, in Kristeva's phrase, 'strangers to ourselves'.[25]

At the same time, cross-reading is also one of the means by which our disparate, stranger selves can converge into a multifaceted presence. Jacqueline Rose threw down a gauntlet to children's literature specialists by arguing that adult interests unconsciously predominate in children's fiction. Her provocative, illuminating study, *The Case of Peter Pan,* 'instead of asking what children want, or need, from literature . . . asked what it is that adults, through literature, want or demand of the child'.[26] In a sense, crossover fiction is simply children's fiction which is becoming conscious of and acknowledging that adult presence. But as the consciousness of a self and other within children's fiction grows, so too do the possibilities of interillumination. Crossover fiction thus invites us to rephrase Rose's question and ask: What is it that adults and children, through literature, want and demand of each other?

One of the distinctive aspects of children's literature as a field of academic research is that it is genuinely interdisciplinary, and brings together readers from many different backgrounds, with widely differing areas of expertise. The approach adopted here is an attempt to reflect the richness and range of the dialogue that typically goes on in this field. In developing my reading of crossover fiction, I have also drawn on previously published academic criticism, newspaper and other media reviews, statistical studies, governmental and other institutional reports, Internet fan sites, published reviews and interviews with child and adult readers, the comments of Sheffield University students, and conversations with children and adults, interviewed in the course of writing this study. Harold Bloom asked about Harry Potter, 'Can 35 million readers be wrong?' and notoriously he answered, 'Yes.'[27] But gone are the days when a famous critic's *ex cathedra* pronouncement could make or break a novel's reputation (if such days ever existed). What were the 35 million readers wrong about? What questions were they asking anyway? Bloom doesn't appear to be interested in finding out. On the other hand, his comment does pay Rowling the compliment of reading her writing according to a set of specifically literary, rather than sociological, criteria (though we can argue about whether his criteria are well chosen). Although crossover fiction is interesting for cultural reasons, the fact that children's fiction is crossing to adult readerships should also afford us the opportunity to appreciate these works for their formal attributes: their characterisation, emplotment, style, structure and all the other distinctive aspects of the ways these texts work as fictional narratives. This study will, I hope, contribute to the growing body of work which considers children's literature as literature. The fact that the academic community devoted to the study of children's literature is growing in strength and numbers might be understood as one more indication of the way in which a decade of crossover has transformed the shared spaces between children's and adult's reading of fiction.

Chapter One
Kiddults at Large

Children's fiction has always crossed over to different age-groups in the sense that, historically, it has nearly always been written and published by adults, and purchased by adults for children. Before the invention of a distinct market for children's literature in the mid-eighteenth century, adult texts regularly crossed to child readerships. Such crossings were often facilitated by adaptation, abridgement and illustration. Bunyan's *The Pilgrim's Progress* (1678), Defoe's *Robinson Crusoe* (1719) and Swift's *Gulliver's Travels* (1726) were adapted for children very soon after they were first published for adults, and they have retained their place amongst children's books until the present day. Adult fiction has not ceased to cross over to child readers, and nineteenth-century realist fiction by Charles Dickens, George Eliot, the Brontës and Jane Austen, for example, can all be found shelved in the older children's sections of bookshops and libraries today. But traffic moving in the other direction, from child to adult readers, is historically much more unusual, and the sheer scale of the flow of traffic in this direction which took place in the millennial decade is unprecedented in British publishing history.

The Ghost of Crossovers Past

This is not to say that child-to-adult crossover has no historical precedent at all, however. On the contrary, there is a strong tradition of children's literature being adopted by adult readers in Britain. Children's nonsense, magic and fantasy fiction, by writers such as Hilaire Belloc, Edward Lear, A.A. Milne, Beatrix Potter, Kenneth Grahame, Lewis Carroll, Roald Dahl, C.S. Lewis and J.R.R. Tolkien, have long attracted a broad spectrum of readers, and this existing horizon of expectation has helped pave the way for the more recent, meteoric rise of the so-named crossover novel in Britain. This sense of lineage is reflected in the frequent mentions of Dahl, Lewis and Tolkien in reviews of Rowling, Pullman and other contemporary children's authors. But the tendency to hybridise the categories of child and adult fiction can be found much earlier than in these earlier twentieth-century classics. It is present, for instance, in British Romantic writers, themselves influenced by the theories of Locke and Rousseau concerning ideas of childhood and education.[1] Sometimes this interest in childhood produced new kinds of writing for children, such as Charles and Mary Lamb's stories for children; elsewhere it produced writing of or about childhood, as in William Blake's *Songs of Innocence and Experience* (1789). Mary Wollstonecraft and William Godwin wrote both for and about children. Many Romantic writers aimed to produce a childlike language, which they defined as simple, direct and natural, as part of a broader aim to revolutionise poetic discourse.

In the Victorian period, George MacDonald's *At the Back of the North Wind* (1871) and *The Princess and the Goblin* (1872), and Charles Kingsley's *The Water-Babies* (1863) were considered to be works of serious, literary fiction, which though published for children could also be appreciated by adults. MacDonald in particular was (and still is) praised by adult readers for his luminous, visionary prose.[2] Christina Rossetti's sexually suggestive fable 'Goblin Market' (1862) was given to children to read, but published with her poems for adult readers.[3] Carroll's *Alice's Adventures in Wonderland* (1865) and *Through the Looking-Glass and What Alice Found There* (1871) were famously written for a real child, Alice Liddell, and her sisters, but even the dedicatory poem sounds elegiac, as if it the little girl were already lost (i.e., too grown-up) for the author:

> *Alice! A childish story take,*
> *And, with a gentle hand,*
> *Lay it where Childhood's dreams are twined*
> *In Memory's mystic band,*[4]

The book sold well from the first, but reviews of *Alice's Adventures in Wonderland* were mixed. Some found it delightfully appropriate for a young reader, others deemed it unsuitable for children, and still others commented on its crossover appeal:

> It is most amusingly written, and a child, when once the tale has been commenced, will long to hear the whole of this wondrous narrative. (*The Press,* 1865)

> We fancy that any child might be more puzzled than enchanted by this stiff, over-wrought story. (*The Athenaeum,* 1865)

> This is the book for little folks, and big folks who take it home to their little folks will find themselves reading more than they intended, and laughing more than they had any right to expect. (*The Spectator,* 1865)

A delightful book for children—or, for the matter of that, for grown-up people, provided they have wisdom and sympathy enough to enjoy a piece of downright hearty drollery and fanciful humour. (*The London Review*, 1865)[5]

And thus began the complicated reception history of these two novels, which have haunted the space between 'Childhood's dreams' and 'Memory's mystic band' ever since.

Less ambiguously, Carroll's *The Hunting of the Snark* (1876), like Lear's *Book of Nonsense* published thirty years earlier, appealed instantly and equally to child and adult readers. As well as producing works for 'the nursery' (i.e., for younger children), the Victorians also segregated books by gender and these gender-specific books tended to cross fluidly between child and adult readerships. Thus Charlotte M. Yonge's domestic novels were read by girls and women, while adventure novels by G.A. Henty, Rudyard Kipling and Robert Louis Stevenson were read by boys and men. Brian Alderson argues that the 'real secret' of the popularity of Stevenson's *Treasure Island* (1882) and other adventure novels was 'not that boys delighted in tales meant for men, like *Robinson Crusoe*, . . . but that men, Victorian men, were eager for tales meant for boys.' (295) Similarly, Rider Haggard's *King Solomon's Mines* (1885), one of the many Victorian adventure novels being re-edited for twenty-first century crossover audiences, was originally dedicated 'to all the big and little boys who read it.' (296) In the same period, Jules Verne's scientific fantasies were being published, serially and in translation, in *The Boy's Own Paper*, a journal which, from its inception in 1879, attracted a readership of 'big and little boys.' In the late twentieth century, 'chick lit' novels such as Helen Fielding's *Bridget Jones's Diary* proved equally gender-specific but age-neutral, although (despite the labelling) 'lad lit' such as Nick Hornby's *About a Boy* were less successful in excluding female readers.

At the beginning of the twentieth century, J.M. Barrie's *Peter Pan* idealised a separate world of childhood adventure and magic, first in the form of a play (1904) and then revised and expanded as a novel (1928). This composite work has arguably had more influence on the subsequent history of children's literature than any other work besides Carroll's Alice books. But as Jacqueline Rose and other critics have shown, Neverland was always an adult projection of childhood, in whose very separateness adults were passionately invested.[6] With Geraldine McCaughrean's officially nominated sequel, *Peter Pan in Scarlet* (2006), we may measure our distance from this early twentieth-century credo, the belief in a *puer eternus* reigning princelike over a separate and eternal realm of childhood. *Peter Pan in Scarlet* begins with a strange series of scenes in which Wendy and the Lost Boys, now grown into adults, squeeze themselves into children's clothes in order to become children again, as they were in Barrie's play/novel. Once they have successfully metamorphosed, their task is to rescue Peter, who is slowly being destroyed by the seepage of time into Neverland. This continuation of the Peter Pan myth reveals the twenty-first century adult's investment in the idea of aging as a reversible process, and of childhood and adulthood being metamorphic, rather than fixed, states of being. But if Barrie's strict prohibition against adults entering Neverland has been overturned, paradoxically we continue to believe in the myth of eternal childhood; the difference is that now we think that adults as well as children have right of access to this world of eternal play. McCaughrean's novel reproduces this contemporary investment in the Peter Pan myth in order, finally, to deconstruct it. Although in a jauntily upbeat Afterword, McCaughrean describes 'Neverland heal[ing] up just like that', she also firmly closes the door to her kiddult protagonists. Wendy and the Lost Boys have grown into adults again, and this time they are glad to be leaving Peter and returning home. Moreover, it is only by remembering his adult training as a doctor that Curly is able to operate on Peter, and remove the mysterious splinter that had been slowing killing the eternal boy. So as it turns out, the safety of Neverland depends on adults learning to value themselves as adults.

In the 1940s, Tolkien began writing *The Lord of the Rings*, a trilogy which began as a sequel to his children's story, *The Hobbit* (1937). By the time it was published in 1954–55, however, *The Lord of the Rings* had developed into an epic fantasy for adult readers. Within ten years of its publication, Tolkien had attracted a cult following which spanned older child and adult, male and female readers in Britain and North America. It has remained one of the most popular works of fiction produced in the twentieth century. Although somewhat dwarfed by the enduring success of *The Lord of the Rings*, Richard Adams's *Watership Down* (1972) should not be overlooked as an important example of twentieth-century crossover fiction *avant la lettre*. Like Carroll's tales of Alice underground and Tolkien's tales of hobbits and goblins, *Watership Down* grew out of stories told to children, but the finished novel is an epic work that draws richly on Biblical and classical myth and literature (Exodus; Aeschylus; Virgil's *Aeneid;* and Joseph Campbell's study of myth, *The Hero with a Thousand Faces*) as well as the author's own military experiences in the Second World War. While published as a children's book, it was also read by millions of adults, and reputedly influenced George Lucas in developing the storyline of that colossus of crossover films, *Star Wars*.[7] In a lighter vein, Douglas Adams's *The Hitchhiker's Guide to the Galaxy* was first broadcast on BBC Radio 4, in 1978, and on TV, *Doctor Who* attracted another cult following, while the enormously prolific Terry Pratchett published his first *Discworld* novel, *The Colour of Magic*, in 1983. Such comic science fiction fantasies, like the boys' adventure stories of a century earlier, seemed to pass effortlessly across age categories, and indeed continue to do so, to the present day. *Doctor Who* was revived both on film and in a 2005 TV series.

The first thing that distinguishes the present millennial situation from this historical context, however, is the sheer volume and diversity of children's fiction crossing from child to adult audiences. The second major difference is that, due to the volume of traffic passing across once distinct publishing markets, crossover fiction has helped to change the map of mainstream literary culture in Britain, altering previous boundaries not only between children's and adult-, but also between literary and popular fiction, as well as print fiction and the film industry. Even within the popular genre of fantasy, there has been a much greater diversity of subgenres crossing to adult readers than heretofore, ranging from best-selling stories of magic for younger children like Eoin Colfer's *Artemis Fowl* series and Lemony Snicket's *A Series of Unfortunate Events* to high fantasy, such as Anthony Horowitz's *Alex Rider* and *The Power of Five*, Garth Nix's *Old Kingdom*, G.P. Taylor's *Shadowmancer* and William Nicholson's *The Wind on Fire*.

Realist fiction has a much more limited history of crossing from child to adult readerships in Britain, though again there are notable precedents, especially from the mid-twentieth century. Examples of social realist novels as well as realist dystopias for young adults that were, and are still, widely read by adults include George Orwell's *Animal Farm* (1945) and *1984* (1949), J.D. Salinger's *The Catcher in the Rye* (1951), William Golding's *Lord of the Flies* (1954) and Harper Lee's *To Kill a Mockingbird* (1960). But in recent years, realist children's fiction has begun to appear on adult best-seller lists with some regularity, with examples ranging from Mark Haddon's *Curious Incident* to Markus Zusak's *The Book Thief*, a novel 'narrated by Death' about a young girl in Nazi Germany, which became a *New York Times* best seller. Documentary narrative such as Bernard Hare's *Urban Grimshaw and the Shed Crew*; realist fiction about street children such as Elizabeth Laird's *The Garbage King*;and school and family stories such as Polly Shulman's delightful homage to Jane Austen, *Enthusiasm*; Linda Newberry's *Sisterland*; and Rachel Klein's *The Moth Diaries* were all marketed as crossover fiction, with Klein's most strikingly described as a novel for '15- to 25-year-old' readers. Perhaps most distinctively, the hybrid fantasy/magic-realist novel crossed in large numbers from young adult to adult readerships. Amongst these generically hybrid crossover novels are Malorie Blackman's *Noughts and Crosses* series, David Almond's *The Fire-Eaters* and Helen Oyeyemi's *The Icarus Girl*.

Hogwarts Express to Fame and Fortune

But unquestionably, what kick-started the millennial crossover phenomenon was the unforeseen popularity of J.K. Rowling's Harry Potter series with adult readers. Rowling proved to publishers and retailers that children's fiction could be big business, equally as lucrative as popular adult fiction and more so. By 2007, Rowling had broken practically every sales record in publishing history. To mention just a few of the landmarks: In 2000, Rowling's fourth volume, *Harry Potter and the Goblet of Fire*, took sales of the series to over forty million in two hundred countries, with translations into forty languages. The fifth volume, *Harry Potter and the Order of the Phoenix*, became an Amazon.com bestseller six months before it was even published in June 2003. The sixth, *Harry Potter and the Half-Blood Prince*, broke records as the fastest selling book in history, selling nine million copies on its first day in July 2005. The final volume went even further and broke sales records on both sides of the Atlantic, selling eleven million copies in its first 24 hours. On the day of its release, 21 July 2007, *Harry Potter and the Deathly Hallows* sold 2.7 million copies in the UK and 8.3 million in the US, and was published simultaneously in more than ninety countries.[8] The running total for Harry Potter book sales over the ten-year period from the publication of the first to the seventh volume, and before the release of the final volume, was 325 million copies, making Rowling the richest author in literary history.[9]

Rowling is said to have awakened a new generation of children to a love of reading, and few would criticise her for this achievement.[10] What was even more surprising was that she appeared to have won many adults back to reading as well. In Britain, the seven novels were published by Bloomsbury first as children's books. They appeared at fairly regularly spaced intervals: 1997, 1998, 1999, 2000, 2003, 2005 and 2007. Recognising how many adults had enjoyed the first Harry Potter, Bloomsbury took the unprecedented step of issuing an 'adult edition', that is, the same text, but with a different cover (in this case, the black and white photo of a steam train) in 1998. This was followed by further adult versions of the next four novels, issued in 1999, 2000, 2001, 2003, in each case, roughly a year after the release of the children's edition. In 2004, a new adult edition of the series was released and from then until 2007, the child and adult editions were released simultaneously, indicating the growing importance Bloomsbury attached to Harry's adult fans. Harry grows from an eleven-year-old child to a young man over the course of the series. And as Rowling's original readers would also be growing up as the series progressed (indeed, growing up at twice Harry's rate, since the later books came out every other year), there are several inbuilt reasons why the series would attract an ever greater number of adult readers. However, it remains to be proven that issuing an adult edition contributed in any substantial way to attracting new, adult readers to the Potter series. For the most part, the children's editions sold much more strongly than their adult counterparts. It was not until the last volume, *Harry Potter and the Deathly Hallows*, that sales of the adult edition of the seventh book were seen to outstrip sales of the children's edition.[11] By that time, Waterstone's was estimating that 60% of Rowling's readership was made up of teenagers and young adults, a substantial number of whom must have grown up alongside the series itself.

Crossover Fiction Goes to Market

It has been much debated whether the success of *Harry Potter* had a stimulating effect on the children's publishing industry or the reverse.[12] The answer is probably mixed, but what is certain is that the nature of the industry changed during this period, with publishers offering huge advances to a few, potentially best-selling authors. One of the beneficiaries of the 'Potter effect' was Michelle Paver, a first-time author who was awarded a record 2 million-pound advance from Orion Books, for a series entitled *Chronicles of Ancient Darkness* which, following the well-worn track of Jack London and Rudyard Kipling, promised to trace the adventures of a wolf-boy named Tora.[13] Ridley Scott was also reported to have offered Paver 2.7 million for the film rights to the series.[14] The first edition's dust jacket of *Wolf Brother*, the first chronicle, had a simple, cave-painting design set against a muted red-brown background, which insured that, as one journalist put it, the book 'could discreetly be read on the train by adults on their way to work.'[15] Some critics would argue that such inflated advances meant that children's publishing in general became less diverse and less generous to the majority of children's authors. But Waterstone's claimed that sales of children's books *excluding* Rowling's novels grew at a rate of 2% per year from 1997 to 2005, and that the number of children's titles being published increased by tenfold.[16] If these statistics are reliable, Rowling's effect on the industry must be considered a beneficial one, at very least in economic terms.

By 2002, 'crossover' had become the buzz word at the Bologna Children's Book Fair, the leading trade fair dedicated to buying and selling rights to children's literature. Children's fiction had also become a major presence at the Frankfurt International Book Fair, the leading international book fair and a much vaster institution than Bologna. But it is at the Bologna Fair that one can see most clearly the emphasis on crossover emerging from within the children's literature market. In 2002, interest in picture books, series fiction and books for younger children (six to eight years) was in decline; what was most in demand was fiction for older children with a sophistication that could appeal to adults. As Mary Tapissier, the Managing Director at Hodder Children's, said at the time, 'the big crossover market we've been talking about for years is finally with us'.[17] Trading in fantasy fiction and edgy realism for older children was particularly strong. For example, Hodder paid a six-figure sum for UK and Commonwealth rights to David Lee Stone's medieval fantasy trilogy, while Puffin battled to win paperback rights to three hard-hitting, teenage novels by Melvin Burgess.[18] This was also the year in which leading publishers created new lists such as Young Picador at Macmillan and Collins Flamingo at HarperCollins that were designed to blur the distinction between adult and children's book markets.

By 2004, publishers and agents had become even more strategic about presenting their titles in Bologna and elsewhere. Literary agents and publishers aimed to seal deals for rights in several countries at once, as well as film rights if possible. The US and UK markets had become more integrated, as Jean Feiwel, publisher and senior vice president of Scholastic in the US, indicated. 'What we hope to do now is to cue each other to our markets, to listen to our sister companies more', she said. 'With the kind of sums you have to spend, you want marketing programmes to work globally. You also have to make a bigger and bigger noise to make a book heard'.[19] The Managing Director at Puffin, Francesca Dow, commented that publishers were seeking distinctive one-off titles that had a potentially global appeal. Within this globalised industry, British fiction was seen to occupy a market-leading position. As Dow put it, 'in the US especially, they look to the UK for literary, interesting fiction and regard us as an important source of individual talent'.[20]

There had been strong interest in securing television and film rights to children's fiction since the new millennium, but by 2005 Hollywood had become an influential and ubiquitous presence at the Bologna Fair. Representatives from Walden Media, Fox, Nickelodeon, DreamWorks and New Line were all present, seeking franchises for family feature films. 'L.A. has woken up to Bologna', remarked Fiona Kenshole, a former children's publishing UK executive.[21] The Harry Potter films were already proving to be hugely popular, as were film adaptations of Lemony Snicket's *A Series of Unfortunate Incidents* and Sachar's *Holes*, not to mention Jackson's toweringly successful adaptation of *The Lord of the Rings*. Adamson's first *Narnia* adaptation was already in production, as was the adaptation of Colfer's *Artemis Fowl* series. L.A. had not only woken up to Bologna; it had also woken up to the concept of the crossover film, and directors and producers descended like Nazgûl on the once peaceful backwater of children's fiction.

Impressing the Cultural Gatekeepers[22]

If it was new to the glamour of Hollywood, children's fiction had never had any difficulty in achieving recognition as popular literature. What people were slower to recognise was that children's fiction could have a place in 'high' culture. It could be fêted and fanfared and ushered in to the white-tie events with a guest pass that read Literature with a capital 'L'. When children's fiction began to be read by millions of adults, its place in the literary canon was also radically altered. Evidence of this transition in cultural status can be seen in the increasing number of children's novels that competed successfully against adult fiction to win major literary awards in the first years of the new millennium.

After the Man Booker Prize, the most prestigious national literary award for contemporary fiction in Britain is the Costa (previously Whitbread) Award.[23] Established in 1985, the structure of the awards was changed in 1996 when the Whitbread Children's Book of the Year was awarded as a separate category. The prize money was considerable (£10,000), but the Children's Book of the Year was not judged against the other four adult categories. Previous to 1996, winners of the Children's Book category included Anne Fine's *Flour Babies* (1993) and Geraldine McCaughrean's *Gold Dust* (1994), that is to say, works aimed at younger children (up to about aged 9 or 10). After 1996, when children's books were competing for a substantial monetary prize, the Whitbread produced a different kind of award winner; David Almond's *Skellig* (winner in 1998) went on to become crossover best seller and was successfully adapted for the national stage in London. In 1999, the Whitbread Award changed its rules again to allow books from the Children's Literature category to be submitted for the overall prize of Book of the Year, that is, to compete directly with adult fiction. In that year, Rowling's third novel, *Harry Potter and the Prisoner of Azkaban* won the children's category award and came close to unseating two venerable poet laureates, Seamus Heaney and Ted Hughes, for the overall Book of the Year award. The following year, the children's category award was won by another crossover novel, Jamila Gavin's *Coram Boy*. And in 2001, Philip Pullman broke through the glass ceiling, winning both the children's category award and the overall Book of the Year with *The Amber Spyglass*. As Boyd Tonkin wrote on the occasion of Philip Pullman's success, 'children's writing has moved from being a dowdy Cinderella on the edges of the literary world to the star of the show'.[24]

Following Pullman's strong precedent, children's fiction with either proven or potential crossover appeal continued to win the children's category award throughout the decade. There was Almond's gritty, magic realist *The Fire-Eaters* in 2003, McCaughrean's feminist version of Noah, *Not the End of the World* in 2004, Kate Thompson's *The New Policeman* in 2005 which succeeded against Frank Cottrell Boyce's *Framed* and McCaughrean's *The White Darkness*, and Linda Newberry's *Set in Stone* in 2006, all of which were felt to have a strong crossover appeal. Moreover, in 2003 Mark Haddon confirmed how confidently children's fiction could compete against adult literary fiction when his novel, *The Curious Incident of the Dog in the Night-time*, which had been published in dual editions for children and adults, was entered in the *adult* fiction category, and won the award not only for this category but also the overall Book of the Year. Reviews of all these novels rather pointedly avoided any reference to the age of the intended readership of the work in question. For example, the Costa Award Web site describes the 2006 winner, *Set in Stone*, as 'beautifully crafted,' an 'emotionally charged narrative' that 'will thrill all lovers of intelligent fiction.'[25]

Nor will it be long before children's fiction begins to appear amongst the winners of the Man Booker Prize. Crossover novels have already crept into the long-lists (Pullman's *The Amber Spyglass* in 2001 and Haddon's *Curious Incident* in 2003).[26] And adult novels focalised through young adults, and narrated in a hybridised 'young/old' narrative voice, or obviously drawing on the model of children's magic or fantasy literature, have fared even better. Thus the 2002 Man Booker Prize was won by Canadian writer Yann Martel, with his Crusoe-esque novel *Life of Pi*, depicting an Indian boy's coming-of-age at sea, in the magic realist company of a zebra, an orangutan, a hyena and a Bengal tiger named Richard Parker. The novel conflates questions of religious belief and faith in 'magic' and childhood imagination in much the same way C.S. Lewis does in *The Silver Chair* (see Chapter Seven of the present study). Susanna Clarke's *Jonathan Strange & Mr Norrell*, touted by Bloomsbury as a 'Harry Potter for adults,' was short-listed in 2004, while Ishiguro's hauntingly bleak novel *Never Let Me Go*, which is narrated by a teenage clone, was short-listed in 2005.

Meanwhile, two of the most prestigious national awards specifically for children's literature, the CILIP Carnegie Medal and the Guardian Children's Fiction Prize, also strongly favoured children's literature with adult appeal in the years spanning the millennium. The Guardian Prize aims to discover 'innovative new children's fiction before it is known elsewhere' and during this period, 'innovative' meant tackling subjects, or more accurately, a complex attitudinal stance on the part of the narrator to certain subjects, hitherto deemed 'off-limits' for child readers.[27] Thus Sonya Hartnett's *Thursday's Child*, the 2002 winner, unsentimentally depicts a family's struggle to survive the great depression in Australia. Haddon's *Curious Incident*, the 2003 winner, is narrated by a boy with Asperger's syndrome. And Meg Rosoff's *How I Live Now*, the 2004 winner, moves breezily from a 'utopian' opening situation, in which an anorexic New York teenager begins an affair with her underage, chain-smoking English cousin, to a dystopic fantasy of foreign invasion, flight and starvation, murder and genocide. No less eager to select fiction that transgressed the traditional boundaries of children's fiction, the Carnegie Medal judges selected Pullman's *Northern Lights* (first in the *His Dark Materials* trilogy) in 1995; Melvin Burgess's *Junk* (a novel about drug addiction for teenagers, which was considered controversial for its overly 'adult' treatment of the subject) in 1996; Aidan Chambers's brilliantly postmodern *Postcards from No Man's Land* in 1999; Jennifer Donnelly's *A Gathering Light* (a Richard and Judy show best seller, discussed below) in 2003; Frank Cottrell Boyce's *Millions*, which was later adapted for mainstream family cinema in 2004; and Macmillan's hot crossover novelist Meg Rosoff's *Just in Case* in 2007.[28]

In terms of winning critical recognition from national judges, critics and reviewers, 2003 was the crossover novel's *annus mirabilis*. This was the year that Mark Haddon's *Curious Incident* proved beyond doubt that the same text could work as brilliantly for a child reader as for an adult. This was also the year that the Carnegie Medal judges chose to showcase 'writing that is as enjoyable for adults as it is for children and young people', according to Chair of Judges Colin Brabazon.[29] Along with American writer Jennifer Donnelly's *A Gathering Light*, the judges short-listed *The Curious Incident*, David Almond's *Fire-Eaters*, and Michael Morpurgo's *Private Peaceful*, a historical novel about the young soldiers who were court-martialled and executed for cowardice during World War One. Because of the bleakness of its conclusion, *Private Peaceful* is arguably the most adult-oriented novel that this former Children's Laureate has produced to date. *A Gathering Light*, the eventual winner, was praised by the judges for 'the striking luminosity of its prose, its tangible sense of place and the integrity of its vision'.[30] (The date of Donnelly's award is 2004, because the Carnegie is awarded to winners the following January.) The judges' assessment was echoed by reviews of the novel in the national press. 'If ever a novel for teenagers deserved a crossover audience, *A Gathering Light* . . . is it', declared Adèle Geras. Geras advises us to overlook the fact that the novel is narrated by a teenager, since 'a whole community is revealed in these pages', conveyed with 'unmatched authenticity' due to the biographical connections linking Donnelly to the historical murder of Grace Brown. As she writes in her 'Author's Note', Donnelly was inspired to write her novel by reading the letters of Grace Brown, a real girl who had been murdered during pregnancy in the Adirondack in 1906. Her lover was eventually convicted and executed for her murder.[31] Donnelly's own grandmother had been a waitress at the hotel where Grace Brown was murdered (though not at the time of the crime). For these reasons, Donnelly's fictional rendition of Grace Brown's history was felt by reviewers to be a 'genuinely authentic' account with which adult readers could engage as if it were local history.

But if the Carnegie panel thought the novel had adult appeal, they were overlooking the author's stated intention, since Donnelly specified that she meant to address female teenagers with her novel.[32] Growing up in a rural community in upstate New York, the protagonist Mattie Gokey is a gifted but plain-looking girl who finds herself being courted by the local golden boy, Royal Loomis, though it turns out he wants her because of a piece of land that adjoins both their fathers' farms. As she struggles to choose between Royal and her cherished ambition to become a writer, she learns to resist the allure of romance by uncovering the tragic history of Grace Brown, murdered at the hotel where Mattie works. In interview, Donnelly insisted that contemporary teenagers needed to hear the message of Grace's story: 'I wanted to tell them that the world is a tough place for young women; always has been, always will be. I hoped teenagers would relate to 16-year-old Mattie and her struggle to build a life of her own choosing'.[33] And teenage reviews of *A Gathering Light* suggest that Donnelly succeeded in her aim. One fifteen-year-old female reviewer writes, 'many of the things people have to deal with nowadays were the same sort of things people had to cope with back then' while another comments 'the main character experiences what it feels like to believe your boyfriend is too good-looking for you'.[34] *A Gathering Light* works on several levels to validate a sense of identity and self-worth in its intended female young adult readership. In Donnelly's revisioning of the story, Mattie exposes the murder by making public Grace's letters, despite Grace's request that they be destroyed; her heroine thus provides a strong and positive role model for teenage readers. But the response of the Carnegie judges demonstrated that this sense of identification could be transferred to a wider age of reader. Looking beyond the specifics of teenage pregnancy, Brabazon described *A Gathering Light* in more general terms as a 'book about hard choices and the power of language to free us from the constraints of everyday'.

The Carnegie judges' decision to showcase children's fiction that was also 'enjoyable for adults' was not a conscious attempt to promote a new publisher's category of fiction. Colin Brabazon said that he referred to 'crossover novels' in his press release because the term 'crossover' was in use in the trade press (*The Bookseller* and other publishers' journals) at the time, and because it seemed a good way of introducing a unifying theme to the judges' range of selected books.[35] Thus, although the Carnegie panel in 2003 helped to sell the concept of the crossover novel, the judges were themselves responding to changes in the market that were already taking place. As will be explored below, this change was in part due to the greater likelihood that adult readers would identify with a young adult protagonist or narratorial voice than they might have in the past.

Cross-reading on TV

If they were moving up the ranks culturally, crossover novels also gained ground on the popular front by being featured on national television book clubs, such as the BBC's *Page Turners* hosted by Jeremy Vine, and Channel 4's *Richard and Judy Book Club*, both of which emulated the huge success of the USA's Oprah Winfrey, whose television book club was initiated in 1996. In 2005, *Page Turners* featured several children's books on its list, which was predominantly aimed at an adult televisual audience. These included McCaughrean's *Not the End of the World*, Oyeyemi's *The Icarus Girl* and Shriver's *We Need to Talk About Kevin*. Similarly, Donnelly's *A Gathering Light*, which had appeared as a young adult novel in the USA, under the title, *A Northern Light*, was published by Bloomsbury in two editions, a children's hardback and an adult paperback. The adult edition was selected by Richard and Judy for their first Summer Reads programme. The husband-and-wife duo's Summer Reads included six novels which offered adult readers 'an eclectic mix of perfect escapist holiday reads' including a 'murderous coming-of-age tale'; 'a compelling family saga; comic and tragic revelations about life, love and friendship'; 'a political thriller/love story set in Chile'; 'the scariest serial killer in years'; and 'a romantic comedy.'[36] Although an eclectic mix of genres, all six books focused strongly on family and romantic relationships. Five of the six writers featured were women (including one mother-daughter writing duo), and the one novel by a male writer was a love story. The cover of Bloomsbury's adult edition of *A Gathering Light* bears the photograph of a tranquil, royal blue lake, and an extract from a *Sunday Telegraph* review running across the top of the page: 'if George Clooney had walked into the room I would have told him to come back later when I'd finished it.' All of these paratextual signifiers, including its place on a mostly female-authored, summer reading list, steered this novel toward an adult female reader looking for light, but not too light, holiday reading.[37] The adult paperback edition made a natural choice, then, for Richard and Judy's list of recommended Summer Reads. And there is no question but that the selection helped the novel reach a much wider base of adult readers; a glance at the sales figures confirms just how valuable a mention on Richard and Judy's show could be. Before its selection, the adult paperback edition of *A Gathering Light* was selling about a thousand copies a week in the UK. The novel featured on the Richard and Judy show on 9 June, and by two days later, sales had leapt to nearly 12,000; and from 19 June to the end of the summer, sales remained at about 15,000 copies per week.[38]

Given that she had so explicitly addressed teenage female readers, Donnelly expressed some surprise that her novel had attracted such a wide adult readership in the UK. But after her Carnegie win, she defended the adult reader's interest, arguing that it showed a respect for children and the issues they faced: 'what is so important about the crossover novel is not what it says about adults, but what it says to children—that the stories which matter to them matter to us as well'. ('Paperback Writer') Since we encourage children to learn about adulthood through the medium of literature, 'why shouldn't we repay the courtesy with a visit back to the realms of childhood and adolescence?' As sound as this argument is, it was not the argument that Richard and Judy were using to sell the book to their readers. Like Geras, Richard and Judy praised the novel for its 'atmospheric' setting in the Adirondack Mountains and its 'tremendous authenticity' in relating 'the true story of a murder that took place in the Adirondacks at the time; a story that rocked America, and that is so captivating itself, that it has already inspired one other novel and the film *A Place in the Sun*, starring Elizabeth Taylor and Montgomery Clift.' With this nod to film history, Richard and Judy guarantee their readers a great story—that is, a gripping fictional narrative, and at the same time, an 'authentic' account of a historical community. There are aspects of the novel which strike me as egregiously inauthentic, for example, the characterisation of Mattie's friend Weaver, 'the only black boy in North Woods,' who almost magically surmounts every racial obstacle to win a scholarship to a New York City college. But it seems to have been the mixture of apparent authenticity and compelling fiction, as well as a young but exceptionally articulate narrator with whom an adult reader could identify, which provided the magic formula to cross over to a mainstream adult audience.

Competing to be 'Best Loved'

Another aspect of the magic formula, however, was the competitive element which Channel 4 introduced into the book club format. Each of the six chosen novels on the Richard and Judy programme was talked up by a guest celebrity, after which viewers were invited to vote for their favourite novel (in this case, choosing Donnelly's over the other five entries). An indication, perhaps, of the decline of original writing for popular television, competitions of every conceivable kind flourished on the four main television channels in Britain over the millennial decade. The BBC exploited this competitive structure to maximum effect in its 2003 Big Read competition, which invited celebrities to champion a favourite book as part of a television campaign to discover the 'nation's best loved book.' Three quarters of a million votes were collected from televisual audiences, and a list of the top one hundred books compiled. Unsurprisingly, J.R.R. Tolkien's *The Lord of the Rings* came in first (it had done so in a similar national poll conducted in 1997[39]). In fact, it came in well ahead of the runner-up, Jane Austen's *Pride and Prejudice*, despite Professor John Carey, one of the illustrious critics invited to participate in the closing ceremonies at the Royal Opera House, dismissing the trilogy as silly. Perhaps more surprising, but confirming the importance of children's literature to a majority of adult readers, was the fact that over fifty percent of the top one hundred best loved books turned out to be children's and young adult fiction. Many of these were classics, but some were contemporary children's novels that had recently crossed to adult readerships. Amongst the former were: *To Kill a Mockingbird* (which came sixth), *Winnie-the-Pooh* (7), *Nineteen Eighty-Four* (8), *The Lion, the Witch and the Wardrobe* (9), *Catch-22* (11), *Wuthering Heights* (12), *The Catcher in the Rye* (15), *The Wind in the Willows* (16), *Little Women* (18), *The Hobbit* (25), *Alice's Adventures in Wonderland* (30), *Charlie and the Chocolate Factory* (35) *Treasure Island* (36), *Anne of Green Gables* (41), *Watership Down* (42), *The Count of Monte Cristo* (44), *Animal Farm* (46), *A Christmas Carol* (47), *The Secret Garden* (51), *The BFG* (56), *Swallows and Amazons* (57), *Black Beauty* (58), *The Magic Faraway Tree* (66), *Matilda* (74), *The Twits* (81), *I Capture the Castle* (82) and *Gormenghast* (84). Amongst the works of contemporary children's fiction in the top one hundred novels were: Pullman's *His Dark Materials* (3), Rowling's *Harry Potter and the Goblet of Fire* (5), *Harry Potter and the Philosopher's Stone* (22), *Harry Potter and the Chamber Of Secrets* (23), *Harry Potter and the Prisoner Of Azkaban* (24), Wilson's *The Story of Tracy Beaker* (31), Colfer's *Artemis Fowl* (59), Blackman's *Noughts And Crosses* (61) and Sachar's *Holes* (83). Of course one can question how meaningful such lists are. Some might dismiss as unreliable any list which ranked Tolstoy's *War and Peace* just below *Captain Corelli's Mandolin* and just above *Gone with the Wind* (although, it should be borne in mind that the object was to discover the nation's best loved book, not the best). It is also questionable whether any television programme could accurately reflect the nation's tastes in reading, because the most dedicated book addicts would presumably be reading, not watching television at all. But the Big Read competition was also an invaluable exercise in demonstrating how thoroughly book reading had been assimilated into popular culture. Indeed, even the fact that a competition about reading could attract millions of viewers is an indication that fiction, particularly children's fiction, can easily hold its own against other forms of popular entertainment in the twenty-first century. Another virtue of the competition was that it provided a talking point for readers across the country to exchange their views about their own favourite books. Although reading is often a solitary experience, it is also a very difficult experience to keep to oneself. Like any other passion, reading asks to be shared and argued over and made present through conversation. As Proust remarked, it is one of those rare activities that bridge the solitary and the communal.[40] The Big Read programme raised awareness of how fiction can contribute to social cohesion, not necessarily by producing a homogeneity of opinion, but by bringing dissenting views into a dialogic frame. And the very high percentage of children's books figuring amongst the top one hundred is a further indication of the heightened adult interest in childhood culture and experience, both present and remembered, in the millennial decade.

All Dolled Up: Dust Jackets for Dual Editions

Whether or not it actually led to an actual increase in sales to adult readers, Bloomsbury's idea of publishing Harry Potter in a dual edition, one for children and another for adults, soon caught on with other publishers. The 'dual edition,' that is, a single text published separately for adults and children, and generally distinguishable from each other only by their differing dust jackets, remains to this day the most visible sign of the historical oddity that is crossover fiction. Mark Haddon's *The Curious Incident of the Dog in the Night-time* was the first novel to be published simultaneously in dual editions, the adult edition by Jonathan Cape, and the children's edition by David Fickling, in 2003. Haddon's was an unusual case, as we shall see in Chapter 4, but generally speaking, the demand for two editions seems to have arisen from the practical difficulties of knowing where physically to place a book that was being marketed for a mixed age audience. Dual editions circumvented the problem booksellers faced in deciding where to place a children's book that might also attract adult readers; they could simply be shelved in two sections of the shop, as two different books (although there was nothing except convention preventing booksellers from shelving a book with a child-oriented cover in the general fiction section). On the other hand, many people now shop for books by Internet, where shelving is not an issue. And in any case, many of the new dual edition dust jackets fail to make a clear distinction between child and adult cover designs. Jonathan Cape's dust jacket for *The Curious Incident* is not more noticeably 'adult' than Fickling's. Both feature a stylised outline of a dead dog. Cape's is upside-down and has a pitchfork sticking out of it, while Fickling's has only the bloody marks left by the fork (and the image of the dog is offset by that of a toy car). Both covers are minimalist, using a limited pallet of colours, which could be said to appeal to children's tastes, or to modernist adult ones. Lian Hearn's *Tales of the Otori* series (2002–2007) was published in Britain both by Picador and Young Picador, respectively the adult and young adult lists of Pan Macmillan.[41] The adult and child dust jackets of the 2003/2004 editions of the first book, *Across the Nightingale Floor*, are identical in every detail except colour, one being blue, and the other, red. Hearn's medieval Japanese fantasy has since been translated and published in thirty-six countries, each edition bearing a distinctly different cover appealing to a diverse range of age-groups. The Pan Macmillan website advertises the series as 'an epic story for readers young and old.' With or without the alternative dust jackets, it seems likely that in the climate of millennial crossover, the books would have sold successfully to a mixed age adult readership.[42]

Dual editions were not the only design innovation that publishers introduced to promote crossover fiction. A more successful route, in the long run, was to be to find a single cover design that would work for both child and adult readers. At the 2002 Bologna Children's Book Fair, Judith Elliott, publisher at Orion Children's Books, commented on the meticulous attention being paid to a striking cover design. 'Children's covers have got very exciting', she said. 'There used to be boundaries but these have now crashed down'.[43] The boundaries in question were those that were previously thought to exclude adult readers, so what the designers set themselves to find were images that would continue to attract children, while newly appealing to a potential secondary readership of adults. At Puffin, the children's literature branch of Penguin, there was a clear decision to market Meg Rosoff's *How I Live Now* as a crossover novel, in a single edition that would also attract adult readers.[44] Rebecca McNally of Puffin recalls that she and her colleagues, all in their thirties, had 'a strong emotional response' to the novel which convinced them of its crossover potential. They also felt that Rosoff's cataclysmic vision of Britain at war was particularly timely, given recent terrorist bombings in Madrid. Convinced that they had a special, dual-audience book to sell, they aimed to place the novel at front of store, thus obviating the need to decide between child and adult sections. The dust jacket cleverly combined lighthearted 'girl's diary' images (flowers and butterflies) with darker notes (thorns and wire), thus ambivalently addressing a sophisticated young adult and/or *faux-naif* adult reader. And directly under the title was a line from a review by Haddon, the reigning crossover star, declaring the novel to possess 'a magical and utterly faultless voice,' a description that might equally entice child and adult readers. The first reviewers of *How I Live Now* confirmed the response of the editors at Puffin. Geraldine Bedell's review in *The Observer* began: 'a novel ostensibly written for children. Adults should read it too'.[45] In any event, both children and adults did read the novel in their millions. It became a crossover best seller, followed two years later by the equally successful *Just in Case*, again published by Puffin, the children's list, with a similarly ambivalent dust jacket design.

So What *Is* Crossover Fiction?

Geraldine Bedell's byline nicely encapsulates the working definition of crossover fiction as it emerged in usage by publishers and reviewers in the early years of the new millennium: A crossover novel is one 'ostensibly written for children' which 'adults should read too'.[46] But if one is hoping to define crossover fiction as a distinct genre, with a set of shared characteristics, this pragmatic definition becomes immediately problematic. There simply are no stable set of traits, no themes or motifs or modes of address or narrative dynamics, which are common to all—or even, most of—the fiction 'ostensibly written for children' which has recently been taken up by adult readers. 'Crossover fiction' represents too varied a group of novels to be identified as a distinct genre or class of fiction. The assumptions behind the phrase 'ostensibly written for children' is a minefield in itself, as Jacqueline Rose has shown with her deconstruction of the idea of writing 'for' in *The Case of Peter Pan*. Beyond this, the hortatory element, illustrated by Bedell's appended sentence 'adults should read it too', raises another host of problems. If crossover fiction is not limited to books that have crossed to adult readers, but also includes children's books that, in the opinion of the reviewer, author, publisher, critic or general reader, should be read by adults, how on earth could one set the limits for this category of novel? The label 'crossover' is at least a neutral one, unlike the despised earlier term 'kiddult,' but it is also so open to interpretation that it does little to distinguish and define this group of texts as a distinct literary genre.

This is all to the good, however, since the inconclusiveness of the term accurately reflects the amorphous nature of the corpus of literature which we have in view. In fact, there seems to be no limit to the number of children's books that could potentially be reinvented as crossover fiction. It is not simply that, as Nikolajeva suggests, contemporary children's fiction is more sophisticated than children's fiction in the past and thus can appeal to adult tastes, because classic children's fiction is also being reread and read for the first time by adult readers.[47] Enid Blyton, J.M. Barrie, Rider Haggard, George Henty—all those books one might previously have assumed were 'for children' or 'for boys' or 'for girls' are being re-edited and reissued for a mainstream readership, including adults and children of both genders.

So is there such a thing as 'crossover fiction'? One answer would be: 'Yes, potentially everywhere'. In such a case, it seems more productive to rephrase the question to ask, not what is crossover fiction, but what does it do?[48] In my view, crossover fiction excels at increasing a reader's awareness of the areas of overlap as well as the differences between children's and adult fiction. It prompts a reader to interrogate everything that happens in these in-between territories, invites us to measure our difference from the recent past and the speed with which we are hurtling towards new concepts of self, of childhood, of aging and dying. Crossover fiction is fiction that calls into question the boundaries which used to define children's fiction by prescribing what it should contain or exclude. In 1976, Myles McDowell compiled a list of 'essential' features of children's literature, nearly all of which would require revision in the light of recent children's fiction that has crossed to adult readers. According to McDowell, 'children's books are generally shorter' than adult fiction, whereas

Pullman's *His Dark Materials* trilogy is over 1200 pages long, and the last four Potter novels are over 600 pages each. Traditionally, children's books 'favour dialogue and incident rather than description and introspection', but very little actually happens in David Almond's *Clay*, the introspective narrator of McCaughrean's *The White Darkness* talks mostly to a figment of her imagination, and Pullman's *His Dark Materials* is opulently studded with epic similes, extended metaphors and set-piece descriptions. Children's books are said to 'develop a clear moral schematism which much adult fiction ignores' but there is no overt moralising in Haddon's *Curious Incident,* and Almond and Pullman invite their readers to challenge orthodox Christian morality. McDowell continues, children's 'plots are of a distinct order, probability is often disregarded, and one could go on endlessly talking of magic, and fantasy, and simplicity and adventure', an odd assortment of characteristics to which crossover fiction could provide many counterexamples. In Haddon's *Curious Incident,* fifteen-year-old Christopher Boone is scathing of adults who find comfort in fantasy, magic and religion. Rowling's *Half-Blood Prince* and *Deathly Hallows* could hardly be described as having simple plots, though there is no lack of magic and adventure. As David Rudd points out, McDowell 'measures children's literature according to adult literature, which collapses difference into sameness' because implicitly both categories are being measured against one standard, which is that of adult literature.[49] Clearly, the binaries are not reversible, or we would be able to define adult literature as: longer than children's books, full of introspection and long descriptions, focalised through adults, morally ambivalent, fact-based, realistic, complex, depressing, with adult-oriented language and chaotic or minimalist plots. Such a definition would strike anyone as weirdly prescriptive, and yet it is no more so than previous definitions of children's literature that are still widely accepted today. Crossover fiction helps to heighten the reader's consciousness of the constructedness of both categories, children's and adult fiction.

Cross-reading reveals the limitations and presuppositions inherent even in less formally prescriptive definitions of children's fiction. For example, in *The Narrator's Voice*, Barbara Wall defined children's fiction by its mode of narratorial address, which could be one of three types: 'single address' to a child reader alone, 'double address' to a child reader and an additional adult reader 'over the child's head', and, most infrequently but least condescendingly, 'dual address' to two equal, but separate readers, a child and an adult.[50] This approach, while much more defensible than McDowell's, is again called into question by contemporary crossover fiction. Wall's thesis would suggest that in a novel like Pullman's *Northern Lights*, the narrative could be divided into layers or levels of difficulty, with a simple level (the adventure plot) aimed at child readers, and a morally sophisticated level (the questioning of institutional religion) aimed at adult readers. But judging from the reviews posted by children on Internet discussion boards, young readers are equally interested in the book's complex themes. They are as, if not more, likely to ponder questions such as the existence of God and the ethical limits of science as adult readers of the novel are.[51] There may be differences between child and adult responses to the novel, but these are not as easy to codify into different levels of address as we might suppose.[52] Cross-reading calls attention to the fact that narrative communication flows in two directions, and levels of address are determined not only by addressers but also by addressees. Regardless of the mode of address of author, implied author or narrator, a book can be read in many ways, on any number of levels, by an actual reader. As an adult reader, one can read 'as if' one were any number of things or people one is not: a child, a nonagenarian, a dog, a tree, or a house. A child reader can exercise exactly the same freedoms. Reading draws us into Rosalind's magic circle at the end of *As You Like It,* where obstacles can vanish on the breath of an 'if'.[53] Crossover fiction makes us especially aware of these freedoms, precisely because we retain a sense of transgression, of crossing a threshold from somewhere that feels like home, to somewhere that feels strange and at least a little alienating. Janice Alberghene rightly argues that 'children's books help create childhood for us'[54] But crossover fiction helps create both states while making us aware that they are provisional and subject to constant change. As David Rudd writes of children's literature, 'there is always difference, but it is never complete; it is always in process, for notions of children change across time, gender, race and class. Also, each child changes over time, playing at adulthood in various guises.'. ('Shirley, the Bathwater, and Definitions', 93) So too does an adult change over time, playing at, and with, and against all the phases of childhood and adolescence.

Thus I would disagree with those who argue that crossover fiction augurs the end of children's literature, whether this argument is framed as something positive or negative.[55] In a lecture delivered to the Royal Society of Literature, Philip Pullman pokes fun at those who object to adults reading children's literature, caricaturing them as 'fierce and stern' border guards:

> They strut up and down with a fine contempt, curling their lips and consulting their clipboards and snapping out orders . . . But when we step away from the border post, when we go round the back of the guards . . . we see . . . people are happily walking across this border in both directions. You'd think there wasn't a border there at all. Adults are happily reading children's books; and what's more, children are reading adults' books.[56]

For some readers, this description might suggest that we are approaching a situation in which there will only be one universal literature 'for all'. But to me, what is striking about this description (and indeed, our present situation) is that it represents the border between states as something permeable, which allows free access from both sides. There still are such things as 'children's books' and 'adults' books' in this imagined scenario. The real change is that more people are crossing the threshold to try out fiction they might not have bothered with before. So Pullman is not advocating a 'One Ring to rule them all' view of literature here. Elsewhere, too, he insists there are crucial differences between childhood and adulthood identities, as we shall see in Chapter 3.

But why should a permeable and flexible border between children's and adult fiction be preferable to the more clear-cut distinctions that have prevailed in the past? Because if there is no dialogic encounter, no impersonations of adulthood by children, of childhood by adults, especially in an era in which the contours of child- and adulthood are changing so rapidly, then we may well become mutually incomprehensible to each other.[57] Before coming on to discuss these social changes, it might be worth considering an example of the alternative view, one which insists on a complete separation between childhood and adulthood, and the fiction read by each. Jonathan Myerson encapsulates this view when he argues that children's books 'address the problems and questions of childhood, enact the hopes and dreams of childhood' which, he argues, are 'a completely different set of questions from those that mesmerise us in adult life'.[58] As adults,

> we deal with the constantly muddled nature of good and evil, we take on things like the constraints and longevity of love, we carry a responsibility for the safety of others, we crave success and fear failure, we confront the reality of dreams. And this is why different books are written for these two tribes: there is barely any genuine or useful crossover between the agendas. When I read a novel, I look to it to tell me some truths about human life—the truths that nonfiction cannot reach. These might be moral, sexual, political or psychological truths and I expect my life to be enlarged, however slightly, by the experience of reading something fictional. I cannot hope to come closer to any of these truths through a children's novel, where nice clean white lines are painted between the good guys and the evil ones, where magic exists, and where there are adults on hand to delineate rules. Adult fiction is about a world without rules.

But it is hard to see how any life could be 'enlarged' while it rests on such an absolute distinction between thinking adulthood and mechanically minded childhood. It seems that this adult consciousness would always end up drawing nice clean white lines between a self and an other, if not a child, then some other mythically unknowable 'tribe' whose very existence endangered the present self. Or to put it in plainer terms, as Jennifer Donnelly argues,

> the idea that books for and about children can only be of interest to children is not just absurd, it's offensive. It's like telling a reader not to bother with *Beloved* unless she's black or *Trainspotting* unless he uses heroin. Books are not gated communities; they're open cities where we

can all come and go at will, freely sampling other lives and times, other cultures and realities.

And it is even less tenable to argue that adults and children are completely unrelated tribes, since every adult has been a child once, and *pace* Peter Pan, most children hope to become adults.[59]

A more unexpected source of support for the idea that adult readers should not engage with children's fiction comes from children's literature specialists themselves. Such critics perceive adult interest in children's culture, including fiction, as potentially predatory and invasive.[60] If adults colonise children's fiction, there will be nothing left for children to call their own.[61] A nuanced version of this position is voiced by Deborah Thacker, who writes:

> The recent example of Bloomsbury's project to publish the hugely successful children's novel by J.K. Rowling, *Harry Potter and the Philosopher's Stone* . . . in two editions, one for adults and the other for children . . . indicates the complex positioning of the texts of children's literature within the 'white noise' of numerous adult voices. Such a phenomenon, suggesting the extent to which adult forces seek to subjugate children as readers, but also to colonize and contain childhood itself, demand further investigation through an understanding of children's literature's place within a larger, inclusive map of readership.[62]

but literature is always positioned within a 'white noise' or static of other voices; to shut off that noise would be to silence literature itself. It is true that there is an imbalance of power between child readers and adult writers within the field of children's literature (although see below, on the new generation of child writers), but this does not necessarily mean that the relation will be one of 'subjugation' and 'colonisation'. It does mean that we need to reconceive how children's literature operates within the 'larger, inclusive map of readership' as Thacker suggests. Crossover fiction provides a spotlight on these areas of intersection between the child's interests, and the adult's. And cross-reading increases our consciousness of difference, even as we traverse and retraverse the boundary lines that once divided us more strictly. But whether one is 'for' or 'against' it, it is worth stressing is that 'crossover fiction' can really only be defined by what it does, rather than what it is.

Kiddults and Cool Britannia

So far, we have considered the rise of crossover fiction and cross-reading in literary and popular culture in Britain from around 1997 to 2007. But while dual editions and publicity campaigns, awards and increased media coverage can help to explain the increasing visibility of children's literature in mainstream, adult literary culture, it cannot really account for the sea change that made this change in status and visibility possible. Although many contemporary children's novels are rich, complex and beautifully written, the shift in status of children's fiction from the marginal to the mainstream of fiction publishing cannot convincingly be explained by a sudden rise in the quality of children's fiction alone. Some have described the recent expansion of children's literature as a new Renaissance or Golden Age, but if so, it differs markedly from the first 'Golden Age' (around 1865–1910), in which critics often discern a shift from an earlier didactic mode towards an emphasis on pleasing and entertaining the child reader (the turn of the century pleasuremongers are said to include Carroll, Barrie, Grahame, MacDonald, Nesbit, Stevenson, Kipling and Burnett, amongst others).[63] What characterises the present phenomenon is the hybridisation of child and adult perspectives within contemporary children's fiction, which reflects and responds to a more pervasive hybridisation of child and adult cultures, one indication of which is the expanded reception of children's fiction in Britain (and indeed, elsewhere in the developed world). To explain the shift in reception, as well as the more complex commingling of perspectives in contemporary children's fiction, there are many broader issues that need to be considered, including changes in Britain's political climate, as well as developments in science and technology.

In May 1997, Tony Blair's New Labour was voted into government in a historic, landslide victory over the Conservatives, who had been in power for eighteen years. Labour's majority (66 % in the House of Commons) was unprecedented and unexpectedly decisive; they had gained 146 seats, while the Conservatives had lost 178. Whether or not Britain 'deserved better' as the slogan went, 1997 seemed like a political new dawn. New Labour lost no opportunity to associate itself with new youth, as illustrated by the occasion on which Peter Mandelson appeared on a children's programme *Pass the Mic*, having declared himself unavailable for interview on BBC Newsnight.[64] It was a time when it was extremely fashionable not just to be young, but to be overtly childish. The older the mutton, the more extravagantly it should parade itself as lamb.

A cult of 'the inner child' or the 'kiddult' was permeating adult cultural life on many levels in the late 1990s, which not coincidentally was when Rowling's early 'childish' Potter novels became popular with adults. Possibly the earliest use of the term 'kidult' was by Peter Martin in an article in *The New York Times* in 1985, and it was used to describe not just fiction but any form of entertainment that would be likely to appeal to a mixed age audience.[65] A few years later, the noun 'kid(d)ult' had become the term for an adult who trespasses into children's culture, and the sense of breaking a taboo was paramount. Thus Ben Summerskill describes a typical kiddult as a single, professional male in his thirties: 'He wears Caterpillar boots and Levis. He rides a motor scooter, with a pavement model for warm weather. When he gets home, he watches *It's a Knockout* before turning on his Sony PlayStation. However, he's not 15. He's 35'.[66] In 2000, it was estimated that ten thousand people a week in Britain were buying Sony PlayStations, that the sale of small scooters went up by 31% and large scooters and motorbikes by 47%, and that the consumers of these products were aged anywhere from 18 to 40.[67] As kiddult fashion took hold, with a proliferation of 'Babe' T-shirts, Reeboks and Adidas trainers, the Spice Girl singer Emma Bunton became a cultural icon in her role as Baby Spice, following in the tracks of teenager Britney Spears who topped the charts with an unexpected hit single in 1999. Elspeth Gibson modelled one season's collection on Tolkien's *The Lord of the Rings*, while Gucci modelled another on baby-doll dresses, and the 'Lolita look' became a global fashion trend.[68] High fashion, as ever, impacted on the High Street. In 2001, *The Guardian*'s Weekend section featured four full-page spreads on male fashion, in which the models were posed in scenes from children's books such as Lewis's *The Lion, the Witch and the Wardrobe*, and fairy tales such as Sleeping Beauty, Little Red Riding Hood and Goldilocks.[69] The oddness of this cultural trend is perhaps best exemplified in 2001, with a CD by American actor/singer Mandy Patinkin released to rave reviews in the UK. Entitled *Kidults*, it bizarrely mixes Broadway musical songs for children together with sentimental songs for adults about childhood.

Even at the height of its popularity, the kiddult craze attracted fierce criticism in the national press. Philip Hensher blames the sexualisation of young children on the kiddulterous behaviour of adults, maintaining—contentiously—that 'there is a direct connection between something like School Disco and the shops that enable five-year-olds to dress like King's Cross prostitutes'.[70] Meanwhile Will Self describes the reality TV programme *Big Brother* as 'a voyeuristic "kidult" soap opera', standing as a 'ghastly synecdoche of the truly loathsome society we have become'.[71] And, rather more persuasively, Gareth McLean criticises what he sees as the ageism of contemporary British culture. Praising a BBC 1 documentary, *Through the Eyes of the Old*, for its attention to such an unfashionable subject as old age, he berates Britons for being 'youth obsessed', arguing 'you have to stop being a kidult sometime'. [72]

Kiddult Politicians: A Return to Mordor?

It must be said, though, that in many quarters the media response to the kiddult craze was positive, as it represented a welcome shaking up of entrenched social attitudes, and outmoded Tory tastes. Thus one *Times* journalist commented approvingly on the hybridisation of child and adult clothes fashions: 'The risqué nature of today's adult fashions and the consumer power of the under-teens is resulting in some seriously hot tots, shopping like "It Girls" and dressed to kill'.[73] Others, however, associated the hybridity of the kiddult with New Labour's brave new world of spin, orchestrated by the archillusionist, Peter Mandelson. Thus Catherine Bennett commented acerbically in *The Guardian* that since there are "'kidults", those unwieldy, 35-ish, Harry Potter-reading, *Stuart Little*-watching, trainer-wearing scooter riders who feel no shame in sharing a hobby with Po from the *Teletubbies*, then perhaps there are kidult voters, too, who want kidult politicians who understand about PlayStations'.[74]

And as Britain's role in global politics changed after 9/11, many became distinctly uncomfortable with the cult of new, or rather borrowed, youth. It was hardly the fault of the film producers, but the first instalment of Peter Jackson's epic adaptation of Tolkien's *The Lord of the Rings* was released just as British troops invaded Afghanistan as part of an allied response to the terrorist bombing of the World Trade Center in New York City. The Afghan war was begun in October 2001, and Jackson's film version of *The Fellowship of the Ring* was released just two months later. The year that was crossover fiction's *annus mirabilis, 2003,* was also the year that George W. Bush and Tony Blair took Britain and America to war against Iraq. This rapidly deteriorating political climate helped to polarise opinion over the phenomenon of adults reading children's literature, and fuelled the argument that adults were dangerously 'dumbing down' when they chose to watch or read about fantasy wars at a time when real wars were being waged against international law. In an article surmounted by a photograph of two adults sticking their tongues out at each other, Timothy Garton Ash excoriated the 'three main British exports of 2001—Harry Potter, Frodo Baggins and Tony Blair', all of whom concealed under high-tech packaging a dangerous and 'remarkably traditional Englishness'. One ingredient in this traditional English package is the courageous but reluctant hero, a role undertaken by Prime Minister Blair. Thus, 'Britain must be Gryffindor among the houses of Europe, and Harry Blair—Sir Frodo of the Shire—will lead us there'.[75]

It would, however, be equally possible to interpret the adult turn to children's fiction in positive terms, as a reaction against the polarisation of global politics into a Western 'us' versus an Eastern 'them.' The epic wars that unfold in Lian Hearn's *Tales of the Otori* and Philip Pullman's *His Dark Materials* are morally ambivalent, and force their readers to rethink the genre of fantasy's traditional distinctions between good and evil. One might go so far as to argue that children's fiction was deconstructing the whole notion of epic imperialism, just at the point where political leaders in Britain and the US were succumbing to the most simplistic forms of militaristic rhetoric ('we need to smoke the enemy out of their holes', as Bush said, prior to the attack on Afghanistan). Another role that children's fiction might have played for adult readers in this increasingly bellicose environment was to provide a ground for rethinking and reasserting personal values at a time when public opinion became divided over the British and American governments' response to the threat of global terrorism. But however one interprets the politics of reading children's literature during this period, the masquerading of politicians as kiddults effectively came to an end in Britain when, in 2007, the Labour Party ousted Tony Blair as

Prime Minister and replaced him with the unmistakably grown-up, cautious and dour-seeming Gordon Brown.

I, Bratz-doll

With the benefit of just a few years' hindsight, it already seems strange that Britain once fetishised its politicians for seeming childlike. But to understand this phase in Labour's, and indeed the nation's, political history, one has to recall the broader social and economic context out of which the kiddult craze emerged. Reasons for the rise in youth culture, and with it the expansion of children's fiction into mainstream, adult markets, must be understood in the light of developments in science, technology and economics, both globally and in Atlantic societies in particular. Western scientists are much more able to intervene in the processes of reproduction and aging than they have been in previous generations. Prolonged youth has become an achievable aspiration for the wealthy, given advances in cosmetic surgery. And, to judge by the extensive coverage that Botox, 'nipping and tucking' and so on, receive on TV and in the print media, the general public is fascinated by tales of the rich and famous 'enhancing' themselves by surgical means. Also, due to advances in fertility treatment, women can now choose to become mothers much later in life, leaving a longer period in which to pursue their own adolescent or kiddult interests. Interestingly, as it becomes a technical possibility, old-age motherhood has attracted a weight of social stigma (which old-age fatherhood seems to have escaped), as was evident in the storm of controversy that broke out over news that a 62-year-old woman was receiving IVF treatment.[76] But that so many people should even want to look, feel and act younger than might be expected of their biological age is an indication of how highly the idea of 'youthfulness' has come to be valued both culturally and economically.

In a special issue of *The Economist* devoted to youth in developed nations, Chris Anderson points out that the Internet 'triggered the first industrial revolution in history to be led by the young'.[77] He cites Don Tapscott who argues in *Growing Up Digital* that for the first time, children are more knowledgeable than their parents about an innovation central to society.[78] Yvonne Fritzche, a researcher in a German market research institute, agrees: 'Technology is one of the reasons that the relationship between the young and old is becoming a dialogue, rather than a lesson.'[79] A rapidly evolving technology is the 'defining event' of the current generation of young people, much as economic depression or wars were for a previous generation, Anderson argues ('Bright Young Things' 7). Not only the Internet, but also mobile phones and personal stereo systems have transformed the lives of teenagers in Western, developed nations, and left some adults struggling to keep pace with the waves of technological change.[80] Anderson argues that since the restructurings of Western business corporations in the 1980–90s, the workplace has been tailored for young or 'youthful' employees who are rewarded not, as previously, for length of service, but for meeting short-term goals and challenges. 'Flitting from job to job, once a trait of fickle youth,' he writes, 'is now an admired sign of ambition and initiative.' ('Bright Young Things' 5)

But on an individual level, the freedom to extend childhood or adolescence indefinitely can induce anxiety in the would-be (or rather, would-not-be) kiddult. In her memoir, *Confessions of a Failed Grown-Up*, Stephanie Calman represents herself as an adult who wants to grow up but no longer knows how it is done ('surely, by the time you get lines on your face the teenage angst should start to recede').[81] Growing up seems to have become an infinitely reversible process: 'Just as computers have internal modems, I have an internal Tardis which shoots me around in time'.(223) In a song released in April 2007 with his new band, Grinderman, Nick Cave has a baffled and aging protagonist sing, 'we're free and we're lost'. That a fifty-year-old singer should be writing and performing hard-edged rock songs about an 'elderly man in crisis' is in itself a sign of our strange, crossover times.[82] The freedom to be whatever you want, to act whatever age you feel, can induce a sense of vertigo which ironically leaves you unable to act at all.

Moreover, if adults are feeling slightly queasy about the limitless possibilities of 'growing down', children are feeling the pressure of growing up very quickly as they become more thoroughly absorbed into the networked global economy than ever before. For 'tweenagers' (children acting like teenagers), there are positive and negative aspects to participating in the economy on a par with adults. On the one hand, children's voices are more often heard alongside adults' in public debates about politics, education and the environment. And they are also increasingly taking leading roles in the arts, from acting to writing and directing their own work. When Jacqueline Rose described children's literature as an 'impossibility', she based her argument on the assumption that the literature so-termed was always produced by adults, for children but with adult interests in mind. But there is nothing impossible, in the sense she meant, about young adult literature that is written by and for young adults. Still less does she consider the possibility that these novels would cross to adult readerships. Christopher Paolini published *Eragon* first privately and then with Knopf in 2003. By the age of nineteen, he had become a best-selling *New York Times* author. A successful feature film followed in 2006, and was released on DVD in 2007. By 2007, *Eragon* and its sequel in the *Inheritance* trilogy, *Eldest*, had sold over eight million copies. Other children and young adults who successfully published novels in the UK that crossed to adult readerships include the Nigerian writer Helen Oyeyemi, who wrote *The Icarus Girl* at the age of nineteen, and two Scottish writers, Emma Maree Urquhart (*Dragon Tamers*, written aged thirteen) and Robert King (*Apple of Doom*, written aged fifteen) both of whom have sold thousands of copies with Aultbea Publishing in Inverness.[83] And, calling into question the critical view that sees the relation between child and adult as comparable to that between colonised and coloniser, are the coequal child-adult writing partnerships that have emerged in recent years. The best-seller *Lionboy* was written by 'Zizou Corder', an alias for Louisa Young and her daughter Isabel Adomakoh Young, and the *Corydon* trilogy was written by 'Tobias Druitt', a pseudonym for Diane Purkiss and her son Michael Dowling. 'P.J. Tracy', the author of a series of murder mysteries, is an alias for another writing pair, P.J. Lambrecht and her daughter Traci Lambrecht. In the States, the documentary film director Chaille Patrick Stovall was just twelve when he released his first feature length film, *Party Animals, or How to Get to the White House in 5 Easy Steps* (2001). Stovall's camera and sound crew were also children. *Party Animals* featured interviews with President Bush, Vice President Al Gore and former presidents Clinton and Carter; it won a national award and was critically acclaimed internationally.[84] Such artistic highfliers show the possibilities that are open to children and young adults in a social economy where youth and youthfulness are so highly valued and respected.

On the other hand, this can also place an unrealistic burden of expectation on children who have no wish to enter a public arena at such a young age. There is also a great deal of evidence to suggest that children and young adults are much more exposed to commercial interests than in previous generations. According to a government report, 'The Commercialisation of Childhood,' the child-oriented market in the UK was said to be worth about £30 billion in the early 2000s. In 2001, a BBC 2 documentary, *Little Women: A Day in the Life of a Tweenager,* documented the lives of a group of seven- to twelve-year-old girls from southern England who shopped at Harrods, watched wrestling on Sky Sports, discussed rape, and dressed like their favourite pop idols.[85] In a 2006 report, 78% of children interviewed said they 'enjoy shopping'. These children, aged ten or younger, were found to have 'internalised 300 to 400 brands—perhaps 20 times the number of birds in the wild that they could name.' The report concluded that British children were among the most materialistic in the world, ahead of American children.[86]

In *Toxic Childhood*, Sue Palmer argues that living 'at electric speed' benefits adults more than children, and that children are being cheated of the 'slow time' development in which empathy for others, the ability to sustain focus, and the capacity to defer gratification all emerge as ingrained habits and values.[87] Technology is replacing parenting and ordinary playtime adventures, as children are kept entertained indoors with electronic games (145, 61). Palmer cites research indicating that children under the age of eleven or twelve (who in the US, UK and Australia are exposed to between 20,000 and 40,000 advertisements a year) lack a critical framework for understanding marketing messages, 'and by this age many have been effectively brainwashed.' (230) In *Sticks and Stones*, Jack Zipes too argues that children are dangerously exposed to financial exploitation: 'everything we do to, with, and for children is influenced by capitalist market conditions and the hegemonic interests of ruling corporate elites'.[88] However unwittingly, we are 'turning [children] into commodities'. (xi)

Meanwhile, if owning a Bratz doll accessorised with spray-on glitter jeans and champagne glasses is the aspiration of middle-class ten- to twelve year olds, very poor children in the UK are living in increasingly distressing conditions, as a recent report by Shelter spells out in detail.[89] A 2007 UNICEF report on child poverty concluded that British children are amongst the worst off of all children in economically advanced nations.[90] According to a 2007 study by researchers at Cambridge University, primary school children, especially from economically depressed areas, feel anxious, stressed, and unsafe playing outside.[91] Reflecting on the government's 'zero-tolerance' policy towards child criminality and the public's extreme reaction to the James Bulger case, Mary Riddle concludes that 'a generation which observes fluid rules about its own evolution is curiously inflexible about the changing patterns of children's lives'.[92] In other words, contrary to what one might expect, kiddults may be the least likely adults to sympathise with children who transgress the law.

Moreover, if young children are growing up faster, and adults are growing down, twenty-first century Britain seems to offer little space or motivation for teenagers to progress from adolescence to adulthood. John Coleman, a psychiatry lecturer at the Royal London Hospital, and Director of the Trust for the Study of Adolescence, believes that 'the transition to adulthood in western societies has become problematic during the last few decades'.[93] In his view, getting into the labour market is much more difficult now than it was during the latter half of the twentieth century (59). Coleman points out that from 1984–99, the number of young adults (16–24) entering the British labour market shrank by 35% (60). Family structures are also becoming more fluid, with more single parents raising children and teenagers. British teenagers are more sexually active than in previous generations, and Britain currently has the highest rate of teenage pregnancy amongst European Union countries (67). As a group, young adults are also often stressed, and according to a 2000 study, more than 10% may suffer from mental health problems such as depression, eating disorders, conduct disorders, drug addiction and suicidal tendencies (73). Government reports have also shown that young people, especially those growing up in 'high deprivation' areas, are increasingly involved in crime, either as victims or offenders. The film *Kidulthood* (where in a rare usage, 'kiddult' is applied to teenagers) depicts this young adult experience of violence on city estates. The experience of adolescence, for these individuals, may be nothing like the beautiful youth to which aging kiddults aspire.

So British children and young adults have a very mixed reputation to live up to. Adults may see them as materialistic consumers or cutting-edge innovators, as victims of crime or criminals, as free agents and free thinkers, or as vulnerable and innocent, in need of adult protection. This contradictory picture of young people might be summed up in the juxtaposition of two half-hour documentaries, broadcast one after another on the same evening on BBC Radio Four.[94] In the first, Simon Cox investigated the rise of knife and gang cultures in British cities, concluding that 'being a teenager has become a potentially deadly business'. In the course of the investigation, he interviewed one seventeen-year-old Glaswegian teenager who had been jailed 32 times. Immediately following this programme, however, came an upbeat business report from Peter Day, which presented 14- to 18-year-olds as the most powerful, sophisticated, flexible and media savvy of all age groups, and the 'grail' of marketing companies across the country. But perhaps it is adults who are pursuing the 'grail' of a mythically idealised adolescence, while real adolescents and children struggle to cope with the conflicting expectations that contemporary society places on their shoulders.

The Kiddult as Soft Capitalist

The value that society places on youth and youth culture, which was particularly apparent in the late nineties and early 2000s, can be explained, too, as part of a general shift from a 'hard' to a 'soft' capitalist ideology. In Costea, Crump and Holm's analysis, this shift took place in Atlantic societies during the 1980s–90s, as a Protestant work ethic of 'salvation through self-abnegation' gave way to a new 'ethics of "self-work"' and the 'cultivation of an "authentic self"'.[95] In soft capitalist corporations, the employee ceases to observe a rigid distinction between work and leisure, but sees both as opportunities to express the self creatively. Corporate management has taken a 'Dionysian turn' towards 'a spirit of playful transgression and destruction of boundaries, a new bond between economic grammars of production and consumption, and cultural grammars of the modern self'. ('Dionysus at Work?' 141)[96] The model for this new 'grammar of the self' is the child at play because whereas adult play is often 'too focused on a specific goal, too competitive' and focussed 'too much on the rules of the game', child's play 'is less conscious, more in touch with the "inner self"'. (143) By emulating the child's more instinctive play, the adult can paradoxically rise above 'playing games, . . . getting back in touch with forgotten powers within'. (143)

Thus soft capitalism reverses the configurations of value and power which previously characterised the relation between adult and child in a Protestant-based, modern work environment. Costea, Crump and Holm argue that,

> for the last two centuries, children were those who were not adults from an ethical standpoint: they were urged to become adults by internalising adult values and overcoming the imperfections of childhood. In the 21st century, the vectors of self-action have been reversed: adults are encouraged to find and preserve the 'inner child', to give up adult reserve and treat life as continuous play as the most important opportunity for free self-expression. (148)[97]

This emphasis on the right—and indeed the duty—to express one's authentic self emerges out of what Charles Taylor describes as the twentieth century's emphasis on the 'affirmation of ordinary life'.[98] If at first this ideology stressed the need for individual emancipation, now in a 'postliberational culture' where (theoretically) individual freedoms are protected by legislation, it has mutated into 'a mythology of worldly *self-assertion* and of everyone's right and responsibility to be happy'. (146) We are thus seeing a revolt against the Apollonian rationalism which underpinned industrial capitalism, and the emergence of a freer expression of the Dionysian, irrational 'will to power', which Nietzsche so polemically advocated. (146)

It might seem odd that one of the signifiers of this new mythology should be the child at play, since real children are generally the last in society to be able to express a Nietzschean 'will to power.' But the child is a second-order signifier in this myth system, as mythmaking was understood by Roland Barthes in *Mythologies*. The myth of the adult's 'inner child' is the product of a signifier which has been emptied of historical content, i.e., has ceased to refer to an *actual* child.[99] We see this in the paradoxical situation discussed above, in which 'youthfulness' is something to which increasing numbers of adults aspire while at the same time, real children and young adults remain trapped in poverty or oppressed by a 'toxic' weight of advertising. Moreover, if the ideological goal of soft capitalism is not only to be free, but to be permanently 'well' and 'happy', then clearly aging and death impose natural limits on this aspiration. By reversing these temporal vectors, so that aging becomes a matter of growing down rather than up, soft capitalists are able to set themselves a goal of attaining a state of permanent innocence and 'continuous happiness'. (148)

Costea, Crump and Holm are ambivalent in their judgement as to whether 'this spirit of play' in the corporate environment is to be welcomed or not. On one hand, the more flexible conception of 'playful work and playful leisure' might encourage the emergence of new and hybrid subjectivities (149). On the other hand, the relentless pursuit of happiness leads to the suppression of any 'tragic dimension of existence'. (148) But surely a more fundamental problem is the vision of endless economic expansion to which this idea of 'limitless play' contributes. Ecologically, we no longer think of the planet as having limitless resources which we can 'exploit' at will; there is, rather, an increasing awareness of the necessity to manage resources sustainably, to find a system that is balanced rather than endlessly expansive. Of necessity, the capitalist drive for limitless growth must, at very least, mutate into new forms. The cult of the 'inner child' may have been one of the forms of its metamorphosis. But the kiddult entrepreneur is a cultural icon with as short a shelf life as the kiddult politician. As the public demand for ethical business management grows, the emphasis on work as creative playtime will change. Indeed, it would seem that from the States we are importing a new personal rhetoric of 'making a difference' which appears to be at odds with the kiddult focus on self-expression.[100]

The emergence of children's literature into the cultural mainstream must be assessed in the light of all these cultural and economic changes, not all of which have necessarily been positive. But it would be erroneous to conclude that the children's fiction written and read during this period is merely reflecting the soft capitalist mythology of self-discovery through play/work. While some novels do reproduce this mythology rather uncritically, there are many others which subject these capitalist myths of childhood and youthfulness to the most stringent critique. Indeed it is in children's fiction—particularly fiction which addresses the theme of adolescent crossing from childhood to adulthood, that we can discover the most careful and sustained scrutiny of contemporary myths of limitless youth. And while there is a myriad of reasons why adults read children's literature—sometimes it may be to escape or to find solace in the known and familiar—one of the reasons we do is to remind ourselves how to live in a timely way, rather than in the vain hope of transcending time altogether. Contemporary children's fiction is of particular consequence to adult readers because in many cases, it is discovering ways to give consecution, consequence, and depth to the unreality of a suspended adolescence which troubles adults, no less than children, at the beginning of the twenty-first century.

Chapter Two
Harry Potter, Lightness and Death

Despite the global popularity of the Potter novels, Rowling's work has attracted fierce criticism from many different quarters. Writing in the *New York Times*, A.S. Byatt criticised J.K. Rowling's Harry Potter series and its readers, describing the former as a 'patchwork' of 'derivative motifs', and the latter as 'people whose imaginative lives are confined to TV cartoons, and the exaggerated . . . mirror-worlds of soaps, reality TV and celebrity gossip'.[1] Frank Furedi argued that the success of Harry Potter was symptomatic of a general, cultural infantilism in late twentieth century and millennial Western society.[2] Harold Bloom, Byatt, Furedi and others would have us believe that for adults to read such lightweight fiction is degrading and infantilising. But are J.K. Rowling's Potter novels really lightweight, and are readers really infantilised by engaging with them? It would seem obvious, to anyone who has actually read it, that the series begins lightly but darkens considerably as it progresses. My argument in this chapter is twofold: that the lightness of the early books is a quality for which they should be celebrated, and that the increasing darkness and seriousness of the later books demonstrate Rowling sharpening her critique of some aspects of contemporary life, while never betraying the original vision expressed at the outset. [3] Before coming on to discuss this thesis, however, I would like to explore the charge of 'lightness' and 'infantilism' in more depth, since this is an accusation frequently aired in debates about adults reading children's fiction in general.

Harry Agonistes

A number of critics have argued that Harry Potter is either intellectually or aesthetically lightweight, and/or that it has the effect of infantilising adult readers, although 'infantilism' turns out to mean different things for different people.[4]

Some accuse Rowling of degrading the genre of high fantasy, the greatest practitioners of which are said to be Tolkien and Ursula LeGuin. In 'From Elfland to Hogwarts', John Pennington argues that Rowling violates 'fantasy literature ground-rules' by failing to depart wholly from consensual reality to create a separate fantasy world, as Tolkien both advocated and illustrated with *The Lord of the Rings*.[5] But Rowling clearly did not set out to create a self-standing mythology, as Tolkien did. The early books in the Potter series are indeed a patchwork of many mythologies, such as one also finds in C.S. Lewis's *The Chronicles of Narnia*. And like Lewis, she freely adds her own monsters to the mix, so that the classical Cerberus can be found barking his three heads next to Rowling's own Blast-ended Skrewts. Like *The Chronicles of Narvia* and other magic fantasy fiction, Harry Potter moves frequently between two worlds, the 'consensually real' and the magic one. In fact, as Suman Gupta points out, there are three worlds present in Harry Potter: the wizarding world, the world of 'Muggles' (humans), and the real world which is implicitly satirised by the former two.[6] In its sustained parody of the real world, Harry Potter can also be classed as a satiric fantasy, together with Jonathan Swift's *Gulliver's Travels* and Roald Dahl's stories, to which the early Potter novels are often compared. So rather than seeing her as a failed high fantasist, we would understand Rowling better if we approached her as a writer who systematically and playfully hybridises different genres.[7]

Another branch of the 'lightweight' argument is that Harry Potter is devoid of literary merit, but has become popular through a relentless campaign of marketing and publicity. In my analysis below, I hope to contribute to the opposing camp which does find merit in the novels. But as to whether Rowling's success is due to marketing alone, Julia Eccleshare has argued convincingly that Rowling established her popularity with younger readers first, through normal publishing channels, and only afterwards accrued an adult readership.[8] The crossover marketing followed the word-of-mouth commendations of child readers, in a distinctly secondary phase. Rowling attracted a children's fan base and won prizes voted for by children, such as the Nestlé (formerly Smarties) Children's Book Prize. Her first three Potter books carried off the Gold Award of the Nestlé Prize (fiction for 9–11 year olds) for three years running, from 1997 to 1999). Indeed, as Eccleshare argues, *Stone* was so popular with children that it seemed unlikely to win critical recognition from adult readers. Prior to Rowling, the most popular children's authors, such as Enid Blyton and Dahl, tended to be ignored by academics and reviewers (*A Guide*, 33). After Dahl's death in 1990, publishers were looking for a potential successor: a writer who would appeal directly to children without necessarily making any great claims to be serious literature (*A Guide*, 34–35). Rowling's generic similarities to Dahl, especially in her first three books, suggested at the time that Harry Potter would quietly bed down in this segregated world of children's books.

As everyone knows, it did anything but. Even while conceding that the initial success came from word of mouth, though, some critics wonder whether

Harry Potter met with such commercial success because the books themselves celebrate a consumerist culture.[9] Rowling's wizard children love to shop; they are shown buying text books, sweets, wands, pets and broomsticks. They are surrounded by catchy advertising slogans. In *Prisoner*, Harry is particularly tempted by an advertisement of a Firebolt, a top model broom (43). Fred and George Weasley know how to exploit the Hogwarts pupils' hunger for anything tasty, weird or frightening, and they soon develop into successful enfantrepreneurs. As Gupta argues, Harry himself is the capitalist's dream: 'someone whose entire sense of the world—the Magic world—is sieved through impressions gathered in the marketplace while having plenty of money in his pocket'. (135) Nevertheless it seems to be stretching the point to argue that the *Potter* books are 'designed to advertise themselves', simply because they reflect the consumer-saturated society in which real children grow up in the developed world (140).

Others have objected to the fact that Harry is a famous wizard from the start of the series, as this apparently panders to our own vacuous celebrity culture. But fame is always a mixed blessing in the series, and Snape is always present to make Harry and the reader feel uncomfortable about it. '"Ah, yes", he said softly, "Harry Potter. Our new—*celebrity*"'. (*Stone*, 101)) Much later, Harry will earn his inherited mythic status as 'The Boy Who Lived', but even then he will be reluctant to acknowledge his celebrity. If anything, readers are likely to become more critical of celebrity culture by reading the series, rather than desirous of stepping into Harry's gold-gilt shoes.

In response to the charge that the series is aesthetically lightweight, Potter fans point out that the later novels are obviously weighty, both in length and content. From *Goblet* onwards, each novel runs to over 600 pages, and each depicts its young protagonists experiencing self-doubt, betrayal, depression and despair as they struggle to cope with the deaths of friends and family. Rowling depicts fascistic prejudice against mixed races; sadistic torture, especially of children; the casual and calculated murder of people and animals, individually and *en masse*. Clearly, there is no lack of gravity in the later books. In their mood and tone, while the first three books are at times light, fizzy and satirical, the succeeding four books more than compensate for this exuberant beginning by being, at times, exceedingly gloomy and portentous. Stylistically, there is less variation across the series as a whole, but there is almost no hint of Rowling's trademark linguistic inventiveness in the opening chapters of *Hallows*, the last volume. As the series progresses, characters are fleshed out and made more complex, the mythic world is given a richness and temporal depth. And, an obvious point but an important one: The protagonists grow up over the course of the series. Aging one year per volume, they start out as eleven-year-old first-year pupils and finish up as seventeen-year-old graduates (with—for good measure—an epilogue which sees them safely into middle age). Rowling's fans surely have good reason to argue that the Harry Potter novels are serious, often dark and sufficiently challenging for adult readers.

An Apology for Lightness

Here, however, I would like to adopt a slightly different tack, to argue that the first three books in the septology are indeed governed by a principle of 'lightness', both aesthetically and ethically, but that this should be viewed in positive terms. Nadine Gordimer described the quality of contemporary life as being such 'where contact is more like the flash of fireflies, in and out, now here, now there, in darkness'.[10] If this is our condition within the foreshortened time-spaces of contemporary western societies, it is easy to understand why lightness, mobility and speed are qualities much in demand.[11] Rowling's series is both a product of this contemporary mind-set and a thoughtful response to it, which eventually leads her to critique some of its key aspirations. Her skill in producing a buoyant, effervescent narrative reflects, in part, the influences of a postmodern society that, as argued earlier, values playfulness, flexibility and spontaneous creativity.

Rowling's work first came to prominence in the late 1990s, when the figure of the childlike adult, or kidult, was ascendant in many aspects of adult life, whether at work or leisure. Following on the success of Harry Potter, many other magic fantasy novels for younger children began to cross over to adult readerships. Prominent amongst these were Eoin Colfer's *Artemis Fowl* and Lemony Snicket's *A Series of Unfortunate Events*, which now sell in translation throughout Europe and farther afield; like Harry Potter, Lemony Snicket's *A Series* has been adapted into a highly successful blockbuster film.[12] In their very different ways, all the early novels in these fantasy series emphasise childhood as a time of life in which one can buoyantly recover from disaster (like Harry, the later books in the Artemis series have darkened over time, while the Snicket books were playfully dark from the beginning).

If lightness, or buoyancy, is often an intrinsic characteristic of these fictional children, it is also represented as a state of mind that can be activated, or in adults, reactivated, by narrative circumstances. This idea was illustrated in the highly successful British crossover film, *Billy Elliot*, directed by Stephen Daldry, with Jamie Bell in the title role. The film tells the story of a young boy growing up in a coal-mining community in County Durham. Ignoring the derision of his father and brother and the increasingly desperate conditions of life during the miners' strikes of 1984–85, he secretly pursues his passion for ballet and eventually wins a place at the Royal Ballet School in London. First released in 2000, *Billy Elliot* won BAFTA awards for best British film, best actor and best supporting actress, and was nominated for Oscars in best director, screenplay and supporting actress categories in 2001. It was adapted, no less successfully, into a stage musical which ran from 2005 in London, Sydney and New York. One reason for the film's success, I believe, is that it celebrates lightheartedness and artistic, uncommercial ambition, in terms that make these equally available to adults. So iconic a cultural figure had the light-footed Northern boy become by 2007 that a scene from the musical was included in the 50-year birthday celebrations of the BAFTA awards, televised on ITV (7 November 2007). To an audience composed of adults in black-tie dress, a troupe of young performers enacted the moment when Billy recognises what dancing means to him. Billy sings,

> And suddenly I'm flying, flying like a bird,
> Something sparks inside of me like electricity, like electricity
> And I'm free, I'm free.[13]

In the film, this description of an electric surge of energy convinces the Royal Ballet judges of his genuine ambition. They award him a place at the School, thus releasing the boy from his constricted existence in a strike-riven community, and freeing him to develop his extraordinary talent. The energy and talent are his own but they need to be magically released, and in a sense, it is the function of narrative to provide him with this release. For the adult onlookers, this electric energy is visually associated with childhood, but the 'inner spark' that frees the soul is implicitly within reach of anyone, young or old.

The buoyant tone, mood and storylines of these works thus connote an ethics of radical freedom, but like Bakhtin's theory of carnival, they can also suppress a sense of individual accountability or 'addressivity' in a particular historical situation.[14] In *Billy Elliot*, a continued allegiance to northern roots is implied, but there is not much practical connection between Billy's individual success down south and the continued closure of the mines and the destruction of a northern community and way of life. In magic fantasy fictions, such as *Billy*, and the early Harry and Artemis novels, narrative time is virtually arrested, art gaily satirises life and characters distance themselves from the past as they are tossed and transformed on a sea of adventures which, while they are sometimes unfortunate (as in Snicket's *Events*), they are never irreparably tragic for the individual hero concerned.

The vision of life as magic metamorphosis expressed in the first three Harry Potter books, eventually yields to a different vision later in the series, though not because 'real life isn't like magic'—in fact, contemporary 'real life' is saturated with the possibility of magic transformations. Indeed it is less a sense of magic possibility than the weight of cultural expectation which now presses us to overhaul our existing identities (bodies, wardrobes, houses, gardens, souls, Internet connections, etc.). In this sense, children's magic fantasy fiction is simply imitating the pressure to metamorphose that consumers feel in a capitalist culture.[15] But at its best, this fiction is also more than mimetic, and strives to depict deeper and more meaningful forms of metamorphosis than are expressed in the illusion-and-bang! universe of advertising.

Bearing in mind J.K. Rowling's claim (and we have no reason to disbelieve her) that she had worked out the entire series in advance of publication, nevertheless between the third and fourth books, respectively published in 1999 and 2000, the emphasis of her work may be seen to shift from expressing the magic 'lightness' of childhood to representing the child as master of death. Beginning with *Goblet*, the narrator shows a consciousness of addressing a global, well-informed, adult and young adult readership, in contrast to the British children implicitly addressed in the first three books. The later books are still centrally concerned with, and do still address, children. But the image of the child in the later books has been mythicised into a quasi-holy being with the power to redeem adult lives. The idea of blood sacrifice is centrally important in the last four books, and in the last, it is a child who must willingly sacrifice his life for the greater good. Here the carnival spirit with its amnesiac energies has largely receded, and characters are driven by grief to remember and haunt and plunder the lost past. *Hallows* ends with a simple, quietly uttered spell. Harry says '*reparo*' and magically mends his broken wand. This is the moment to which the last four books tend: a tiny act of reparation to set against enormous loss of life and innocent blood. If the lightness celebrated early in the series is an expression of ludic postmodernism in its most positive aspect, then the later books subject this optimistic vision to stringent critique. In the end, the carnivalesque spirit gives way to a sense of timeliness and polyphonic freedom, a sense of being framed, but not overdetermined, by the finality of death.

A Memo from Calvino

However, before turning to the later books, since 'lightweight' and 'lightness' have quite different connotations, we need to be clear exactly what qualities of the latter attribute are being celebrated in the first three books. This is crucial because in a sense, Rowling never abandons this original vision, though it is reworked and tested against progressively darker circumstances. What is meant by 'lightness', and why should this be regarded as a positive feature of children's magic fantasy novels, and the early Potter novels in particular? Flexible capitalism puts a premium on lightness, smallness, and mobility, and yet in certain respects, these are the very qualities of life which capitalism tends to erode. Increasingly, we live in crowded, noisy and hectic places, and the Internet, while liberating, can also contribute to a massive sense of information overload. Articulated on the eve of the new millennium, Italo Calvino's remarks on lightness and weight in literature are even more pertinent today. In the first of a series of six intended lectures, published posthumously as *Six Memos for the Next Millennium*, Calvino reflects on Milan Kundera's famous novel, *The Unbearable Lightness of Being*, arguing that Kundera in fact confirms 'the Ineluctable Weight of Living' which 'consists chiefly in constriction, in the dense net of public and private constrictions that enfolds us more and more closely'.[16] If Kundera was describing what he saw as a universal human condition, he was nevertheless arguing from the position of an East European writer, in a country oppressed by state communism. Calvino writes from Italy in the mid-1980s, where the enemies of lightness are different and more diffuse. But he finds them no less powerful: 'At certain moments, I felt that the entire world was turning into stone: a slow petrifaction, more or less advanced depending on people and places but one that spared no aspect of life'. (4) What Calvino writes to defend is 'the liveliness and mobility of the intelligence', which he sees threatened by 'the weight, the inertia, the opacity of the world'. (4) At one level, this is just an argument against narrative realism, but more generally, it can also be taken to suggest the weight of living in a globalised society in which, as Wordsworth prophetically wrote, 'the World is too much with us; late and soon,/ Getting and spending, we lay waste our powers'.[17]

Calvino's thesis is that reading certain kinds of literature can develop mental qualities or capabilities that are essential to combating the 'weight, inertia and opacity' of contemporary life. The qualities he enumerated were lightness, quickness, exactitude, visibility, multiplicity and consistency (although the first of these turns out to encompass all six), and these qualities, he argues, can be strengthened and sharpened by reading certain kinds of narrative. Just as Perseus survived Medusa's gaze by looking at her indirectly, so certain fictions can 'free up' the world, and diminish its weight by presenting it to us lightly:

> Whenever humanity seems condemned to heaviness . . . I think I should fly like Perseus into a different space. I don't mean escaping into dreams or into the irrational. I mean that I have to change my approach, look at the world from a different perspective and with a different logic. (*Six Memos*, 7)

The ability to escape aporetic, oppressive conditions of life by means of a shift of perspective is celebrated in such works as *Billy Elliott* and *Harry Potter and the Prisoner of Azkaban*. It is not that the more serious aspects of life are denied in these works; rather, they are reflected back to us through a defamiliarising lens, a point to which I will return in Chapter 4. Calvino cites a passage from Boccaccio's *Decameron* in which the poet Guido Cavalcanti escapes from an aggressive crowd by leaping lightly over a wall.[18] In praising 'lightness', Calvino celebrates a number of related ideas, amongst which are: physical lightness, mental agility, precision, determination, the philosophy of atomism expounded by Pythagoras and set to verse by Lucretius and Ovid, and most importantly for the antirealist Calvino, the capacity of words to remove the weight of substance from reality (3–29). In all these different manifestations, lightness is something we deploy agonistically against the intractable heaviness of contemporary life.

Though a collector of folk and fairy tales and a writer of children's stories himself, Calvino was not arguing here specifically for the mental qualities that could be fostered by reading children's literature.[19] But he might very well have, given that children's literature has a long history of celebrating precisely these qualities, as Jerry Griswold's study, *Feeling Like a Kid,* demonstrates.[20] Peter Pan, Mary Poppins, Superman, and the flying boy-wizard, Harry Potter himself, are examples he cites of protagonists in children's literature who overcome evil by outflying or outfloating it (75–102). Again, for Griswold, this 'lightness' has an agonistic force; mental flexibility is something that characters in children's literature habitually deploy against various gravid forces, whether these be the forces of evil, or simply the weight of accumulating time. Griswold's observation that lightness is a recurrent theme in children's literature, taken together with Calvino's thesis that lightness is precisely what we need to thrive in the new millennium, may begin to explain the attraction of certain types of children's literature to contemporary adult readers. For although Griswold does not specifically draw attention to it, the adult interest in 'feeling like a kid' is implicit throughout his study. Presumably a reader can only feel '*like* a kid' if he or she is not actually a kid at that moment. Similarly, lightness is valued more highly, perhaps, by those who have experienced its opposite.

A sense of lightness is one of the first impressions an early Harry Potter novel is likely to make on its older readers. It is not just that Harry and the other wizard children fly on broomsticks, nor that Rowling's use of punning language and classicisms is 'lighthearted', nor even that a narrative pattern is established whereby three children outwit an adult embodiment of evil over the course of each book. Lightness is also integral to the narration, plotting and characterisation of the first three books. In agreement with those who argue that early Harry Potter novels 'offer both simplicity and complexity', I would add that the ease with which a reader can switch between simple and complex levels of interpretations is another sign of narrative lightness.[21] In Calvino's words, the Potter novels are constantly urging readers to 'change [their] approach, look at the world from a different perspective and with a different logic'.

The Adult on Platform 9¾

For an adult reader, this urge to shift one's normal perspective is felt from the moment one steps across the threshold of the first book in the series. The sense of trespassing into foreign territory is part and parcel of the adult experience of reading *Harry Potter and the Philosopher's Stone.* Rowling addresses child readers in a tone that invites a conspiratorial resistance to adults and adult modes of perception. The narrator begins, 'Mr and Mrs Dursley, of number four, Privet Drive, were proud to say they were perfectly normal, thank you very much'. (*Stone,* 7) The narrator's use of free indirect discourse here undercuts the Dursleys' speech, and invites children to laugh and mock at the adult worldview they represent. In the phrase 'normal, thank you very much', Rowling sums up an entire suburban, middle-class world of work and social aspiration which is implicitly inimical to the imaginative child's well-being. So for an adult, this child-complicit address immediately presents the narrative as 'not for us', or for us, but once removed. Just as Harry will later need to pass through an invisible barrier on Platform 9¾ to access the magic world of Hogwarts, so adult readers need to shift perspective right from the beginning to participate fully in the role of the text's narratee.[22] In Geraldine McCaughrean's sequel to *Peter Pan*, the grown up Wendy has to fit herself into her childhood clothes to get back to Neverland. Likewise here, Rowling's adult readers have to enter Harry's world as if they were children. This is, of course, the aspect of reading *Harry* that many critics have objected to, but as I will argue further in Chapter 4, adopting the child's eye view can liberate an adult reader, and help us to read 'lightly' in new ways.

Lightness Spells

While fantasy fiction traditionally privileges lightness over dark, Harry Potter rather differently privileges lightness over weight. Wizard life is implicitly superior to Muggles' because it is not bound by gravitational laws. Already capable of flight, witches and wizards further transform their circumstances by charming people and objects into lighter states of being. Consider, for example, how many of the spells cast in the Potter series have to do with making things lighter, with levitating and floating, with unbinding and unfastening, and in general with removing and releasing people and objects from constricting circumstances.[23] '*Wingardium leviosa*', one of the first spells to be taught to Hogwarts students causes an object to levitate; the incantation derives from 'wing' and *levare*, Latin for 'raise up'. Ron Weasley puts this spell to comic use in *Stone* when he causes a mountain troll's club to rise up in the air, then crash back down on the troll's head. Similarly, the incantation '*levicorpus*' causes a person to be suspended upside-down in the air (*Half-Blood*, 78; *Hallows*, 26). Any incantation beginning with '*mobili-*' removes an object that is causing an obstruction, hence: '*mobilicorpus*' for moving a body out of the way (*Prisoner*, 19) and '*mobiliarbus*' for moving a tree (*Prisoner*, 10). A 'feather light' spell is one that can make your luggage lighter, an option Harry considers when on the run with a heavy trunk in *Prisoner* (3). In *Chamber*, the house elf Dobby uses a hover charm to float Aunt Petunia's pudding in the air (2). Uttering '*glisseo*' (from the French word, *glisser*) can transform stairs into a slide, for smoother and speedier descent, as Hermione shows in *Hallows* (32). '*Expelliarmus*', disarming an enemy by causing his wand to fly out of his hand, becomes one of Harry's trademark spells, showing his reluctance to use more physically harmful forms of combat. It is the first spell he teaches fellow students in their underground resistance movement (*Phoenix*, 18), and he employs it against the advice of his friends, twice against Voldemort and once against Stan Turnpike (*Hallows*, 4, 36). There are also spells to clear the air passages of the throat ('*anapneo*', from the Greek for 'breathe' [*Half-Blood*, 7]) and spells to open locked doors ('*alohomora*,' *Stone*, 9). But perhaps the most important of the lightening spells is cast with the incantation, '*expecto patronum*' (from the Latin, *exspectare*, meaning either 'look for' or 'expel from the chest', and *patronus*, meaning 'patron saint'). This is a spell used to fend off depression and despair, in the form of 'Dementors'; if the caster can summon enough optimism in the face of terror, a silvery phantom creature will burst forth from the tip of the caster's wand, effectively creating a protective wall around the caster for as long as the spell lasts (for example, *Prisoner*, 12; *Goblet*, 31; *Phoenix*, 1; *Hallows*, 13).

Ranged against these lightening spells and charms are the spells, jinxes and curses that weigh down, freeze, bind, constrict and silence their victims. These spells are cast by Dark Arts practitioners, Death Eaters, and Lord Voldemort, but they are also used by Ministry of Magic wizards, by Harry and the other pupils and ex-pupils of Hogwarts. Draco Malfoy casts a '*locomotor mortis*' spell on Neville, which locks Neville's legs together (*Stone*, 13). A cry of '*impedimenta!*' impedes the progress of a person or object. Binding spells can throw snaky ropes round a victim; for example, Snape ties up Lupin in the Shrieking Shack (*Prisoner*, 19), while in the wizards' court, the accused is routinely roped to a chair in the middle of the courtroom (*Phoenix*, 8). A more extreme form of physical constriction is produced by the spell '*petrificus totalus*', a full-body curse which renders the victim's entire body rigid. (*Stone*, 16; *Half-Blood*, 28). '*Stupefy!*' knocks the target of the spell unconscious. Harry will later make use of it with some regularity—for example, against the Dark Arts wizard Yaxley (*Hallows*, 13), the Death Eaters (*Hallows*, 4), and the goblins in the Gringotts vaults (*Hallows*, 25). And, an invention of the half-blood prince, '*langlock*' freezes the tongue to the roof of the mouth, disabling the victim from speaking (*Half-Blood*, 12, 19). In a more extreme version of language-binding, the 'unbreakable vow', which Snape swears to Narcissa Malfoy in the opening of *Half-Blood* (2), binds the swearer forever to the letter of his or her oath. The three most constricting curses in the wizarding world are the *imperius*, *cruciatus* and killing curses, cast with the incantations, '*imperio*', '*crucio*' and '*avada kedavra*'. All three, known as Unforgivable Curses, submit the victim to the total control of another witch or wizard, respectively by mind control, torture and death.

Until the final book, it is generally only Voldemort and his Death Eaters who cast Unforgivable Curses, but otherwise, wizards on both sides of the conflict make use of the full range of magic spells of which they are individually capable. This is one early indication that Rowling's moral universe is not as simply divided into black and white as it first appears. Both 'good' and 'evil' wizards value lightness, and wreathe themselves in magic spells that make their own lives lighter, while weighting and binding the lives of their enemies where possible.

Harry the Seeker

Harry is the chief signifier of lightness in the early books, not because he is the most morally good (he isn't), but because his life is most radically capable of metamorphosis. From the start, his fortunes are shown to be subject to reversal from low to high, dark to light, and vice versa. Like Cinderella at midnight, and indeed like the reader, Harry has to leave his beloved magic world at the conclusion of each of the first three books. In order to recover his place in this other world, Harry has to practice his lightness 'skills', which might be said to include: sharpening one's ability to read complex and misleading situations; becoming precise and agile in one's response to danger; learning to act determinedly in accord with one's moral values, especially when these conflict with institutional rules. As a boy who shares a strange kinship with the evil Lord Voldemort and can speak the 'dark' language of Parseltongue, who is offered a place in the 'Dark Arts' house of Slytherin by the Sorting Hat, Harry is no white knight in the making. In the process of fulfilling his seven heroic tasks, he regularly breaks rules, cheats, lies and steals.[24]

On the other hand, Harry does not quite fit the pattern of the typical antiestablishment hero. He nearly always depends on his friends to overcome Voldemort. In *Prisoner,* for example, it is Hermione who provides Harry with the technical ability and the determination to break the time-travel rule ('never to change anything in the past'), which brings about the novel's comic resolution. In the series as a whole, it is rarely a good thing to become obsessed with a private vendetta, or even a private sense of the good, because characters who do so invariably end up making disastrous mistakes. So there is a lightness to Harry's educative process in that it involves balancing competing perspectives and value systems and finding an individual way through to a sense of the collective moral good. Pertinent to this argument is Sarah Maier's thesis that the 'Einsteinian relativity' of time, mass, density, volume, energy and velocity in Rowling's magical world teaches Hogwarts pupils to exercise 'emotional and intellectual vigilance' and helps them to understand the complexity of magical knowledge and its relation to power.[25]

The reader identifies with Harry, moreover, because he is new to the wizarding world and has to work out how its systems operate, just as the reader does. As Ziegler points out, all fantastical worlds are relational, requiring us to contrast primary and secondary worlds; 'reality, like patchwork is relative'.[26] But in Rowling's text, three worlds are held in a constantly shifting, comparative relationship. Like Harry, we are constantly balancing the realities of one against the other, which lightens our footprint in either world and provides a distance from which we can view both from a comic or more complex perspective. Within each world, there is a further moral split between 'light' and 'dark' values, social practices and systems of government. This internally divided, triworld fictional universe complicates the normal binary oppositions we would expect to find in good-versus-evil fantasy fiction. Here the binaries are constantly shifting, with aspects of two worlds contrasted with a third. Thus, both 'light' and 'dark' wizard worlds are superior to Muggle-dom because witches and wizards are more advanced in evolutionary terms than humans. On the other hand, light wizards and Muggles align against Dark Arts wizards in a binary of moral good versus evil. And yet again, light wizards employ the immoral practices of Dark Arts wizards (Sirius Black and James Potter were child bullies; both sides of the conflict use Unforgiveable Curses, slave labour and tormenting demons), so there is no absolute division between these worlds in moral terms.

Omniscience vs. Apian Instinct

Before the connection between Voldemort and Harry becomes apparent, the Dark Lord's moral antithesis is the patriarchal Headmaster Dumbledore. In the first three books we are given little reason to doubt Dumbledore's omni-science though we might, like Harry, question his decisions about when to intervene in his pupils' adventures. In this respect, he is clearly a godlike char-acter but even in the early books, he represents the moral good of bearing pain lightly, rather than the divine attributes of absolute goodness or power. The quality of lightness is connoted, for example, in Dumbledore's appear-ance. When Harry meets him, he notices the Headmaster's 'silver hair, the only thing in the whole hall that shone as brightly as the ghosts'. (*Stone*, 91) Dumbledore's name mixes etymologies from different languages: Albus, from the Latin for 'white'; Percival and Wulfric from Middle English and Anglo-Saxon; Brian, also British but comically ordinary (perhaps even Pythonesque), and Dumbledore, an onomatopoeic word intended to suggest the sound of a bumblebee, humming along the castle corridors.[27] This mixture of names helps create the impression of a composite character, who plays out a num-ber of different roles, some of them more successfully than others. William Wandless has described Dumbledore as a figure of 'enlightened reserve' in the series, but one who is himself learning how much reserve to apply in a given situation.[28] Later, Dumbledore will admit to Harry the mistakes he has made, which mostly consist of underestimating Harry's courage and constancy in the face of danger (*Phoenix*, 838; *Hallows*, 577). He has a grand design, and a complicated dance by which he works out his design; but his methods and outlook seem to me more apian than absolutist. He can never be sure he is going to succeed, and sometimes he misses his way.

Dumbledore's key role seems to be that of a paternal figure who can teach Harry to face death lightly. Although we will learn in *Hallows* that this wis-dom was hard won, in *Stone* he is presented as the powerful wizard who can lightly cast aside the chance of achieving immortality by means of possess-ing the philosopher's stone. In this respect, he is Voldemort's binary oppo-site since Voldemort has one abiding obsession, to make himself immortal.

As Rowling has commented in interview, 'my books are largely about death. They open with the death of Harry's parents. There is Voldemort's obsession with conquering death and his quest for immortality at any price . . . We're all frightened of [death]'.[29] Like C.S. Lewis and LeGuin, Rowling's work develops from the consciousness of mortality.[30] Rowling's position in the earlier books is chiefly that one needs to maintain a mobile perspective, to be able to change directions swiftly and avoid becoming too bogged down in the past. But even here, the importance of lightness is neither facile nor superficial, since it is consciously chosen as a response to loss and death.

Lightness in *The Prisoner of Azkaban*

The third novel in the series, *Prisoner*, in my view represents the culmination of this celebration of lightness, both as a moral value and as an aesthetic principle. *Prisoner* is still addressed primarily to younger readers, in contrast to the much heftier *Goblet* which follows. But just as Harry reaches the threshold of adolescence, turning thirteen in the third book, so *Prisoner* takes us to a point of major transition in the series as a whole. In terms of the novel's hybridisation of genres, we begin to see stresses opening up between magic and heroic or 'high' fantasy, while the comic tone is more often disrupted by realism and tragedy. Within this darker frame, the theme of lightness emerges as a strategy for combating psychological depression, buoyed along by a leitmotif of images of floating, flying, and galloping light-footedly across dangerous territory. Rowling's skill as a light writer, in Calvino's sense, should not be forgotten as she develops her myth-making credentials in the later books. To be able to blend so many genres and tones into a fast-flowing, suspenseful narrative is a rare art, whereas the high fantasist art of creating self-standing mythic worlds is (alas) hardly in short supply.

To illustrate the lightness of *Prisoner*, I will focus on three aspects of the text: first, the opening conflict, which demonstrates the increasing tension between different tones and genres as Harry is depicted in combat with his first 'petrifying force'; second, the climactic episode towards the end of the novel, where Harry saves his godfather's life by casting an 'enlightening' charm on a demon of despair; and third, the role of the reader in producing a light and buoyant narrative.

Exploding Aunts

In the second chapter of *Prisoner*, we find Harry at home with the Dursleys, prior to his annual apotheosis to the magic world of Hogwarts. As in the first two books, the Dursleys are presented as Dahlesque caricatures. But whereas previously, the Dursleys appeared simply to be dull and narrow-minded, here their social prejudice takes on a more sinister edge. Uncle Vernon growls at the news of a convict escaping from prison, 'when will they *learn* . . . that hanging's the only way to deal with these people?' (*Prisoner,* 19) Harry then learns to his dismay that Vernon's sister is coming for a visit. In some respects, Aunt Marge is simply a comic double of her brother ('large, beefy and purple-faced, she even had a moustache, though not as bushy as his' [22]), but she is also several shades more vindictive. She shows a sadistic pleasure in torment-ing Harry, and in this, she is a prototype for the more poisonous villains of the later books, Dolores Umbridge and Bellatrix LeStrange. Aunt Marge repre-sents the first 'petrifying force' that Harry will encounter in *Prisoner,* and her metamorphosis is the first of many examples of a child's imagination 'making light' of an adult oppressor. Forbidden from responding to her verbal taunts directly, Harry unconsciously channels his resentment into a curse that—to his surprise, transforms Aunt Marge into a helium balloon, thus exemplifying on a literal level what Calvino says about 'light' writing having the power to remove the weight of reality from words. Harry's charm notably removes the power of speech from Aunt Marge as her bitter taunts are reduced to 'apoplec-tic popping noises.'

The way Harry physically lightens his portly aunt is imitated in the narra-tion of the episode. Calvino identifies repetition and repetitive verbal patterns as a characteristic ingredient of light-footed prose, and in this chapter, the narrator alludes repeatedly to two sets of Dursley facial features: little eyes and a large, red face, which together emblematise the mean-spiritedness and monstrous aggression of both brother and sister. But these very features are transformed in a comic contrapasso: Marge's littleness of spirit is punished by her transformation into an inanimate object and her puffed-up aggression is punished by a physical inflammation of the limbs. With a wicked delight worthy of Dahl, the narrator recounts how Uncle Vernon's 'mean little eyes' became 'slits in his great purple face', Aunt Marge 'narrowed her eyes', 'her great ruddy face dripping', 'her huge face very red', until 'swelling with fury', her 'great red face started to expand, her tiny eyes bulged and her mouth stretched too tightly for speech' and finally, she becomes 'entirely round, now, like a vast life buoy with piggy eyes . . . her hands and feet stuck out weirdly as she drifted up into the air'. (20–27)

All of the above is narrated without a trace of sympathy for the unfortunate aunt. But the episode concludes on a jarring note which exposes the fragility of this comic resolution. Harry storms from the house, chased by Uncle Ver-non who bellows after him, 'COME BACK AND PUT HER RIGHT!' But by now, Harry is full of 'reckless rage'. He draws his wand, points it directly at his uncle, and 'breathing very fast', he threatens, 'she deserved it . . . She deserved what she got. You keep away from me'. (28) According to the classic rules of comedy, Uncle Vernon is in the right; the comic villain is meant to be restored to normality once his antisocial humours have been purged. And in most children's literature, when characters are floated in the air, they are generally brought gently down to earth (as happens in *Mary Poppins*, George MacDonald's *The Light Princess* and Erik Linklater's *Wind on the Moon*). But Harry is not looking for comic restitution; he wants revenge. With his threatening gesture towards his uncle, he steps into a morally ambivalent role. He is suddenly aware that he is more powerful than either of the Dursleys; but at this point, his power is unstable and unfocussed. Thus Harry emerges as the potential hero of a heroic, epic fantasy, since an epic hero typically has to master forces of good and evil within himself before he can complete his predestined task.[31] In the preceding volume, *Chamber of Secrets*, Harry has had to overcome an antagonist which literally froze its victims. Here, with this surprisingly dark twist concluding a farcical episode, Rowling shows that countering 'petrifying forces' has become a more complex and difficult matter than before.

Fathering the Man[32]

After this ambivalent threshold crossing, Harry and his friends encounter a series of challenges, each of which they have agonistically to make light of, in different ways. The simplest of these tasks is learning how to overcome a Boggart, a demon that springs out of wardrobes, terrifying its victims by taking on the shape of their worst fears. Harry discovers Mrs Weasley weeping over a Boggart which has assumed the form of a dead Ron. These demons thus embody the fear of death, as well as other childhood nightmares. Yet they are presented lightly as monsters that can be quite easily defeated once the correct techniques have been mastered. Hogwarts pupils are taught how to neutralise the fearful image by overlaying it with a comic one, this incongruous juxtaposition causing the Boggarts to self-destruct and explode. These are comic lessons in overcoming unhappiness. But the pupils find it harder to overcome a stronger, more psychologised form of demon, known as a Dementor. The Dementors' normal function is to guard the wizard prison, Azkaban, but here they penetrate the school grounds in pursuit of the escaped convict, Sirius Black. With their hooded, empty faces, and grasping, corpselike hands, the Dementors bear a strong physical resemblance to Tolkien's nine Wraith Lords, and like them, they overcome their victims by draining them of hope and optimism. In Rowling's novel, the Dementors are represented as transgressors in the world of childhood. Their presence on the periphery of Hogwarts is only reluctantly tolerated by Dumbledore, and they break wizard law when they cross into its grounds. Even in the adult world, their function is morally ambivalent. Though clearly wielders of dark magic, they are employed by the state to drive its prison convicts to madness and despair. Their magic is not externally imposed, but drawn from the victim's own memories of tragedy and loss. While they would appear to represent a particularly adult form of depression, their methods prove equally effective with child victims, particularly children who have witnessed death. In contrast to the wardrobe-haunting Boggarts, then, Dementors represent a form of unhappiness that cannot be boxed up as alien to the child or adult, nor can they be easily dissipated by carnivalesque laughter.

During his incarceration in Azkaban, Harry's godfather Sirius has been driven half-mad by Dementors. The dark memory on which they have been preying is his unwitting betrayal of Harry's parents, an event which led to their deaths. Sirius has come to Hogwarts to protect Harry, but in fact, it turns out that he is the one most in need of salvation. As his name connotes, his despair is 'serious', and his black melancholy is beyond the reach of ordinary comic redemption. Harry shows he has mastered the art of lightness in the climactic episode where he saves Sirius from these dark and disabling memories. After a complicated series of plot reversals, Harry comes upon his godfather lying prone beneath a Dementor as it prepares to administer the kiss of death and suck the soul from Sirius's mouth. Harry himself is helpless to intervene, but at that moment, across the lake, he catches sight of a distant figure, strangely resembling himself, who summons a powerful patronus charm in the form of a silvery stag. The stag gallops swiftly across the glassy lake and drives off the Dementor. A short time afterwards, by means of Hermione's secret time-turner, Harry revisits this incident. But this time, he finds himself standing in the place of the figure he has seen across the lake. Realising that this mysterious other must have been himself in a parallel reality, Harry is able to do what no other Hogwarts child has yet done, summon a powerful patronus. He accomplishes this adult-level task deriving strength from the certainty that, as he explains later to his friends, he had 'already done it' and so he could not possibly fail (301).

But before he works out that the figure across the lake must be himself, Harry wonders whether it might have been the ghost of his dead father, especially when he learns that his father's patronus spell took the form of a silver stag. Dumbledore, as usual, corrects his mistake: 'You did see your father last night, Harry . . . you found him inside yourself'. (312) To save Sirius, Harry has had to harness two temporal perspectives at once: the forward-looking spontaneity of a child, and the retrospective experience of an adult. This image of two Harrys, gazing at each other across the lake, the one sending a powerful deliverer to the other, illustrates graphically Calvino's principle of shifting perspective to escape the world's petrifying forces. Here in *Prisoner,* the shift of perspective needed is specifically a temporal one. The child fathers the man by imagining he sees his father in himself. Harry 'fathers' Sirius, moreover, in the sense that he saves his godfather's life and gives him a reason to hope. This is the first sign of Harry's fully fledged role as the semi-divine redeemer of *adult* lost souls, which emerges at the end of the final book.[33]

In *Prisoner,* the serious Sirius theme (the need for the child to discover the adult within) is presented within a lightly comic frame, another sign of this novel's successful balancing of tones. Hermione's time-reversal device, an instrument she has on loan from Professor McGonagall, is so reassuringly implausible that it restores the comic frame of the novel, and reconfirms the idea of magic as a form of instant, effortless transformation. While rescuing Sirius from the Dementors, Hermione and Harry also save the winged creature, Buckbeak, who for different reasons has been sentenced to death and indeed already executed by the time they come to rescue Sirius. In a final, enlightening twist of plot, the two children turn back time to save Buckbeak's life, and deliver him to Sirius, leaving the two condemned creatures to fly off together into the night.[34]

Dialogic Reading

As we have seen, *Prisoner* blends together the generic features of magic and high fantasy, but it also plays with another set of generic expectations drawn from detective fiction. And it is within this generic horizon that Rowling develops her distinctively dialogic relation to her readers. Several critics have commented on the way Rowling engages a reader's detective instincts, 'planting clues while simultaneously entrapping the careless reader',[35] and 'deliberately creat[ing] and correct[ing] these misapprehensions in the reader's mind as well [as] . . . persistently revisiting events from a different perspective a second time'.[36] The proliferation of Harry Potter Internet discussion sites, such as Mugglenet and Harry Potter for Grownups, where readers predicted what was to come in future novels based on existing clues, shows the extent to which Rowling succeeded in actively involving her readers in unraveling her complicated twists and turns of plot.[37]

The mystery in *Prisoner* revolves around the incomplete history of four former pupils of Hogwarts: Sirius, Harry's father, Lupin the current Dark Arts professor, and Peter Pettigrew—whose name mysteriously appears on a magic map of Harry's, though he seems to be nowhere present himself. One of these characters has betrayed the other three to Voldemort in the past and is currently acting as his spy at Hogwarts. Harry and the reader have to discover the identity of this spy, and solve the riddle of why Peter's name should appear on Harry's magic Marauders' Map, when he is by all accounts long dead. As in the other books in the series, Rowling provides a plethora of false clues to lead Harry and the reader astray. The major red herring is Sirius Black, his name already infelicitous, his appearance savage (the image of the escaped convict's face, with its sunken eyes and overgrown hair, is visible on police notices everywhere), and the common knowledge of his evil crime seemingly conclusive. Vernon is the first to condemn the convict out of hand, as we saw earlier; Harry's initially negative impressions of Sirius are confirmed by the conductor of the Knight Bus and later by Mr Weasley. It isn't until the climactic encounter with Sirius in the Shrieking Shack that Harry hears the true version of events, which vindicates his godfather of the crime of killing Peter Pettigrew and several bystanders (266–67). There are also other clues that falsely suggest Sirius's evil intent, or in some other way mislead Harry and the reader. There is the huge black dog which crosses Harry's path several times, seeming to augur his death, but which turns out to be Sirius in disguise. As an animagus, Sirius has the capacity to transform into one particular animal, and the form he takes is suggested in his name: Sirius [Dog Star] + Black = black dog. There is also Hermione's new pet, Crookshanks, a suspiciously vindictive cat who turns out to be the only one to recognise that Ron's rat, Scabbers, is the real spy and ally of Voldemort, Peter Pettigrew. Finally, there is the ailing Professor Remus Lupin, whom Snape appears to be poisoning but who turns out to need Snape's potions in order to resist turning into a werewolf at full moon (again, the name is a riddle concealing/ revealing his true nature: Remus [legendary founder of Rome, mothered by a wolf] + *lupus* [Latin for wolf]).

Following the trail of these clues, and trying to second-guess where Rowling might be leading, constitute a large part of the pleasure of reading *Harry Potter*. As Wolfgang Iser has argued in *The Implied Reader* and elsewhere, leaving interpretive gaps in a text encourages a reader to engage with it dynamically; the more gaps there are, the more space there is for the reader's free play.[38] Rowling specialises in setting several shadow narratives in motion at once. For example, the prophetess Madame Trelawney is obviously a charlatan much of the time, so Hermione discounts her as a source of information. But Trelawney turns out to be unreliably unreliable; she is wrong about the black dog auguring death, but she utters a prophecy about Harry and Voldemort which turns to be true. A major aspect of the lightness of Rowling's novels is the way she proliferates the number of such shadow narratives competing at once. In doing so, she opens up a spacious maze which her characters, and readers, are expected to work through individually. Hogwarts's one hundred and forty-two mazelike staircases provide a chronotopic image of this teasing system of emplotment:[39]

> There were ... wide, sweeping ones; narrow, rickety ones; some led somewhere different on a Friday; some with a vanishing step halfway up that you had to remember to jump. (*Stone*, 98)

The second person address embraces the reader in the process of finding a way along these passageways, which are temporally as well as spatially unreliable, but pleasurably challenging to both younger and older readers.

No less than plots, characters are also presented as moral mazes, unreliable in their apparent allegiance to either Dumbledore or Voldemort. In *Prisoner,* a whole range of characters, including Sirius, Crookshanks, Lupin, the black dog, and of course, Professor Snape are mysteries, seeming to be one thing and turning out to be quite another. Some of them are meant to be mysterious from the start, and readers are invited to scrutinise their actions and question their motives. The case of Snape, however, illustrates how Rowling extends the interval we are required to withhold judgment from one book to the next in the series. Because Snape's character is subject to moral reversal in two opposing directions—seemingly evil but actually benign in the earlier books, and seemingly trustworthy but apparently evil in *The Half-Blood* and most of *Hallows*—none of the earlier books' final revelations about this character turned out to be reliable in the next book. Readers had no choice but to speculate and to wait for the final moment of revelation in *Hallows*. Given that the seven Harry Potter novels were published over an interval of ten years, Rowling's readers became accustomed to suspending judgment over long arcs of time, not only about Snape's character, but also about Dumbledore's history, and Harry's mysterious bond with Voldemort. By the time readers had come to the third novel in the series, most would have grown accustomed to Rowling's method of wrong-footing them, and reversing the apparent meaning of a series of clues in a final, furious-paced denouement. Not only would readers be used to engaging actively with the text, they would also have become accustomed to misjudging characters and events and subsequently being corrected. In the process, they might well have acquired a mental agility and flexibility of which Calvino would have approved.[40]

That adult readers enjoyed being drawn into this process as much as child readers did over the decade of the series' publication was obvious from a glance through any of the adult-fan discussion boards, where one found readers trying to second-guess Rowling's unfolding plots. To take one example, Daniela Teo constructed an elaborate matrix of seven 'keys', seven paradigmatic categories, which she found recurring through the seven volumes (the syntagmatic axis in her analysis). This matrix allowed her to predict, before its publication, how the key mysteries of the series would be resolved in *Harry Potter and the Deathly Hallows*.[41] Teo's densely logical editorial shows how adult readers could be drawn into the game of riddling and unriddling, conjecture and correction, which Rowling fostered with her elaborately constructed yet open-ended plots.

Reading Harry Potter over the course of a decade, in the company of millions of other articulate and opinionated fans allowed for an extraordinary degree of dialogic interaction between text and reader, and between heretofore divided readerly communities. Over this decade, child and adult readers were drawn together into a shared conversation in a way that had rarely occurred before on such a scale. Suman Gupta dismisses children's responses to Harry Potter as 'unintelligible', but this seems to me highly contentious.[42] To anyone who cared to engage with readers across the border, as it were, it was immediately that children and young adults followed the clues laid down by Rowling with as minute an attention to detail and textual nuance as did any dedicated adult fan. Such a close involvement in the dynamics of plotting is evident from this response, sent to me by Hermione Dawson, aged 15, immediately after she had finished reading *Half-Blood*:

It explained so much stuff you didn't even realise you didn't understand. It brought forward with more definition the power of Voldemort,
and his knowledge as a boy which helped him be so successful, i.e. that
Draco Malfoy would be so scared for himself and family that he'd kill
Dumbledore, Voldemort's knowledge of the horcruxes, his powers of
manipulation. It also showed what everyone had been dying to find out,
whether Snape was good or evil, but in the end I was disappointed by
that. I think [J.K. Rowling] chickened out. Chapter 2 with the unbreakable vow made me really wonder, but from the very start, you knew
he was evil because he had the Defence against the Dark Arts post . . .
However, Snape actually killing Dumbledore was too unexpected, and I
think she should have found a subtler way to show Snape's true colours.
Having said that, of course I did cry for about an hour over the last fifty
pages. I had to keep stopping because my eyes were too swollen to see!
The prospect of Harry Potter not going back to Hogwarts is so upsetting! It's obviously the dream school for everyone, which just makes
me think the next book is going to be really black. But at least we have
so much to ponder. Is Harry in fact one of the horcruxes? Is the person
who got the horcrux they thought they'd found in fact thingy-thingy-
Black? Was Dumbeldore, as well as Crabbe and Goyle, in fact someone
else under the polyjuice potion (I don't think so, but others do) and
who're going to be the survivors in the last book's final chapter? excitement, excitement.[43]

Hermione clearly relishes the space she has been given to work things out for
herself, and there is a sense in which the increasing complexity of the series
has corresponded with her own intellectual maturation. She sees herself as
part of an interpretive community, as she concedes the influences of 'others'
and 'everyone' in the formulation of her own response. She is emotionally
invested in Hogwarts as an educational institution and in Dumbledore, its
benevolent patriarch. But she is also intellectually invested, in the sense that
she enjoys guessing answers to the mysteries Rowling creates (with hindsight,
one can see that she guessed wrongly about Snape but rightly about Harry).
The reader confidently raises not only proairetic questions ('what will happen next?'), but also questions about Rowling's competence as the architect of
the labyrinth through which she enjoys finding her own way. For this reader,
Harry Potter functions as a 'light' text in that it leaves generous gaps for her to
exercise her own reason and imagination.

Chiaroscuro

I have been arguing here that the early Harry Potter novels demonstrate the
degree to which 'lightness' as an aesthetic principle deserves to be taken

seriously in this series, and indeed in children's magic fantasy fiction more generally. However, as the series progressed, these enlightening strategies appear to have become inadequate responses for Rowling's maturing characters, faced by the fear of loss and the sense of imminent mortality. Whether she considered these strategies to be sufficient for younger readers but not older ones, or whether her views changed and developed while writing the series is a question that lies beyond the present study. But *Prisoner* approaches an aporetic moment in this celebration of life as playful metamorphosis. As Tim Parks says, in a different context, fiction that imitates this postmodern notion of ludic existence requires 'everything . . . to be maintained in a fizz of promise, potential, multiplicity, and openness'.[44] This sense of infinite promise and potential is widely associated with childhood in British millennial culture, as was discussed in Chapter 1. But in Rowling's fourth Harry Potter, the children's party is interrupted. At the level of plot, the caesura is unsurprisingly caused by death: the death of an old man in the first chapter and the death of a boy in the conclusion of *Harry Potter and the Goblet of Fire*.

Enter the Deathly

The opening of *Goblet* disrupts the pattern established in the first three books, in which we meet Harry amongst the Dursleys where a satiric interchange takes place before he is transported off to the magical world. In *Goblet,* the first chapter, 'The Riddle House', is straight out of the horror genre: there is a haunted house, village gossip about ghosts and past misdeeds, a disabled old man who dares to venture into the house, a monstrous evil lying in wait for him, and a murder. The only children represented in this chapter are taunting boys, focalised through a fearful, adult perspective. Thus while Rowling naturally addresses her established audience of maturing children, here adult readers are able to take up the narrative with none of the shift of perspective required of us in earlier books.

What most strongly disrupts the previous narrative pattern is not so much the murder of the old man, which is only to be expected from Voldemort, but the sadistic exchange between the killer and his victim. *Hallows* opens on a very similar note, with Voldemort mocking and humiliating a prisoner before killing her. Fantasy fiction is, of course, full of sadistically mocking villians, but what is particularly striking about these two instances is that they replace the episode where we would normally expect to find Rowling's mocking representation of the Dursley family. It is as if Rowling is drawing an invisible connection between her own satiric impulses and Voldemort's cold-blooded sadism towards his victims. This might strike some readers as far-fetched, but it is no less far-fetched to imply, as she does at the beginning of *Hallows,* that the benevolent Dumbledore might turn out to be as fascistic towards physically weaker races and as hungry for absolute power as Voldemort himself.

Rowling sets out quite deliberately to undermine the moral certainties she has set up in previous books. More than this, she disrupts the sense of certainty and control that a reader gains on an aesthetic level from unravelling her carefully constructed plots. Instead she provokes us to question the instinct for power, and particularly the instinct to master, escape or mete out death.

Plotting and the Death Drive

Why should this question embrace her narrative method, and the satirical impulse from which her lighthearted vision of the world springs? As Peter Brooks argues in *Reading for the Plot,* one psychoanalytic explanation for a reader's desire to engage with narrative is so that he or she can vicariously experience death, the summative moment to which, Freud argues, all living organisms unconsciously tend.[45] Narrative allows us to play off two basic drives, the pleasure drive and the death drive. The first is played out in the digressions and deferrals of plot, and the second, in the meaningful closure (neither too soon nor too late) of the narrative. In *The Sense of an Ending,* Frank Kermode argues that many modernists aimed to disrupt closural endings because they felt the latter to be forged in a strategy of *mauvaise foi,* faked closures that offered false consolation for the messy inconclusiveness of real death.[46] In Kermode's reading, Sartre viewed fiction as a kind of magic that could provide the reader with a false illusion of control over his or her destiny, and an illusion of a meaningful end (*Sense of an Ending,* 135). For Sartre, all fictional endings are fake in that they obscure the fact that reality is deterministic, but still, some fakes are better than others, ranging from good, magic illusion to *mauvaise foi* (135).

In the early Harry Potter novels, the consolation for death lies in the intricate plotting, the increase of mystery leading to a crescendo of conflict followed, crucially, by explanations, clarification and reassurance. It does not matter much that Voldemort lives to fight again (in fact, it is good that he does as his survival ensures the series will continue). The ending is still felt by Harry and the reader to be a victory in the sense that it retrospectively delivers meaning and coherence to Harry's adventures. As Gupta usefully observes, the Potter series combines two different kinds of structural repetition: variation on a theme, which is commonly found in series fiction such as Christie's Poirot novels, and progression within a given world, which is characteristic of fantasy series (*Re-reading,* 93–94). The Potter novels establish a basic pattern, which would include a satiric beginning at the Dursleys', a heroic task for Harry, a friend who will turn out to be an enemy, a magic instrument, a moment where friendship is put to the test, a furious crescendo of dangerous adventure which culminates in Harry saving the day, a day which is brought to a close with a celebratory feast. Each book then introduces variations to this pattern. But the series also progresses in the sense that the characters age, the plots become more convoluted, and the dangers they face become more extreme. Gupta terms this combination of repetitions 'elaboration', and he sees this principle governing the series as a whole (*Re-reading*, 95).

But the grossly extended plots of the fourth through seventh books suggest that this dynamic elaboration has come to feel less like narrative magic, and more like a case of *mauvaise foi*. As Harry, Ron and Hermione camp in the wood, bickering and festering for nearly two hundred pages of *Hallows*, it seems clear that endless plot elaboration eventually ceases to foster a mental agility in either protagonist or reader. At the same time, the plots have to work harder and harder, because they lack conviction of their potency to deliver consolation for death. The later books betray the artifice of their art and expose the illusory nature of the magic gift of narrative coherence. In *Hallows*, rather than a choice of several shadow plots, we get a veritable explosion of possible narrative trajectories. Should Harry and his friends be searching for Horcruxes, slivers of Voldemort's fragmented soul? If so, they must undertake seven tasks, seven series of adventures, to find and destroy them. Or should they be attempting to unite the Deathly Hallows? If so, three magical objects (Elder Wand, Cloak of Invisibility and Resurrection Stone) need to be mastered, again requiring three separate sets of adventures. How are they, and the reader, to choose which trajectory to pursue: destruction of Voldemort or the promise of absolute power? Rowling's title misleads the reader, but Hermione, as usual, turns out to be correct in her instincts; they should remain faithful to Dumbledore's instructions and search for Horcruxes. But the two boys disagree; first Harry is consumed by the desire to recover his dead parents and guardian, and later Ron wants revenge for the death of his brother (514). In fact, though the protagonists have to choose a single path through one consecutive series of adventures (Horcruxes), Rowling manages retrospectively to deliver all ten magical objects and ten plot sequences into the hands of the reader by the end of the novel.

But how satisfying is it? It is as if, like Harry, Ron and Hermione, we have been trapped in the enchanted vault at Gringotts, where to touch any precious object causes it to multiply but also to scald the toucher, so that eventually he or she is buried and burned alive. If we continue to read like detectives as previously, sifting clues to discover the whereabouts of all these magical objects, we risk losing sight of the characters' humanity completely, as indeed does the novel itself. None of the three major characters develops psychologically in the seventh book. Their adolescence, so awkwardly explored in *Order* and *Half-Blood*, is put on hold in *Hallows*. Ron and Hermione are now firmly matched though they continue to squabble in the same vein as before, while Harry's love interest in Ginny is simply deferred until the resolution of *Hallows*.[47] Dumbledore is dead, and remains so, despite what must have been a mountain of pressure on Rowling to reverse the shocking conclusion of the penultimate volume. But disturbingly, his death appears to have made no difference to his narrative function. As before, he appears to Harry at the end of the novel to answer questions and elucidate mysteries. And most importantly, he is there at the end to watch and praise, and be tearfully proud of Harry in his moment of victory ('the pride and gratitude emanating from him filled Harry with the same balm as phoenix song' *Hallows*, 599). These consolations are offered, however, from within the frame of a painting, since Dumbledore now only exists as a magically animated portrait. The return of Harry's mentor to his former advisory role despite—as Voldemort keeps reminding Harry—his being irretrievably dead (593), is thus an egregious instance of a faked ending, suggesting the thinness of any consolation for death which consists of nothing more than the tidy resolution of a complicated plot.

Wingardium Graviosa

One indication that lightness no longer governs as the series' dominant ethical and aesthetic good is that in the last four books, enlightening spells come to be used for horrifying ends. Thus in *Goblet*, the Death Eaters form a lynch mob in the aftermath of a Quidditch game. They set fire to a Muggle campsite, and levitate a human family in the air above:

> The floating people were suddenly illuminated as they passed over a burning tent, and Harry recognised one of them—Mr Roberts, the campsite manager. The other three looked as though they might be his wife and children. One of the marchers below flipped Mrs Roberts upside-down with his wand; her nightdress fell down to reveal voluminous drawers; she struggled to cover herself up as the crowd below her screeched and hooted with glee.
>
> 'That's sick', Ron muttered, watching the smallest Muggle child, who had begun to spin like a top, sixty feet above the ground, his head flopping limply from side to side. (*Goblet*, 108)

Here farcical elements, such as 'voluminous drawers', are caught up in a repellent description of fascistic violence. Ron's abject response, 'That's sick', implies a certain horrified recognition of himself in this display of antigravity magic. This is a world in which humans can be tossed lightly in the air because compared to witches and wizards, they are almost entirely powerless. 'Magic is Right', as the title of Chapter 12 of *Hallows* sardonically indicates, but here too, lightness manifests itself as Might. Rowling's self-critique might equally be turned on other examples of ludic postmodern fiction, suggesting that kid-dults who play at being children can do so, in part, because of the greater wealth and power that, as adults, they possess vis-à-vis real children.

Instead of levitation spells, other forms of magic come to the fore in the later Potter books, which interestingly have more to do with binding, sealing and locking disparate objects together. Snape's declaration of an Unbreakable Vow in *Half-Blood* is one instance of this, but so are the *fidelius* and Secrecy charms cast by Dumbledore and his followers. By degrees, Rowling reveals that all her characters are bound together by unbreakable blood ties. The most powerful spell cast by any witch or wizard in the series is Lily Potter's protection charm over her son. She offers her life's blood to save her child, and Voldemort steals a fraction of this powerful charm from the infant Harry in order to make himself invincible. The theft of blood binds Voldemort and Harry together in life and death so that, as Harry works out at the end of *Hallows,* only by willingly sacrificing his own life can he destroy Voldemort and the fragment of Voldemort's soul that he carries in himself (554). This blood-bond makes itself evident in the growing telepathic connection between Voldemort's mind and Harry's. While the reader knows that Harry is not responsible, nevertheless it is disturbing to witness him focalising through Voldemort's eyes and emotions, and experiencing Voldemort's sadistic crimes as if he himself were committing them.

At the level of plot, this is simply a technical problem: How to sever the magic link between Voldemort and Harry? Thematically, however, Rowling is suggesting that dark and light wizards are united by ties of blood and destiny over which they have little control. Comedically, this ties them together in love, as Harry is bound in a protective relationship with his mother, and as, more generally, wizards protect each other by means of *fidelius* pacts, etc. Infernally, the blood-bond yokes wizards together in hatred as well. The deterministic power of both aspects of this blood-bond increases exponentially in the final book. The dark wizards fear the contamination which this predestined blood-bondage implies, which is one reason why, under Voldemort's aegis, they so obsessively pursue their fascistic dream of purifying the wizard race.[48] Harry and his friends are equally fearful of the blood-ties uniting them with Dark Arts wizards (Sirius, especially, is ashamed of his kinship with Bellatrix) but they combat this fear by delving into history to understand these bonds more fully. While the psychological development of the young protagonists is put on hold in *Hallows,* the plot loops backward to explore the adolescence of the major adult characters: Snape, Lily and James Potter, Voldemort and Dumbledore. Thus in a sense if the first book is about learning to forget (Harry forgetting his upbringing with the Dursleys), the last is about the necessity of remembering. This burden falls largely on the young protagonists, whose task it is to uncover the childhood secrets of their elders. Of all the adult characters whose past is recovered, Snape's is the most complex and engaging, because he alone experiences this sense of a blood-bond both comedically and infernally. Loving Lily Potter, he is bound to protect her son, but equally he is bound to hate Harry for being the sign of Lily's love for another man.

'He took my blood'

Not only must they uncover the past, the young characters also seem destined to bear the consequences of their parents' histories. Harry, Neville, Hermione and many other young characters are tortured, maimed or killed in *Hallows* because of some parental link with the past. When Dumbledore asks Harry what his connection with Voldemort in essence consists of, Harry answers 'easily, without effort. "He took my blood"'. (568) This idea of love and blood-guilt binding generations is underlined with the first of Rowling's two epigraphs, an extract from Aeschylus's *The Libation Bearers*:

> Oh, the torment bred in the race,
> > the grinding scream of death [. . .]
> But there is a cure in the house
> > and not outside it, no,
> > > not from others but from *them*,
> their bloody strife. [. . .]
> Now hear, you blissful powers underground—
> > answer the call, send help.
> Bless the children, give them triumph now.[49]

In this play, Orestes and his sister Electra have to expiate the crime of their mother, Clytaemnestra, who killed their father, Agamemnon upon his return from the Trojan War. Orestes knows that if he commits matricide he will incur the wrath of the furies, who only pursue murderers of kin, not those related by marriage, but he also knows his father's soul will not rest until it is avenged. The children are trapped either way, and while they feel allegiance to their father, the audience also knows that Agamemnon was hardly an innocent victim. Clytaemnestra killed her husband because he had earlier sacrificed their child Iphigenia to obtain the gods' favour before setting sail for Troy. Yet here the chorus call up the infernal gods and chillingly bless Orestes and his sister for taking up the task of killing their mother. The cycle of revenge would seem to be endless, as the 'cure in the house' entails one child after another offering their lives in sacrifice to an earlier generation. Electra placates her father's soul with these self-denying words,

> though you died, you shall not yet be dead, for when
> a man dies, children are the voice of his salvation
> afterward. Like corks upon the net these hold
> the drenched and flaxen meshes, and they will not drown. (505–507)

The idea of being *miaros*, stained or infected by proximity to a blood-crime was a central preoccupation of Greek tragedy.[50] The only thing that could soak up the infected blood was the blood of an innocent sacrifice, an idea that the tragedians derived as much from medicinal theory as from religious practices.[51] Aeschylus's *Oresteia* breaks the cycle of bloodshed and martyrdom by introducing a rational legal system to take the place of vengeance at the end of *The Eumenides*, the third play in the trilogy. Orestes is brought to court, tried and acquitted by human jurors, and the furies are driven off by Apollo.

The Master of Death

Rather than this reproducing this classical resolution, however, Rowling draws on a Christian model of sacrifice, in which Christ's offer of his own, divine life cancels the need for any further shedding of human blood. Divine love soaks up the infection of inherited guilt, to extend Aeschylus's medicinal image. While visiting his parents' graves in Godric's Hollow, Harry comes across two tombstone engravings: 'the last enemy that shall be destroyed is death', on his parents' grave, and 'where your treasure is, there will your heart be also', on the grave of Dumbledore's mother and sister (*Hallows*, 266–68). These New Testament verses (Matthew 6:19 and 1 Corinthians 15:26) together denote the promise of resurrection through the Son of God's consent to die.[52] In interview, Rowling has stressed that these two quotations 'sum up—they almost epitomize the whole series'. (*ibid.*) In a movingly written chapter ('The Forest Again'), Rowling has Harry come to a decision to give up his own life, to invite Voldemort to kill him so that the Dark Lord would also be destroyed:

> He felt his heart pounding fiercely in his chest. How strange that in his dread of death, it pumped all the harder, valiantly keeping him alive. But it would have to stop, and soon . . . Terror washed over him as he lay on the floor, with that funeral drum inside him. (554)

Rowling here powerfully conveys Harry's fear of death through his heightened awareness of ordinary physical sensation. She makes us feel the simple miracle of the heartbeat, and the enormity of the decision of her hero to extinguish it willingly for his friends. In one sense, Harry's self-sacrifice is strongly Christian in tone, as he imitates Christ's sacrifice. In another sense, though, it is humanistic to attribute this Christ-like power to a mortal being.

Whether one approves the narrative manoeuvre or not, it seems undeniable that Harry steps into a Christ-like role at the end of *Hallows*. Having committed himself to die, he acquires Christ's powers of raising the dead, much as Aragorn does at the end of Tolkien's *The Return of the King* (there are also parallels with Aslan's self-sacrifice at the end of Lewis's *The Lion, the Witch and the Wardrobe*). Harry opens the Resurrection Stone (gifted to him by Dumbledore), and the ghosts of all his dead family and friends gather to accompany him in his walk through the forest to reach Voldemort. He thus illustrates the Christian sentiment of Rowling's second epigraph, taken from the Quaker William Penn's *Fruits of Solitude*: 'death is but crossing the world, as friends do the seas; they live in one another still'. While this can be taken to mean that none of us should fear death, as we all can revive the lost through memory, it also seems to apply more specifically to Harry in his Christ-like role. Unlike the reader, he can literally walk amongst the dead and converse with them. Harry also ceases to puzzle through Dumbledore's tasks, on the same level as the reader. He acquires a temporary omniscience during his final battle with Voldemort, as repeatedly he discovers that 'without having to think' he knows what must be done: 'understanding was coming so fast it seemed to have bypassed thought. . . . And again, Harry understood, without having to think.' (559) But he is at his most Christ-like after his resurrection from near death. The Great Hall of Hogwarts is ablaze with celebrating witches and wizards:

> They wanted him there with him, their leader and symbol, their saviour
> and their guide, and that he had not slept, that he craved the company
> of only a few of them, seemed to occur to no one. He must speak to the
> bereaved, clasp their hands, witness their tears, receive their thanks,
> hear the news . . . (596)

This passage, and indeed the entire concluding section of *Hallows,* reveals the enormity of the task facing Rowling: to bring a ten-year writing project to a close which has (despite its critics) fed the imaginations of millions of readers. If narrative closure is an imaginative enactment of the death wish, as Peter Brooks argues, then how could the death, or the miraculous survival, of this single, fictional character be made to bear the burden of so massive and global a desire?

In one sense, this is achieved by elevating Harry from an ordinary boy into a demigod, apotheosing him into myth so that he becomes simply 'The Boy Who Lived'. In his Christ-like role, he is the wizards' sole redeemer. But in another sense, he is more simply an *exemplum* of the ordinary individual's power to exercise choice over his destiny. He does not survive Voldemort's curse by accident, as in the past.[53] He returns to an in-between threshold space (the ghostly version of King's Cross) where he is given the choice to live or, in Dumbledore's simple phrase, to go 'On'. This recuperates Rowling's earlier stress on lightness, but here, to put it in Bakhtinian terms, she has progressed from the carnivalesque to the polyphonic.[54] As Bakhtin notes of Dostoevsky, Rowling places her character on a par with his authorial creator, mediated through Dumbledore. Although clearly he is still a scripted fictional character, Harry is represented here as having the choice to decide the direction of his own narrative. And this is the profound sense of lightness that narrative can give us: an image of a human being acting freely.[55] As Sartre wrote, in life 'all ways are barred and nevertheless we must act. So we try to change the world; that is, to live *as if* the relations between things and their potentialities were governed not by deterministic processes but by magic'.[56] For Harry, lightness is no longer a condition into which he and the other wizards are born; it is a condition he creates for himself by exercising his choice to return and help his friends.

Lightness Revisited

At the end of *The Prisoner of Azkaban*, Harry is depicted staring across the Hogwarts lake at an older double of himself, a figure Harry mistook to be his father. This visual image showed us the child fathering the man, while deriving imaginative strength from the thought of what that man had successfully achieved. This image might also be taken to represent the harmoniously constructed plots, styles, and tones of the earlier Potter novels, in which a sense of lightness was communicated, to the adult reader in particular. The later books, however, reveal a darker and more archaic relationship between adults and children, where adults desire not only children's lightness but also their greater distance from death, that is, their life. Harry demonstrates his willingness to fulfil the sacrificial role, but then discovers that in Dumbledore's or Rowling's comedic universe, the gift of death preserves his life.[57] As Harry asks wonderingly, 'I live while he lives? . . . I thought we both had to die? Or is it the same thing?' (*Hallows*, 568)

Choosing how and when to end one's life, then, appears to be the highest good in Rowling's series, a theme likely to speak as potently to an adult reader as to a child. It is the secret knowledge of Dumbledore's death that Harry hurls at Voldemort to disarm the dark wizard: 'he chose his own manner of dying, chose it months before he died, arranged the whole thing'. (593) Still the benevolent patriarch in death, Dumbledore returns to give Harry this same ultimate choice. Unafraid of dying and untempted by absolute power, Harry proves himself to be, in Dumbledore's eyes, 'the true master of death, because the true master does not seek to run away from death. He accepts that he must die, and understands that there are far, far worse things in the living world than dying'. (577) Elevated to this plateau of wisdom exceeding even Dumbledore's, Harry now reverses roles in respect to the adult protagonists in *Hallows*. He is present to receive Snape's memories, so that the dying man knows he will be posthumously exonerated. And he is present to reassure the dead Dumbledore that his good reputation will be restored. As Dumbledore receives this blessing, he seems 'less than an old man, much less. He looked, fleetingly, like a small boy caught in wrongdoing', and 'like a child seeking reassurance'. (571)

Most of all, though, Harry plays the role of redeemer to Voldemort, offering the powerful wizard a chance to apologise and repent, as an adult would a child. When he enters the clearing in the forest to give himself up, he sees Voldemort standing there silently, like 'a child counting in a game of hide-and-seek'. (563) Even when Voldemort raises his wand to deliver the death curse, he still appears childlike in comparison to Harry: 'his head was still tilted to one side, like a curious child, wondering what would happen if he proceeded'. (564) When Harry returns from semi-death to confront Voldemort for the last time, he tells the dark wizard, 'try for some remorse . . . It's your one last chance . . . I've seen what you'll be otherwise . . . be a man . . . try'. (594) During his conversation with Dumbledore at King's Cross, Harry has seen a 'thing' in 'the form of a small, naked child, curled on the ground, its skin raw and rough, flayed-looking . . . unwanted, stuffed out of sight, struggling for breath'. (566) This creature cannot fail to remind the reader of the orphan Harry, abandoned outside number 4 Privet Drive in the first book, and indeed Harry himself seems to identify with the child, wanting to comfort him despite a sense of revulsion. But Dumbledore tells him shortly, 'you cannot help'. (566) How Harry later comes to realise that the abandoned child is Voldemort's soul in the afterlife is not made clear; this is simply one of the things he magically understands. Voldemort's punishment constitutes a twist on the fate of the unfortunate Cumaean sibyl, who requested eternal life but forgot to ask for youth. As T.S. Eliot quotes Petronius in the epigraph to *The Waste Land*: 'I have seen with my own eyes the Sibyl hanging in a jar, and when the boys asked her "What do you want?" She answered, "I want to die"'.[58] Rowling reimagines this *contrapasso* to suit Voldemort's crimes; having attempted to steal the life of an infant, he will be condemned to inhabiting forever the body he once stole. Voldemort misses Harry's allusion to his future, being too shocked at the reversal of roles, whereby a mere child could address him from a position of greater power. Unlike Dumbledore, he misses the chance to turn his own history into a narrative of redemption by means of this grown child's belief in his capacity to change. There could be no more severe indictment of the kiddult who refuses to listen to a child urging him 'to be a man, try' than this image of a soul arrested forever as an infant 'thing', suffocating and struggling for air.

When Harry chooses to put away the Elder Wand rather than using it (with echoes of Frodo and the Ring of Power), he also steps down from this Christ-like heroic role. Ceasing to act extratemporally, as the redeemer of older, more powerful wizards, he also re-enters ordinary, chronological time. Nineteen uneventful years pass between the penultimate and final chapters of *Hallows,* underlining the point that Harry reaches adulthood by the normal, unheroic channels. In the epilogue, Harry is depicted as the father of a child, in the normal, biological sense, and he appears for the last time, in the midst of seeing his anxious son, Albus, off to his first day at Hogwarts. Albus admits to his father that he is afraid of ending up in Slytherin House, like Voldemort, and Harry reassures him with a lightness worthy of Dumbledore: 'the Sorting Hat takes your choice into account'. (607) It is a low-key, prosaic ending, but it nevertheless conveys the insight that Harry brings back from his supernatural journey through the suburbs of death: that one can choose, or at least influence, the trajectory of one's own fate.

Chapter Three
Coming of Age in a Fantasy World: Philip Pullman's *His Dark Materials*

Looking back from near the end of the millennium's first decade, it would not be an exaggeration to say that Philip Pullman's *His Dark Materials* has permeated cultural life in Britain, with some version of its influence felt across all the major national media. In 2003, the trilogy came third in the BBC's Big Read competition, adjudged the nation's 'best loved' book, after Tolkien and Jane Austen. It was adapted for the National Theatre, under the direction of Nicholas Hytner, and showed to sellout audiences in London for two seasons (December 2003–March 2004, November 2004–April 2005). A three-part radio adaptation of the trilogy was also broadcast on Radio 4 in 2003, and later issued in CD and cassette form. But the trilogy reached the stratospheres of world renown when a major film adaptation from New Line Cinema was released to mainstream cinemas around the world in early December 2007. Movie gossip and speculation had fuelled the Internet fan sites devoted to Pullman's trilogy, especially BridgetotheStars.net and HisDarkMaterials.org, for at least two years prior to the release of *The Golden Compass* (so named after the American title of *Northern Lights,* volume one of the trilogy), so the film opened to an audience well primed to experience what the movie trailer promised, 'the next epic adventure' 'from the producers of Tolkien's *Lord of the Rings*'.[1] Philip Pullman's global success, coming so soon after Rowling's, confirmed that British fantasy fiction had become an international crossover phenomenon.[2] According to the *Los Angeles Times,* 15 million copies of Pullman's trilogy had been sold by December 2007, even before the release of the film adaptation that same month.[3]

Strange to say, success did not come to *His Dark Materials* overnight. *Northern Lights* did win the CILIP Carnegie Medal for children's literature when it was published in 1995, but at that time, winning the Carnegie did not necessarily guarantee big sales figures. Between 1998 and 2000, *His Dark*

Materials was still selling only three to seven hundred copies a week in each of Scholastic's paperback editions for children. These are good runs by the standards of the pre-crossover Blockbuster decade, but a few years later, once it had attained its crossover status, the trilogy was accumulating over 10,000 new readers weekly.[4] Critical acclaim was confirmed six years later, when *The Amber Spyglass,* third volume in the trilogy, won the children's category of the Whitbread award, and then—a historical first for a children's book—the 2001 Whitbread Book of the Year Award. During the month or so of the media coverage of the Whitbread and its aftermath, sales figures of the whole trilogy soared, and the National Theatre production in 2003 produced similar spikes in sales of the books. Following the precedent of Bloomsbury's Harry Potter, adult editions of *His Dark Materials* were available from 2001, but these seem not to have made a huge impact on the sales figures. In 2001, the adult editions sold less than a fifth of the numbers of the children's editions.[5]

Perhaps one reason that adults were happy to be seen reading a children's edition was that *His Dark Materials* seemed to legitimise cross-reading more convincingly than did Rowling's Harry Potter series. Pullman's Whitbread Award was hailed as a long overdue recognition of the serious literary merits of children's fiction. Although Pullman himself declined to draw parallels with Rowling, most critics certainly did when the trilogy gained a widespread adult readership. Pullman's style is undoubtedly more sophisticated, his 'multiverse' of parallel worlds more complex and his moral universe much more clouded and ambivalent than Rowling's. It may also have helped to silence the sharpest critics of children's fantasy fiction that Pullman was himself a harsh critic of the genre. Most fantasy, he claimed, 'does nothing . . . except construct shoot-'em-up games', a sentiment with which Harold Bloom and A.S. Byatt would no doubt concur.[6] Despite its obvious fantasy elements, Pullman provocatively insisted that *His Dark Materials* was realist, since it 'deal[s] with matters that might normally be encountered in works of realism, such as adolescence, sexuality, and so on; and they are the main subject matter of the story . . . what it means to be human, to grow up, to suffer and learn'.[7]

Moral Education and Fantasy

'What it means to grow up, to suffer and learn' more specifically describes the narrative trajectory of a certain kind of realist narrative: the bildungsroman, or novel of education, which emerged to prominence in the late eighteenth century. In a sense, the bildungsroman is a natural crossover genre, because it typically represents a protagonist developing from child to adulthood. Charles Dickens's coming of age novels attracted a mixed age readership almost immediately, with *Oliver Twist* being adopted by child readers in his own day, and *David Copperfield* abridged for child readers soon after publication.[8] In his lecture, 'Miss Goddard's Grave,' Philip Pullman expresses his admiration for nineteenth century realist fiction in which he argues, quoting Jane Austen in *Northanger Abbey,*

> the most thorough knowledge of human nature, the happiest delinea-
> tion of its varieties, the liveliest effusions of wit and humour are con-
> veyed to the world in the best chosen language.[9]

But what attracts Pullman most is that nineteenth-century realist fiction (and theatre) offered its audience 'a moral education.' Readers (and viewers) of such fiction would see that,

> some kinds of behaviour, such as generosity and forgiveness, led to
> happy outcomes, and were praiseworthy; other kinds of behaviour, such
> as greed or deceitfulness, led to unhappy outcomes, and were disap-
> proved of; yet other kinds of behaviour, such as renunciation or noble
> self-sacrifice, led to sad outcomes in the short run, but were highly
> praised, because they led to happy outcomes for others in the long run.
> (*Miss Goddard's Grave,* 2)

In our own times, Pullman argues, readers are deprived of this kind of moral education by the destructive influence of two opposing schools of thought, 'theocratic absolutism' on the one hand, and postmodern scepticism on the other. If the former insists on a single, correct way of reading which disallows 'ambiguity, or mystery, or subtlety' (6), the latter produces 'contradictions and fractures and disjunctions and subversions and an endlessly regressive series of dialectical readings' which, in Pullman's view (and many would agree with him), 'undercut a certain moral idea, namely responsibility' (11).

On one level, *His Dark Materials* offers readers a moral education of the nineteenth-century realist kind. In *Northern Lights*, the twelve-year-old hero-ine Lyra Belacqua discovers that a corrupt Church organisation, led by her own mother, has been performing scientific experiments on children (375). In addition, Lyra's mad scientist father, Lord Asriel, is exploring parallel worlds in search of a mysterious energy referred to as 'Dust' (original sin, in the Church's conception, and dark matter, in the scientists' view). His aim is to destroy this Dust from whence, he wrongly assumes, 'all the death, the sin, the misery, the destructiveness of the world' derives (377). In the second volume, *The Subtle Knife,* Lyra travels into another world and meets another twelve-year-old, Will Parry, who is on the run after accidentally killing a man while protecting his ailing mother. Will is also in search of his scientist father, who has mysteriously disappeared, and Will suspects has been kidnapped. In this multiverse filled with ambitious, untrustworthy adults, then, the two children have to discover their own moral code. At key points, both choose not to obey adult authority but to follow their own instincts: Lyra at the end of *Northern Lights,* when she decides that 'Dust' must be a force for good, and Will at the end of *The Subtle Knife,* when he decides to help Lyra, rather than deliver a magic instrument to Lord Asriel. The climax of their disobedience, which constitutes their moral awakening, occurs in the third volume, *The Amber Spyglass,* when Lyra and Will release the 'Authority' (Pullman's ironic portrait of God) from a glass bottle in which he has been imprisoned, allowing Him to evaporate and disappear. They also negotiate the release of the souls of the dead from the underworld, thus ending a long regime of religious tyranny which promulgated the fear of death in its followers. And they consummate their attraction to each other, in defiance of religious and social prohibitions.

The question is, though, why Pullman chose to represent this bildungsroman-style moral education in the genre of fantasy, which he has elsewhere decried as shallow. In defence of his claim that the trilogy is an instance of 'stark realism,' Pullman argues that, unlike many fantasy novels, his trilogy has the texture of material reality, his characters are presented as fully rounded and realistically complex individuals, and his moral and ethical concerns are characteristically realist.[10] But this explanation does not address the fact that his pair of children come of age in multiple universes populated by talking armoured bears, witches, tiny knights mounted on dragonflies, angels and harpies (rather than, say, nineteenth-century London). The fuller answer seems to be that we exist in a postmodern world that is inescapably drawn to fantasy. In part, this is because the nature of contemporary life has itself become fantastical, insofar as we live and work in magically compressed spaces, in virtual communities, on screen (and are surrounded by the promise of magic metamorphoses, as discussed in the previous chapter). In this sense, fantasy *is* the new realism. At the same time, many contemporary readers crave contact with lost material worlds, so that fantasy has to deliver a kind of hyperrealism, with accelerated action sequences, and plenty of blood, death and horror to remind us of our visceral existence in the world.

This is not quite how Philip Pullman has defended his choice of genre, and I am sure it is not how he would describe the action sequences in his own work. In 'Miss Goddard's Grave', for example, he explicitly criticises 'the sheer relentless *busyness* of modern life, the *crowdedness,* the incessant thumping music and braying voices, the near impossibility of finding solitude and silence and time to reflect'. (12)[11] Nevertheless, I would maintain that there is just such a restlessness in the plotting of *His Dark Materials,* where one crisis—and, more significantly, one emotional extreme—follows hard on the heels of another. For example, at the end of *Northern Lights,* Lyra realises her father is about to sacrifice her friend Roger in order to create the energy to build a pathway between worlds. She summons the armoured bear, Iorek, and they ride furiously through the snow to rescue the boy. As if that excitement were not enough, they are attacked from the sky by enemy witches. Lyra then has to leave Iorek behind as she makes her way across a fragile, ruined bridge. She crosses just in time to see Roger being killed, at which point she also sees her parents together for the first time, which arouses another host of confused feelings. Lord Asriel and Mrs Coulter are hovering on the brink of entering a new world together; meanwhile the Aurora is blazing in a 'brilliant and extraordinary' display of radiating light, as if it 'knew that the drama was taking place below.' (382) Lyra is torn between fascinated resentment at the sight of her cruelly amorous parents, amazement at 'such a vault of wonders she had never seen' in the sky, and feeling 'wrenched apart with unhappiness' at the death of her friend (397). Any one of these emotional crises would have sufficed for Dickens, and I doubt that Austen would have strayed into the territory of such baroque emotions at all, or at least, not without a considerable dose of irony.

But this very narrative drive is one of the aspects of Pullman's writing which appeals to contemporary readers, as the makers of the film adaptation are perfectly aware, when they promise Pullman fans a 'rollercoaster ride' of adventure on screen.[12] Pullman himself has admitted to being surprised 'to find that my imagination was liberated when it found itself in a world where people have personal daemons, and polar bears make armour.' ('Writing Fantasy') Expressing sentiments with which many contemporary readers of fantasy would agree, Pullman writes,

> With fantasy I felt that in some odd way I had come home. This was where I was connected with all the things that gave me strength; where the air I breathed was full of the scents I recognized and relished, where my feet were on the soil where the bones of my ancestors were laid, and where the language I heard around me was the language I thought and spoke and dreamed in. ('Writing Fantasy')

In this essay, however, Pullman suggests that the contemporary attraction to fantasy is the product of a postlapsarian imagination. Realist fiction is still rated highest in his moral hierarchy of genres, but in contemporary times, we seem to have lost the taste for it. 'The tricksiness and games-playing of modern and postmodern literary fiction' are signs of our postlapsarian 'self-consciousness' that arises when 'we lose our innocence about texts and about language'. If this is true, if 'the Fall happened in literature . . . when the first text noticed that it was a text', then the only remedy is to press forward through self-consciousness, to strive to reach the more complex state of 'self-possession'.[13] *His Dark Materials* enacts this dialectic development of genres by representing Lyra first as a fantasist (a 'liar', as her name suggests, or 'Silvertongue' as she is named by Iorek), and then by having her realise at the end of *The Amber Spyglass* that true stories are better and more morally nourishing. In this way, the dialectic of genres comes to be mapped onto a narrative of coming of age. When we grow up, in the moral sense that Pullman means, we come to appreciate the quieter truths and insights of realist fiction. Thus can fantasy be made to 'serve the purposes of realism'. ('Writing Fantasy')

In my view, this aim leads to a split in the argument of *His Dark Materials* which cannot easily be reconciled. On the one hand, the implied reader is morally educated through the examples of Lyra and Will, who use their childly intuition to develop their own sense of right and wrong in a morally ambiguous world. For adult readers, following their example means unlearning adult ways of thinking, becoming less sceptical and self-conscious, rediscovering the powers of empathy and imagination that are most evident in Lyra and the other child protagonists of *His Dark Materials*. On the other hand, childhood imagination and intuition come to be associated with fantasy, with the genre that reflects the diseased nature of contemporary consciousness. So in order to complete their moral education, Will and especially Lyra have to choose realism over fantasy, and a sense of themselves as no longer roving and free children, but 'fixed' and 'settled' adults. Pullman underlines this shift to realism via adolescent awareness in a climactic episode in the underworld when Lyra Silvertongue has to promise to give up spinning tall tales, and take up truth-telling instead. (*Amber Spyglass*, 332) The pact that Will and Lyra strike with the harpies is this: if the harpies will release the dead souls, then in future years, the dead will return to 'feed' the harpies with stories about their actual lives. As Pullman himself glosses this passage, Lyra 'leaves fantasy behind, and becomes a realist. (As the whole story does, you might say)'. (Writing Fantasy') Both trajectories of these two moral educations aim to develop a sense of responsibility, centredness, and 'self-possession' in the adolescent protagonists and, by extension, the empathising reader. But they seem to propose two conflicting ways in which these qualities can be drawn out: the first suggests we should put aside postmodern scepticism and develop intuitive modes of thinking, while the second suggests that loss of intuition is an inevitable, and even a desired, by-product of growing up. As adults, we should seek knowledge through conscious, rational means. Since I find it difficult to square the argument that childhood and adulthood are fundamentally different states of being with what actually happens in the trilogy, and the response it invites from the adult reader, here I would like to approach this apparent schism from a slightly different angle.

As a starting point, I would argue that Pullman's *His Dark Materials* represents an exciting fantasy multiverse that dynamically mirrors our own chimerically unreal world. The ability of Will Parry to cut through to different worlds with a magic knife reflects the telescoping of space in a globalised world, where half a day's travel can deliver us to the opposite side of the globe. And Lyra's alethiometer might well serve as a symbol of the mighty Internet, with its powerful search engines, Google *et al.*, which offer to deliver us all the knowledge we seek if only we can master its mysterious mechanics. This fantasy world is a place in which, like Pullman, many of us can feel 'at home' because in fact, we lack a sense of material home or *heim*.[14] Like rootless nomads, we make our 'home' anywhere, for example, in the transitory world of fiction. Fantasy appeals especially because, as John Durham Peters argues, it 'arises from the human condition of incompleteness'.[15] Fantasy is inescapable because 'the self always constructs itself first as a fantastic other; thereafter, all identity passes through otherness'. ('Exile', 37) If this is true of the human condition in general, it seems to be a particular feature of contemporary Western consciousness that we are hyperaware of identity as something incomplete, a work in progress, a doubleness that is both self and other. In my view, *His Dark Materials* represents this contemporary state of being both affirmatively and critically. In particular, it dramatises our anxieties about coming of age, which in a sense, are indicative of a more pervasive uncertainty about who to be, and where and when to be 'at home' in oneself. Whether or not one agrees with Pullman's polarisation of child and adult states of being, and whether or not one is persuaded by the turn to realism in *Amber Spyglass*, it is still possible to find in *His Dark Materials* a serious, passionate and thought provoking response to the contemporary condition of *unheimlicheit* or homelessness.

Coming of Age in the New Millennium

To place Pullman's fantasy bildungsroman in context, we should consider how fraught the subject of coming of age has become in British and other Atlantic societies in recent years. To appreciate this, one might contrast Shakespeare's *As You Like It,* where the malcontent Jacques mockingly describes the seven ages of life:

> At first the infant,
> Mewling and puking in the nurse's arms.
> Then the whining schoolboy, with his satchel
> And shining morning face, creeping like snail
> Unwillingly to school. And then the lover,
> Sighing like furnace, with a woeful ballad
> Made to his mistress' eyebrow. Then a soldier.
> Full of strange oaths, and bearded like the pard,
> Jealous in honour, sudden and quick in quarrel,
> Seeking the bubble reputation
> Even in the cannon's mouth. And then the justice,
> In fair round belly with good capon lin'd,
> With eyes severe and beard of formal cut,
> Full of wise saws and modern instances;
> And so he plays his part. The sixth age shifts
> Into the lean and slippered pantaloon,
> With spectacles on nose and pouch on side,
> His youthful hose, well sav'd, a world too wide,
> For his shrunk shank; and his big manly voice,

Turning again towards childish treble, pipes
And whistles in his sound. Last scene of all,
That ends this strange eventful history,
Is second childishness and mere oblivion,
Sans teeth, sans eyes, sans taste, sans everything.[16]

From a contemporary perspective, what is striking about this description is not so much Jacques's melancholy conviction of the futile circularity of life, but that he is able to discern the different phases of life so clearly and distinctly. A schoolchild's preoccupations would bear practically no relation to the lovesick obsessions of a teenager. At thirty-something, a man might be hot tempered, 'sudden and quick,' but by middle age, he would be 'full of wise saws' and comfortably settled in his own skin.

But how would one characterise the seven ages of life now, assuming that different stages are still even distinguishable? A hornet's nest of neologisms has sprung up to describe the new virtual age categories. The infant might 'mewl and puke' as before but by age two to eight, he would have developed into a tweenager, while at twenty he would be a thresholder, experiencing a 'quarter-life crisis' about the difficulties of finding work and a place to live, which stresses would transform him in a few short years into a kipper or boomeranger, an adult child (thirty +) living or returning to live with his parents. If by thirty-five, he had managed to fly the nest, he would emerge fully fledged as a kid(d)ult, a.k.a. rejuvenile, adultescent, or middlescent, in which stage of life he would remain entrenched through his 'middle youth' (up to mid-fifties).[17] By this time, he might be ready for early retirement and a surreptitious slide into a second childhood, where he would find himself in sync again with Jacques's sardonic portrait of the aging infant, sans teeth, sans eyes.

The defining feature of contemporary coming of age is that it could happen at any age of life because age, like gender, has become a conscious construction rather than a biological fact. 'Now we are six' could mean a virtual age of sixteen or sixty. Witness Bill Watterson, creator of the comic strip *Calvin and Hobbes*, who identifies with the child Calvin ('many of Calvin's struggles are metaphors for my own'), rather than the wise, adult tiger Hobbes. Watterson suspects 'that most of us get old without growing up, and that inside every adult (sometimes not very far inside) is a bratty kid who wants everything his own way'.[18] Forty could mean thirty for Desperate Housewives and those with deep enough pockets for plastic surgery, while sixty could mean twenty for rock stars like Lou Reed, still fuelling their songs with adolescent rage.

In contrast to Philip Pullman, twentieth-century psychologists have described adulthood as a stage of life that is not in any way settled, but full of major transitions. Following Jung, Erik Erikson writes extensively about the changes that occur in the development of an adult.[19] And J.A. Appleyard, drawing on Erikson, posits that adults work through the challenge of these life transitions through their reading, as well as other activities. Issues pertaining to adult development include:

> whether a person can share this self with others in friendship and genuine intimacy, then whether he or she will invest in the establishing and guiding of the next generation that Erikson calls generativity, and finally whether the aging person will accept the triumphs and disappointments of his or her life and the significant people in it and achieve the ripeness, coherence, and wholeness that Erikson calls integrity.[20]

But even if there is some uncertainty about whether or not the adult will accomplish these transitions successfully, Appleyard's thesis that there are five distinct stages of life, and five ways of reading to accompany them, seems dated in the present context of virtual-age fluidity. Klaus Riegel's description of the aging process as fluid and cyclical captures the complexities of the contemporary zeitgeist: 'development consists of a ceaseless flux involving four major dimensions (inner-biological, individual-psychological, cultural-sociological, and outer-physical) along which an individual moves simultaneously'.[21] Adults not only undergo the transitional challenges Erikson identifies. They may also re-experience, or experience for the first time, any of the crises of so-called earlier phases of life: infant primal scenes, childhood insecurities, adolescent existential angst, etc. Nor are the time-slips only retrospective. Some very young children now feel adolescent-type social and sexual pressure from peers or adults, while adolescents are experiencing 'adult' anxieties about careers and financial security.

Reflecting this increasingly fluid social context, Pullman's child protagonists are of an uncertain mental or virtual age, even though their biological age is twelve. When Will first meets Lyra, he notices that 'her expression was a mixture of the very young—and a kind of deep sad wariness.' (*Subtle Knife*, 25) Will himself is preternaturally old for his years, having been the primary carer for his mentally ill mother, and now, an accidental murderer. Sometimes his observations are indistinguishable from an adult's, as when he first sees Lyra's mother, Mrs Coulter: 'The woman herself was beautiful ... Will saw that with a shock—lovely in the moonlight, her brilliant dark eyes wide with enchantment, her slender shape light and graceful'. (*Subtle Knife*, 213) And Lyra herself can behave either as a very young child or as an adult. In the conflict between bear kings, she exercises conventional feminine wiles over Iofur, flattering him as Pan urges her to do (341) and feeling an 'intoxicating' power when this masculine figure is rendered 'helpless' by her deception, but remembering just in time to act 'modestly'. (343) With the other bear king, Iorek, she becomes the lady of courtly romance, urging her knight to succeed in battle: 'Fight well, Iorek, my dear. You're the real king, and he en't. He's nothing'. (348) When his blood is spattered during the fight, she presses a drop of it into her hand 'like a token of love' (351); 'she thought anxiously of how tired he would be', (341) 'trembled at the weight of those blows (351) and wept to think 'her dear, her brave one, her fearless defender, was going to die'. (352) In *The Subtle Knife,* she comes to behave with a similarly conventional feminine deference towards Will. For example, she quickly understands how the subtle knife works but since this is his challenge, not hers, 'she held her tongue and clasped her hands'. (192) Indeed Lyra surpasses even Milton's prelapsarian Eve in her deference to Adam, so much so that one wonders if Lyra's exaggerated performance is meant to underline that she is acting, rather than inhabiting, the dutiful wifely role.

This blurring of mental ages is a characteristic feature of a large number of protagonists in contemporary children's and young adult novels. As we shall see in Chapter 6, the child protagonist of Almond's *Clay,* Stephen Rose, makes sculptures that might pass for 'the work of a thirty-year-old professional' (50), while Davie, the child narrator of the novel, wearily observes, 'Time moves forward, so we're told . . . Past, present, future. Child, teenager, adult. Birth, life, death. But sometimes time gets stuck. We can't move on'. (271) Sometimes time gets clotted, as in *Clay,* and sometimes it hemorrhages and flows too fast. In Garth Nix's *Sabriel,* the eponymous heroine tells an adult soldier, 'I am only eighteen years old on the outside . . . But I first walked in Death when I was twelve . . . I don't feel young any more'. (46) At the end of McCaughrean's *The White Darkness,* a young man is embarrassed to discover that the girl he has just asked out is only fourteen (258). And at the beginning of Meg Rosoff's *How I Live Now,* the worldly-wise, anorexic fifteen-year-old from New York City is a little stunned to be collected at the airport by her fourteen-year-old, driving, chain-smoking British cousin (5). Not much later, she is even more surprised to find herself involved in a passionate love affair with the same underage cousin. While at one level, these protagonists matter-of-factly accept their unstable social positions as simply the way things are, they also betray deep anxieties about how they should act in this borderless social context.

In *Sabriel,* the visual symbol of this social disintegration is the crumbling wall that once preserved a strong division between the north and south of the country. In the south is rational, modern Ancelstierre, while north of the border is the magic Old Kingdom, where souls move fluidly between life and death. Since the wall has begun to disintegrate, a southern soldier reports:

> 'Corpses wouldn't stay buried . . . Soldiers killed the day before would turn up on parade. Creatures prevented from crossing [the Wall] would rise up and do more damage than they did when they were alive'. (*Sabriel,* 38)

It becomes Sabriel's heroic task to restore the wall, return the dead to the underworld, and seal up the magic leaking from the North. Lyra is destined to fulfill a similar role in *His Dark Materials.* In *The Subtle Knife,* she and Will stumble into another world, Cittàgazze, where as a result of a biological-ecological disaster, adults are preyed on by alien Spectres and reduced to zombies, while children roam the streets in warring gangs. As in *Sabriel,* the situation stems from Cittàgazzan citizens having opened up too many passages between their own and other worlds, leaving their own world exposed to alien dangers. Similar dangers loom in *Northern Lights,* when Asriel opens a window into another world, and in *The Amber Spyglass,* when Will learns that by cutting doorways between worlds with the subtle knife, he has made the uni(or multi-)verse dangerously unstable (515).

Northern Lights and Nomadism

In Lyra's world, then, there is—or there should be—a distinct difference between the states of childhood and adulthood. All human beings and other species in her world have personal, visible daemons, or souls, which accompany their hosts everywhere in the shape of animals. Whereas adults in this other world have daemons of a fixed shape, children's daemons are unfixed and can take on the shapes of different animals, depending on the child's emotional state, or stage of psychological development. When the child's daemon 'settles', he or she is said to have crossed into adulthood. Thus Pullman connotes that adults are—or should be—settled into stable, unchanging identities. In interview, Pullman has spelled out this view explicitly. When asked 'what would happen if humans changed dramatically in later life? . . . Would their daemons change also?' Pullman replied: 'do people change dramatically in later life? I think their basic stance towards the world is pretty constant'.[22] In his introduction to *Paradise Lost,* Pullman again stresses his view that there is, or should be, a clear demarcation between childhood and adulthood: 'innocence is not wise, and wisdom cannot be innocent, and if we are going to do any good in the world, we have to leave childhood behind'.[23] But this clear demarcation between children and adults turns out to be a lost ideal in Lyra's world, since a theological organisation called the General Oblation Board (loosely modelled on the Catholic Church) is supporting Mrs Coulter's research into the possibility of severing children from their daemons, and entrapping the children in a permanent state of immaturity. As Lord Asriel explains to his daughter at the end of *Northern Lights,* Mrs Coulter's experiments are based on a hypothesis that,

> the two things that happen at adolescence might be connected: the change in one's daemon and the fact that Dust begins to settle. Perhaps if the daemon were separated from the body, we might never be subject to Dust—to original sin. The question was whether it was possible to separate daemon and body without killing the person. (375)

This then is the basis for Mrs Coulter and the Oblation Board's interference in children's coming of age in *His Dark Materials.* And one might assume this is also Pullman's swipe at concepts of childhood segregated from adulthood entirely, such as are expressed in Barrie's Neverland or in Pullman's reading of Lewis's Narnia.[24] For although he sees childhood and adulthood as distinct states, Pullman insists there is and should be a natural continuity between them. This conviction also informs the manner of his address to children as a writer: 'I was once a child, and so were all the other adults who produce children's literature; and those who read it, the children, will one day be adults . . . there must be some sort of continuity'. ('What! No Soap?' 43) In *Northern Lights,* this natural continuity is disrupted when Mrs Coulter attempts to cut through the chronotope, the time-space of adolescence, which links childhood to adulthood.

Lyra undertakes to rescue the kidnapped children, with the help of her 'gyptian' allies. Thus her heroic task is to restore the 'natural' coming-of-age process which has been disrupted by corrupt, religious adults. Lyra and Will's correspondent heroic tasks thus consist of closing up leaks and fissures between disparate social worlds; this joint work is bound up with the trilogy's eventual rejection of fantasy for realism. This manoeuvre would surely disappoint a celebrant of nomadism like Salman Rushdie, who argues that the ending of *The Wonderful Wizard of Oz,* where Dorothy declares that Kansas is better than Oz, is an instance of the radical 'dream of Away' being betrayed by a conventional 'dream of Home'.[25] But if Pullman seems to be falling into the same trap here, we should remind ourselves that the home-worlds Lyra and Will decide to limit themselves to are still fantastical to the reader, measured against the reader's own, actual world. In terms of defining the new social order, while Will and Lyra claim their right to experience adolescence without interference from theocratic adults, Pullman at the same time creates a fictional universe in which 'childlike' qualities are given a higher status and value than those associated with adulthood.

When I say that Pullman valorises the 'childlike', I mean specifically those qualities and characteristics which he attributes to childhood, above all in his characterisation of Lyra. Neither obedient nor well mannered nor truthful like C.S. Lewis's Lucy Pevensie, Pullman's iconic child is daring, wilful, independent, empathetic and devious. Lyra is physically light on her feet, and as agile as a goat, as is evident from the opening scenes of *Northern Lights,* which depict her skipping sure-footedly across the rooftops of Jordan College. Later, it will be a sign that her childhood is over when she slips and falls while crossing a narrow ledge around an abyss in the underworld (*Amber Spyglass,* 378). Pullman's sense of childliness indeed encompasses many the qualities of lightness celebrated by Calvino in *Six Memos,* as discussed in the previous chapter.

'Childliness' also means here being emotionally agile, in the sense of being prone to extreme emotions oneself, and empathetic towards the emotions of others. Empathy is Lyra's signature key, while it is a trait often found lacking in adult characters in the trilogy. After the tortured child Tony Makarios dies, she demands to know what has been done with a piece of dried fish which Tony had been clinging to in place of his severed daemon. She wants to bury it with him in a mark of respect ('Don't you *dare* laugh! I'll tear your lungs out if you laugh!') A man admits 'uneasily' that he gave it to his dogs, 'Not thinking he had a need for it . . . I do beg your pardon'. But Lyra replies, 'It en't my pardon you need, it's his'. (221) Later, meeting her mother at the laboratory where the severing is carried out, she demands to know, 'why were they going to do that? . . . why are they so cruel?' (283) Mrs Coulter soothingly appeals to Lyra's self-interest ('They won't ever do it to you . . . you're safe'.), but Lyra instantly rebukes her ('they do it to other children! Why?'). Throughout the trilogy, Lyra identifies intensely with the suffering of others (not only Tony and the other children at Bolvangar, but also Iorek, Roger *et al*) but she can also use her ability to read others' emotions to her own advantage (for example, when she plays off the rival bear king Iofur's insecurities).

Lyra is also clever and mentally flexible and intuitive, rather than rational. This is demonstrated by her ability to read the alethiometer, an instrument which allows her to discover a limited number of hidden facts and future events. Although as an adult, she will have to relearn the skill through diligent study, as a child she can read the instrument instinctively:

> Without even having to think about it, she found her fingers moving the hands to point . . . felt her mind settle into the right meanings like a complicated diagram in three dimensions. At once the needle began to swing round, back, round and on further, like a bee dancing its message to the hive. She watched it calmly, content not to know at first but to know that a meaning was coming, and then it began to clear. She let it dance until it was certain. (*Northern Lights*, 204)

The learning here is unforced, as Lyra allows the instrument to dance its meaning 'like a bee'. Pullman elsewhere explains, 'I intended this power of hers to be a sort of . . . grace . . . a function of her lack of self-consciousness, so to speak, a sign of primal innocence'. ('Writing Fantasy Realistically') Being 'content not to know, but to know a meaning would come' sums up a child's relation to knowledge in *Northern Lights*. It is not that Lyra is content to be ignorant, but rather that the knowledge she needs comes to her quasi-magically. She is still in Eden, but a Miltonic Eden where one dreams and wakes up to find one's dreams are true.[26]

The other sign of childhood flexibility in this text is, of course, that children's daemons change their shapes rapidly and constantly. And Lyra's daemon Pantalaimon seems nimblest of them all; he changes from mouse to insect, to bird, to pine marten (his final form) and to ermine, the creature in the Leonardo da Vinci painting said to have inspired Pullman's portrait of Lyra.[27] All this shape-changing and mental agility suggests that in *His Dark Materials*, children are adept at thinking 'as if': as if they were somebody else, as if they lived somewhere else, or as if they existed at some other time. In other words, they are more attracted by the dream of Away than the dream of Home, and they are instinctive masters of time travel (evidenced in Lyra's alethiometer), magic space travel (Will's subtle knife), disguise, mimicry, imaginative empathy and many other forms of escaping to an 'elsewhere'. If these are childish attributes that Will and Lyra seem eager to relinquish at the end of *The Amber Spyglass,* they are nevertheless a fundamental part of the fictional world that Pullman has invented in *His Dark Materials.*

This is not to suggest that this fictional world is a Neverland, where children rule because adults have been excluded. Pullman's Cittàgazze is indeed such a world, but Pullman represents this as a Hell not a Paradise, for both children and adults. Lyra's own world is fully populated with adults and, for the most part, the children there are governed by adult rules. But many of these adults share Lyra's childish qualities of mobility, flexibility and empathetic imagination. The first community to help Lyra are the 'gyptians', led by John Faa and Farder Coram, a nomadic people who inhabit the borderless Fens, 'that wide and never fully mapped wilderness of huge skies and endless marshland in eastern Anglia'. (111) Accustomed to a free life, moving by boat through 'a thousand winding channels and creeks and watercourses', the gyptians are able to respond to Lyra's plea and send a rescue mission to the north, because like Lyra herself, they are an unfixed and rootless people. Indeed, most of the benevolent adults in *His Dark Materials* are nomadic, if not physically airborne. The Texan aeronaut Lee Scoresby, the flying witch Serafina Pekkala, the mounted Chevaliers and the angels are all adults who move freely and lightly through space, and who imaginatively empathise with the children they choose to protect.

Although Pullman might recoil from the association, the nomad is a figure much celebrated and romanticised in postmodern theory. For Deleuze and Guattari (and before them, Emerson and Nietzsche,) the nomad, like the philosopher, challenges and unsettles entrenched authority.[28] In Peters's paraphrase, 'nomads liberate thinking from dogmatism, break through convention to new life and beauty, and prize the mobile diversity of being'. ('Exile', 33) This principle of liberation is deeply embedded in the characterisation, plotting, style, narratorial voice, and even the history of the reception of *His Dark Materials.* Adult readers may be drawn to Pullman's trilogy precisely because of its promise of release from entrenched attitudes and settled modes of being. As Peters writes, 'ultimately at stake in the concept of nomadism is the dream of radical liberty, of roaming at will, beholden to nothing but the wind and the stars'. ('Exile', 33) *Northern Lights* is the most uncritically nomadic of the three books, and it concludes with just such an image of radical liberation: 'Lyra and her daemon turned away from the world they were born in, and looked towards the sun, and walked into the sky'. (399)

In the contrast between the two bear-kings, we might identify two types of postmodernism, the one presented as superficially ludic, and the other, as genuinely nomadic. The narrator says, 'there were two kinds of beardom opposed here, two futures, two destinies'. (349) On the one hand, there is Iofur Raknison, gaudily dressed in gold and jewels, with gold-leaf painted claws, who has decorated his granite throne with 'swags and festoons of gilt that looked like tinsel on a mountainside'. (336) He is not quite one of the drag-queens in *Priscilla, Queen of the Desert*, but he is still unmistakably postmodern camp.[29] Iofur no longer knows who he is (a bear) and longs for a personal daemon, like the ones humans have in his world. By contrast, the true bear-king, Iorek Byrnison, is 'pure and certain and absolute' in himself, which does not sound particularly postmodern until one realises that what he is most certain about is that he is a nomadic creature who has no need of golden palaces or daemons since he carries his soul on his back (quite literally, as *panserbjørne* bears' souls are their armour). When Iorek wins the duel, the other bears come to their nomadic senses immediately: 'every single badge and sash and coronet was thrown off at once . . . They swarmed to the Palace and began to hurl great blocks of marble from the topmost towers'. (354)

His Dark Materials also evinces a sense of the nomadic in its narrative emplotment. As is characteristic of fantasy in general, but this one more than most, there are multiple plots and mini-narratives which unfold over vast sweeps of space. *The Subtle Knife*, whose central protagonist, Will, is a boy in exile, develops this nomadic plot structure almost to the point of entropic disintegration. The narrative also moves swiftly, indeed relentlessly, through a whole series of death scenes, from which the surviving characters appear to recover with remarkable rapidity. This is most pronounced in the morally corrupt characters, as one might expect. Lord Asriel instantly forgets having killed a child in his excitement of finding a pathway through the Aurora at the end of *Northern Lights*. But even when the child, Roger, gets to experience death again, this time as a pantheistic dispersal of atoms, the sense of cheerful, almost carnivalesque amnesia predominates:

> The first ghost to leave the world of the dead was Roger . . . [he] laughed in surprise as he found himself turning into the night, the starlight, the air . . . and then he was gone, leaving behind such a vivid little burst of happiness that Will was reminded of the bubbles in a glass of champagne. (382)

Individual readers' responses to this description of death are likely to vary widely (I find it uncomfortably reminiscent of the happy deaths of angelic children in Victorian fiction). But the point to stress here is how 'drifting apart' in death, to be 'out in the open, part of everything alive again' (335) is in many ways the fitting consummation to a postmodern nomadic life.

Not coincidentally, Pullman's writing is at its best when describing light, dust, and any form of atomic dispersal. To my mind, there is no finer writing in the trilogy than such dramatic descriptions of the Aurora:

the first veils trembled and raced to one side, and jagged curtains folded and unfolded above, increasing in size and brilliance every minute; arcs and loops swirled across from horizon to horizon, and touched the very zenith with bows of radiance. (*Northern Lights*, 383)

More problematically, however, the rapid alteration of scene and action in this kind of epic fantasy may produce a sense of dislocation, a lack of 'addressivity' in the nomad or observer, to invoke Mikhail Bakhtin's concept.[30] No single world, or person, or other, will hold our attention for long, because we do not belong in, and hence do not address ourselves to, any one place. The 'we' here may equally signify the protagonist, the reader or the writer of fantasy. As Pullman perceptively comments, 'this is one of the great joys . . . in writing fantasy. You can do this: you're in danger in one world so—*slash!*—you cut out into another one'.[31] This carnivalesque sense of existence with a loophole, with 'a permanent alibi for being' as Bakhtin puts it, is one of the negative aspects of nomadism which is specifically redressed in *The Amber Spyglass*, when Pullman has Will close up all the loopholes he has cut open.[32] But *Northern Lights* for the most part communicates the joyous and liberating aspects of the nomadic *mode de vie*.

One catches the scent of this intoxicating freedom, not only in the rapid shifts of scene, but also in the treatment of myth and source texts. For example, Lord Asriel reads from a bowdlerised version of Genesis in *Northern Lights* where daemons feature in the temptation of Adam and Eve: 'your daemons shall assume their true forms, and ye shall be as gods, knowing good and evil'. (*Northern Lights*, 372) With equal boldness, Pullman rewrites Virgil's *Aeneid* in *The Amber Spyglass*, as the travellers in the underworld here manage to alter the fates of the dead.[33] 'The old dispensation', that is to say, the law of the Christian and classical underworlds, is summarily dispatched as a miniscule character, the chevalier Tialys, persuades a giant flock of terrifying harpies to release the souls of the dead (*Amber Spyglass*, 333). Pullman thus shares with other iconoclastic writers the instinct, not so much to pour new wine into old bottles, as to burst the bottles asunder altogether.[34] His narration of the descent into the underworld is comparable in this respect to Angela Carter's *The Passion of New Eve* or Alice Notley's *The Descent of Alette*.[35]

'Sprite narration'

The sense of liberation from fixed categories of being is also communicated to the reader through the voice and stance of the narrator. Maria Nikolajeva has argued that recent children's fiction has moved away from omniscient, third-person narration, since 'it is no longer possible to write about the innermost thoughts and feelings of a child in the old traditional manner'.[36] Contemporary writers tend to prefer first-person narration, she argues, because this kind of narrator 'is more subjective and insightful and therefore more suitable for conveying the deeper feelings of a child'. In this new fiction, 'we find a fundamentally different authorial attitude towards the character'. (*Children's Literature*, 99–100) In her view, modern children's literature has shifted from epic to polyphonic narration. In the latter type, according to Bakhtin, the narrator 'retains for himself no essential "surplus" of meaning and enters on an equal footing with . . . [his characters] into the great dialogue of the novel as a whole'.[37]

By contrast, Philip Pullman has often stressed his preference for 'the old, traditional manner' of third-person narration. Yet there are two important ways in which his narrative is polyphonic, despite the 'essential "surplus" of meaning' of its omniscient narrator. First, the polyphonic novel is structured so as to allow characters to argue on equal terms with each other and the narrator. As Bakhtin writes, the novelistic hero's words and actions are 'not uncontested'; his 'position is always open to contest'.[38] This is true of many of the ideas expressed in *His Dark Materials*. Pullman's characters are constantly caught up in ideological conflicts relating to science and ethics, religious faith, good and evil, youth and adulthood. Some readers might feel that the trilogy's antireligious stance is so extreme as to be absolutist in itself, but the trilogy does not present atheism as a given truth. Many characters polemically argue the question of whether there is a God or not. There is a polyphonic openness, in terms of the structuring of characters' voices, which invites debate both within the text and without. Indeed, the trilogy's contentious reception is proof in itself of how successfully the text is structured to provoke debate. For Bakhtin, the special work of the novel is to increase self-consciousness, that is, to make narrators, characters and readers more conscious of their ways of speaking and to make language more conscious of itself.[39] While Pullman has expressed a strong distaste for subjective narration, nevertheless I would argue that the great debates which run through *His Dark Materials*, many of which are unfinalised, contribute to this novelistic work of making life and art more conscious. Indeed Pullman's concept of Dust, which is variously defined as original sin, dark matter, adult self-awareness, and the dispersed souls of the dead, works very well as a visual image of Bakhtin's thesis that the novel should generate and sharpen consciousness.

But there is another way in which Pullman's narration resembles the subjectivity of (post)modern writing rather than objective realism. In my view, the third-person narrator of *His Dark Materials* is mobile and fluidly empathetic, rather than omniscient or objective in the classic sense. This is suggested in Pullman's description of his preference for third-person narrative:

> In third-person, omniscient narration, a 'consciousness' seems to wander about at will, entering first this mind and then that, moving forward in time . . . moving in close enough to see the slight narrowing of a character's eyes, moving out far enough to describe the lights of a whole

city at night from space—or whatever . . . what sort of consciousness is it that can do these things? The closest I've come is to suggest that the omniscient narrator . . . is in fact not a human being at all.[40]

In this description, the narrator's roving eye operates rather like a camera lens, though with the extra capacity to move inside its subject's head. Like the eye of the camera, this narratorial figure sees with something other than a human gaze, and with a voice that is not settled in one human shape. It is rather, he suggests,

> some kind of sprite. Certainly he-she-it is both ancient and youthful, male and female, sceptical and credulous, sophisticated and innocent, wise and foolish, all at once.

Omniscient narration is an aspect of nineteenth-century realist fiction for which Pullman has explicitly stated his admiration. But this hyper-omniscience seems rather to belong to the world of fantasy, whose chronotope allows characters to travel vast distances and time zones. Clearly the narrator is not a child. It introduces Lyra to us as a 'coarse and greedy little savage', evincing an affectionate but certainly not childlike perspective on the heroine (37). But neither is this narratorial voice that of an adult, at least as the latter is defined in the cosmology of *His Dark Materials,* because its identity is anything but settled or fixed in one shape. What this third-person narrator seems to resemble most is the daemon of a child; both are restless metamorphs who are constantly drawn to testing out new discoveries and experiences. Like Lyra and her daemon Pan, the narrator of *His Dark Materials* is also distinctively empathetic, entering characters' minds not just to reveal their thoughts, but to present them passionately to the reader. This daemonic narrator wraps itself around its characters' thoughts, actions and words, just as closely as Pan wraps himself in the shape of an ermine round Lyra's neck. It huddles affectionately in its characters' thoughts, just as Pan takes the shape of a mouse to burrow in Lyra's pocket. This narrator is not so much omniscient as anxious that the reader should hear, smell, taste and above all, feel the world as it is being experienced by a particular character.

If it resembles a child's daemon, however, the narrator of *His Dark Materials* is also something more. Within the diegesis, daemons attach themselves to only one individual, whereas this sprite narrator has the capacity to function as the daemon of any character it chooses. In the following passage, he-she-it begins by empathising with Lyra when she is forced to leave her daemon behind at the entrance to the underworld:

> And she looked back again at the foul and dismal shore, so bleak and blasted with disease and poison, and thought of her dear Pan waiting there alone, her heart's companion, watching her disappear into the

mist, and she fell into a storm of weeping . . . all along the shore in in-
numerable ponds and shallows, in wretched broken tree stumps, the
damaged creatures that lurked there heard her fullhearted cry and drew
themselves a little closer to the ground, afraid of such passion. (*Northern Lights*, 296)

The empathy eddies outward to encompass the entire shoreline in an Orphic
pathetic fallacy, as creatures are animated into human consciousness by the
narrator's sorrow for Lyra's pain. Could this be an alternative development of
the child's imaginative psyche to the one explicitly proposed in the diegesis?
In other words, rather than having to settle into a fixed shape, could a child
and his or her daemon 'come of age' by becoming *more* empathetic, *more* able
to flow into the thoughts and feelings of others?

Sprite Reading?

Not only could the narrator of *His Dark Materials* be compared to a child's
daemon which has come of age in this sense, but he-she-it could also produce this effect on its narratee or reader. At one level, the reader hears the
explicit thesis of *The Amber Spyglass*, as Will, like a Miltonic Adam, imparts
it to Lyra: 'my father . . . said we have to build the republic of heaven where we
are. He said that for us there isn't any elsewhere'. (516) Their enforced separation, along with Lyra's rejection of fantasy, seems to shut the door with equal
firmness on the reader's, especially the post-adolescent reader's, craving for
an elsewhere. But at another level, the daemonic narrator also speaks to us
about adult selves that can be pried free of the familiar and cast into strangely
altered territory, where places and souls are doubled.[41] Here, for example, is a
reader registering a sense of the uncanny when entering Lyra's Oxford, which
is like but unlike the real place:

From the opening scenes at the school or on the streets of Oxford, we
feel the grasp on the ordinary world slipping. This is our world—almost. These real people in this slightly altered time and place create a
world of wonder. It is as though you [are] looking at the unfolding of
events through a shimmering silky black fog. It is not only mysterious
in the sense of plot development, but also in more profound ways as we,
through Lyra's eyes, let go of our firm holding of our ideas of how things
should be.[42]

Like Salman Rushdie, Pullman writes 'at a slight angle to reality', mixing
descriptions of the real (Turl Street, Jericho, the River Isis as the Thames
is named while it flows through Oxford, Port Meadow, the old nunnery at
Godstow) with the imaginary (Jordan College, Gabriel College) to create

an imaginary homeland for Lyra.[43] Thus 'Lyra's Oxford' assumes more and less fantastic shapes like a daemon reflecting, confirming and distorting the actual city.[44] Other places are altered in different ways; for instance, some are given new names with a comical historical inference. Thus, one finds New Denmark for USA, New France for Canada, and the German Ocean for the North Sea. Similarly, ordinary things are defamiliarised by slightly altered names. Pullman invents the word 'anbaric' for electric (which is derived from the word for 'amber' in Greek), 'photogram' for photograph and 'gyptian' for gypsy (derived originally from 'Egyptian'). All these familiar-but-strange words heighten the reader's sense of an uncannily doubled reality.

Pullman has said that his intended audience is not 'a particular age group, or a particular gender, or a particular class or ethnic group or anything specific at all'.[45] Clearly, he means that he welcomes all ages of reader. But a secondary effect of his prose, I would suggest, is for the reader to become unfixed from any of these 'particular' categories. The implied reader of *His Dark Materials* is someone who grows to be like its narrator: 'ancient and youthful, male and female, sceptical and credulous, sophisticated and innocent, wise and foolish all at once'. Moreover this metamorphosis will not be limited to the reader's interaction with the text, but will spill outwards to spark off debates and arguments and agreements with other readers. This is also the image of the reader which emerges from Pullman's speech on acceptance of the Astrid Lindgren Award:

> as we talk about the book with other people, with our friends or family, so the circles of democratic understanding spread out around it ... when we read a book, we are active about the process. We decide for ourselves how we want to read it ... We retain our freedom—in fact, in reading just as in politics, when we exercise our freedom, we enlarge it.[46]

The following reviews strikingly demonstrate readers (child and adult) putting to one side their most deeply held convictions, to experience the liberation of reading 'as if' they were or could be someone or somewhere else ...

> When reading the trilogy, prepare to put your life on hold as you are guaranteed to be encapsulated by the intricate ideas Pullman has woven into the marvellous story.[47]

> I am a Christian and I still enjoy these books ... Yes, there is a war on God, but it is very original, something fresh and exciting.[48]

> You have to open your mind and put your religious beliefs behind you. If you do that, this trilogy will blow you away.[49]

Art and Answerability

The major debates and dialogues between characters in *His Dark Materials* remain open-ended, while the narrator moves fluidly into the minds of those on either side of the arguments. Most of the characters who tramp, fly or sail through the text appear to feel fulfilled in their nomadic existence. Since these dialogic aspects of the narrative reflect the qualities of childhood celebrated in Lyra and her friends, in what sense can it be a good thing to close the door on childhood, fantasy and freedom of movement in the closing chapters of *The Amber Spyglass*? Pullman's reservations about the limitlessness of fantasy may be compared to the critique of nomadism, articulated by John Durham Peters and others, and it also has parallels with Rowling's later Potter novels, as discussed in the previous chapter. If nomadism privileges the idea of endless self-invention, Peters points out that 'the resources for self-invention are unequally distributed' and that 'nomadic identification often preys on the other without giving anything back'. ('Exile', 34) This brings us back to Pullman's concern for 'a certain moral idea, namely responsibility'. To address oneself to, and in, a particular time and space is to begin to make oneself answerable to the other, as Bakhtin argued in *Art and Answerability*.[50] Lyra makes herself answerable when she seeks out the soul of Roger, the boy whose death she is responsible for, so that she can tell him she's sorry. In my view, *The Amber Spyglass* does not reject the idea of 'Away' altogether, but rather stresses the need to fully acknowledge the other within the framework of a nomadic existence. When Lyra and Will are forced to go back to their separate worlds, it is hardly comparable to Dorothy returning to Kansas by clicking her heels and chanting, 'there's no place like home'. Pullman's couple are left in a state of *unheimlicheit* since they are not permitted to live together in one world. Lyra expresses an exilic sense of loss:

> 'I'll be looking for you, Will, every moment, every single moment. And when we do find each other again we'll cling together so tight that nothing and no one'll ever tear us apart. Every atom of me and every atom of you . . . We'll live in birds and flowers and dragonflies and pine trees and in clouds and in those little specks of light you see floating in sunbeams'. (*Amber Spyglass*, 526)

To Lyra it appears that they will only meet again after death, when their souls will be permitted to re-enter the world(s) and mingle as Dust. Until then, she will be estranged from Will and in this sense, a stranger to herself. This idea, central to Kristeva's *Strangers to Ourselves*, is also comparable to Judeo-Christian notions of exodus and/or life as a pilgrimage on the way to heaven.[51] Between the extremes of nomadic amnesia and exilic longing, Pullman has his two protagonists willingly defer their homecoming in each other, so that they can concentrate on 'build[ing] a republic of heaven where [they] are'.

While Pullman's stated aim was to rewrite Milton's *Paradise Lost* to make the Fall a happy one, his conclusion is paradoxically more tragic than Milton's. Not only are the lovers separated from God (in *Amber Spyglass*, He ceases to exist), but they are also separated from each other, as they 'make their solitary way' into separate worlds (cf. *Paradise Lost* 12.646).[52] Furthermore the movement at the end of Milton's epic is from an enclosed space to an open one: 'the world was all before them'. By contrast, Will and Lyra are being shut in at the end of *The Amber Spyglass*, and multiple, spacious worlds are being closed off from them. This representation of coming-of-age as a process of learning to inhabit a smaller world has a particular resonance in the contemporary context. Due to globalisation and environmental crises, we *do* need to recognise the world as a finite space with limited resources, which somehow we have to inhabit responsibly. On the other hand, as *His Dark Materials* connotes, in a more limited space we have even greater need for an imagination such as Lyra's, which will perceive the infinite within the finite world, and recognise the stranger within the fissured self.

Chapter Four
Seeing Things Big: Mark Haddon's
The Curious Incident of the
Dog in the Night-time

As we have seen, Philip Pullman's *His Dark Materials* depicts an extraordinary journey through multiple fantasy worlds which culminates in a resolution to find the present world equally extraordinary. It seems eminently fitting, then, that the next major step in the expansion of crossover fiction in millennial Britain should be with a work of luminous realism. Like Pullman, though via a very different route, Mark Haddon aimed to convey a sense of 'the extraordinary inside the ordinary' with his novel, *The Curious Incident of the Dog in the Night-time*.[1] Haddon explains that he set out 'to take a life that seemed horribly constrained, to . . . show that if you viewed this life with sufficient imagination it would seem infinite'.[2] He chose to write from the point of view of a boy with a mental health condition, because 'disability is a way of getting [to] some extremity' that is 'also terribly, terribly ordinary'. His fifteen-year-old narrator, Christopher Boone, has a form of Asperger's syndrome which makes him brilliant at mathematics and logic but limited in empathy or certain forms of imagination.[3] Growing up in Swindon, a market town lying to the south of Oxford's ethereal dreaming spires, the monosyllabic Christopher Boone is the very antithesis of Philip Pullman's charismatic, silver-tongued Lyra, and at the time, seemed to be an unlikely fictional child to enchant an adult reader. Nevertheless it was this novel that brought home the point that realist fiction for children could cross over to adult readers as easily as fantasy.

Prior to the publication of Mark Haddon's *The Curious Incident of the Dog in the Night-time* in 2003, the received opinion amongst critics and reviewers was that crossover fiction would be limited to the genre of children's fantasy fiction.[4] But when Haddon won a handful of mainstream adult literary fiction awards with what appeared to be a children's novel, the assumption that only fantasy had the magic crossover ingredient had to be revised. Expressed in the most general terms, one could say that Rowling attracted greater numbers of adult readers to children's fantasy fiction than ever before, that Pullman legitimised that adult interest by elevating children's fantasy to the status of the seriously 'literary', and that Haddon's *Curious Incident* greatly increased the numbers of adults reading children's realist fiction.[5]

Moreover, the unconventional route by which *Curious Incident* came to the attention of adult readers raised even larger questions about whether or not books for children and adults were any longer distinguishable. Rowling and Pullman both had adult editions published subsequent to the children's editions of their novels. By contrast, Mark Haddon's novel was published simultaneously in two editions, one for adults, the other for children. According to David Fickling, publisher of the children's edition, this was not a conscious decision to market the novel as a 'crossover' text.[6] Mark Haddon had intended *Curious Incident* for an adult audience, while his literary agent thought it should be marketed for children.[7] So, unusually, the manuscript was offered simultaneously to David Fickling (whose children's list included Pullman's *His Dark Materials*) and Jonathan Cape, a publisher of adult literary fiction. As it happened, both publishers liked the manuscript; rather than compete for it, they decided to collaborate on a dual edition.[8]

First published on 26 April 2003, *Curious Incident* went straight to the top of the adult bestseller list, with Jonathan Cape selling 1,866 copies of the adult edition and David Fickling selling 559 of the children's edition in the second week of publication.[9] The dust jacket of both editions featured a stylised drawing, in primary colours, of a dog with limbs splayed and a wound in its side. The adult dust jacket additionally bore words of praise from the novelist Ian McEwan and the neurologist Oliver Sacks, two specialists of the 'curious gaze', a key feature of this novel and of some kinds of cross-reading generally, to which I shall return presently. Unlike Donnelly, who arguably acquired her massive adult readership through selection for a popular TV show, Haddon's novel seems to have acquired its adult readership by word of mouth in the publishing industry. Even before the novel's publication, the rights for foreign editions had been sold in forty countries, film rights acquired, and negotiations begun with screenwriter Steve Kloves (author of the screenplays for the Potter films, as well as *The Fabulous Baker Boys*).[10] Soon after publication, *Curious Incident* was favourably reviewed in *The Guardian*, and by Germaine Greer on BBC Newsnight.[11] It was long listed for the Booker Prize, an award which no children's book has yet won, and the Chair of judges, John Carey, publicly criticised his fellow judges for failing to select it for the short list.[12] All this adult interest emboldened Haddon's publishers to enter *Curious Incident* for the 2003 Whitbread Award in the category of Best Novel, rather than Best Children's Novel. Not only did it win the award, it went on to win the overall prize of Book of the Year (like Pullman's *The Amber Spyglass*), substantially boosting the sales figures of both child and adult hardback editions. *Curious*

Incident was awarded the South Bank Show Award on 23 January 2004, and the Whitbread Book of the Year the following week, and in that week, adult hardback edition sales more than doubled while sales of the children's hardback edition went up by a third.[13]

The success of *Curious Incident* in the adult fiction market led reviewers to debate whether the novel should be properly considered a children's book or one for adults. As Haddon's literary agent had maintained, novels narrated by adolescents very often appeal to that age of reader. The novel depicts a teenage boy's coming of age in the context of his parents' marital breakdown, a theme that might be expected to appeal to a teen readership. In addition, Christopher narrates in plain, straightforward language which presents few difficulties for the younger reader. Although the adult edition continued to outsell the children's edition by a factor of roughly two to one in the months and years after publication, the sales figures for the children's edition were still extremely strong. [14] The official Mark Haddon web-site lists seventeen awards for *Curious Incident*, amongst which are many for a work of children's fiction. Thus by many measures, it belongs in the category of fiction for older children. On the other hand, none of these features preclude it from being a work suitable for adults. As far as the flat style of narration is concerned, one could point to a host of 'inadequate narrators' like Christopher in adult fiction: Camus's *L'Etranger*, Hemingway's short stories, or novels by William Faulkner or Kurt Vonnegut.[15]

Approaching this debate from a slightly different angle then, I wish to suggest in this chapter that Christopher Boone embodies what Gaston Bachelard has called the child's ability to 'see things big'. Thus Christopher is both a narrator characteristic of children's fiction, and a fictional child in whom adults are particularly invested. Christopher's limitations as a storyteller—his deadpan tone, his fussy literalism, the fact he cannot intuit other people's thoughts or take in, let alone describe, a crowded, busy scene—are all aspects of the narrow gate by which the reader accesses a spacious, new perception of the world and the capacity to 'see things big'.

'Infinite riches in a little room'

On one hand, Christopher Boone seems to be an absolutely unique character and narrator in children's literature. The striking individuality of his voice and gaze is often what impacts upon the reader first, whether that reader is a child or an adult. Thus remarks Robert Hanks: 'the world is seen entirely through Christopher's tunnel vision [and] it is his uninflected voice that gives the book its particular charm'.[16] Equally conscious of the limitations imposed on the narrator, a twelve-year-old girl from Stoke writes: 'the logic of Christopher was just incredible, especially for someone who was so restricted in other ways'.[17] Upon first reading the manuscript, David Fickling was similarly struck by the way the novel 'imprisons you in a restricted voice'.[18] On the other hand, Christopher can be viewed as one of the latest examples in a long tradition of fiction which associates the restricted gaze of a child or small person with the spaciousness of a creative intellect or visionary imagination. In this literary tradition, one stumbles across the extraordinary within the context of the mundane; 'infinite riches' are found in 'a little room'.[19] More often than not, the infinite is perceived through the eyes of a child who is underestimated and literally overlooked by adults. To place *Curious Incident* in context, then, we might briefly contrast a number of other texts which develop the concept of a restricted voice or gaze paradoxically producing a sense of the infinite.

In *The Poetics of Space*, Gaston Bachelard notes in passing that 'les enfants regardent grand'. This quotation from de Boissy loosely translates as 'children see with an enlarging gaze': whatever they look at, they make bigger with their eyes.[20] In agreement with de Boissy, Bachelard assumes firstly, that children perceive objects on a different scale to adults because of their comparatively smaller size, and secondly, that they perceive objects with a greater attention to detail. Whether or not this view is scientific provable, fictional children are very often represented as seeing things on a different scale, and often with a more intensely focused gaze.[21] In *Feeling Like a Kid*, Jerry Griswold cites many examples of children's books that reproduce the child's sense of 'smallness', from which comes their perception of the world as spacious and infinite.[22] As he points out, children's fiction is full of tiny characters with big imaginations: Petit Poucet or Tom Thumb, Stuart Little, the Deptford Mice, and Charlotte the spider in *Charlotte's Web*. But again, it should be emphasised that this observation implies an adult perspective on children's modes of perception. A child's gaze is only 'enlarging' to an observer who is aware of the differences in scale involved. Children may perceive themselves as small in relation to adults; but it is only the adult who is likely to be surprised by the small child's 'enlarging' gaze (to a child, it would just be their normal mode of perception). It is an adult reader who is most likely to be affected by the way fictional children 'see things big'. Christopher Boone is fifteen, and hence hardly small, but he also is drawn to 'really little spaces':

> Sometimes when I want to be on my own I get into the airing cupboard in the bathroom and slide in beside the boiler and pull the door closed behind me and sit there and think for hours and it makes me feel very calm. (65)

There is a certain pathos in this image of a teenager behaving like a little child, but on the other hand, it also functions as a gateway for the adult reader who, though perhaps not as willing to act on it, may well share this impulse to hide away and feel protected. The boiler cupboard is also Christopher's imaginary spacecraft (though he says he does not imagine things), so that when inside the cupboard he thinks about 'machines and computers and outer space'. (65) From the boiler cupboard, Christopher draws the reader out to a sense of the infinite, informing us that the stars he will see from his spacecraft window 'are the places where the molecules that life is made of were constructed billions of years ago. For example, all the iron in your blood which stops you being anaemic was made in a star'. (66) He produces a similar sense of the infinite later, when he imagines himself in a 'spherical metal submersible' observing ecosystems in the depth of the ocean, 'one of the quietest and darkest and most secret places' on the earth (100).

Bachelard himself mentions the 'enlarging gaze' of children in the context of adult modes of perception. The botanist carrying a magnifying glass is the lucky adult who can recapture this childlike ability to see things big. He or she becomes like a child in a garden, intensely absorbed by the tiny movement of insects, colour of blossoms, the prickly or velvety touch of stems and petals. There are, of course, many associations between gardens, whether magic or ordinary, and fictional children. Two well-known novels on this theme are Frances Hodgson Burnett's *The Secret Garden* and Philippa Pearce's *Tom's Midnight Garden*.[23] Haddon satirically alludes to this tradition when he has Christopher go out to the garden with the aim of describing it in his diary: 'the garden wasn't very interesting or different. It was just a garden, with grass and a shed and a clothesline'. (85) However, he is soon captivated by the cloud formations above, and goes on to describe and illustrate these at length, producing the same effect of the child's eye enchanted by natural wonders. For Bachelard, the botanist with his magnifying glass is a symbol of 'youth recaptured', as the glass rejuvenates (from the Latin, *juventus*) his tired adult eyes. Thus while Bachelard normally thinks of the magnifying glass belonging to an 'old man trying to read his newspaper, in spite of eyes that are weary of looking', in the botanist's hands the glass becomes the instrument of a man who 'takes the world as though it were quite new . . . He is a fresh eye before a new object'. (155)

Amongst contemporary British writers of adult fiction, perhaps none has been more preoccupied with the contrast between perceptive children and sluggishly unobservant adults than Ian McEwan.[24] McEwan's *The Child in Time* demonstrates vividly how a child's gaze can function as a magnifying glass for a world-weary adult observer. In the following passage, the narrator is remembering his dead daughter, and recalling how closely she used to observe the natural world:

> The wood, this spider rotating on its thread, this beetle lumbering over blades of grass, would be all, the moment would be everything. He needed her good influence, her lessons in celebrating the specific; how to fill the present and be filled by it to the point where identity faded to nothing. He was always partly somewhere else, never quite paying attention, never wholly serious. (105–06)

In this passage, it is the child who once taught the adult how to observe things closely, how to 'celebrate the specific'. There is both a spatial and a temporal aspect to this facility for close observation. The adult narrator is 'always partly somewhere else' while the child, as he remembers her, 'filled the present', occupying the here and now in space and time. In his *Confessions*, Augustine famously described what he understood to be the threefold nature of time, in which every present-tense moment actually contains three temporal orientations—expectation of the future, attention to the present, and memory of the past.[25] In *The Child in Time*, the reminiscing adult narrator expresses his need for the child's gaze to restore what is for him now lost: attention to the present, the middle term of Augustine's sense of time.[26] Implicit in McEwan's text is the Augustinian sense that redemption lies in being able to repair the threefold wholeness of temporal perception. If the reader can follow the child's example and restore attention to the present, he or she may be able to move beyond the adult's disabling self-consciousness, to reach a point 'where identity fades to nothing'.

This capacity to 'see with an enlarging gaze' is one of the qualities, I would suggest, which an adult reader hopes to gain from certain kinds of children's fiction. The childlike ability to 'see things big' is often perceived by adults, rather circuitously, as an essential tool for acquiring mature 'self-awareness' (in Philip Pullman's sense), while for children, of course, 'seeing big' is a way of imitating adult modes of perception. Besides the botanist, the other class of adult who typically carries a magnifying glass is the detective. Sherlock Holmes, often iconically represented with glass, deerstalker, and pipe, is Christopher Boone's particular hero. Christopher's own 'murder mystery' narrative is named after a Sherlock Holmes case which hinges on Holmes noticing how a dog failed to bark when it should have.[27] In *Curious Incident*, Christopher discusses the trail of clues in his favourite story, *The Hound of the Baskervilles* (*Curious Incident*, 90–91), and in imitation of Doyle's detective, frames his own narrative as a 'murder mystery novel' with a major puzzle to solve: who killed the dog, Wellington? (5)

While the child can straightforwardly mimic the adult, for an adult reader there are two stages to the process of acquiring a child's enlarging gaze: one has first to shrink, metaphorically, to the size of a child before one can then perceive the world on a magnified scale. Lewis Carroll's Alice, who shrinks to mouse-size and then directly afterwards shoots up to the height of a giant, is often interpreted as the sign of a child whose identity is unfixed (cf. *His Dark Materials*). But this shape-changing Alice can also be understood as a figure for the adult reader as he or she works out how to get through the miniature gate into the child's magic garden.[28] Though not a children's text, Milton's *Paradise Lost* provides another illuminating gloss on the notion of a change of size leading to a shift in perception. Milton describes the fallen angels, having built their palace in Hell, being forced to shrink to insect-size to get through the gateway in all their numbers, into the inner court of

Pandemonium. Milton underlines the reduction of stature by comparing the demons clustering at the entrance to 'bees in spring-time', then to dwarfs, then pygmies and elves:

> . . . so thick the aerie crowd
> Swarmed and were straitened; till, the signal given,
> Behold a wonder! They but now who seemed
> In bigness to surpass Earth's giant sons,
> Now less than smallest dwarfs, in narrow room
> Throng numberless-like that pygmean race
> Beyond the Indian mount; or faery elves . . .
> Thus incorporeal Spirits to smallest forms
> Reduced their shapes immense, and were at large,
> Though without number still, amidst the hall
> Of that infernal court. (*Paradise Lost* I.775–92)

Although the lesser devils remain in miniaturised form while they are inside the hall, the narrator emphasises the spaciousness of the hall, once they have all got through the gate. In particular, the line 'Reduced their shapes immense, and were at large' conveys the idea of constraint leading to spaciousness.[29] I would argue that there can be a similarly double-edged address to the adult reader of children's texts: you may come in, but you will have to stoop to get through the entrance. As Matthew 18.3 has it, 'except ye . . . become as little children, ye shall not enter into the kingdom of heaven'. Or in Bachelard's secular terms, 'the minuscule, a narrow gate, opens up an entire world'. (155) This double-edged invitation was discussed in Chapter 2, in the context of Rowling's child-oriented early novels. I would distinguish 'double-edged' from Barbara Wall's concept of double or dual address, because in my concept, not only the narration is doubled, but the reader herself is; i.e., she reads with a split perspective, as if adult and child.[30] It is this paradoxical combination of a restricted point of view and forbidden/magic access to a spacious other world which a child's capacity to 'see things big' provides for the adult reader.

Sardine Tin Eyes

In many classic children's books, the curious child's gaze is the instrument by which the reader gains access to a world of magic transformation and redemption. In *The Lion, the Witch and the Wardrobe*, one reason that Lucy is the first Pevensie to find her way into Narnia is that she is naturally observant and more curious than any of her three siblings. And Carroll's Alice is, of course, the iconically inquisitive child, whose response to Wonderland is to exclaim, 'curiouser and curiouser!'[31] For the adult reader, this curious child's gaze can function as a Shklovskian device for defamiliarisation or *ostranie* ('making strange').[32] Like the glass-wielding botanist, the reader is distanced from an overfamiliar object in order to be able to see it again with fresh eyes. Roman Jakobson identified this process as the 'poetic function' of language, and in this sense, all consciously literary language shares this aim to defamiliarise. But implicitly, the fictional child's gaze is of central importance in this theory, since it is the 'freshness', the 'first-time-ness,' of the child's gaze to which, according to this theory, all poetic language aspires. Shklovsky writes, for example, that Tolstoy 'describes an object as if he were seeing it for the first time, [or] an event as if it were happening for the first time'. However, in this description of estrangement, the 'as if' is as important as the 'first-time'. An actual first-time view of an object or scene is often notably inaccurate or limited; the 'as if for the first-time' view conjures an image, rather, of an observer returning to the scene after a period of absence. Arguably, then, Shklovsky's defamiliarising gaze belongs to an adult remembering, imagining or reconstructing the child's gaze.

In *The Case of Peter Pan,* Jacqueline Rose's chief objection to the narrative dynamics of children's literature is that adults demand something from the child in fiction, and by extension from actual children, without declaring their stake in the exchange (the exchange being the 'gift' of the book from adult writer/buyer to child reader/consumer).[33] In my view, however, adults in recent years have become increasingly conscious of their interest in the exchange, and this self-consciousness may be the basis for a freer and more equable dialogue between children and adults, both within fiction and without. This is particularly evident in the recent developments in this literary tradition of the curious child gaining access to magic, and not-so-magic worlds. Such fictional children are represented as curiosities in themselves—hence, objectified and overdetermined in a way that lends weight to Rose's thesis. In addition, they are the adult reader's conduit to becoming more inquisitive, more actively curious. Thirdly, however, they fix the beam of their curious eyes, in both active and passive senses, on the adult reader, unsettling the latter and destabilising the implicitly unequal power relation between the child's and the adult's gaze. This third sense of the curious gaze might be compared to the effect described in Jacques Lacan's celebrated anecdote of the sardine tin floating in the sea, discussed in his Seminar XI.[34] While taking a trip on a fishing boat, Lacan recalls looking out to sea and catching sight of a sardine tin floating along on the surface of the water. A sailor joked at him, 'at least it's not looking at you'. But Lacan was made uneasy by the thought that this nonconscious thing might actually be looking at him. Lacan was discomfited by the thought of how he might appear to such an alien gaze. Craig Raine's poem 'A Martian Sends a Postcard Home' exploits this idea to comic effect, as does Kurt Vonnegut with the Trafalmadorian perspective in *Slaughterhouse-Five.*[35] And to the extent that it is represented as alien to 'normal', adult understanding, the curious (odd/inquisitive) child's gaze may startle and discomfit an adult viewer in a similar way.

Ofelia's Curiosity

As an excellent, recent example of how self-consciously contemporary adult writers deploy the device of a curious child's gaze, we might also consider Guillermo del Toro's film, *Pan's Labyrinth* (2006), which introduces itself specifically as 'a fairy tale for adults'.[36] Del Toro's film is largely focalised through the eyes of a young girl named Ofelia, who in several shots is dressed in a pinafore dress with white apron, reminiscent of Sir John Tenniel's illustrations of *Alice's Adventures in Wonderland*. As her name suggests, though, Ofelia is also strongly associated with death and sacrifice from the opening scene of the film. This is a film, then, which advertises its stake in the child's curious gaze and its capacity to access marvelous new wonderlands. We need the curious child's magic gaze, del Toro suggests, particularly in those moments when adult reality has become aporetic, when there seems to be no escape from a fatal, historical nightmare. Strikingly, the first shot of Ofelia shows her sprawled on the ground, blood coming out of her nose, apparently dead. But in the next frame, miraculously, the blood starts to flow back up into her nose; her eyes fly open, and she is alive. An adult, male narrator then begins to narrate a fairy tale about a princess who lived in an underworld kingdom, 'where there are no lies and no pain'. This princess became curious about the overworld and escaped her own world to explore it, thereby exposing herself to mortal sickness and suffering. Her immortal father, the king, is said to be still searching the world for his lost princess. Both these opening scenes underline how the child Ofelia is conjured into life by an adult desire for redemption. The camera then switches to the primary plot to reveal the reality in need of redemption by means of this curious child's gaze. The narrative takes place in 1944, just after the Spanish Civil War, when Franco was imposing fascist control over Spain, and Ofelia's mother is on her way to marry a captain in the fascist army, then engaged in crushing the democratic resistance movement.

The first episode demonstrates how, within this oppressive environment peopled by brutal or hopelessly crushed adults, Ofelia finds her way into an alternative reality by means of her natural curiosity and sense of wonder. It shows Ofelia and her mother being driven by soldiers to Captain Vidal's outpost in the woods. Ofelia's mother is pregnant with Vidal's child, and is suffering from car sickness, so at one point the driving party is called to a halt while she gets out for fresh air. The camera then follows Ofelia as she wanders up the road on her own. She stubs her toe against a stone in the road, then notices it bears the carving of an eye. Having picked it up, and been drawn wonderingly to a statue in the woods, she notices her stone fits exactly into a hole in its carved face. A tiny stick insect pops out of the statue's mouth as she inserts the eye. The adult viewer of this scene begins by looking at Ofelia, a naturally curious child who notices more than other people around her. But the viewer ends up looking with her, following her eyeline, and becoming curious, in the active sense, about the objects she discovers: the stone fragment, the statue in the forest, the insect. Her curious gaze becomes the viewer's conduit to another level of reality, accessed via a different mode of perception. The entry into the magic or fairy-tale world is initiated with two gestures: first, Ofelia replacing the eye of the statue, and second, the insect popping out of the statue's mouth. So one could say that the child's gaze, signified by the statue's eye, unlocks the tale that can only be told by an otherworldly, magic narrator, signified by the statue's mouth. As the film goes on to demonstrate, believing in this other, magic reality may be one of the ways we can transform our own, material and political reality, just when it seems beyond the point of repair. The child's or statue's alien eye functions as the instrument by which the adult narrator (the voiceover heard telling the fairy tale) gains the storytelling voice that can convey this possibility of transformation.

To access the magic world, the adult viewer stoops to Ofelia's level, following her as she crawls through all the film's many narrow gateways—the hole in the fig tree leading to an encounter with a giant toad, and the chalk doorway she herself draws in her garret room, leading to an underworld hall where a magic banquet has been spread for a slumbering monster. When awakened, this monster implants eyeballs in the palms of its hands and holds these up, horrifically, to see and pursue the fleeing Ofelia. In scenes like these, the film registers a constant uneasiness about the ways in which an adult viewer appropriates the child's gaze. But self-awareness is, in my view, the aspect of the film which prevents it reproducing the kind of narrative dynamic Jacqueline Rose criticised in Barrie's *Peter Pan*.[37] Throughout the film, Ofelia's sharpness of vision will be contrasted with the willful blindness of adults around her. In *Pan's Labyrinth,* then, the adult viewer relates to the fictional child's 'enlarging' gaze in three ways: first, the viewer looks at Ofelia; secondly, he or she looks with her upon two worlds, the magic and the real; and thirdly, the viewer is looked at and implicitly judged by Ofelia's gaze.

Curiosity as a Prime Number

In reconfiguring the tradition of the curious child's gaze in fictional narrative, Haddon's *Curious Incident* goes even further than del Toro's *Pan's Labyrinth.* Not only is the redemptive power of a child's marvelous world brought to bear on an aporetic, adult reality, but that aporetic reality is itself revealed to be fantastically marvelous. Christopher begins to investigate the mysterious death of his neighbour's dog, but in the process he stumbles upon a mystery closer to home: the fact that his father had faked the death of his mother in hospital to avoid telling the boy about their marriage breakup. What begins as a consciously narrated detective story opens out into a realistic narrative about a dysfunctional family. Christopher's everyday life also appears at first to be severely restricted by his autism, but the reader gradually comes to experience the spacious intellectual horisons of Christopher's world, and to appreciate the enormity of the challenges he faces and overcomes.

Moreover, in the crossover space of this novel, the child reader and the adult reader find common ground to be made curious (actively and passively) by Christopher's exceptional gaze. This is because both child and adult reader at first possess what Bakhtin would call an essential surplus of vision and meaning vis-à-vis Christopher Boone.[38] Like many protagonists of crossover fiction, his biological age of fifteen does not determine his emotional or intellectual age. Intellectually he is in some respects as mature as an adult, while emotionally he seems very young compared to a modern teenager (he never mentions sex or girls in his diary entries). Because of his limited ability to read emotion or decode figurative language, both child and adult readers understand the tangled situations in which Christopher finds himself, more clearly than he does. And while he says flatly, 'this will not be a funny book' (10) and he doesn't like being laughed at (84), his interchanges with other characters, where both end up startled and confused, do often strike the reader as comic. At the same time, the longer one spends in the company of the brilliant Christopher, the less confident one feels about understanding his inner world, whether one is of Christopher's age or older. And still more, under the cool eye of his estranging gaze, the reader finds his or her own worldview beginning to look increasingly odd and dysfunctional. By the end of the novel, the unequal power relation implicit in the adult *or* the child reader's surplus of knowledge is either reversed, or effectively neutralised by the curious child's returning gaze. This trinity of effects makes curiosity a prime number which cannot be broken down into lesser parts. That is to say, one cannot access the child's magic gaze without also releasing its other, more discomfiting effects.

From the start, Christopher draws the reader into a fictional world that is both bizarrely surreal and crushingly prosaic. He begins his narration in this way:

> It was 7 minutes after midnight. The dog was lying on the grass in the middle of the lawn in front of Mrs Shears' house. Its eyes were closed. It looked as if it was running on its side, the way dogs run when they think they are chasing a cat in a dream. But the dog was not running or asleep. The dog was dead. There was a garden fork sticking out of the dog. (1)

This, the curious incident of the title, is indeed an odd enough event to arrest the reader's attention along with the narrator's. The setting is an ordinary suburb with lawns, dogs, and garden forks—all very prosaic props, but their combination is fantastical.

But even more curious than the incident is the tone of the narrator's voice. The deadpan description and stilted rhythm (especially the last 'dog' coming at the end, rather than the beginning of the phrase) convey this potentially horrifying scene in the mode of farce. And yet, if it strikes the reader as comical, evidently it does not strike the narrator in the same way. So, the reader is led to ask, who is this serious observer with the precise eye for detail, who notices that it is exactly '7 minutes after midnight', and that the dog is lying precisely 'in the middle of the lawn' with its eyes closed, in an attitude of dreaming? The incident is certainly mysterious, but for the reader, the dead-pan voice and mathematically precise gaze may pose an even greater mystery to unravel. Christopher is both our means of access to this surreal portrait of suburbia, and the main object of the reader's fascination. He is curious, in both the active and passive senses of the term.

Christopher introduces himself to the reader almost immediately, making it quite clear what his strengths and weaknesses are: 'I know all the countries of the world and their capital cities and every prime number up to 7,507'. Yet he cannot decipher facial expressions more complex than 'happy' or 'sad'. (2)[39] The reader also learns, though, that he is constantly working out mechanisms for deciphering human interactions he would otherwise find unbearable. At an earlier age made violent and upset by confusing situations, now he says, 'if I don't know what someone is saying I ask them what they mean or I walk away'. (3) Thus, quite apart from his immediate interest in the mystery of the dog, Christopher faces every day as a labyrinth with treacherous paths to negotiate, and for the reader it becomes fascinating to see how he will overcome these daily challenges. His narration, organised as chapters in a prime number sequence, consists of two interleaved sequences. In one sequence (Chapters 2, 5, 11, etc.), he narrates what he calls his 'murder mystery novel', which begins with Wellington and leads on to his attempt to find his mother. In the other sequence (Chapters 3, 7, 13, etc.), a series of diary entries provide more general and disparate reflections on Christopher's memories, likes and dislikes. It is largely through this diary-narrative that the reader builds a more general picture of Christopher's stance and worldview. In the diary sequence, he describes how, in order to determine whether it is a day to take risks or not, he counts the number of cars of a certain colour passing down his street; if the wrong colour car passes, he stays quietly in his room. Certain colours are not permitted to appear on his plate (brown and yellow), and no colours are allowed to mix together; so he drinks strawberry milk-shakes and eats broccoli segregated from other foods. On upsetting days, he writes out timetables which regulate his activities down to the last five minutes. Christopher's obsessive self-regulation will certainly strike many readers as odd, yet many also find traces of their own eccentric behaviour in his descriptions. For example, several of my Sheffield students said that his description made them aware of the bizarre rituals and vaguely superstitious habits they had themselves developed unconsciously.[40] Through such correspondences, the reader comes to identify with Christopher, but this sense of identification is held in check primarily by two things. First, he is a genius with mathematical concepts, a trait he will share with a very limited number of readers. And secondly, he is horrified by other characters' attempts to connect with him emotionally. This is poignantly the case when he finally finds his mother, and she rushes to hug him: 'And I pushed her away because she was grabbing me and I didn't like it . . . And Mother said, "I'm so sorry, Christopher. I forgot"'. (233) Transparency and logical consistency are what Christopher craves from others (and very seldom gets). And so, paradoxically, if one fully empathises with Christopher, as Haddon's narrative certainly leads one to do, one comes to appreciate his point of view which regards consistency as infinitely preferable to empathy. Thus the reader is estranged from his or herself as s/he empathetically sees how distasteful and abject this empathetic blurring of identities must appear to Christopher himself. From this estranged perspective, the reader may come to feel that, as one of my students succinctly put it, 'it's not Christopher who has the problem. It's everybody else'.[41]

A Curious Case of Split Narration

For a reader to reach this stage, though, Christopher must be presented to us by another, much more empathetic narrator, one who can win our understanding and act as the ambassador, as it were, for Christopher's uncompromising worldview. One could describe this other presence as an implied author, Wayne Booth's term, and yet here it intervenes at the level of narration throughout the text, so in my view a more accurate term would be that of implied narrator.[42] In *Curious Incident*, this silent, secondary narrator presents Christopher to the reader in the boy's own words, but he (or she or it) carefully screens and organises those words in such a way as to sustain the reader's curiosity and affection for the primary narrator. As noted above, Christopher's narration is organised in two alternating threads, the first in the genre of a mystery novel (narrated in the simple past), and the second, a series of diary entries (narrated in the present). As Haddon comments elsewhere, if Christopher had his own way as a narrator, he would have narrated only the first thread and rushed quickly to the conclusion.[43] To slow him down, Haddon added the other thread in which Christopher offers the reader his more general reflections. But Christopher himself never offers a rationale for writing this second, diary sequence, and he seems the kind of person who would have no interest in that confessional genre, with its frequent second-person address to an unknown implied reader. Even the first sequence, concerning the murder of Wellington, is resolved halfway through the text, so if had been up to Christopher, the novel would probably have ended there. Clearly, there is another narratorial consciousness driving the story on, knowing that this other mystery will reveal more of Christopher and his parents than he could realise. Just as in *Pan's Labyrinth*, Ofelia places the eye in the statue, and releases the power of magic speech (the stick insect hopping out of the mouth, and thus initiating the fantasy narrative), so in *Curious Incident* a symbiotic relationship develops between Christopher's gaze and the implied narrator's voice which makes that gaze more fully accessible to the reader.

For example, a second narrator clearly shapes the dialogues between Christopher and the adult strangers whom he meets in his solitary journey across London. Often these are comic, revealing not only Christopher's limited understanding, but also that of his adult interlocutors. But the comedy is all in the timing. For example, at the ticket office of the train station in Swindon, Christopher reports the following exchange with the man selling tickets:

> And I said to the man behind the window, 'I want to go to London.'
> And the man said, 'Single or return?'
> And I said, 'What does single or return mean?'
> And he said, 'Do you want to go one way, or do you want to go and come back?'
> And I said, 'I want to stay there when I get there.'
> And he said, 'For how long?'
> And I said, 'Until I go to university.'
> And he said, 'Single, then.' (189)

In this exchange, each speaker is incomprehensible to the other because their linguistic codes don't overlap; the ticket man is as narrowly literalist, in his own way, as Christopher is. Both employ the same deadpan style, but what makes this scene comic is the shaping of their exchange into a perfectly symmetrical stychomachia, concluding with a punch line which is funny for the reader, though not for the participants.

The implied narrator also shapes Christopher's flat-toned speech into a powerful rhetoric in the plain style. Christopher maintains that he cannot lie, and for the same reason, he cannot use figures of speech or metaphors, because they assert things that cannot possibly be true: 'a pig is not like a day and people do not have skeletons in their cupboards'. (20) Truthfulness, combined with total recall, make Christopher an exceptionally reliable narrator of surface images. As he explains, 'my memory is like a film', which he can access simply by pressing 'Rewind and Fast Forward and Pause like on a video recorder'. (96) But neither of these makes him a good storyteller. To shape Christopher's narrative into a compelling narrative, the implied narrator draws on figurative language that Christopher might use, if he were to speak figuratively. Thus when he tells his mother that Mr Boone had pretended she was dead, he writes: 'And then she didn't say anything for a long while. And then she made a loud wailing noise like an animal on a nature programme'. (236) The image captures his confusion, but only by means of a simile ('like an animal') which Christopher says he avoids using.

One of the most brilliant examples of the rhetorical plain style occurs, ironically, in a passage in which Christopher is explaining why he can't lie or use metaphors:

A lie is when you say something happened which didn't happen . . . And if I think about something which didn't happen I start thinking about all the other things which didn't happen. For example, this morning for breakfast I had Ready Brek and some hot raspberry milkshake. But if I say that I actually had Shreddies and a mug of tea I start thinking about Coco-Pops and lemonade and porridge and Dr Pepper and how I wasn't eating my breakfast in Egypt and there wasn't a rhinoceros in the room and Father wasn't wearing a diving suit . . . and even writing this makes me feel shaky and scared, like I do when I'm standing on the top of a very tall building and there are thousands of houses and cars and people below me and my head is so full of all these things that I'm afraid that I'm going to forget to stand up straight and hang onto the rail and I'm going to fall over and be killed. (24)

Hastened by parataxis, this stream of consciousness hurtles to a conclusion, inducing in the reader a feeling of vertigo to match Christopher's panic as he contemplates the possibility of things being other than they are. The passage is also a prolonged *recusatio,* a rhetorical figure which proves something by performing the opposite. While there is no use of metaphor, the series of images relates things which aren't true and events which Christopher only supposes might happen. Finally, the sequence also carefully builds from the commonplace *ad absurdam,* thus from Ready Break to the rhinoceros (since Ionesco, surely the totemic animal of the Absurd[44]).

Not only does the implied narrator help Christopher narrate two kinds of story, a diary and a murder mystery. This secondary narrator also has a further two stories to tell: the narrative of Christopher's coming of age, plus another, metafictional narrative about the pleasures of creating and reading fiction. In this fourth narrative, Christopher becomes a figure for the author who enjoys creating narrative order out of chaotic experience. Indeed in Christopher's struggles, one hears echoes of the writer's sometimes obsessive need to regain control: 'And then I thought that I had to be like Sherlock Holmes and I had to *detach my mind at will to a remarkable degree* so that I did not notice how much it was hurting inside my head'. (164) Christopher also functions as a figure for the reader, who in reading makes order from the chaos of words and images in his or her head. But Christopher also becomes a champion for the more specifically realist writer (or reader), for whom fantasy is an unnecessary diversion from the wonders of the actual world. Thus, one hears a realist's credo being articulated by the implied narrator in the following passage, even though it never ceases to sound like something Christopher himself would think:

And I think that there are so many things just in one house that it would take years to think about all of them properly. And, also, a thing is interesting because of thinking about it and not because of it being new. (219)

Perhaps the most intriguing aspects of this metafictional commentary emerge when Christopher reacts badly to the unreliability of other people. After a fight with his father, for example, Christopher retreats into his room and comforts himself with a savage daydream which kills off nearly the whole human population:

> And in the dream nearly everyone on the earth is dead, because they have caught a virus. But it's not like a normal virus. It's like a computer virus. And people catch it because of the meaning of something an infected person says and the meaning of what they do with their faces when they say it. (242)

Through the implied narrator, who has Christopher write these thoughts down (again, improbably), one intuits the boy's rage and frustration over words and faces that hide meaning, rather than convey it transparently. On the metafictional level, these lines also convey the writer's frustration with the medium of language, and perhaps his or her anxiety over the unknowability of the reader. Christopher's fantasy might be understood, then, as a reflection of the adult narrator's fantasy, imagining a situation in which 'eventually there is no one left in the world except people [who] are all special people like me. And they like being on their own and I hardly ever see them'. (242–43)[45] In such passages, Christopher unknowingly turns an estranging gaze on his implied narrator, revealing aspects of this secondary narrative voice that might not have been intended or foreseen.

The Magnifying Glass and the Postmodern

The central *peripateia* of *Curious Incident* occurs during Christopher's solitary journey from Swindon to his mother's flat in London (174–232). Christopher is frightened by his father's confession of having killed Wellington, and lied to him about his mother's disappearance, so the boy decides to run away. He makes his way from Swindon Train Station to Paddington, and thence via the Tube to his mother's flat in northwest London. This otherwise ordinary journey is made extraordinary by the fact of Christopher's hypersensitive, first-time gaze (he has never traveled alone before). As he tells the reader, 'when I am in a new place, because I see everything, it is like when a computer is doing too many things at the same time and the central processor unit is blocked up' so that sometimes, 'I have to close my eyes and put my hands over my ears and groan'. (177–78) This is what he does in the train stations, when the cacophony of noise and visual information overwhelm him (181, 208, 216). The implied narrator, however, brilliantly reproduces the effect of Christopher's experience, delivering the reader an *as if* first-time gaze, by presenting in a blocked-off text a digest of the typographic signs which are overwhelming the boy in Paddington. This text appears twice in the narration, first as an undifferentiated block of signifiers in various typefaces: 'Sweet Pastries **Heathrow Airport Check-In Here** *Bagel Factory* **EAT** *excellence and* **taste**' etc., and then 'after a few seconds' in which we infer Christopher's mounting fear, the same signifiers reduced to a garbled jumble of letters and graphic signs: 'Sweathr♟♟■ow○Airpheck-I*agtory*EA*enceandtaste*'. (209–09) This climactic episode presents a distilled example of the triple force of the curious child's gaze. Firstly, one feels sympathy for Christopher and irritation at the unhelpfulness of the other passengers (in this sense, he is the curiosity who provokes the reader's pity). In addition, one identifies with Christopher because most people experience this kind of fear upon entering a confusing new place. On the metafictional level, this passage registers the effect that a fast-paced, 24/7, postmodern information-dense culture can have on any individual consciousness, be it autistic or not (in this sense, we share his eyeline). And third, as the possessor of an alienating gaze (that of someone who does not [and does not want to] belong here), Christopher shows us that most people can only survive in this absurdly oversignifying space because, unlike himself, 'most people are almost blind and they don't see most things'. (178)

Metafictionally, the observant Christopher provides the reader with two possible responses to postmodern, transitory urban spaces. On the one hand, one can feel a paranoiac sense, as Christopher clearly does, that strangeness, transience and linguistic excess represent a threat to the individual's identity. On the other hand, however, one can read this scene as an instance of joyous postmodernism, in which the subject is exhilarated and transformed by the encounter with plurality and otherness. After all, Christopher does make his way successfully through the station, drawing on reserves of courage and mental focus that presumably have not been tested to this extent before. The frightening experience leads to his emotional coming of age because, as he later says, 'I solved the mystery of Who Killed Wellington? and I found my mother and I was brave . . . and that means I can do anything'. (268) And, moreover, while the signs become scrambled in his brain, there is, in fact, no breakdown of communication between Christopher and the reader, because the implied narrator uses the fragments of words and graphics to convey with precision and humour all the complex emotions that Christopher is experiencing. Thus if one reads the garbled block-text closely, one finds graphics and emoticons that Christopher presumably does not actually see in Paddington Station (graphics of skull and crossbones, lightning, bombs, sad faces, etc.) but which nevertheless convey his feelings in a clear, visual language which he would understand and might plausibly use himself.

In order to contain his terror, Christopher physically cups his hands into the shape of a magnifying glass, and peering through this restricted frame, he steers his way through this bewildering labyrinth of signs: 'I made my hand into a little tube with my fingers and I opened my eyes and I looked through the tube so that I was only looking at one sign at a time and after a long time I saw a sign that said [I] **Information**'. (210) This might be read as a final instance of the power of the contemporary fictional child's gaze to neutralise power relations between adult observer and child observer/observed. Here the magnifying glass does not magically enlarge his view; on the contrary, it prosaically but helpfully restricts it. In terms of its place in a literary tradition of curious children gazing into Wonderland, Christopher's gesture is a salutary reminder of the fictitiousness of this literary device, and of the adult interest that may be implicit in its application. Huddling in a tiny space, speaking with a low voice, seeing through a small person's eyes may not always guarantee the possessor of these traits access to a free and spacious new world. But even if the child does not want to find his way into an adult memory of a magic garden, he can still make use of the restricted gaze to find his own way in the real world.

Chapter Five
Adolescence and Abjection: Geraldine McCaughrean's *The White Darkness*

As we have seen in previous chapters, adult readers over the millennial decade flocked to children's fiction in unprecedented numbers. In the cases we have considered so far, what adult readers would have found there were texts which reimagined the borders and transitions of life and conveyed a sense of wonder at both prosaically ordinary and fantastic other worlds. But it seems more difficult to account for the crossover to adult readerships of children's novels which centre on themes of violence, death and brutality. The emphasis on violence manifests itself across all genres, from realism to fantasy, and across all media from text to film, graphic art and television. To an extent, an emphasis on death in fiction for, and about, adolescents, is unremarkable if, as Haddon suggests, awareness of death is what separates an adult's consciousness from a child's, 'not literal death . . . but death's smaller harbingers: illness, failure, loss, the irony that we have infinite dreams but find ourselves stuck in one body for one life'.[1] Just as Pullman depicted Lyra being guided across the threshold of the underworld by her own 'death' in *The Amber Spyglass*, so the representation of death in young adult fiction helps escort the child reader into adolescence.[2] But many contemporary young adult novels dwell not on these 'small harbingers' but on violent, gruesome, horrifying deaths, which cannot be explained by reference to this function of escorting a child across the threshold into adolescent and adult awareness. In this latter type of fiction, scenes of torture and brutality are depicted with minute attention to detail, while the impact of such scenes on a young protagonist is meticulously recorded, so that the protagonist's feelings of revulsion strike a reader as viscerally as the description of the violence itself. I would argue that in such cases, a primary aim is to induce in the reader a feeling of abjection at the sight, smell and sound of the deathly, rather than to impart any rational understanding of death. This raises the question, not only why abjection has become such a central feature of young adult fiction, but also—and for this study, more pressingly—why adult readers should be drawn to reading violent fiction for younger readers. To put the question differently, why should adult readers (or film viewers) choose to experience abjection from the point of view of a child or teenager?

The Abject as Contemporary Theatre

Violent fiction has been around a long time, of course, in both children's and adult fiction. And signs of an interest in the abject are not at all exclusive to the contemporary period. In *Dombey and Son* (1848), Dickens describes the suicide of James Carker with evident relish; the villain throws himself in front of a speeding train, his body explodes on the impact, and the 'white teeth of his dismembered smile' flash as they are flung through space.[3] There is no doubt that violence has been with us as long as art, but it seems a distinctly twenty-first century form of art which requires not only this degree of horror but this much attention to how it affects an observer. This emphasis is evident in many spheres of contemporary writing, and in fiction for adults as well as children. To take an example from the former, which should help put the fiction of this chapter in some perspective: Haruki Murakami's *The Wind-up Bird Chronicle* (2003) contains a leisurely, three-page description of a man being skinned alive which no one who has read it, is ever likely to forget.[4] Lieutenant Mamiya, the character forced to witness this act, tells the novel's narrator: 'it was something like a work of art. One would never have imagined there was any pain involved, if it weren't for the screams'. (159) Mamiya himself is closely observed by soldiers as he is forced to witness this murder, and is beaten with a rifle butt whenever he tries to close his eyes.

It would be hard to find an example as extreme as Murakami's in young adult fiction, but sadistic violence features prominently in two best-selling crossover fictions: Lian Hearn's four-volume, medieval Japanese fantasy, *Tales of the Otori* and Meg Rosoff's dystopian novel, *How I Live Now*.[5] In the former, the fifteen-year-old protagonist returns from mushroom picking to find that his entire village has been massacred. He picks his way through the dismembered corpses on page four of the first novel in the series, *Across the Nightingale Floor*. Later, he witnesses men hung out to die on castle walls, and risks his life to save his adoptive father from the same fate. He does manage to cut down the dying Lord Otori, but only so that he can administer poison and cut off Otori's head for burial. In the invasion of Britain which Rosoff imagines in *How I Live Now*, Daisy, a visiting New Yorker, also aged fifteen, and her nine-year-old English cousin are witnesses to killing at close range. They look on as a boy named Joe exchanges insults with a guard at a military checkpoint: 'And then in an almost lazy kind of way the checkpoint guy who'd been looking at [Joe] raised his gun and pulled the trigger and there was a loud crack and part of Joe's face exploded and there was blood everywhere'. (98) Their friend

Major McEvoy sees that Joe is still alive and tries to intervene, but is mowed down by machine-gun fire. Daisy recalls,

> the momentum of the blasts hurled Major M. backwards across the road away from Joe with blood welling up in the holes all over him and this time you could see Joe's condition was a hundred percent dead with brains splattered everywhere and our driver didn't wait around to see what might happen next but just stepped on the gas and as we drove away I felt tears on my face but when I put my hand up to wipe them it turned out to be blood and nobody made a single sound but just sat there shell-shocked and all I could think about was poor Major M. lying there in the dust though I guess he was much too dead to notice. (99)

This unbroken stream of words (the full sentence is twice as long again) issues from the shell-shocked narrator like the vomit that spews from Mamiya as he is forced to watch the prisoner being flayed. But like Mamiya, Daisy also, at some level, witnesses this murder as a form of art, a cinematic scene unfolding 'in slow motion'. (99) Nor does the horror entirely efface her teenage sense of humour either here or at the end of the novel, when she observes sardonically that at least starving due to lack of food cured her of anorexia.

As Kristeva suggests in *Powers of Horror,* the staging of abjection is an art akin to ancient Greek theatre. The sense of revulsion generated in the onlooker (protagonist and audience) is meant to produce a catharsis, a purgation of mind and spirit.[6] Anything that threatens to disrupt the border between identity and nonbeing, 'a wound with blood and pus, or the sickly, acrid smell of sweat, of decay' and above all, 'the corpse, seen without God and outside of science' may be defined as abject; these things show us 'death infecting life'. (*Powers,* 4) Rather than rationally 'signifying' death, corpses and suppurating wounds 'as in true theater . . . *show me* what I permanently thrust aside in order to live'. (3) Thus in her horrified rejection of the abject, the viewer or reader re-enacts the very forma-tion of herself as a subject. Kristeva understands adult abjection to be a repetition of a psychic drama first played out in infancy, between four and eight months of age, when the infant becomes aware of itself as separate from the maternal body. This is, she writes, 'a violent, clumsy breaking away, with the constant risk of falling back under the sway of a power as securing as it is stifling'. (*Powers,* 13) Abjection is re-experienced in adult life whenever one is confronted by some-thing that threatens to disrupt a border that differentiates the self from the other. The abject 'draws me toward the place where meaning collapses', and where the self would dissolve back into undifferentiated being, or indeed, non-being (*Pow-ers,* 2). Kristeva's theory of abjection extends the Lacanian model of subjectivity, in which identity is forged out of a primary act of repression (in his model, one suppresses the Real to enter the Symbolic order of language and signification[7]).

This notion of a primary psychic repression, which ultimately derives from Sigmund Freud, has been challenged by other theorists, notably Deleuze and Guattari.[8] But the Freudian concept of a 'return of the repressed' is still widely accepted, and is certainly a prevalent motif in contemporary fiction. The contemporary 'theatre of war', marked by 'acts' of terrorism such as 9/11, is often interpreted in precisely such psychoanalytic terms. For example, Slavoj Žižek comments,

> The shattering impact of the bombings can only be accounted for only against the background of the borderline which today separates the digitalized First World from the Third World 'desert of the Real'. It is the awareness that we live in an insulated artificial universe which generates the notion that some ominous agent is threatening us all the time with total destruction.[9]

In the above analysis, 9/11 was an abject experience not only for New Yorkers but for all developed nations, in the sense that it 'drew us toward the place where meaning collapses'. Abjection brings self-awareness and realisation of a connection with the suppressed other ('the Third World "desert of the Real"'); but it also induces a violent rejection of the perceived threat of otherness.[10] Thus abjection might be thought of as a single act of theatre combining *peripateia* (reversal) and *anagnorisis* (recognition).[11] In this act, two opposing movements unfold simultaneously: (a) 'this thing of darkness I acknowledge mine,' and (b), this thing of darkness I expel.[12] The catharsis of abjection arises from this double movement of recognising in oneself the disease or inner 'agent of destruction', and thrusting it away or purging oneself of the connection. It may be that the contemporary political context has sharpened readers' tastes for the abject in fiction, because terrorism provides an instance of hidden, 'viral' evil which appears to erupt from within the body of the state.[13] Perhaps, too, because we share Žižek's awareness of economically 'living in an insulated artificial universe,' we—or some of us—feel the need for the catharsis of 'true theatre' or abjection. Finally, amidst the resurgence of religious fundamentalism, contemporary fiction may be finding its place 'on the far and near side of religion', as Kristeva writes (*Powers,* 17). Though I would not claim, as she does, that all literature enacts a version of the catharsis of religious apocalypse, it does seem true of the violent fictions alluded to above. Such fiction might well be described as rooted 'on the fragile border . . . where identities (subject/object, etc.) do not exist or only barely so—double, fuzzy, heterogeneous, . . . metamorphosed, altered, abject'. (*Powers,* 207)

Adolescence and the Abject

All the same, this does not explain why adult readers should be looking for this kind of catharsis in young adult fiction. The current popularity of what I would call abject adolescent fiction is particularly arresting, given that teen fiction, until very recently, was generally understood to have a very restricted and transient audience. As Karen Coats wrote, 'most young adult novels have a relatively short shelf life'.[14] Well, evidently this is not the case any more. Over the millennial decade, adolescent abjection began to reach a very broad audience of readers in Britain. Writing in *The Independent* in 2005, Boyd Tonkin noted that not only is teenage fiction more nightmare-filled than ever, but for the first time, adult readers are rushing to escape into these unhappy fictional childhoods.[15] Among the crossover titles he mentioned were Malorie Blackman's best-selling *Noughts and Crosses* trilogy, which has since been adapted for a major theatre production at the RSC, Melvin Burgess's *Bloodsong* (following the equally violence-soaked *Junk* and *Lady: My Life as a Bitch*), and Geraldine McCaughrean's *The White Darkness*.[16] Meg Rosoff's *How I Live Now*, quoted above, was serialised for Radio 4 Woman's Hour in 2007.[17] But a novel need not be brutally violent to be abject in Kristeva's sense. McCaughrean's *The White Darkness*, which I will come to discuss below, contains little brutality but a great deal of suffering and pain. If *Bloodsong* was an example of the violent abject, Michael Morpurgo's *Private Peaceful* (2003) was equally harrowing, with its quiet, intense depiction of two brothers in World War I, one of whom is shot on a charge of cowardice. This novel, too, was successfully adapted for a mainstream theatre audience. Directed by Simon Reade for Bristol Old Vic in 2004, the stage play of *Private Peaceful* was performed to sell-out audiences in Edinburgh, London's Soho Theatre, provincial theatres throughout the UK, the London West End and Off-Broadway, New York.[18]

So why all this adult interest in adolescent abjection? One reason might be that the adult reader or viewer's sense of horror is heightened when the violence is filtered through the eye of a younger, more naive witness.[19] Conversely, the contemporary teenage protagonist might be thought of as precociously sophisticated, hence indistinguishable from an adult witnessing the abject. Most frequently, the adolescent protagonist appears to combine both viewpoints, with a surface of apparent sophistication masking a core of inexperience and comparatively greater innocence. Karín Lesnik-Oberstein suggests that the adult reader's appropriation of the child's innocent gaze constitutes an act of 'colonization' whereby adults strive 'to create, control, and finally to become the child themselves'.[20] But this view must be questioned in the light of Kristeva's thesis that adolescent abjection is already a re-enactment of an earlier psychic drama. In Kristeva's scenario, the 'child's' subjectivity is not simply a neutral entity waiting there to be appropriated. It is already internally divided, as the older child looks back on, and partially collapses into, a younger sense of self. Moreover, it is not only the adolescent, defined in terms of biological age, who can re-experience this dramatic reversal. Kristeva defines adolescence as 'an open psychic structure' which an individual may re-experience at any stage of life, whenever he or she becomes vulnerably open 'to that which has been repressed'.[21] In her view, the activities of writing and reading fiction tend to open up the psyche, thus re-creating in any age of reader a measure of the adolescent's 'state of incompleteness'. (139) Indeed, Kristeva suggests that novel writing may be inherently 'the work of a perpetual subject-adolescent'. (139) While Kristeva explicitly associates adolescence with the Lacanian order of the Imaginary, Karen Coats convincingly demonstrates the connections between Kristeva's view of adolescence and her concept of abjection.[22] As Coats argues, 'adolescence, like abjection, breaches and challenges boundaries'. (*Looking Glasses,* 142) In both psychic states, the individual experiences 'a reassertion of the Real body' where a contradictory 'desire to fuse with the Other' conflicts with the need to reaffirm 'the paternal law' which secures the boundary of identity (143). Thus, argues Coats, young adult fiction has always had a particular interest in abjection, the doubled sense of horror in which psychic identity is both threatened and reaffirmed. This insight helps to explain why the transient category of teen fiction is gaining a wider audience today. If adult readers are seeking a new theatre of abjection, one place they will almost certainly find it is in adolescent fiction.[23]

'The time of abjection is double'[24]

For the adult reader drawn to 'edgy', difficult, sublime and cathartic adolescent fiction, there is one recently published novel that, in my opinion, stands head and shoulders above the rest: Geraldine McCaughrean's *The White Darkness* (2005).[25] Although it has not yet attracted the millions of readers that novels by Rosoff, Hearn, Blackman, Burgess and others have done, *The White Darkness* received glowing critical reviews ('as good as it gets'; 'one of the very best children's books I have read in the last 10 years'; 'with any luck it'll be read by everyone, whatever their age'), and was shortlisted for both the 2005 Whitbread Children's Award and the Carnegie Medal.[26] McCaughrean had already broken into crossover territory with her Calvinoesque collection of linked stories, *A Pack of Lies,* and her feminist retelling of Noah's Ark in *Not the End of the World.*[27] But in *The White Darkness,* she relates a semi-real, semi-mythic journey into Hell which impacts as powerfully on adult readers as adolescent ones.

One obvious reason for the novel's crossover appeal is that the first-person narrator speaks with two voices, one a teenager's and the other, an adult's. The double perspective is emphasised by the Oxford University Press dust jacket design: on the front cover, a young girl gazes out of a white mist directly at the reader, while the back cover reproduces a photograph of a young man in Edwardian dress, staring out with equal directness. The first-person narrator is the bright, socially maladjusted, awkward Sym Wates, who is obsessed with Antarctica and the history of its exploration. As her father lies dying in hospital, she is watching a box set of DVDs, *The Last Place on Earth,* about Scott's expedition to Antarctica in 1912 (*White Darkness* 12–13). Just as her father dies, a voice jumps into Sym's head; the voice belongs to Captain Richard or

'Titus' Oates, one of the men killed on Scott's fatal expedition. The novel thus begins with Sym telling the reader, 'I have been in love with Titus Oates for quite a while now—which is ridiculous, since he's been dead for ninety years. But look at it this way. In ninety years, I'll be dead too, and then the age difference won't matter'.(1) In one deft sentence, Sym establishes the adolescent tone of her narration while signaling to the older reader that, as far as she is concerned, age is immaterial. It is prophetic of what's to come that she establishes this inclusive audience by picturing herself as a corpse, like Titus. It is via this abject image that she conveys the doubleness of her temporal perspective. Titus is an adult she not only desires but also desires to be.

Much of the dialogue in the novel consists of exchanges conducted in Sym's head between herself and this projected self/lover. They are in some respects opposite: she is shy and awkward while he is composed and self-assured. She is fourteen and female; he is 125 and male. She is alive, he is dead. But they share the same self-deprecating, morbid humour. Sym flicks her mousy hair and says, 'I wish I could have been blonde', to which Titus responds, '*I wish I could have been grey*'. (27) When Sym is tricked into undertaking an Antarctic expedition in the company of her mad scientist uncle, Titus comes with her. His memories of the Scott expedition function both as analepsis and prolepsis of Sym's own adventures. Chronologically, the Scott expedition precedes hers by nearly 100 years, but Titus is also a figure of the post-apocalyptic self she is to become. As the novel progresses, and the character of Titus comes more clearly into focus, it becomes more difficult to categorise one character as 'real' and the other as imaginary. After all, Sym is a creation of McCaughrean's, while Titus Oates is a historical figure. He is particularly well known for the understated bravery with which he died. On the company's return from the South Pole, Oates was wounded and having to walk more slowly than the others. So that they would be able to get to safety more quickly, he took the decision to walk out alone into a blizzard to die. As McCaughrean reminds us in her epilogue, Oates left the tent, saying to his companions, 'I am just going outside and I may be some time.' The speaker of these words becomes more and more present to the reader and to Sym as she approaches the place where the historical Oates's body may lie still buried under ice.

Quite apart from the adult voice Sym invents in her head, her voice as a narrator also often sounds more adult than a fourteen-year-old's. Although she loves Antarctica, it is doubtful whether, unaided, she would be able to produce the many soaringly eloquent descriptions of the continent in her narration. There almost seems to be a Cyrano de Bergerac whispering in the wings, for example, when she gets her first sight of the continent from an airplane window:

> It churned up such foaming, fuming feelings. Antarctica doesn't need anyone's admiration, so why should it go to the trouble of being so beautiful? Of riming ice caves with emerald green and turquoise? Or

pumping vuggy ice full of rhinestones? Why moon logs and corniches
of snow like freeze-frame waves? Why, when we overflew the coast
were there turquoise sculptures of ice rolling over and over in waves of
indigo? It terrifies me . . . I know this whole continent would kill us if
it could once sink its teeth into us. (58–59)

For some readers, the unlikeliness of such virtuosic description issuing from
an adolescent speaker constitutes a flaw in the novel. Peter Bramwell argues
that 'the imagery and range of reference that make McCaughrean one of the
greatest stylists in children's fiction are in tension with the constraints of a
first-person narrative voice'.[28] This is a valid point, and yet I think the effect of
McCaughrean's intense prose is rather to demonstrate a fluidity and nonfix-
ity of being that allows the authorial voice of a great stylist to flow into that of
an adolescent narrator's. In the same way, her adolescent protagonist is able
to imagine into being the speaking voice of a long dead, adult, male Polar
explorer. In an interview with McCaughrean, Nicholas Tucker suggests that
the author remains 'caught up with her discontented teenage self', a version of
which features in Sym Wates.[29] In the novel itself, what emerges clearly is that
the teenage narrator and the authorial voice are equally prone to 'foaming,
fuming feelings' and both feel the burning need to realise a fantasy. Eyes fixed
on the DVD of Scott's expedition, Sym 'watched so intently—concentrated so
hard that there was no sofa, and no screen . . . And it came real. So real. So real.
So real. So real. So real'. (12) Just so do the sublime descriptions of Antarctica
work to 'make real' a landscape that seems, by definition, to exceed description
in prose. Confronted by a vivid mirage of a castle in the snow, McCaughrean
has Sym tell herself, 'I wanted it to be Aeolus, brass-walled home of the King-
of-the-Winds, shipwrecked here in the days of myth. I wanted so much for it to
be real'. (152) Here one hears a distinctly authorial voice, since McCaughrean
is renowned for her rewriting of mythology for children.[30] As Bramwell suggests, such descriptions are probably beyond Sym's linguistic range (as well as
her interests, since we know her singular obsession is with Polar exploration).
Yet there is little sense here of an implied narrator's surplus of knowledge
vis-à-vis the adolescent protagonist, as we found earlier in Haddon's *Curious
Incident*. Rather both voices betray an adolescent longing to be submerged in
myth or fantasy.

Sym and the adult authorial voice share another desire, specifically in relation to Captain Oates. For Sym, Titus is not only an imaginary friend (more
usually created by younger children), but also a teenage crush, as corporeally
real as Sym can imagine him to be:

so sublimely beautiful that his image passed clean through my retina
and scorched itself on my brain. And his voice flowed into me, so sensu-
ous that I was wading across the River Jordan, up to my ears and deeper
in milk and honey, towards Paradise on the other side. (13)

As Coats suggests, in adolescence the body reasserts itself as Real in the Lacanian sense: overflowing, self-obliterating, sublime. Titus has a touch of the abject about him from the start. Flowing through her like maternal milk, as Sym says, 'he set up a ferocious pain inside me'. (13) The pain in part derives from Sym's foreknowledge of his tragic death: 'I was powerless to rewrite the past—to change the outcome of the story'. (13) But by conjuring him into life in her head, Sym is attempting precisely to rewrite the past. In the same way, McCaughrean invents a fantasy narrative for the historical Oates in which his sacrifice does save another's life, and against all expectation he does survive. Intertextual allusions to *Glass Town* (1826–32), a fantasy saga written by Charlotte Brontë in her teens, further emphasise the connections between the adult writing, and the adolescent living and narrating, the descent journey into the Antarctic (119).[31]

The fluidity of identity that allows adolescent and adult voices to mingle so indistinguishably is in part facilitated by the novel's extremely fluid social context. Like *His Dark Materials*, *The White Darkness* reflects a kiddult-oriented world, in which traditional borders separating adult and child cultures have begun to break down. Like Pullman, McCaughrean does not represent this social context in a particularly favourable light. Sym is an introverted teenager, and she is shocked by her friend Maxine's revelation that the latter is dating a thirty-year-old man, met over the Internet (19, 45). Sym is not immune to similar virtual attractions, of course, since her imaginary boyfriend is also aged thirty-two (the age Oates was when he died). But neither Sym nor Titus are fond of the aggressive sexuality of contemporary adolescence, epitomised in Maxine, and Sym consciously retreats into 'the quaint, chivalric chastity' of her imaginary friend's 'Edwardianland'. (132)

But that she can so successfully retreat into fantasy may also be read as a sign of her contemporariness. The 'Pengwings Expeditionary Force' which gathers in Antarctica under her uncle's leadership, comprises a group of adult fantasists (including a film director, a novelist and a journalist) as prone to escapism as Sym is herself. These Icarus-like souls arrive in Antarctica laden with expensive gadgets ('all possessed lots of everything and had brought most of it with them'), in marked contrast to the Spartan company that Scott led to the South Pole in 1912 (37). Sym's Uncle Victor manipulates these postmodern adultescents into funding his Polar expedition; 'every direction he looked there was some rich old idiot begging to be ripped off, begging to put their money into a movie about themselves or their bloody passions'. (164) But the brilliant Victor is in the grip of a delusion bigger than the rest combined. With echoes of Jules Verne's Professor Lidenbrock, who sought out the earth's core by descending into the glacier-peaked volcano Snæfellsjökull, Victor is convinced that he will discover a habitable world beneath the hollow drum of ice known as 'Symmes's Hole'.[32] His niece Sym is a key player in his fantasy, as he intends her to live in the underworld and populate his colony with the offspring of an adolescent partner he has chosen for her. Sigurd, the boy chosen to be Sym's partner, seems perfectly comfortable with the uncle's arrangement (until he realises it means being fed into a bottomless well of ice). As a well-adjusted, contemporary teenager, Sigurd is also unfazed by Sym's account of Maxine, merely assuming that the girl must be a fortune hunter like himself. He looks at Sym with 'a smile of such understanding and wisdom that he might have been forty-five'. (127) The subtext of sexual/colonialist exploitation of children in an adult fantasy-driven world could scarcely be more explicit.

In McCaughrean's earlier novel, *Not the End of the World,* there are fantasists (mostly male, and headed by the arch-fantasist, Noah) and there are realists (generally female and/or children). But in *The White Darkness* no such clear-cut distinctions apply. Sym is increasingly disillusioned with her mad uncle, but unlike Noah's daughter, she never entirely rejects his vision of an Antarctic Wonderland. At first, she is glad to be counted 'an honorary man' by her uncle since women and children clearly have no place in the Antarctic. Titus himself dismisses women as 'a great nuisance' (241, cf. 130). Setting off with her uncle, she casts a backward glance at her mother, who having had her passport stolen by Victor, is forced to remain behind at the station. Sym sees a *pietà,* a 'Madonna holding someone dead on her lap, head cocked sideways in grief', but being more of a fantasist than a realist at this point, Sym is not moved to turn back (11). Gradually she learns what a villain her Uncle Victor is. She watches him leave a fellow explorer to die in the snow, learns how he has murdered her own father, and discovers how he intends to sacrifice her in his thirst for glory. And yet she never ceases to feel a kinship (although he turns out not to be a real uncle). She tries to turn him back from a suicidal descent into an ice chimney, 'hugging him and hugging him . . . feeling the scales of peeling skin sharp as a dogfish, and the big pulse hopping in his neck, and me saying, "I love you, I love you"'. (164) And she really does seem to, because she and Victor have long shared the same obsession with ice continents. Titus tells her that he also loved his leader, despite a historically documented antipathy to Scott: *'early on, I couldn't abide him . . . But in the end? Out on the Barrier? In the end, I loved the man. We all did . . . who else* was *there to love?'* (225) Thus the adult need for fantasy is treated much more sympathetically in *The White Darkness* than in *Not the End of the World* or indeed, in Pullman's *The Amber Spyglass.* Instead McCaughrean explores the core of abject longing which seems equally able to possess, or more accurately *Dis*possess, both the adolescent and the adult.[33]

This fluidity of temporal perspective is well illustrated in the climactic scene in which the two remaining explorers, Sym and Victor, reach a hollow plateau of ice known as 'The Devil's Ballroom.' Here they come across ice chimneys which, seen from a distance, look as uncannily human as the prehistoric humanoid which Axel glimpses in the underworld in Verne's *Journey to the Centre of the Earth.* Sym sees through the illusion: 'they're not robed guard or placid ambassadors from another world; they're bulgy outcrops of craggy ice'. (219) But Victor falls victim to the force of his own dream; he 'turns on me a face so agitated that I think the figures in the fog, the tantalizing illusion of life, must have finally broken his heart'. (220) Victor thinks they have arrived at Symmes's Hole, the entrance to the underworld, and he wants them both to descend through the chimneys of ice. Adult becomes child and child becomes adult, as Sym screams at her uncle, 'What the hell are you doing, you fool?' (221) When she resists being fed into the mouth of the ice chimney, he rages 'like a toddler in a tantrum', a 'demented child . . . wanting, wanting, wanting his own way, thwarted by a world that won't do as it's told'. (222) Although she can fight off her uncle's attack, she is not able to prevent him from clambering into the mouth of the ice chimney himself. She watches in horror as he drops himself into the abyss. Like Conrad's Marlow standing before the dying Kurtz, she faces an abject image of her alter ego. She witnesses a fantasy-driven adult throwing himself, as it were, into the Real, the womb of the Antarctic. As he drops down, he turns his face up at Sym: 'I see the look that crosses it. Realization. True enlightenment. Dark takes him in the blink of an eye'. (223) In the instant of infernal 'enlightenment', just as the abject yields himself to darkness, he realises that all the darkness contains is death; return to the Real is impossible.

'The mind is its own place, and in itself can make a heaven of hell, a hell of heaven'[34]

Happily for Sym and the novel's readers, one can stand at the edge of non-being and still return safely from the experience. The above epigraph, borrowed from Milton's *Paradise Lost,* along with the echo of Conrad's *Heart of Darkness* in McCaughrean's title, suggests how Antarctica's sublime landscape will become a psychological Hell through which Sym and her companions descend; some of the Pengwings company will be lost, but those who are lucky enough to escape will emerge transformed.

The irony latent in the Miltonic passage is also operative in McCaughrean's novel. In the above lines, Satan is boasting that he is free to make a heaven anywhere, but by the end of *Paradise Lost,* he knows the opposite to be true: he is inescapably in Hell, because it is a construction of his mind which he cannot escape. Embarking on her adventure with a similar confidence, Sym thinks she is setting off for a Carrollian Wonderland, where she will discover a confident new self:

> The idea of it took me in thrall. It was so empty, so blank, so clean, so dead. Surely, if I was ever to set foot down there, even I might finally exist. Surely, in this Continent of Nothingness, anything—anyone—had to be hugely alive. (53)

But she comes to life via an unforeseen route, a *via negativa* which entails the near obliteration of her former self (one thinks of Dante at the bottom of Hell, saying, 'I did not die and and I did not remain alive').[35] During her journey,

Sym suffers the physical extremes of cold, starvation and exhaustion. Straining to see through the arctic fog, she feels her 'optic nerves stretch like threads of bubble gum'. (138) She witnesses the murder of a fellow explorer, as her uncle drives their jeep away, leaving Manfred Bruch running to catch up until he breaks an ankle: 'it was easy to read it in his face: how it felt to break a bone. I saw him pitch on his face; saw the unnatural angle of his foot as he dragged himself upright'. (159–60) Reaching shelter after being exposed in a blizzard, she experiences a torturous thawing of the flesh: 'I am burning on a grid-iron ... My skin is scalding. My tendons shrink and shrivel up short till the bones crack'. (240) Under the pressure of this ferocious metamorphic landscape, Sym experiences the abjection of her companion, her own body, and even the body of her imaginary friend. As Titus accompanies her back to the scene of his death, his body too undergoes an infernal transformation in her mind. His hair falls out and he begins to limp; 'his beauty has been blackened and pitted and eroded away like old stone'. (236–37)

Along with this physical abjection, there is a psychological regression to painful memories Sym thought she had successfully repressed. One memory above all torments her: 'My father didn't like me, and now he's dead there's nothing I can do to make him like me. I thought I'd got over that. But wounds unheal here'. (178) Kristeva writes of the abject that 'we may call it a border', where the subject reaches the edge beyond which subjectivity dissolves (*Powers*, 9). On her hellish journey, Sym discovers that such an edge exists in material reality and even has a name, the Ross Ice Shelf:

> Geographers can't map the chaos of the Shear Zone; it is always changing. This is where the Ice Shelf hinges against solid land, flexing, blistering, and gaping, like a scar that won't ever heal. (147)

The memory of her father's indifference returns to haunt Sym, while at the same time, a wound on her leg refuses to heal, since 'in the cold, wounds don't heal, they reopen. It's Nature in reverse'. (178). Sym herself compares her journey to Odysseus's descent into the underworld (79, 218). But her descent is also Dantean in that here, in the underworld, she relives *in vero* the mental anguish she has already suffered in a former life. Prior to her journey, she had felt herself to be locked up and 'frozen' inside. Her hearing impairment, caused by her uncle's experimental 'vitamins', had reduced her world to a 'blizzard' of sound. These and other psychic states take on a material reality as the *contrapassi* of damned souls, as she and her companions descend through the Antarctic *inferno*.

Tedium and Bliss

Once Victor has separated out his three chosen travellers and turned back the rest of the Pengwings company, there is very little discernible narrative development in *The White Darkness*, despite several literal cliff-hangers. Sym and her three fellow travellers reach a point of 'pure terror' as a white abyss opens up beneath their jeep. The ground 'simply unzipped beneath the tank, opening on the left of us, passing under the tracks, and out to our right, dropping compacted snow into the nothingness below it. It can't have taken more than three seconds for the ground to fall from under us'. (142) Sym and Sigurd also survive a fall off the side of a glacier, and Sym has to hack the ice out of the boy's eyes to save him from going blind. Having put her characters through such extremes of exhaustion, suffering and fear at such an early point in the novel, it is difficult to know what McCaughrean can do to maintain the same level of adventure and suspense. The four travellers press on through endless whiteness and cold. Manfred is abandoned, and then Sigurd steals the jeep, leaving Sym and Victor to search for Symmes's Hole on their own. Each of these events is suspensefully narrated, while Antarctica's sublime landscape continues to dazzle and terrify. But when it is not being ripped open by craters and crevasses at their feet, the landscape is an undifferentiated white desert. There is no visible horizon, nothing to mark their progress through the mist and snow. Unlike Verne's *Journey to the Centre of the Earth,* the fantasy of an underground Wonderland conspicuously fails to materialise in *The White Darkness.* Thus, despite all the terrors they endure, the journey and the narrative of the journey begin to border on the tedious. This is, I think, a deliberate effect. In *The Pleasure of the Text*, Roland Barthes defines a text of *jouissance* (or bliss) as 'one which imposes a state of loss' and which 'discomforts (perhaps to the point of a certain boredom)'.[36] *The White Darkness* does not assail its protagonists with one thrill after another because, I would argue, its aim is to discomfort its readers in this 'blissful' way. At the end of the novel, McCaughrean quotes a letter of Kafka's (whom Kristeva incidentally cites as a master of abject writing), in which he writes, 'a book must be an ice-axe to break the sea frozen inside us'.[37] McCaughrean takes us across a vast frozen sea which, before it can be broken, has first to be endured. Sym recalls a line from Coleridge's 'The Ancient Mariner' ('*water, water everywhere, nor any drop to . . .* ' (135)), and her Antarctic journey might well be compared to the long penance which the mariner suffers as a prelude to his psychic rebirth.[38]

As well as Coleridge's mariner at sea, *The White Darkness* recalls Marlow sailing his boat up the Congo River and feeling the malignity of a 'great and invincible' wilderness, 'like evil or truth, waiting patiently for the passing away of this fantastic invasion'.[39] As in Conrad's novella, evil and truth are inextricably linked in McCaughrean's representation of the descent journey. Again and again, on this relentless adventure, Sym confronts the horror of the real body, on the verge of being broken and emptied of life. Even more importantly, she is forced to confront the illusory nature of her fantasies. From her uncle, she learns that her father had loved her after all, and in fact was poisoned because he was trying to protect her. Rather like del Toro's Ofelia, Sym comforts herself with fairy tales; she compares herself to an enchanted princess, tightly bound by three bands of iron. Upon this news of her father's loyalty, she feels one of the bands of iron breaking (183). But before the princess can be freed, Sym needs to accept the falsity of other delusions which she is much more reluctant to let go. Sinking drowsily into the snow, overcome by a desire to sleep, Sym is enlightened by an angry Titus: '*Because I'm perpetually thirty-two, maybe you think I'm Christ Almighty? Maybe you think I went for a three-day warm in Hell, then rose again on the third day?*' Paradoxically, it is the voice of her own invention that forces Sym to acknowledge her solitude: 'All right! You died! Lawrence Oates died!' But this is more than a rational concession. She abjectly visualises the scene of his death, a horror from which she has so far shielded herself: 'he crawled on and on until the pain paralysed him—until the walls of his lungs froze and blinded him, and his arms wouldn't lift his face off the ground any more and his damaged thighbone snapped. Then he froze to death and the snow buried him!' (210) The scene 'comes real' for Sym not only imaginatively, but literally, as she lies paralysed and wounded, facing a repetition of his death.

Even so, she feels the abject's fascination with death, and she takes some comfort in the thought of Titus's corpse perhaps somewhere near, frozen in the ice. As Karen Coats argues, abjects 'organize their existence around the pole of . . . nonbeing—the unsublimated expression of the death drive'. (*Looking Glasses*, 145) But for Sym, the lowest point of abjection occurs simultaneously with the realisation of a thoroughly material form of catharsis. While she retains in her mind the image of Titus's body in the snow somewhere nearby, she seems willing to face the idea of dying herself. But Titus tells her (and she takes pains to point out that this was a fact she did not know herself) that corpses don't stay put in the Antarctic, so his can no longer be there: 'The surface is moving! . . . Carrying everything with it . . . all carried along inside a river of ice—all the time sinking lower, like dead fish . . . Lawrence Oates hasn't been in Antarctica for years!' (235) Sym is revolted at the thought, both that her friend's body would be so degradingly dispatched, and that she could be facing the same fate: 'what kind of graveyard spews out its dead? I hate it! It's like a patch of leprosy on the planet—can't feel cold, can't feel pain . . . All the time it's sloughing its dead, white skin—purging itself . . . I don't want to be in this frigid bitch of a place! I don't want to be in a dead place that doesn't even want my dead body!' (236) If abjection is felt as a collapse and return to the maternal body, it is not insignificant that Sym finally rejects Antarctica as a 'frigid bitch'. The thought of Antarctica's blank, insentient purgation of its dead is finally what purges Sym of her latent death wish.

'On the far and near side of religion'

Having come to this realisation, Sym (no less than the reader) expects the imaginary Titus to disappear for good: 'once you understand about madness, you're not allowed to go on being mad, are you? You have to grow up, buck up, shape up, wise up, get real'. (211) But unlike Pullman's Lyra, Sym does not entirely leave her instinct for fantasy behind in the underworld. Contrary to her own expectation, here and at the end of the novel, Titus reappears:

> there, ten metres ahead, back turned on the perpetual wind . . . Captain 'Titus' Oates flashes me the most dazzling of smiles. It is all the smiles I have craved from every face I have ever met. *'Thank God for sanity!' he says . . . We know this place, you and I. That's what's going to get you out of here'.* (211)

One might say that from this point on, Titus is more explicitly a product of Sym's own knowledge; he has been internalised as a voice of reason in her head. At the same time, he is clearly more than this, as his image appears mirage-like before her. Though a figure of sanity, standing her in good staid, in contrast to her uncle, Titus is also the projection of an ideal which she refuses to give up: 'when the whole world's on fire around you, you use a blind-fold. Everyone needs someone like Titus for a blindfold'. (227) An important aspect of Sym's 'growing up' and 'getting real' is learning when and how to keep hold of her imagination.

But this shift to a more mature perspective cannot entirely account for Titus's magical reappearance. First, there is the puzzle of Titus telling Sym something she doesn't already know (the fact that Antarctica recycles its corpses and refuse). And secondly, there is the fact that she finds her way through the blizzard back to Sigurd and the Hagglund jeep. If she didn't have Titus to follow, how did she find her way? Titus has already sardoni-cally challenged her quasi-religious thoughts (*'maybe you think I'm Christ Almighty?'*) which seems to rule out a religious interpretation of his presence. But the words she hears in the blizzard are certainly Christ-like: *'give it to me to carry . . . the pain . . . Because I'm the one who loves you enough'.* (231) And she responds in the manner of a disciple, trustingly following 'his shape . . . blurred by the swirling snow'. (236) Later, she wonders who 'that figure beside me' might have been (257), which recalls the speaker in T.S. Eliot's *The Waste Land*, questioning:

> Who is the third who walks always beside you?
> [. . .] when I look ahead up the white road
> There is always another one walking beside you
> Gliding wrapt in a brown mantle, hooded . . . [40]

So the presence of Titus might be understood as something 'on the far and near side of religion' (Kristeva, *Powers*, 17). Either his intervention is miracu-lous; whether a figure of Christ, an angel or some other supernatural being, he saves Sym's life. Or she saves herself, by means of courage, wits and good luck, and Titus is a product of her imagination. If the latter is so, then it is the strength of her imagination which keeps her alive: 'everyone needs a reason to stay alive—someone who justifies your existence . . . They just have to be there to love'. (231) A third way of interpreting Titus is as a troubled ghost who cannot rest until he has freed himself of the burden of knowing that, despite sacrificing his life for Scott and the company in 1912, they had failed to return to the camp alive. Such a ghostly Titus would be waiting for a life like Sym's to save, so that he might be saved himself. On whichever side of religion it stands, the sense of redemption at the end of this novel is double: lover and beloved, the living soul and the lost, are both regained from the underworld.

Unlike Dante, though, the modern subject does not travel through the infernal abyss just once. Abjection, as we have understood it, can be experienced at any stage of life, and not once but many times. As a result of her cathartic experience, Sym returns to what promises to be a relatively prosaic adolescence (although she still hears Titus's voice in her head). Some of the more traditional boundaries between age groups seem to have been reaffirmed, as Sym is asked out by an older boy, who then backs off when he learns she is 'only' fourteen (258). But for the reader, this is not quite the end of the adventure. McCaughrean concludes with a historical chapter, 'Scott of the Antarctic', in which an undramatised, third-person narrator relates the outlines of Scott's last expedition. We learn how Scott failed to heed Oates's advice about where to place their return camp depot—a willed deafness (like Victor's) which cost the company their lives. On 16 March, his 32nd birthday, Oates 'crawled out into a blizzard to die'. (262) But despite his heroism, the rest of the company froze to death eleven miles short of One Ton Depot. McCaughrean does not attempt to efface the historical tragedy, but instead leaves it juxtaposed with her own redemptive fantasy narrative of Titus saving Sym Wates. The White Darkness offers not so much a cure for abjection as a spectacle of 'true theatre' which returns the reader (whether adult or adolescent) to the edge of death, so as to recognise our deepest loves and desires, for the sake of which we cling to life.

Chapter Six
The Search for Roots:
David Almond's *Clay*

While death, as we have seen in earlier chapters, is a major theme of many of the crossover novels published in the millennial decade, it seems that many adult readers in the same period have turned to children's fiction, on the contrary, to discover (or rediscover) a sense of the energy and potential embedded in the beginnings of life and art. In children's fiction, adult readers are seeking to recover the earliest memories of childhood, the perceived roots of language and culture, and narrative in its allegedly most archaic and primitive forms. This search for roots can be interpreted as a resistant response to the disorienting aspects of contemporary life: accelerations of time, collapse of space, rapid developments in technology, and so on. Moreover, in a decade which has witnessed spectacular and repeated collisions between religious fundamentalism and modern secularism, children's fiction has emerged as a significant arena in which to explore the roots of the religious and/or spiritual instinct in the individual psyche. In this chapter, I would like to make a case for one particular novel's excellence in probing these related concerns. David Almond's *Clay* tells the story of two boys who combine their imaginative powers to create a living monster out of clay.[1] Set in Felling-upon-Tyne in the 1960s, the place and date of Almond's own childhood, and drawing on the Frankenstein and golem legends as well as the Genesis story, in which Adam and Eve are fashioned out of the dust of the earth, the novel raises questions about where the human instinct to create comes from, whether the instinct to destroy is equally inherent in us, and whether there are or should be limits to creative aspiration.[2]

The subtitle of Mary Shelley's novel *Frankenstein* is 'The Modern Prometheus', which underlines the latent kinship between the Frankenstein and golem legends.[3] In Greek mythology, Prometheus first created man out of clay, the same materials that Rabbi Loew used to create the golem in sixteenth century Prague. Contrary to the will of Zeus, Prometheus also stole fire to give to the human race, for which act of hubris he was ferociously punished by Zeus. For Percy Bysshe Shelley and other Romantic writers, Prometheus thus became a tragic hero, unjustly made to suffer for his rebellion against tyranny.[4] Mary Shelley's brilliant scientist Victor Frankenstein, however, is a much more morally ambivalent figure. By creating life *ex nihilo*, he transgresses divine law, but he also transgresses human law by failing to nurture and protect his creation. Rabbi Loew had fashioned the golem monster to protect the Jews from persecution, but the golem turned out to be an unreliable protector who, in many fictional and film versions, broke out of control to wreak general havoc before his creator was able to withdraw the breath of life and return him to inanimate clay.[5] In *Clay*, Almond draws on these legends to question the ethical limits of science in an age where bringing monsters to life has become a scientific possibility.

Prague being the city of alchemy, the golem is also a figure strongly associated with the magic realist narrative tradition. By combining Romantic ideas about Frankenstein/Prometheus with magic realist treatments of the golem legend, Almond not only tests the reader's credulity concerning the magic elements of his plot, but invites us to question why we seem to need to believe, and why we are attracted by the idea of *ex nihilo* creation. As is characteristic of magic realist fiction, Clay is a monster in which the reader hesitates to believe or disbelieve, to explain naturalistically or to accept as a marvellous and/or demonic reality.[6] But an even greater mystery is presented by one of the two main protagonists in the novel, Stephen Rose, a fourteen-year-old version of Victor Frankenstein, whose precocious talent at clay modelling extends to an ability to breathe actual life into the clay. On the other hand, since his grandfather is reputed to have been a powerful hypnotist, it may only be that Stephen has inherited this ability to persuade others to believe in whatever he says. In either case, his uncanny power seems to stem from a demonic instinct to destroy, in contrast to the novel's first-person narrator, Davie, who is naively drawn to Stephen because he is fascinated by the possibility of creating life.

In narrating this story, Davie employs a strong north eastern dialect polished and pared down to a concentrated, lyric intensity. As Almond has remarked, *Clay* 'is a very Geordie book, relentlessly Tyneside'.[7] Stylistically, then, *Clay* might be said to speak from the margins, like many magic realist texts; for, Almond says, 'the north east is an undiscovered country in literary terms; you might think it's a place that's . . . excluded from mainstream culture'.[8] At the same time, Davie's youthful idiom has an economic simplicity and directness that makes it easily accessible to non-Geordie readers. On several levels, then, Almond takes the reader on a 'search for roots': the roots of life in dust or clay, the origins of good and evil creativity, the origins of belief and of the need to persuade others to believe, and the roots of marginal cultures obscured by the mainstream. In my view, *Clay* is one of the outstanding crossover novels to address the question of roots and origins in the millennial decade, because it not only draws upon, but is also willing to challenge and interrogate resurgent Romantic notions of the divinity of children, as well as magic realism's sometimes simplistic binary oppositions between the child, the 'primitive' and the irrational on the one hand, and the adult, the 'civilised' and the rational, on the other. But before reading *Clay* in more detail, we should consider the broader context of adult cross-reading in an atavistic quest to reconnect with lost, cultural origins.

Millennial Atavism

In the responses to children's literature published by adult readers, reviewers, authors and critics over the millennial decade, several common themes emerge which associate the turn to narrative fiction for children with a conscious rejection of (post-) modern secularism, irony or 'knowingness' in western art and culture.[9] As Jonathan Stroud, author of the best-selling crossover *Bartimaeus* trilogy, put it, 'a successful book for children must have a strong narrative . . . The kid is not going to be impressed by trendy, pretentious, hifalutin stuff which some adults will be enraptured by'.[10] In this view, narrative aimed at a primary audience of children becomes a touchstone of authenticity for jaundiced, post-postmodern older readers. The inauthenticities of contemporary, 'hifalutin' adult fiction can be countered by fiction aimed at child readers in at least three ways: stylistically, children's fiction is perceived as being more closely linked to oral tradition and the ancient craft of storytelling; ideologically, it speaks from the margins and for the marginalised; and thematically, it addresses a timeless core of experience and accesses a latent spirituality and/or hope of redemption within (post)modern, secular culture.

One of the most commonly articulated defences of cross-reading is that in returning to children's fiction, adult readers are expressing their preference for strong, clear narratives with their roots in oral tradition. Authors of such fiction often refer to themselves, and are referred to, as storytellers rather than novelists, because it is stories which are 'the thread of life itself.'[11] For example, on the occasion of Michael Morpurgo's election to the Children's Laureateship, Joanna Briscoe described Morpurgo's style as 'remarkably uncluttered: neither poetic nor edgy with contemporary vernacular, it simply conveys a story in plain prose'. In the same article, Morpurgo described himself as 'a storyteller rather than a novelist'.[12] Nicholas Clee opined that cross-reading 'seems to reveal an appetite for strong, old-fashioned if you like, storytelling'.[13] In publisher David Fickling's view, children's fiction returns us to 'the trunk of the tree of narrative', which partly explains why many children's novels seem to possess a mythic quality (*pace* Maria Nikolajeva's view that the mythic element is in decline in contemporary children's fiction).[14] Thus reviewing Richard Adams's *Watership Down* on the thirtieth anniversary of its publication, S.F. Said described the novel as a 'work with ancient roots', which 'tap[s] into the power of narratives that have survived for millennia', recreating 'their timeless, profoundly enriching sense of depth'.[15] Adams's novel alludes extensively to Greek and Roman literature, but in other works, the sought-after sense of antiquity is specifically Anglo-Saxon and Celtic. Kevin Crossley-Holland's Arthurian trilogy was widely admired, and the first book, *The Seeing Stone*, won the Guardian Children's Fiction Prize in 2001.[16] Claire Armistead described Crossley-Holland's style as 'lean and plain, with no syllabic fat—one of the lessons Old English taught him'.[17] Michelle Paver attributed the crossover success of her *Chronicles of Ancient Darkness* to the fact that it revived the 'magic' of 'ancient superstition, spiritualism and ancestor worship'.[18] This renewal of interest in what might be described as narrative primitivism (which, it must be pointed out, has marked similarities to modernist interests in the 1920s) is well summed up in Bel Mooney's assertion that 'the need for narrative is ageless and timeless: [narrative is] a magic art to keep the darkness at bay, as surely as when the cave dwellers told tales around the fire'.[19]

In such reviews, the question of whether 'cave tales' are actually more appealing to children seems almost beside the point. The language of children (or rather, the language addressed to children), like the folk tales praised by Wordsworth and Coleridge in the preface to *Lyrical Ballads,* is understood to express something elemental and universal about the human condition.[20] Thus in a review of John Boyne's Holocaust novel *The Boy in the Striped Pyjamas*, Shame Hegarty writes, 'the child's voice is the common voice. It's the language we all spoke once'.[21] All the following reviewers cite a pared down, uncluttered style as a feature of contemporary children's fiction that should make it particularly appealing to adult readers (and all the works cited did, in the event, attract a substantial adult readership in the millennial decade): Meg Rosoff's *How I Live Now* is 'a haunting book with a deceptively spare style';[22] the 'purity of the language' of Lian Hearn's *Tales of the Otori* series was much praised;[23] according to Philip Pullman, 'the plain, uninflected telling' of American Louis Sachar's *Holes* 'has the quality of a fable', a 'bright clarity';[24] in Sonya Hartnett's *What the Birds See,* 'the writing is spare, the images crystalline' according to Jan Mark;[25] and Julia Eccleshare finds David Almond's 'spare writing' 'both beautiful and compelling'.[26]

But if spare, clean, crystalline writing with resonant depth has a strong appeal for post-postmodern adult readers, it does not follow that such fiction is betraying the interests of its primary audience of children. On the contrary, it is implicit in the comments above that the child reader will be able to sound out the truth and authenticity of the work, and that the adult reader's tastes should be guided by this implied child's more instinctive literary judgement. Although Barbara Wall argued that 'dual-addressed' narration (in which children and adults are addressed as equals) constitutes the rarest category of children's fiction, very little contemporary crossover fiction overtly addresses adults over the heads of children (her definition of the more common form, 'double address').[27] As Boyd Tonkin, I think rightly, argues, none of the children's fiction that is most widely read today, whether written recently or not,

> sets out to speak with a forked tongue; one part aimed at youngsters, while another whispers over their heads at some knowing adult behind ... On the contrary: they seek a comprehensive truth within the emotional world of their child characters ... The crossover moment arrives, if it does, not because grown-ups want to shed their sober mental suits in favour of shorts and gymslips—like some literary answer to the ghastly School Disco craze that now fills the nation's nightclubs. Rather, it's a matter of adult readers (and adult authors) recovering within themselves the special intensity, and the special focus, of the pre-adolescent vision ... Every reader in the world, after all, either has been—or remains—a child, with access at some level to the child's capacity for rapture, terror, boredom and excitement. This is, perhaps, the only sort of universality that literature can claim.[28]

In the previous chapter, I discussed the special focus of the fictional child's gaze, which adult readers may re-experience through engaging with children's fiction. Here what I would draw attention to is Tonkin's emphasis on the centrality of the child's experience in identifying the contours of a 'comprehensive truth' lying hidden within an 'emotional world' that is common to all readers of any age.

If the child's perspective is central in such fiction, the implicit reproach is directed at adult readers: we have 'forgotten' the fundamental verities by which we should be governing our adult lives. Even if these truths are no longer accessible through religion (for secular readers), they can be found buried in the most ancient narratives and myths and, like our eroding natural environment, they must be protected and sustained if we are to survive. In his children's fable, *Haroun and the Sea of Stories,* Rushdie dramatises this idea by picturing an ocean of ancient stories being polluted by poisonous 'anti-stories'. Iff the Water Genie, a custodian of the Ocean, guiltily admits,

> It's our own fault ... We are the Guardians of the Ocean and we didn't guard it. Look at the Ocean, look at it! The oldest stories ever made, and look at them now. We let them rot, we abandoned them, long before this poisoning. We lost touch with our beginnings, with our roots, our Wellspring, our Source.[29]

Iff's tone borders on the mock tragic, but he is expressing an idea that recurs throughout Rushdie's writing. The free circulation of myths—as stories, rather than as doctrine—seems to be as essential as water and air to Rushdie's protagonists. Indeed, retelling stories is part of the 'great work of making things real': 'turn right on this forking path and you find god; turn left and there is art, its uncowed ambition, its glorious irreverent over-reach'.[30]

Romantic Revivals

For Rushdie, there is a definite fork in the road separating religious stories from secular ones, the difference being that only religious stories ask to be read as absolute truth. Yet even he insists they come from a common source. It is not insignificant that Rushdie chose the form of a children's fable to articulate this view during the years he lived in hiding from Ayatollah Khomeini's death threats. For many contemporary authors and readers, children's fiction is the best vehicle to explore the theme of (post-) secular spirituality, because human divinity is understood to be most strongly present in children. This is a favourite theme of nineteenth century Romantic writers, many of whose ideas are being revived today in discussions of childhood and children's fiction. For example, on the BBC Radio 4 discussion board, which was set up to invite responses to the *Lebrecht Live* debate, 'Why Are Adults Reading Children's Literature?' one contributor posted the following comment:

> When we are born we have a spirit shining bright inside us . . . but without a mind filled with clutter to obscure clear vision . . . Without any doubt children see much better than adults what is important because they see with the spirit/intuition, call it what you will, rather than the mind. Also, they live in the present, adding to that clarity . . . This happy state is allowed for a while and then broken . . . And yet that bright spirit is still there inside us somewhere.[31]

Both the sentiment and the vocabulary ('bright' 'shining' 'inner' 'intuition' 'present' 'clarity') are strongly reminiscent of Wordsworth's 'Ode: Intimations of Immortality from Recollections of Childhood', one of the most influential representations of the child in Romantic poetry.[32] Wordsworth's fifth stanza includes these famous lines:

> The Soul that rises with us, our life's Star,
> Hath had elsewhere its setting,
> And cometh from afar:
> Not in entire forgetfulness,
> And not in utter nakedness,
> But trailing clouds of glory do we come
> From God, who is our home:
> Heaven lies about us in our infancy!

Wordsworth's Ode intimates that the child is closer than the adult to the soul's divine origins. Together with Coleridge, Lamb, DeQuincy and other nineteenth-century writers, he helped popularise an image of the child which mingled eighteenth-century sentimentalism with John Locke's ideas about the child's malleability, and Rousseau's belief in 'natural' education fostering the innate goodness and innocence of children.[33] Historians of the nineteenth century have been at pains to point out that actual nineteenth-century children are unlikely to have borne much resemblance to their projections in Romantic literature.[34] But this does not appear to dampen our current enthusiasm for the concept of divinity residing in childhood rather than institutionalised religions.

If Heaven really does 'lie about us in our infancy', then one of the ways we can rediscover the faraway home of the Soul is by engaging with children's literature. This Romantic idea, implicit in the Internet posting quoted above, recurs frequently in contemporary discussions of children's literature and culture. When children's books are adapted for the stage, the adaptation process often involves tailoring the material to a mixed age audience. For theatre director Laurence Boswell, who adapted 'Beauty and the Beast' for an RSC production at Stratford in 2003, 'there's a timeless core that society doesn't really touch, and it's up to us to find the archetypally true moments, comic or tragic, that reach that core'.[35] Implicit in this concept of a 'timeless' core is the Romantic association between the child and immanent, rather than transcendent, forms of the divine. On BBC Radio 4's *With Great Pleasure* (aired on Sundays, as a spiritual, rather than explicitly Christian, programme), Adrian Mitchell introduced a reading of children's poetry for adult listeners with a quotation from William Blake: 'for everything that lives is holy'.[36] David Almond's best known novel, *Skellig*, makes references throughout to William Blake, and depicts a child protagonist discovering innate powers of spiritual telepathy. In *Clay*, Almond draws on the rituals and iconography of his Catholic upbringing to explore what his novels suggest is a basic need to believe in a spiritual dimension to reality. Similarly, William Nicholson argues explicitly for the idea that children's fantasy literature can answer a spiritual need in both child and adult readers: 'there's a type of psycho-spiritual adventure story that appeals very strongly to quite a wide age group—10 to 30. It is as if the appetite for other worlds has to be met somehow. Perhaps one would call it fable-telling. Secretly I have a suspicion that these things are almost religious at base'.[37]

Turn right and one finds God, turn left, and one finds art, asserted Rushdie's irreligious narrator in *The Ground Beneath Her Feet*. But travel back up the road to where the two forks join (in other words, travel back to childhood), and one may discover a world where spiritual and material worlds are still intertwined. This is the main argument of Ted Hughes's essay, 'Myth and Education', in which he describes the contemporary adult psyche as destructively split into two 'worlds': an inner, spiritual world and a material, outer one.[38] The inner world is 'elemental, chaotic, continually more primitive and beyond our control'. ('Myth', 15) When cut off from the outer world (as happens to Davie midway through *Clay*), this inner world becomes 'a place of demons' while the outer world, when cut off from the inner, becomes 'a place of meaningless objects and machines'. ('Myth,' 15) In the decline of religion, and the failure of psychoanalysis to fulfil its role, only the creative imagination retains the capacity to bring the two worlds together, to produce a meaningful sense of being. Echoing Coleridge on the secondary Romantic imagination, but with more confidence in its operation, Hughes declares, 'the faculty that makes the human being out of these two worlds is called divine'.[39] Even more Romantic is Hughes's assertion that children are naturally suited to inhabit this undivided world, but they are blocked from doing so by spiritually depleted adults:

> Children . . . want to escape the ugliness of the despiritualized world in which they see their parents imprisoned. And they are aware that this inner world we have rejected is not merely an inferno of depraved impulses and crazy explosions of embittered energy. Our real selves lie down there. Down there, mixed up among all the madness, is everything that once made life worth living. All the lost awareness and powers and allegiances of our biological and spiritual being. ('Myth,' 15)

Here at least, Hughes makes it clear that if we accept the Romantics' ideas about the child's natural divinity, we will also have to take on board their more unsettling ideas about demonic energies smouldering at the core of the psyche, the child's as well as the adult's. After all, Blake not only wrote that 'everything that lives is holy'; he also declared in the same poem that the Protestant poet Milton was 'of the Devil's party' and that Hell was the best place to generate unfettered, revolutionary creativity.[40] Like Almond's *Clay*, Hughes's essay also demonstrates the ways in which Romantic notions of childhood and immanent divinity are being deployed in a critique of capitalist consumer culture. It may be slightly paradoxical that adults are turning to children's literature for an escape from aggressive consumerism just when, as we saw in Chapter 1, certain areas of children's literature are becoming more thoroughly commercialised than ever before. Nevertheless, neo-Romantic children's literature can still produce powerful, utopian images that can inspire adults and children to challenge the dominant consumerist ethos.

Magic Realism and 'the view from underneath'

The theme of ecological *hubris,* of man presuming too far on Nature's bounty, was central to many Romantic texts, and it resurfaces strongly in David Almond's retelling of Mary Shelley's *Frankenstein*. This is also a theme found in many magic realist novels, of which *Clay* could be considered an example.

In *The Jaguar Smile*, Rushdie argues that countries like India and Nicaragua share a common, 'underworld' perspective vis-à-vis the developed world:

> those of us who did not have our origins in the countries of the mighty West, or North, had something in common—not, certainly, anything as simplistic as a unified 'third world' outlook, but at least some knowledge of what weakness was like, some awareness of the view from underneath, and of how it felt to be there, on the bottom, looking up at the descending heel.[41]

If this ideological perspective is implicit in many works of magic realism, 'the view from underneath' is also a feature of many children's novels, in particular those, like David Almond's, written from a position outside the cultural mainstream of London and southeast Britain. For example, *Skellig* is a retelling of a short story by Gabriel García Márquez, in which a decrepit, bizarrely winged man appears without explanation on the margins of an impoverished, rural community.[42] Magic realist fiction is frequently focalised through a child's gaze, but in this case it is Almond who adds the child protagonists to the story of a winged man's inexplicable appearance.[43] While Márquez focuses satirically on the villagers' readiness to exploit the angel for financial gain, in *Skellig* Almond dwells on the children's capacity to believe in a creature whose existence their parents and teachers would deny.[44] Almond's novel thus exaggerates a magic realist tendency to attribute credulity in the supernatural to children.

In some magic realist fiction, the child's 'view from underneath' is deployed simplistically to criticise the way developed nations exploit the rest of the world's natural resources. In Isabel Allende's crossover ecofable, *The City of the Beasts*, for example, the binary oppositions are extremely clear-cut: children, women, native Amazonians (irrespective of age and gender), animals and 'nature' are all good, while male westerners, technology and 'civilisation' are mostly bad.[45] In Rushdie's *Haroun*, there is an unambiguous distinction between the fabulists and the anti-fabulists, the latter represented as 'scurrying, cloaked, weaselly, scrawny, snivelling clerical types'. (152) But these oppositions can be unconvincing if presented without qualification or nuance. Many psychologists have contested Piaget's view that children are unable to distinguish between real and imaginary levels of reality, and hence that children are naturally more credulous than adults.[46] The allegedly 'primitive' spiritualism of these works can also seem more a product of western culture than the native cultures they are intended to reflect. Carol Birch, for example, remarks of Allende's *The City of Beasts*, 'it feels as if you've wandered into a meditation class: "Seek your centre . . . Breathe. When you inhale, you are charged with energy, when you exhale, you rid your body of tension"'.[47] It seems questionable, sometimes, whether Allende's spiritualism derives from a genuinely Amazonian tradition, or whether it is a product of western/northern fantasies and desires.

Unlike other magic realist children's fiction (including Almond's earlier novel, *Skellig*), *Clay* does not represent its 'magic' level of reality to be automatically superior to the realist one. Before Stephen's arrival, Davie is a contented child, well loved and befriended in a close-knit community, while the discontented outsider, Stephen Rose, is presented in terms that constantly vacillate between the naturalistic and the demonic. The spirit world that Davie accesses through Stephen is represented as being neither entirely believable nor unambiguously good. For example, Stephen may be hypnotising Davie in the following passage, so that Davie imagines seeing movement in a clay figurine of a child:

> 'Look deep. Look with the eyes of the spirit, Davie. When I say you'll see it move, you will see it move.'
> He lifted the child towards me. He passed his hand before my eyes again.
> 'Now, Davie,' he whispered. 'You will see it move.' (84)

It is less clear here than in Allende's case whether 'looking with the eyes of the spirit' will lead to the truth or to a delusion. Almond dovetails magic realism's structural hesitation over ontological realities into a morally ambiguous, Romantic quest for forbidden knowledge. The desire to create an ontologically multiple world becomes an expression of masculine Romantic overreach, a desire to supplant both the Father (God) and the human mother to create life from dust.[48] When they succeed in bringing Clay to life, Davie expects to be struck down by God's wrath. He is bewildered by the lack of divine punishment and stumbles into an alienated state of consciousness in which he no longer knows who he is or where he belongs. As Clay and Stephen become more real to him, the rest of the Felling community, including his best friend Geordie, become 'like characters in a story, beings from another world'. (235)

Davie's loss of faith in God leads to his loss of faith in human identity also, illustrating the Nietzschean idea that, as John Milbank writes, 'the coherence of the self collapses when it is no longer referred to stable transcendent goals, and the redemptively unifying reclamations of divine grace'.[49] Or, as Davie puts it, in his strong Tyneside dialect: 'let God be gone. Let the soul be nowt but an illusion. Let death be nowt but rotting flesh and crumbling bones. . . . Let it all be nowt but a bliddy joke. God, world, soul, flesh . . . Nowt but nowt, bliddy nowt'. (169) Thus in *Clay*, Almond moves beyond *Skellig* to explore this crux at the heart of contemporary magic realism: the need to believe and to be believed at precisely that point where belief becomes most difficult. At the same time, the novel explores and interrogates the Romantic myth that human beings come into the world instinct with divinity but lose this divine power as they approach adult consciousness.

Postmodern Spiritualities

While many commentators assume that the adult reader's turn to 'spiritual' children's literature constitutes a rejection of postmodern philosophy, there has, in fact, been a strong resurgence of interest in a 'divine way of thinking' *within* postmodern philosophy. This is evident in the later writing of Luce Irigaray, Jacques Derrida, Maurice Blanchot, and Emmanuel Levinas, as well as a wide range of novelists described as 'postmodern'.[50] In a seminal article on postmodern spiritualities, John McClure explains:

> Many postmodern texts . . . explore fundamental issues of conduct in ways that honor, interrogate, and revise religious categories . . . their political analyses and prescriptions are intermittently but powerfully framed in terms of magical or religious conceptions of power; their assaults on realism . . . [reaffirm] premodern ontologies . . . that portray the quotidian world as but one dimension of a multidimensional cosmos, or as hosting a world of spirits.[51]

The very instinct to search for roots in children's books in reaction to the surface play of postmodernist texts may indeed be an impulse produced by postmodern economic and social conditions. David Harvey argues that postmodernity produces the craving for its opposite, for a sense of tradition and 'secure moorings in a shifting world'.[52] As further evidence of this, one might point to the recent rise of the genre of 'inspirational novel' in the USA. Ted Dekker, author of the best-selling novel *Obsessed,* aims 'to write books that characterise that redemption overcomes a terrible evil and is available for all mankind". His publisher, Allen Arnold, seems convinced that Dekker has achieved his aim ('I stand in awe at the powerful gift God has poured into Ted').[53] As Harvey points out, the irony is that 'tradition is now often preserved by being commodified and marketed as such' so that 'the search for roots ends up at worst being produced and marketed as image, as a simulacrum or pastiche'. (*Condition of Postmodernity,* 303)

Nevertheless, acknowledging a divine, or in Irigaray's term, a 'dark', way of thinking seems crucial to many during the millennial decade, especially after the catastrophic events of 9/11 in 2001.[54] Since that event, Islamic and Christian fundamentalism has been contributing to a lethal polarisation between East and West, as well as within nations, between opposing religions and between religious and anti-religious worldviews. In Britain, an aggressive atheism, such as that expressed in Richard Dawkins' *The God Delusion,* is taking shape, which seems likely to exacerbate the alienation of religious communities that has already dramatically increased, after the London bombings of 2005.[55] In this context the revival of Romantic discourses in children's literature, along with other postmodern explorations of spirituality, may have an important role to play in bridging the growing divide between atheistic and faith communities. Despite his fierce iconoclasm, Blake's concept of childly holiness is generously inclusive, and is often cited by both secular and religious organisations.

David Almond's secular spirituality, reflecting a Romantic preference for immanent forms of divinity, has long attracted a devoted following of adult readers. This crossover appeal has intensified as his novels have become thematically darker and structurally more complex in recent years. On its publication in 2005, *Clay* was immediately hailed as a children's book with crossover appeal. In *The Guardian*, Claire Armistead wrote that *Clay* 'takes readers into strange new areas of the imagination that are not . . . fileable under "childhood issues"'.[56] Almond's exploration of the nature and origins of the spiritual instinct may thus play a part in this millennial bridging of cultures, not only between child and adult, but also between secular and religious communities.

Clay: A Fall in Four Acts

Clay is narrated in four parts which trace the parabola of Davie's psychic and moral journey from a state of innocence (described in Part I), through temptation (Part II) and fall (Part III), to the beginnings of a recovery (Part IV). Like Philip Pullman, Almond thus represents a child's individual threshold crossing into adolescence as a re-enactment of the Biblical Fall from Eden. Moreover, in *Clay* the adolescent crossing allegorically comes to represent the process of artistic creation so that the two boys' collaboration in producing the monster connotes the codependence of author and reader in creating a 'living, moving' story out of a piece of written text.[57]

The adult reader enters the text of *Clay* on a par with the implied adolescent reader in part because, as in other novels considered in this study, adolescence is represented as a psychic state as well as a biological stage of life. The adult's entry alongside the younger reader's is especially facilitated in this novel by the temporal ambiguities of Davie's narration. It is never made entirely clear how old Davie is when he narrates the text we are reading. Like McCaughrean's *The White Darkness*, the dust jacket of *Clay* depicts a child's face staring directly out at the reader. The image, closely cropped to show only the eyes, challenges the reader in an unsettling way, by suggesting an adult depth of experience behind the young boy's eyes and hinting at their hypnotic power to draw us into that same, estranging depth. But whether this image represents Stephen's face or Davie's, and the latter as a character in the story or as its narrator, remains unclear. At the time of events, Davie and his friend Geordie are about twelve years old, and Stephen about fourteen (7). But Davie does not specify how much time has elapsed before he narrates the story. At the end of the novel, he confesses, 'this is the first time I've told the tale. I've tried to speak it, like Maria said . . . but each time I start, the craziness in it just brings me to a halt. So now I've written it down'. (295–96) This sounds like a fairly immediate process, but we still don't know when the 'now' of the narrator is. Davie begins the novel by describing his earliest memory of Stephen: 'he arrived in Felling on a bright and icy February morning. Not so long ago, but it was a different age. I was with Geordie Craggs, like I always was back then'. (1) The time is at once specific and imprecise. 'Back then' suggests that Davie might be much older now than the twelve-year-old self he is describing, but he also says it was 'not long ago.' Might the sense of a greater interval simply be a reference to the enormity of Stephen's impact on his preadolescent self? 'Not so long ago' also connotes a narrator occupying the same time frame as the reader, so in the first chapter we are led to assume that Davie is narrating in the mid-2000s, when the novel was published. It is not until the second chapter that Davie specifies he was a child 'back then in the 1960s' (7); from this clue, we might correct the earlier assumption to imagine a narrator of the author's own age (around 50), since like Davie, David Almond's childhood was spent in Felling-upon-Tyne in the 1960s. But there is almost no internal evidence of such a major chronological gap separating the narrator Davie from the younger self portrayed in his narrative. The linguistic register of the narration appears to be that of an adolescent although, as noted earlier, the polished and pared down style has also been described by reviewers as 'ageless'. This temporal fluidity reflects Almond's sense of Felling, and the British northeast in the 1960s more generally, as 'a place where all generations lived together . . . I never had a big sense of a generation gap'.[58]

On the other hand, there is a definite attitudinal distance between Davie's former self (the character represented at the outset of the story), and Davie as the text's narrator. We witness a break or caesura between the two selves just at the point where Davie decides to help Stephen in his hubristic aim to create a living monster. From the church where he serves as an altar boy, Davie has stolen crumbs of communion bread and a cloth stained with communion wine, because Stephen has told him these are needed to bring the clay figure to life (though he later laughs at Davie's credulity in believing them to possess any kind of magic power). Now Davie hesitates before delivering these sacred objects into Stephen's hands. He hopes his mother will appear at the doorway to prevent him getting out of bed and going to meet Stephen,

> But it's Davie, of course, who rises from the bed an hour later, Davie who quietly puts on his clothes . . . who steps from the room . . . Davie who opens the door and holds it open . . . Davie who wants his mam to call, 'What are you doing, Davie?' Davie who wants his dad to stamp downstairs and stop him and haul him back, Davie who closes the door behind him when none of this happens, Davie who steps out alone into the night. (170)

Here, for the first (and only) time in the novel, the narrator describes his former self as a separate character; he employs the third person and refers to this 'other' Davie by name, nine times in one sentence. Looking back on this younger, more naïve self, he pictures a child longing to be saved by his parents, but deciding to 'step out alone', to cross the threshold into adolescence and face his moral crisis on his own. To see oneself as an other is a sign of postlapsarian consciousness in Milton's account of the Fall in *Paradise Lost*, just as it is a sign of incipient adult consciousness in what Lacan describes as the 'mirror stage' of psychic development.[59] Thus in the passage above, when Davie sees himself as an alien other, he is anticipating the moment when he and Stephen will transgress divine law by creating life from clay. The language he uses here becomes 'adult' in the sense that the sentence is grammatically complex, lengthy, and rhetorically structured by the eloquent use of anaphoric repetition.

What separates the child Davie from the older narratorial voice is the experience of creating Clay with Stephen, an event which thus comes to stand metonymically for 'adolescence' in the novel. Adolescence here signifies the biological development of a boy into a teenager, as well as the awakening of moral consciousness in an individual (of any age), a community, or an entire society. While in *The White Darkness,* adolescence was characterised by the abjection encounter with death and the deathly, here in *Clay* adolescence is above all about the experience of birth: both giving birth, and being (re)born oneself. Like McCaughrean's Antarctica, the event of creation in *Clay* is described in the paradoxical terms of the Romantic sublime: revelatory and liberating, but also morally abhorrent and terrifying. As with abjection, one can collapse back into this phase of primal creativity from either side of the adolescent threshold, that is, from childhood or adulthood. In *Clay* this is signified by a shift in the tense of narration, from the historical past used in Parts I, II and IV, to the present tense used in Part III to describe the 'Fall' of Davie and Stephen. Thus the memory of creating Clay recurs in Davie's narration as trauma, an unresolved past which may continually resurface 'in a kind of endless present', at any point in later life (271).[60]

At one level, *Clay* represents the threshold crossing into adolescence as a stage in a child's psychobiological development. Davie has just reached the age where he is taking an interest in girls. To his best friend Geordie's consternation, he accepts an invitation to go on a walk with a schoolmate, Maria ('you're gonna do *what* with *who*?' [105]). Stephen's arrival disrupts both the childhood friendship and the incipient, heterosexual romance, as the new boy pointedly excludes Geordie from his conversations with Davie and kisses him in front of the other children, causing a rift between Davie and Maria. For Davie, the older boy represents a wilder, more dangerous mode of being that exceeds Felling's ordinary social norms. He is fascinated and seduced by Stephen's attentions, and instinctively sure that if he wants to grow up, he must go through whatever it is that Stephen is offering him: 'I told myself that Stephen Rose was something strange and new, something that had been sent to me, something that stood before me as I grew from being a boy into a man.'

(127, and cf. 166) Thus one aspect of Davie's adolescence is his willingness to respond to latently erotic encounters which lie beyond the sexual mores sanctioned by his community. Davie's parents attribute his moodiness to a confusion of feelings over Maria, never suspecting that Stephen is anything but a new playmate, which indicates how far the two boys' creative-erotic alliance exceeds Felling's recognised social norms.

On a more allegorical level, though, the entire town of Felling is represented as being on the brink of an 'adolescent' awakening into different and more complex reality. While Felling in the 1960s, according to Almond, was characterised by an optimistic socialism, this political idealism was about to change.[61] In the novel, Stephen half convinces Davie to believe that after 1945, God turned his back on the human race, or 'mebbe a bit earlier. You know: war, concentration camps, gas ovens, atom bomb, all that stuff. Enough to drive anybody away'. (223) Since that time, according to Stephen's theory, human beings have operated in a moral vacuum, with no sense of spiritual aim or purpose. 'Mebbe he was here in the past', says Stephen, 'but these days, man, it's all a bliddy joke'. (223) On an allegorical level, Stephen may be said to represent the secular world post-1945, which, by neglecting the connectedness of inner and outer worlds has devolved into a 'place of demons,' as Ted Hughes argued.

Interpreted naturalistically, Stephen's behaviour is destructive, rather than supernaturally demonic, and his wildness is understandable as a response to a history of parental neglect. As he recalls, his mother always believed that he had not been naturally conceived, but appeared in her womb like a demon (263). So one might interpret his conviction that God had abandoned the human race, and that he himself possesses demonic powers, as the psychological displacement of bitter feelings towards, as he puts it, his 'mental' mother. But whether one chooses the naturalistic or the allegorical interpretation, Stephen is clearly 'on a quest for identity', as Charles Taylor suggests is characteristic of secular, modern subjectivity.[62] For all that he is driven by a sense of purpose to create (and destroy), Stephen is profoundly uncertain about his own identity. He needs Davie, not only to help him make Clay, but also to help him fashion a sense of self. For example, Stephen tells Davie about a horrifying event from his past: one night as he and his parents were sitting around the dinner table, his father choked on his food, suffocated and died. The first time Stephen tells this story, as the two boys are moulding the figure of Clay, he casts himself in the role of his father's saviour. Assuring himself of Davie's credulity before he continues, he relates how he brought his father back from the dead:

> I stare back at him. He waits for me. And I say the true and crazy words.
> 'Yes. I believe you'.
> 'Yes!' he gasps. 'I hold me dad and I call him back, and it starts happening, Davie. I feel the life coming back into him. I feel his spirit move. I feel a tiny breath'. (188)

Later, however, in revenge for Davie's betrayal, he insists that Davie hear the 'true' version of events. Not only did he not save his father's life, he hypnotised and caused him to die: 'I was staring at his face in horror, because he was ugly and horrible and I was sick of him, and inside I start going, "Die, you cretin. Die". . . . and then he does his gagging and his gurgling and his tumble to the floor'. (263–64) Neither version is more verifiable than the other, and Davie and the reader are finally left to choose between three possible Stephens, one a fallen angel, another a demon, and a third 'just an ordinary kid'. (275) But unlike the decision facing the reader at the end of Yann Martel's magic realist novel, *The Life of Pi*, here the choice is genuinely open, because Stephen himself appears not to know who or what he really is.[63]

In this sense, Stephen represents the schizoid identity of the postmodern subject, whose complex nature the innocent adult inhabitants of Felling completely fail to understand. Davie challenges the benign old priest, Father Mahoney, to account for the presence of evil in the world: 'if you believe in God and goodness, should you not believe in the devil and evil?' (283) But Father Mahoney first dismisses his question ('I see that adolescence is truly upon you' [282]), and then answers glibly, 'yes, but I am an optimist, Davie. I believe that God and goodness have the upper hand'. (283) But in the event, Father Mahoney fails to anticipate Stephen's destructiveness, and a local boy dies as a result. The priest admits feebly to Davie, 'I did look out for him. But my flock is large . . . We'll make a better job of it next time'. (284) Commenting on the greater pessimism of *Clay* than his earlier novels, Almond remarked that he was less sure than formerly that goodness was the dominant force in the world: 'you see the actions of the politicians over the last few years and you see that actually they don't [act for the common good]. George Bush doesn't have the goodness of the world at heart and yet this man is rampant in the world'.[64] In the larger historical context, then, Davie is right to feel frustrated by the naive optimism of his elders, and his instincts are correct when he senses that they will be powerless to counteract the destructive force that Stephen is driven to unleash on the world. Still less will they be able to prevent him from being tempted to become like Stephen himself, because they refuse to recognise any of that darkness as their own.

In many respects, the child characters represented in *Clay*, with the exception of Stephen, inhabit a vastly simpler world than the one familiar to child readers in the millennial decade. These characters don't carry mobile phones or watch TV or get driven in SUVs to school, and they go for rambling, unsupervised walks and play outdoors in secret gardens. But in other respects, they are facing changes that seem very contemporary, or at least are still as relevant to readers today. Stephen and Davie create their monster in a clay pit known as Braddock's Garden, the site of an old quarry and ancient gardens which are about to be developed into a housing estate. As Maria complains to Davie, 'they'll call the new streets Pretty Place and Lovely Lane but they'll not see how they've smashed a bit of Paradise'. (112) The children are also aware of growing up in the dawn of a period of rapid technological and scientific change. Davie is aware and afraid of the knowledge that one day soon, society as a whole will be able to play God, as he and Stephen are doing: 'they say that one day we'll be able to make life in test tubes ... we'll be able to create living creatures with chemicals and electricity and nuclear power'. (115) Indeed, he and the other children seem to have a clearer grasp of the future than the adults in the novel. His art teacher, the aptly named Mr Prat articulates some of the moral dilemmas facing Davie, but the teacher's responses seem always too simple and abstract to help Davie decide how he should act. Prat announces to his art class, 'we cannot, like God, create life. But who is to say what the limits of our creativity might nevertheless be?' (97) Davie has to deal with the fact that he can, apparently, create life. Again, Prat says, 'it's the human paradox ... We are creative beings. But our passion to create goes hand in hand with our passion to destroy.' Nevertheless, he concludes lightly, echoing Father Mahoney: 'I am an optimist. I believe that the forces of good will defeat the forces of evil'. (213) But just then, as if to challenge his optimism, Davie catches sight of the clay monster lurching towards the school gates. Thus one gets the sense of a community approaching a period of accelerated social change, for which the adult inhabitants seem particularly ill prepared.

'Earliest things'

To meet this new, more dangerous reality, *Clay* takes its readers and child protagonists on a psychic journey backwards in time, to what appears to be a recovery of original psychic drives. Just as in *The White Darkness* McCaughrean's focus is on the essential instincts that draw us towards abjection, so Almond scours the boys' memories of 'earliest things' to uncover the source of the impulse to create and destroy. The psychic journey that Davie undertakes is a private one, but it leads him backwards or 'down' in time to connect with a vital force that predates his own existence. This Jungian, as opposed to Freudian, emphasis on a pre-individual, collective identity is often found in magic realist fiction, while the notion of digging downward and inward to discover a primeval truth is a common theme in Romantic writing.[65]

From the start of the novel, it is clear that the child characters are more willing and capable of probing beneath the surface than the adults. The two child protagonists are also Romantically represented as being closer to a mythic sense of divine origin than their elders. At Stephen's former school, a seminary college run by Catholic priests, several boys had been caught experimenting with ritualistic practices ('devil worship' and 'Black Masses' according to Geordie), and Stephen was expelled as a result (43). Before his expulsion, Stephen was told by a priest that he was perhaps 'more suited to the wilderness than to the civilised world'. (53) Crouched with Davie and Geordie in Braddock's Garden, he points out that 'saints used to live in caves like this . . . they tested themselves', discovering their innate powers (53). When he thinks about the creation of the human race, as he frequently does, Stephen considers every possibility: before He came to create Adam and Eve, 'mebbe God made . . . thick stupid lumpy things without a soul . . . mebbe there was a time of beasts and monsters before there came the time of us'. (82) This idea appeals to Geordie and Davie because their lives are plagued by an actual 'thick stupid lumpy thing', a school bully tellingly named Martin Mould, who will frequently be compared to the monster, Clay.

Although he does not entirely persuade Davie to agree with his Manichean view of the world, Stephen does infect him with the obsession to uncover a hidden, more primitive spiritual reality. So, while Stephen is represented as a possibly demonic influence, he is also a more powerful spiritual guide than any of Davie's adult mentors. Under Stephen's hypnotic influence, Davie learns to hear with an inner ear (75, 213, 242), to see with inner sight (84), to sculpt clay with an 'inner light' (49). Thus in Stephen, Almond conveys a comparable sense of the demonic to that found in Blake's *The Marriage of Heaven and Hell*: the demonic as a subterranean, creative energy—essentially positive and life-giving until it is fettered or shut off, at which point it distorts and darkens into something suppressed or exorcised as evil.

On the verge of his 'Fall', Davie argues with his parents, is sent to his room, and climbs into his bedroom cupboard: 'I clambered over toys and games to find my earliest things: rattles and building blocks and crayons and board books and found my ancient tub of Plasticine'. (149) In these objects that fascinated him as an infant, Davie rediscovers his earliest impulses to create life from inanimate matter. By presenting Davie as a subject with nostalgic impulses of his own, Almond short-circuits any tendency in the adult reader to objectify him as a romanticised symbol of lost childhood. Like the adult reader, Davie discovers that there is an earlier time to which he must regress in order to recover himself.

This discovery comes from working with clay, a material so basic and yet so easily moulded into forms suggestive of life, that it appears to bridge the divide between matter and spirit. In contrast to Mary Shelley's monster, 'Clay' (so named by Davie) is a low-tech invention, not much more evolved than a snowman: 'sycamore seeds make eyes, ash keys make the ears . . . twigs and grass stems make his hair'. (176) He is a natural monster, 'plant[ed] like a garden' rather than sewn from corpses and animated by electricity (176). If Almond's creature is less exotically alien than Shelley's, it is also more sinister because it can evidently be created by sheer force of will and desire. Any child-reader could fashion the rough figure and repeat the rituals that brought Clay to life. This point is not inessential in an age where young and old have access to bomb-making instructions via the Internet, and as a race, our capacity for destruction is escalating.

But perhaps the strongest contrast between Shelley's monster and Almond's is that the latter is beautiful rather than hideous, and his creation is a work of love.

Stephen has singled Davie out to be the midwife to his creative genius, but by the time they come to sculpt the figure, they are equals in an Edenic partnership:

> We kneel and turn the sticky sloppy clay into the shape of a man. And we become engrossed in it . . . We keep telling each other: 'Make him beautiful'. We keep packing more clay on to the body. 'Make him strong', we say. We run our damp fingers across the surface of the man: 'Make it smooth like living skin'. We keep leaning back from our work. We smooth out the flaws, we touch in details, we smile and sigh at the beauty of our work'. (175–76)

The intensities of Davie and Stephen's relationship surface as they work over the clay. Damp-fingered, sighing, and smiling, they become as-if lovers, or parents conceiving a child, and their individual selves merge into an undifferentiated 'we'. Their pleasure derives in part from the quasi-magical nature of the material with which they are working. The clay, once dampened and smoothed over, resembles living skin and they begin to believe that it could cross the threshold into life. As an image of immanent divinity, they differ from Victor Frankenstein (not to mention the God of Genesis) in one obvious respect: Clay is the product of a partnership, not a solitary act of abiogenesis. Their pleasure clearly derives in part from working together. For the reader, too, there is the pleasure of gliding over these smoothed down, assonant phrases which work over the temporal fissures between child and adult discourse so that the reader, too, becomes part of this shared creativity. At the end of his adventure, Davie wonders if he has been hypnotised by Stephen. And the same doubt might occur to the reader of Almond's novel, because his writing frequently takes on this hypnotic quality, inviting us to step free of the categories of age, gender or class in response to a mesmerising, apparently ageless narratorial voice.[66]

As they sculpt the figure of the giant man, the boys appear not so much to grow older, but to regress to a more primitive state of being. Praying, chanting and singing over the clay figure, they resemble the ancient priests for whom Stephen has earlier professed an admiration:

> And time passes and our whispers change and waver and become like weird singing that comes out of us but that's somehow not part of us, but is part of the night, the air, the moonshine, and the words in the singing are no longer like words but are just sounds drawn from somewhere deep inside ourselves, like creatures' cries, like complicated birdsong, nighttime birdsong. And we ourselves become somehow not ourselves, but we turn subtler, weirder, less attached to our bodies, less attached to our names. (179–80)

Stephen believes that modern day religious practices derive from more powerful and ancient shamanistic rituals, and clearly Almond intends us to see their present metamorphosis as a Jungian regression to this wilder, more instinctual past. The fact that they are children is critical, because the Romantic association between children and Nature facilitates the transformation, but the state to which they are reverting is precivilised and even prelinguistic (they utter cries 'like complicated birdsong'). The narration also loses any semblance of being spoken by a twelve-year-old boy; the punctuation becomes sketchy and the short phrases more incantatory and iterative. The boys become 'less attached to names' and follow the road of evolution, as it were, back to the forking point where matter divides from life. At that distant crossroad, abiogenesis becomes a simple feat of imagination. Stephen leans forward and whispers into the clay man's ear: 'live, my creature. Move'. (189) And it does.

Creatureliness

Another fork in the road presents itself as the two boys respond differently to the animation of their monster: 'Stephen's transfigured. He's filled with dreadful joy. One hand points to Heaven, the other points down to our creature'. (191) This double gesture, pointing upwards and down, captures exactly the ambivalent nature of their Romantic transgression, whose consequences the boys have now to face. Davie flees from the scene in terror, re-enacting the cowardice of Victor Frankenstein. His sudden departure leaves Stephen free rein to act as he will, and Stephen immediately sets Clay on a golem-like mission in pursuit of their persecutor, Mouldy. With the help of Clay's looming presence, Stephen drives the bully to the edge of a cliff, and pushes him over to his death.

Stephen and Davie have gained the Promethean knowledge of how to create life, but as Davie soon learns, this knowledge comes twinned with another realisation. Not only are they divine creators capable of animating matter, they are also creatures dragged into life like Clay, through no conscious will of their own. Davie has been fighting off this growing awareness of being someone else's 'creature' since waking from a dream of being sculpted by Stephen: 'I felt Stephen's fingers on me, like he was forming me, like I was his clay. His fingers slid and slipped across me. I squirmed on the bed, trying to break free'. (76) But once he hears of Mouldy's death, he knows it is too late; he has outlawed himself from the community of Felling and has, in a sense, become what Stephen had meant him to be. His parents, whom Davie imagines dreaming him into life like the Red King in *Alice's Adventures in Wonderland*, can no longer have any idea who he is (268).[67] This sense of entrapment is confirmed when the two boys meet again, and Stephen tells him, 'the only one that understands you now is me'. (235) What Stephen has forced Davie to recognise in himself is that he is fully capable of evil. On the way to meeting Stephen, in a daze of fear, he had stoned a dog, thinking it was about to attack him; the episode is narrated in such an indistinct way that neither Davie nor the reader can be sure if the killing was done vindictively or in self-defence (171–72). Stephen taunts him with this episode later, and challenges Davie's image of himself as morally good: 'you that wanted Mouldy dead. You, that helped to make the thing that helped to kill Mouldy'. (265)

But Stephen, too, begins to see himself as trapped by forces beyond his control. Contrasting his mother with Davie's, he becomes bitterly aware of the sources of his creative rage; 'no way a lovely mam like yours had the makings of madness in her'. (227) Seeing himself through Davie's eyes, he comes to feel still more excluded and shunned: 'are you saying that *I* am the monster?' (218) And through his own savage treatment of Clay, he recognises the origins of his own demonic energy: 'mebbe this is how to make a proper monster, Davie. Drag him back and forward between life and death. Make him suffer, make him bliddy terrified . . . Then give him a job to do'. (257) Thus both boys identify with the creatureliness of Clay, although this self-knowledge compels them to act in diametrically opposing ways. This sense of doubled identity is, in fact, already implicit in the post-textual history of the Frankenstein legend, in which the name of Mary Shelley's creator 'Victor Frankenstein' so often gets transposed onto the monster itself. But by setting up resonances between several different pairs of characters—Clay and Mouldy, Davie and Clay, Mouldy and Stephen, Almond works free the categories of creator and creature to reveal the potential for each character to occupy both these roles at once.

At one level, the knowledge the boys gain is presented as extraordinary and supernatural, beyond reach of the reader's experience. But read naturalistically, these events can also be interpreted as almost prosaically universal. While the legend of Frankenstein raises a reader's expectations of horror and high drama, Almond defeats these expectations by concentrating narrowly on the wonder of Clay's animation, and the moral choice this presents to his two creators. Once brought to life, Clay does little to advance the plot, beyond stumbling uncomprehendingly after his two masters. To Stephen's great disappointment, he turns out to be incapable of murder, and it is Stephen himself who pushes Mouldy off the cliff. The knowledge that the boys gain of their twofold status as creators and creatures can also be interpreted prosaically. As adolescent creators of Clay, their identity faces in two directions, back to themselves as children, and forward to their possible futures as parents. But at one level, any reader could gain the same insight by studying the middle figure in a photograph of three generations. On the other hand, the boys' sense of temporality is superhuman and divine, because they have experienced all these temporal states in a single moment and event. The sense of identity they have gained corresponds to Augustine's notion of an idealised temporality, felt at every moment to possess a threefold awareness of past, present and future time. As creatures of other people's desires and dreams, and lordly creators of their own, the boys are linked into a chain of being, like the middle line of a *terza rima,* which both recalls the rhyme scheme of a previous stanza and anticipates the new rhyme to come.[68] In bringing their giant creature to life, they act out Wordsworth's famous line, 'the Child is the father of the Man'.[69]

Pedestrian Magic Realism

For Davie, this insight into his double status as creature and creator leads to an acceptance of his limitations as well as a sense of responsibility to the being he has created. When Clay turns up at the school gates, Davie goes down to meet him, an act of no small bravery, since at this point, he believes that Clay is responsible for killing Mouldy. Again defeating readerly expectations of a more dramatic turn of events, Davie simply takes Clay on a walk through the town. Having transgressed both divine and human law, Davie feels he has lost his place in the community of Felling. But now, guiding Clay through the town, he consciously rebuilds a sense of belonging, naming things into existence like a postlapsarian Adam. 'This is Felling,' he tells Clay. 'This is the town I come from. This is where I live'. (244) He names places and people, flooding the dialogue with realist detail: 'the baths is that way. Brian Phelps practises diving there. He's been in the Olympics. Over there's where we play football. We support Newcastle. They're not that good but they're the best'. (245) In the course of the walk, he reawakens his emotional ties to people and place, while accustoming himself to the idea that both he and his monster are alive, however unable to explain their origins: 'There's me. There's you. We're together in the world'. (247) If the detail is realist, as at the beginning of the novel, there is a greater sense of temporal and attitudinal distance on the part of the narrator here. Felling has become an 'imaginary homeland,' in Salman's Rushdie's sense of the term, as Davie walks and carefully selects a series of vivid, larger-than-life images and scenes to convey to Clay what the place means to him.[70]

In Almond's novel, then, the search for roots leads to a primal scene which is not, finally, about discovering an individual artistic or heroic self; it is rather about discovering a latent potential in humanity. Davie has a difficult choice to make, but he steps back from Stephen's Romantic solipsism by attempting to integrate Clay into a social world of his own conscious making. In terms of contemporary critical approaches to Romanticism, he might be said to have shifted from the masculine to the feminine type, the latter noted for its greater emphasis on socially constructed identity.[71]

Like Pullman, Almond develops Milton's concept of 'a paradise within thee happier far' in that the postlapsarian sense of place and identity is greater than the prelapsarian because it is consciously chosen (*Paradise Lost* 12.587). There is, however, no rejection of the magic level of reality that might correspond to Lyra's rejection of fantasy in *The Amber Spyglass*. Davie never leads us to disbelieve in the existence of Clay. Indeed, as his salvific walk through the town demonstrates, he needs the presence of this alien other in order to become the artist who can bring Felling and its inhabitants to life in narrative. As such an artist he consciously reaffirms the essentially socialist vision that had been disrupted by Stephen's arrival. But the vision is tempered by a knowledge of 'crazy' forces he can neither explain nor control, which exist not only outside Felling but also in himself.

Don Latham argues that children's magic realism ultimately aims to socialise its primary readers, but that it does so by teaching them first to question adult authority and challenge social norms.[72] In line with this general theory, Davie does conclude his adventures by becoming more closely integrated than ever into the Felling community. All the same, to argue that *Clay* simply socialises its readers would be, I think, to neutralise many of the disturbing and unresolved aspects of the novel. In the struggle between Davie's vision of the world and Stephen's, it is Stephen who proves the stronger. Davie treats Clay like a rational, sentient being, but he receives no look of recognition in return from Clay's eyes, 'sycamore-seed-shaped gaps . . . that nothing enters and nothing leaves'. (245) Despite his efforts, creator and creature fail to understand each other. Once he realises he cannot give Clay consciousness, he tries to put him back to sleep, an ambivalent act that could be interpreted as either selfish or compassionate. Interrupted by Stephen, Davie fails to achieve even this, and Clay escapes them both to perish alone. Stephen disappears from Felling, evading a police investigation, and leaving a trail of rumours about further acts of destruction in his wake.

And yet, however morally ambivalent it is, the 'craziness' that Stephen embodies becomes part of the reality that Davie accepts as true. Thus, by hybridising magic realism and Romanticism, Almond renders them both, in a sense, more 'grown up'. Magic realism's sometimes naïve faith in the irrational is severely tested in this novel, where the irrational takes the form of a demonic transgressor. And, on the other hand, Romanticism's celebration of the rebellious, Promethean hero is modified by a magic realist emphasis on community and the need for an ethical encounter with otherness. What John McClure writes of postmodern fiction's explorations of the spiritual could equally apply to the end of Almond's novel:

> there's a dream of social reconciliation, a healing of the breach that separates the children from the parents, the counter-culture from the mainstream . . . And redemption consists not in a program of escape and individual immortality, but in one of compassionate identification with a creaturely community that suffers, enjoys, and endures. ('Postmodern/Post-Secular')

In *Clay*, such redemption is far from certain, but there is, nevertheless, a conscious and determined faith placed in the ideal of a creaturely community. The basis of this faith is a recognition of the manifold nature of identity in time. Like Janus, the god of thresholds, we look backward to our births and forward to the life we can create in others.

Chapter Seven
Rereading Childhood Books:
C.S. Lewis's *The Silver Chair*

No study of millennial cross-reading would be complete without a consideration of adults rereading the books they once read as children. For as increasing numbers of adults engage with new children's fiction, they are also, not surprisingly, returning to their own childhood favourites. One indication of this trend is the reissue of children's 'classics' (the term is commonly used to denote children's fiction written up to the mid-1970s), and the publication of new editions, often with strikingly sophisticated dust jacket designs. Enid Blyton, George MacDonald, S.E. Hinton, Mary Norton and H. Rider Haggard are among the classic children's authors to have received the marketing makeover in recent years.[1] Alongside contemporary children's fiction, these newly vamped classics are actively marketed to potential adult readers, supported by major publicity campaigns as well as reviews in the national media, from print to television and radio. Like Rowling, Haddon and Pullman, the classics are sometimes reissued in dual editions, in order to entice a double readership of adults and children.[2]

Many of these books have, of course, never been out of print or fashion. Classic British fiction such as *Alice's Adventures in Wonderland*, *Peter Pan*, *The Wind in the Willows*, the Beatrix Potter books, Roald Dahl's stories, *The Lord of the Rings* and *The Chronicles of Narnia* are perennially resuscitated, whether in new issues, abridgements or adaptations into film or theatre. But even these familiar favourites have enjoyed a more than usually high profile in the decade spanning the new millennium. Major film adaptations by Peter Jackson and Andrew Adamson have boosted sales of Tolkien and Lewis respectively, although these authors were never much in need of the extra publicity.[3] The Beatrix Potter books have been a small industry unto themselves for many years, but once again, a feature film of the author's life, directed by Chris Noonan, has helped the industry expand still further.[4] Sales of Roald Dahl and

J.M. Barrie rose due to Tim Burton's screen adaptation of *Charlie and the Chocolate Factory* starring Johnny Depp as Willie Wonka, and Mark Forster's *Finding Neverland*, with Depp again playing the role of Barrie (although Spielberg's *Hook*, based on Barrie's *Peter Pan,* had already attracted a crossover audience more than ten years previously).[5] The City of Oxford now has an 'Alice Day' (7 July), when Carroll's works are celebrated with a wide range of activities for families all across the town and the surrounding countryside. There is a 'Roald Dahl Day' (13 September) in Great Missenden, Buckinghamshire, now home to the Roald Dahl Museum and Story Centre, which opened to the public in 2005.[6] In addition to film, television and radio adaptations, popular classic children's fiction can be expected to mutate into PlayStation games and Internet fan fiction.

What might be some of the reasons behind this upsurge of adult interest specifically in childhood books and remembered reading experiences? One contributory factor must be that children's literature publishing evolved from the marginal to the mainstream over the millennium decade. The change in dust jacket design is one obvious sign of this change in status of classic children's fiction. In 2001, HarperCollins reissued *The Chronicles of Narnia* in an edition aimed to include adult buyers. In line with other new children's fiction covers (the staring eyes featured on the cover of *Clay, The White Darkness* and others), the Collins dust jacket of *The Lion, the Witch and the Wardrobe* depicts the head of a lion gazing directly and challengingly at the potential buyer.[7] This bold, apparently 'age-neutral' design contrasts sharply with the original cover illustration by Pauline Baynes, in which Aslan dances on hind paws with a pair of girls, who are encircling him with a Hawaiian-sized garland of flowers. In 2005, Collins went a step further, issuing a box set which Amazon.com describes as 'a bold and striking contemporary new look, designed especially for adult readers!' featuring an even more menacing-looking lion's head and artwork from the Adamson *Narnia* films.[8]

The problem is, however, that Lewis's *Chronicles* are not in fact age-neutral; they are addressed primarily to children, and pointedly exclude most adult and older child characters from entering Narnia.[9] C.S. Lewis famously wrote, 'a children's story which is enjoyed only by children is a bad children's story' which I take to mean that good stories should reawaken childlike tastes in older readers.[10] Ideologically, too, the *Chronicles* are not modern or age-neutral. In *The Voyage of the Dawn Treader* and *The Silver Chair,* Lewis expresses his disgust for mixed-gender comprehensive schools, female heads, teetotallers and vegetarians. In *The Horse and His Boy,* most of the villains are Middle Eastern in appearance, and in most of the books, girls are excluded from participating in battle. His conservatism is not nearly as thoroughgoing as his detractors make out, but still it is hard to present Lewis as a crossover novelist in the same sense that the term is used of Philip Pullman, Mark Haddon or Meg Rosoff.

Rereading childhood books is a particular kind of cross-reading, where the part of the pleasure for the adult rereader lies in reliving the experience one had as a child-reader. In cross-reading of this kind, the paratextual material (cover, title page, blurbs, illustrations) should all ideally emphasise the text's childliness rather than the reverse; and in this case, what 'childliness' means is that the text should look as it did when the adult reader first encountered it as a child.[11] As Sue Batt, librarian of the Holborn Children's Library, comments, 'it is obvious when adults are borrowing a children's book from the library for themselves, because they will seek out a hardback edition in the format they remember from childhood, whereas an adult borrowing the same book for a child will tend to choose a paperback, picture book edition'.[12] Thus, alongside the more 'grown-up'-looking reissues of the *Chronicles* there are also deluxe box sets in hard cover for adult buyers, featuring all the original Baynes illustrations (and conspicuously not featuring any film tie-in material[13]).

One might suppose that adult nostalgia for their own childhood books would inhibit the expansion of recent children's fiction, of the kind considered in previous chapters. But in fact there seems to be little evidence to support that view; indeed, adults who retain an interest in their own childhood reading are often those who become interested in recently published children's fiction. Surveys suggest there is a lively cross-fertilisation of influence between children who opt for new fiction, and adults who gravitate towards classic children's literature. Thus, for example, Tesco found that among 2,600 readers, children tended to recommend that their parents read works by contemporary authors Haddon, Pullman, Rosoff, Rowling, Sachar, Lemony Snicket and Sue Townsend, while parents encouraged their children to try Enid Blyton, Lewis Carroll, Roald Dahl, C.S. Lewis, Mary Norton, Anna Sewell and Tolkien.[14] According to another 2003 survey by the BBC magazine *Parenting,* the children's book that most parents want to share with their children is Lewis's *The Lion, the Witch and the Wardrobe.*[15] One parent I spoke to declared that the opportunity to read her favourite books to her children was 'one of the major pay-offs of motherhood'.[16] In a list of the nation's one hundred best loved books, compiled from the results of the BBC's Big Read competition in 2003, classic and contemporary children's fiction jostle together for many of the top places.[17] *The Lord of the Rings, Winnie-the-Pooh, The Lion, the Witch and the Wardrobe* and *The Wind in the Willows* came first, eighth, ninth and sixteenth, respectively, while *His Dark Materials* and *Harry Potter and the Goblet of Fire* came third and fifth. Whether contemporary or classic, children's fiction ranked extremely high in the competition as a whole; amongst the top twenty novels, only two could be described as exclusively for adult readers (Louis de Bernières's *Captain Corelli's Mandolin* and Tolstoy's *War and Peace*: in that order!). The rest were either children's books, or novels read by both children and adults. While rereading the classics is a particular kind of cross-reading, it evidently developed over the millennial decade, hand in hand with the expansion of contemporary children's fiction into adult markets.

Because adult readers don't necessarily go out and buy new editions of the childhood favourites they are rereading, it is extremely difficult to get an accurate sense of the extent of this particular trend in millennial cross-reading. But that there was a general increase in public awareness of the activity of rereading is evident from the surge in re-editions, as well as frequent discussion in the national media, of classic children's fiction and the pleasures of rereading. The BBC *Big Read* TV programme provided a weekly venue for well-known public figures to discuss and debate the issue, from April to December 2003. But it was Francis Spufford's memoir, *The Child That Books Built. A Memoir of Childhood and Reading,* which captured the *zeitgeist* most convincingly.[18] In rereading 'the sequence of books that carried me from babyhood to the age of nineteen', Spufford traces his true, though invisible autobiography, since 'the stories that mean most to us join the process by which we come to be securely our own'. (21, 9) As Primo Levi's personal anthology, *The Search for Roots,* demonstrated even more eloquently than Spufford's memoir, we are what we've read.[19] But unlike Levi, Spufford specifically revisits the reading of his childhood because it is during this period, he feels, that fiction exerted its most potent influence, fusing 'with the accelerated coming-to-be we do in childhood'. (9) In returning to these books, then, adult readers can recover something of that magically potent relationship they once had with books and reading.

Rereading in Context and Theory

Spufford's insight would no doubt ring true for readers of many different historical eras. But why did adults become preoccupied with self-reflective reading over the millennial decade in particular? Many have pointed to the growing pace of contemporary life; less time to read meant that adults may have become increasingly reluctant to engage with more dense and abstruse (adult) fiction. Responding to a comment that Dan Brown featured on the cover of *Time* instead of *Portnoy's Complaint,* Philip Roth remarked that readers' 'habit of concentration has shifted away'.[20] In part, it seems to have shifted to children's literature; there is certainly no evidence of a lack of concentration amongst the dedicated readers of Harry Potter and *His Dark Materials.* Looking back to classic children's fiction might be one aspect of the nostalgia industry, which over the millennial decade repackaged and marketed the past in ever more ingenious and consumer-friendly ways. Macrocosmic explanations for the rise of this industry have been touched upon in previous chapters. Postmodern rootlessness paradoxically has produced a desire for historical depth and a sense of personal rootedness. Sometimes what resulted were kitsch and deracinated forms of history, as was arguably the case with *Lawrence Pollard's*

National Treasures, a series of programmes on BBC Radio 4, in which participants argued for the relative merits of an arbitrarily selected pair of 'national treasures': the Thames estuary versus Stonehenge, *Cutty Sark* versus the British Film Institute, and so on.[21] But there were also many other examples of genuine engagement with personal and national histories, and with histories of childhood and children's literature in particular. For example, the Museum of Childhood at the V&A was newly expanded in 2003. Seven Stories, the Centre for Children's Books, was opened in Newcastle-upon-Tyne in 2005, offering visitors 'a treasure trove of original artwork and manuscripts'. An exhibition at the Dulwich Picture Gallery in London explored 'The Changing Face of Childhood' in 2007. So the millennial trend of republishing childhood classics might be situated alongside these exhibitions and new institutions, as part of a broad spectrum of activities designed to preserve and celebrate the treasures of the past (and indeed, in some cases, to preserve the past *as* treasure: precious, in every sense, semi-sacred, and sealed off from the present). As Clifford Geertz argues in *Available Light,* late twentieth-century political and economic globalisation produced 'a sense of dispersion' and of 'uncenteredness'.[22] 'Left with the pieces', we are looking for ways to bind these dispersions, and looking back to childhood can be a way of recovering a sense of centre.

Again at a global level, unstable ecological and political climates may have contributed to readers' desires to seek solace, or a renewed sense of personal values, from familiar childhood reading. On the anxieties produced by terrorism, for example, the American novelist Alice Hoffman commented, 'I felt . . . there was no point in writing [after 9/11]. I mean, what difference would it make to this world? And what I did was . . . I went back to read some of the books I had loved as a child, to see if they still mattered. [Ray Bradbury's *Fahrenheit 451*] made me remember how important fiction can be'.[23]

Nor was this return to childhood reading necessarily a private search for value. For Susan Sontag, the fortuitous connections between her own and a colleague's childhood reading led to a strengthened sense of a community of readers, 'literature was the passport to enter a larger life'.[24] She recalled growing up in southern Arizona and as a ten-year-old Jewish girl in 1943, burying herself in German books while at the same time fearing an invasion of Nazi soldiers. Much later she discovered that Fritz Arnold, a New York publisher, had been a German prisoner of war at a camp in northern Arizona also in 1943, and he had passed his time avidly reading American literature. As an adult, Sontag found a particular resonance in these two chiastically matching histories of childhood reading. Taken together, they illustrate how reading can connote freedom: the freedom to rise above political enmity, and the freedom to escape the circumstances of one's birth.

Or indeed, to escape *to* the circumstances of one's birth. Childhood books can also function as Portkeys (as Rowling would say) to transport the reader back in time. Adults seek out the precise edition they read as children so that the look and feel of the book will, like a *petite madeleine,* conjure up a rush of buried memories and sensory impressions.[25] In my Crossover Literature seminars at Sheffield University, students recall a whole network of associations connected with a book read in childhood. It is not just the book they rediscover, but this whole segment of lost time. Thus Clare Webber recalls how easily her reading spilled out into other forms of play:

> I had not read *The Lion, the Witch and the Wardrobe* since I was very young but from the moment that I started to re-read it, I was reminded of the way in which my sister and I used to make up fantasy games involving being transported to Narnia.[26]

And for Joanna Ecclestone, the same text is a Portkey leading to rich memories of childhood events, voices and identifications:

> Re-reading *The Lion, the Witch and the Wardrobe* brought back a lot of childhood memories, in particular of my Father reading it to me. I was also in a musical version of the play when I was twelve so re-reading the book awoke memories of this . . . I felt a particular allegiance with Lucy, on re-reading the text as this was the character I played and also because I am the youngest child.

In his early essay 'On Reading', Proust begins by remembering how voraciously he had read as a child, to the exclusion of all other, more material interests. Ironically, those same books re-encountered as an adult would bring vividly to mind not so much the books' contents, as the material circumstances in which they were read: childhood reading 'leaves in us above all . . . the image of the places and the days when we did this reading'.[27] And this can only happen with recollected texts which straddle two or more time frames. Proust's *La Recherche*, according to Elisabeth Ladenson, not only recalls lost time; it is also structured as a lost text that can only be recovered by rereading. The novel 'paradoxically depends on the partial incomprehensibility of any first reading', revealing its integrity only when reread.[28]

If not as vividly as Proust, most of us can summon up positive memories of childhood reading, so one might expect the recent revival of classic children's fiction would be universally welcomed. Yet the resurgence of adult interest in these books has been stringently criticised, on two opposing fronts. Some critics fear the overcommercialisation of classic children's fiction, while others have criticised its sanctification. According to the first group, the aggressive marketing of children's classics is an instance of the way our memories and remembered dreams are being exploited for their commercial value and sold back to us as consumable goods. Jack Zipes has written extensively about how thoroughly fairy tales have been commodified in contemporary western culture. As he rightly argues, 'the fairy-tale film has become the most popular cultural commodity in America, if not the world'.[29] Not all modern adaptations and retellings of fairy tales conform to the rules of the culture industry, of course. But whether resisting or conforming, fairy tales indeed provide us with a discourse in which 'we carry on struggles over family, sexuality, gender roles, rituals, values, and socio-political power'. (9) Like fairy tales, classic children's novels are embedded in the collective cultural consciousness, so they are as readily exploited and commodified. Adamson's film introduces us, not to Narnia, but to 'belovèd Narnia', in other words, to an idea that has already become a cultural myth. Even before we see its slow-paced prose translated to an action-packed visual adventure narrative, Narnia has already become a 'stolen and frozen cultural good', as Zipes (following Barthes) describes the commodified fairy tale.[30]

Narnia, an imaginary kingdom of Talking Beasts ruled over by a magnificent lion, stands for many readers as a synecdoche for childhood freedom and imagination, for the possibility of metamorphosis, for suffering and ultimately, for joy and triumph. When asked to reflect on what 'Narnia' meant to them, two of my students responded:

> If Narnia is to conjure any particular idea or image to me it must be that of freedom. Narnia often acts as an escape for the children that visit it. Narnia is also like a blank canvas, or a fresh start for characters such as Edmund or Eustace, and this too is in its own way liberating . . . Aslan comes and goes as he pleases . . . and this freedom is something which is integral to Narnia . . . The children often enter Narnia for the purpose of helping someone else achieve their rightful freedom. (Rebecca Shackleton)

> To me, Narnia represents the freedom and innocence that is often lost after childhood. Lucy's chance discovery of Narnia shows how her open-mindedness allows her to enter another world . . . Narnia is the idea of freedom and a method of escaping the real world. It seems that you can only use this escape route and access the freedom that it offers if you have not yet become too caught up in the real world. (Elizabeth Cameron)

As Elizabeth Cameron's comment suggests, Narnia is also the myth of recollected childhood as the time-space in which such freedom exists, with its promise of magic transformation. As a myth, it is powerfully appealing.

It is also a wonderfully easy concept to sell. On Walden Media's website of the film of *The Lion, the Witch and the Wardrobe*, the viewer who clicked on the 'Games' icon was flash-greeted with three slogans: 'Combine Forces', 'Defeat Evil', and 'Free Narnia!' which impressively delivered the action of all seven Chronicles in under seven words.[31] Some viewers might have been alarmed by the same Web site's profile of 'the ultimate Narnia fan', who was living (with her four children: two boys, two girls) in a house with a replica of the lamppost on her lawn and the *trompe-l'oeil* of a wardrobe framing her front door.[32] Others might have found her account of costume parties, with Narnia-themed buffet food, a lighthearted celebration of Lewis's creation. It all depends on whether you see kitsch as fun or frightening. For the fearful, the danger is that classic children's books may be retold and resold so many times, in so many different versions, that they may, like the god Dionysus, end up being plundered and ripped apart and submerged in a lethal sea of adoring fans.

The Walden Media film of *The Lion, the Witch and the Wardrobe* in fact aimed to be as faithful as possible to the text, which could invite criticism from the opposing point of view, that Lewis's novels are idolised as sacred texts. Cary Granat, head of Walden Media, declared 'the truer we are to the written word the better the film will be'.[33] And the director Andrew Adamson added humbly, 'I share Walden's excitement in giving those fans an epic theatrical experience worthy of their imaginations and driving new generations toward the work of C.S. Lewis'.[34] But in transforming the Chronicles into an 'epic theatrical experience', Adamson was bound to introduce profound changes to the tone of the original text, however faithful he was to the visual detail (a bluebottle buzzing at the window in the spare room, for example).

C.S. Lewis once criticised a film adaptation of *King Solomon's Mines* for altering the tone and pace of the text, in much the way the Adamson film changes Lewis's novel.[35] Lewis objected to the scene in which Haggard's heroes are immured underground; to heighten the terror, the film director added a subterraneous volcanic eruption and an earthquake. Lewis commented scathingly, 'no doubt if sheer excitement is all you want from a story, and if increase of dangers increases excitement, then a rapidly changing series of two risks (that of being burned alive and that of being crushed to bits) would be better than the single prolonged danger of starving to death in a cave'. ('On Stories', 5) But for him, the specificity of the novel's atmosphere had been lost: 'the whole sense of the deathly (quite a different thing from simple danger of death)—the cold, the silence, and the surrounding faces of the ancient, the crowned and sceptred, dead . . . The one lays a hushing spell on the imagination; the other excites a rapid flutter of the nerves'. (6)

In Adamson's film, our nerves are similarly excited by an added scene in which the three Pevensies and Mr and Mrs Beaver are being pursued by the White Witch's wolves (in the novel, the wolves never come within sighting distance). The fugitives narrowly escape the snapping jaws of the wolves by hurling themselves into white water rapids and scrabbling onto huge slabs of ice that are hurtling down the half-thawed river. The scene recalls a very similar one (also not in the original text) in Jackson's rendition of the Fellowship escaping across a river into Lothlórien. But this kind of dramatic action is more integral to the tone of Tolkien's epic trilogy than the Chronicles, which, after all, Lewis classed as fairy tales.[36] For readers who can remember the hushing spell laid on their imaginations by Lewis's writing, there may be a sense of regret that a new generation may only come to the books via this experience of a hyped-up, action-packed narrative.

Still, if it were not for the film, many younger readers might not come to the books at all. And in some respects, Adamson's film constitutes a thoughtful and moving rereading of the Chronicles. If there are critics who resist such reinventions of classic children's literature, there are others who argue that we are far too protective, that we seal them in amber, in an effort to memorialise our own pasts. Savouring memories of 'innocent' reading-as-discovery, we ignore the ideologically questionable content of some of these books, clinging with particular fondness to images of hazy English summers spent rambling in large country houses or neighbouring streams and woodlands. With no sense of awareness of the millions of readers for whom these images must be sheer fantasy, we thus perpetuate archaic notions of Englishness that can only worsen the social and cultural divisions that exist in Britain today.

Philip Pullman's scathing critique of the Narnia myth is an instance of this approach. In an article in *The Guardian,* he denounced the Narnian Chronicles as 'one of the most ugly and poisonous things I've ever read'.[37] According to Pullman, the whole cycle is permeated with misogyny, racism, and a 'sado-masochistic relish for violence'. He describes the scene at the end of *The Last Battle,* when Aslan reveals to the children that in their own world, they have been killed in a railway accident, as 'one of the most vile moments in the whole of children's literature'. To 'slaughter' all your characters, 'and then claim they're better off, is not honest storytelling: it's propaganda in the service of a life-hating ideology'. But this argument is puzzling, because in Lewis's fiction, the children always long to *stay* in Narnia, and the railway accident allows them to stay for ever. It can hardly have the impact of a mass death scene on a reader (child or adult) since we only know the children from their adventures in Narnia; it is in the realistic world of England that they are shadowy and unreal to us. And Pullman himself comes close to celebrating a mass death scene in *The Amber Spyglass,* when all the souls of the dead evaporate into thin air (382). The ideology is different, of course, but one cannot blame an author for trying to find narrative consolations for death.

Pullman goes on to claim that for Lewis, 'death is better than life; boys are better than girls; light-coloured people are better than dark-coloured people', which is accurate up to a point, but also overstated. Death, or rather the after-life, is only better than life in *The Last Battle,* which in my view is the weakest book and atypical of the series. Even there, the Calormene Emeth is saved despite being a follower of Tash rather than Aslan, a rather pointed reminder from Lewis that neither race nor religious creed can exclude the truly righteous from Heaven. As for Lewis's supposed misogyny, it is worth pointing out that many of the Chronicles are focalised through girl characters. Lucy is idealised from the start, but Polly, Aravis and Jill are all complex characters who mature over the course of their adventures; by the end of the series, Lucy, Aravis and Polly have all developed into adult women. Pullman draws our attention to the 'notorious' exclusion of Susan from Paradise on the grounds that, as Lewis has Jill say, 'she's interested in nothing nowadays except nylons and lipstick and invitations. She always was a jolly sight too keen on being grown-up'. (154) For Pullman, this exclusion shows how Lewis is 'frightened and appalled at the notion of wanting to grow up', and of girls wanting to grow up in particular. But it would be more accurate to say that Lewis was appalled by modern forms of adolescence, rather than female sexuality *per se*. Polly, now an adult in *The Last Battle,* adds to Jill's criticism of Susan: 'grown up, indeed. I wish she *would* grow up . . . Her whole idea is to race on to the silliest time of one life as quick as she can and then stop there as long as she can'. (154–55). It is the arrest of development that Lewis is really objecting to, rather than 'being grown up'. As for seductive adult temptresses, of the kind Pullman portrays in Mrs Coulter, C.S. Lewis of course has plenty of those. And even if they are not redeemed by a sudden surge of maternal instinct as Mrs Coulter is, they are still vivid, engaging characters who tend to steal the show whenever they appear in the narrative (Queen Jadis/the White Witch and the Lady of the Green Kirtle are instances of these). But what seems to draw Pullman's ire, in particular, is that Lewis's Narnia books are not so much read and admired as adored and pored over like sacred texts, while their author is revered as a saint.[38] One has to assume that Lewis's Christian apologetics was a major irritant for Pullman, and a source of his ire. But on such issues, writers (and readers) are rarely unbiased.

On the larger question of whether or how one 'should' reread childhood books, received opinion would have us choose between the pedestal and the pit. On the one hand, children's classics like *The Chronicles of Narnia* are in danger of being overcommodified and reduced to junk, and on the other, they are overly worshipped and idolised. But it is possible to feel intensely about one's childhood books without elevating them to the status of Scripture. And it seems to me necessary for any critical evaluation to begin by recognising that adult readers do have a different kind of relationship with their childhood texts. A critique like Pullman's will never convince a Narnia fan, because the text he is criticising is, in a sense, not the same text that the fan is defending. *That* text is somewhere else entirely, half-bound up with memories of another set of circumstances, other places, other voices, another sense of self. Ideologically objectionable elements simply might not feature in this other text as it is summoned up from a past reading experience. Amongst other critics, Knoepflmacher has pointed out that 'the emotional configurations of our childhood affect the nature of our engagement with child-texts', while André Green asserts that 'we can only read a book, in the sense of engaging in an interpretive conversation with it, if something has already happened between the text and the analyst'.[39] Rather than ignoring the 'something that has already happened' between the childhood book and the adult reader, we should take this as the starting point of the investigation into why and how adults reread classic children's literature.

Rereading of this kind is dialogic, not only in the sense that it is often shared with another reader, often a child, but also in that the rereader's response to the text is always split between a former and a present reading.[40] This can lead to an increased consciousness of oneself as a reader, as well as of the text's narrative structures and rhetorical devices. In my Crossover Literature seminars, when students are asked to record their second impressions of reading a childhood book, their comments often describe a doubled experience, a heightened consciousness both of the text, and of the reading process, though this then can lead to a whole spectrum of reactions from a sense of continuity with the past to a sense of radical disjunction. Here, Laura Baker describes her sharpened critical appreciation of the text, while she finds she can be as 'enchanted' by it as she was previously:

> I found that [*The Lion, the Witch and the Wardrobe*] conjured up the same innocence and sense of adventure that it did for me as a child. I love the slow and delicate pace of the book, as well as the old-fashioned diction ... After studying literary criticism I can see the devices that Lewis uses, such as repetition and metaphor, which I would not have picked up on as a child. So I can now more easily explain exactly why I like it! The adventure is still as exciting and enchanted for me now as an adult, as it was for me then as a child.

By contrast, in the next example, Abi Dean is implicitly correcting her earlier reading, and expressing a sense of disjunction between former and present reading selves:

> When I was younger [*The Voyage of the Dawn Treader*] was my favourite book but I hadn't read it for about nine years ... I found myself questioning the authorial voice more than I did as a child. There were certain things that I wasn't entirely comfortable with, such as the suggestion that faith will always save you. There was also an obvious social hierarchy present and the connection of Edmund, Lucy and Caspian to Aslan suggested that the royalty of Narnia had been invested with an almost divine right to rule ... There is also a striking contrast between Edmund and Lucy as 'good' children and Eustace as a 'bad' child, which I found somewhat simplistic. Eustace only becomes 'good' once he has abandoned the things that were once important to him.

Like many other readers of the Narnian Chronicles, Abi Dean found the religious allegory more obvious as an adult reader, and for her, this detracted from the richness and 'innocence' of her childhood reading. But in the following response, Angela Boctor describes how her appreciation of the Chronicles has deepened because of their very religiosity:

I find that on rereading *The Magician's Nephew*, I no longer believe as I used to that perhaps a world like Narnia could exist (I remember my continual disappointment on discovering the back of my wardrobe would not take me into another world) ... I've become like one of the grown-ups 'always thinking of uninteresting explanations' and I dislike the cynicism I now have. However, Narnia holds a new kind of magic for me that I was not so consciously aware of when I was young and that is, my appreciation of the character of Aslan. He powerfully conveys to me the majesty and gentleness of God in a way I cannot remember feeling before. I am more aware of the allegorical aspects of the novel and the Christian metaphors for good and evil. I am more struck with what is real about Narnia than what is imaginary. Aslan's singing creation into being reignites my awe and wonder at the world around, a sense of the idea Lewis so strongly advocated, that life itself is extraordinary.

Angela Boctor's account of her shifting understanding of magic, Narnia and the Real would probably have pleased the Christian Platonist in C.S Lewis very much. And even though the child's and the adult's ways of reading are very different for this reader, both are valued for their different strengths. Arguably, too, the text can only exert its luminous power on the present reader, because of a particularly intense encounter the child had experienced in the past. Rereading can therefore make us aware of our mental horizons, the architecture of the inner self, and it can reveal exactly where and how this architecture took shape. Thus for Francis Spufford, the sequence of books he read as a child constitutes his inward autobiography,

> for the words we take into ourselves help to shape us. They help form the questions we think are worth asking; they shift around the boundaries of the sayable inside us, and the related borders of what's acceptable; their potent images, calling on more in us than the responses we will ourselves to have, dart new bridges into being between our conscious and unconscious minds, between what we know we know, and the knowledge we cannot examine by thinking. They build and stretch and build again the chambers of our imagination. (*The Child*, 21–22)

Of course, rereading need not always provide fresh insights into the 'boundaries of the sayable' inside us. David Galef describes rereading as a 'gain-loss phenomenon'. While we tend to see more of the text's themes, images, rhetorical devices, historical and literary contexts, there may also be 'a loss of spontaneity, a series of distortions' as 'suspense disappears' and 'characters become unmoored from their surroundings'.[41] As Lewis argues, however, it could be viewed as one of the distinctively positive features of reread books that their various elements (character, plot, mood) can drift out of context and find new life in the reader's imagination.

Rereading can stimulate us into better, sharper, more interesting responses to the text, the world, and ourselves, but it is of course up to the individual reader whether he or she *wants* to reread for this kind of stimulus. This leads me to a third commonly voiced criticism of rereading children's classics, which is that adults rereading these texts are generally assumed to be reading lazily and self-indulgently, looking for comfort and security, and deliberately shutting out the unknown and the unsafe. Reading for security is deemed by some critics to be a form of dumbing down more drastic, even, than reading contemporary children's literature because here adults are opting for known comforts rather than new material. For example, in *Lost in a Book*, Victor Nell has argued that 'rereading old favourites renders the formulaic even safer' and that rereaders are people who 'have especially high needs for this kind of security'. (250) Such rereading echoes the repetitious pattern of children's play, and indicates a need to make safe one's immediate environment. As Freud observed, 'in their play children repeat everything that has made a great impression on them in real life, and . . . in doing so they . . . make themselves master of the situation'. (16–17)[42] According to Freud, child readers often insist on sameness and continuity: 'if a child has been told a nice story, he will insist on hearing it over and over again . . . and he will remorselessly stipulate that the repetition shall be an identical one . . . Each fresh repetition seems to strengthen the mastery they are in search of'.[43] Karen Odden notes how adults describe their favourite books using a particular language relating to infant experience; we speak of 'devouring, curling up with, coming home to' these texts. Such language is 'rooted deep in our past' and 'reflect[s] our earliest experiences of comfort, nurturing, and security: oral satisfaction, the experience of being held, a secure space to which we long to return'.[44] Adult rereaders also often recall themselves as child-readers, having consumed books with this form of intensity. Thus Francis Spufford muses, 'I want to know why I read as a child with such a frantic appetite, why I sucked the words off the page with such an edge of desperation'. (*The Child,* 10)

To those for whom such rereading constitutes a 'dumbing down', one might respond that there is surely nothing inherently wrong with reading for comfort. As Galef says, 'in a world of uncertainty, here is something that will not disappoint. If particular books are old friends, rereading allows a communion of sorts' (*Second Thoughts,* 26). Moreover, I doubt whether reading for these therapeutic benefits can be neatly distinguished from a properly aesthetic, 'adult' response to a book. Victor Nell divides rereaders into two types: Type As, who read to dull their consciousness of the world, and Type Bs, who read to heighten consciousness. He is in no doubt about which of these types is superior: 'Type A readers . . . select highly formulaic material, which best meets their needs for safety and predictability but which, in critical terms, is as near to the bottom of the literary heap as prose can get'.[45] In *Becoming a Reader,* J.A. Appleyard cites Nell's two categories, and makes a further distinction in the different ways that adults read (he is no longer discussing rereading, specifically).[46] Based on surveys and interviews with adults from many walks of life, Appleyard identifies three general motives for reading, or uses that adults make of fiction. Adults read first, to escape from the intractable problems of everyday life, second, to enlarge their consciousness of the world, and third, to discover images that have power and meaning for their lives. (*Becoming a Reader,* 14–15)

In line with these distinctions, the activity of rereading has a curiously ambivalent reputation. Rereading popular, formulaic or children's literature is considered escapist entertainment and 'near to the bottom of the literary heap', while rereading classic *adult* literature is a sign of seriousness and professionalism. Vladimir Nabokov begins his *Lectures on Literature* by declaring 'a good reader, a major reader, an active and creative reader is a re-reader', and it seems quite clear that the rereaders he has in mind are all Type Bs.[47] In his study entitled *Rereading*, Calinescu assumes that rereading is always an exercise in deepening one's understanding of a complex and demanding text, and acquiring wisdom through it; needless to say, the texts he uses to illustrate his argument are all classic novels for adult readers.[48] Tamburri's 'retro-lector', celebrated in his study *The Semiotics of Re-reading,* is also an ideal, Type B reader, always challenging his or her limits, becoming enriched by successively more complex rereadings.[49] When Calvino addresses himself to the question, *Why Read the Classics?* he winds up defending the practice of rereading, since a 'classic' is by definition a work with which one is, or pretends to be, already familiar.[50] But even though elsewhere Calvino praises the rereadability of fairy tales, here he makes no mention of rereading 'to escape', 'to master one's insecurities' or 'to be entertained'.

While Appleyard is much less condescending to readers in the 'escapist' category than Victor Nell, his distinctions are still difficult to maintain in practice. Where would one place Tolkien, for example, when he describes the useful escapism offered by the fairy tale: 'Escape is evidently as a rule very practical, and may even be heroic . . . Why should a man be scorned if, finding himself in prison, he tries to get out and go home? Or if, when he cannot do so, he thinks and talks about other topics than jailers and prison-walls?'[51] By this definition, a fairy tale can provide a prisoner (or anyone trapped in negative circumstances) with a temporary 'escape from intractable problems' by projecting images of a better world somewhere else, but these images can 'have power and meaning' for him as they give him the strength to resist his present circumstances; the fairy tale may also 'enlarge his consciousness of the world' in that it may sharpen his sense of dissatisfaction with those present circumstances. Del Toro's film, *Pan's Labyrinth,* subtitled 'a fairy tale for adults', shows how adults can deploy children's fairy tales in the resistance to political tyranny. As Del Toro's Ofelia demonstrates, our motives for escaping into literature may be utopian or, as Tolkien suggests, they 'may even be heroic'.

But even supposing that adults sometimes escape into familiar books for much less heroic reasons than Tolkien had in mind, classic studies such as Q.D. Leavis's *Fiction and the Reading Public* show that 'escapism' can be a serious business for the adult reader.[52] Appleyard concludes from his interviews with adult readers of genre fiction that they are 'escaping from . . . the boredom and frustration that accompany the intractable problems of everyday adult life—or, we might say, by precisely the challenges . . . [of] middle age'. (165) Reading such fiction provides an escape not only from the intractable problems themselves, 'but also from the problematic treatment of problems [i.e., from] the kind of fiction that, with its complicated narrative methodology, ironic perspective, and lack of clear resolution, makes the problems it deals with seem as intractable as those of readers' own real lives'. (165) Such fiction offers the psychological rewards of romance, and one might add, the fairy tale: 'it appears to confront intractable problems of good and evil, reduces them to manageable shapes, and provides the assurance of a happy ending. It offers the image of a central character who can ultimately control threatening circumstances and achieve a glorious destiny'. (167) A little over twenty years ago, Appleyard could assert, in a confident aside, that adults would turn to genre fiction to meet these needs, since 'adults do not after all turn to juvenile and adolescent fiction for escape'. (166) But now self-evidently, they are doing so. The shift to cross-reading can thus partly be explained as an acceptance of the continuities that have always existed between child and adult readers, in terms of their most deep-rooted psychological needs for security and reassurance.

In a psychoanalytic study, Karen Odden argues that adults are re-enacting any of six childhood psychic dramas when they read series fiction. These unfinished 'dramas' are: learning to trust the world as safe; symbiotic bonding through identification; controlling separation anxiety; shifting from egocentricity to acknowledging the world; mastering object relations (understanding that good and bad are mixed together); and managing anxiety.[53] What is particularly interesting about this approach is that it represents the search for comfort and security as a process that must be acted out and may never be satisfactorily concluded. One may never overcome the anxiety of finishing a book, which has a deathlike finality, as Peter Brooks has shown.[54] And so to mask the anxiety, one picks up another book, or the same one. In other words, even if we are rereading to create a sense of comfort and security, we also may be continually falling short of the desired psychic goal.

Such a need to re-enact childhood dramas thus can merge seamlessly into 'Type B' reading: rereading to 'increase consciousness'. Rereading critically gives one the comforting sense of being in control and in the right, as well as enriching one's understanding of textual complexities, as is evident from Wolfgang Iser's description of the process: 'on a second reading, familiar occurrences now tend to appear in a new light and seem to be at times corrected, at times enriched'.[55] Marianne Hirsch characterises first time readers as rather childlike in their dependency on authorial direction, while second time readers are more mature in their control of the reading experience: 're-reading gives the reader a holistic view and a control of the text which is not possible in a first reading during which the reader trustingly and somewhat blindly follows the author's lead'.[56] But this is not far from Freud's description of the child's game of *fort-da,* in which the child plays out the mother's departure from the room with his own toys, so that he can acquire a sense of control over her leaving.[57]

What is more, if rereading is like child's play, this need not imply that the playful rereader is unsophisticated or 'dumbed down'. In *S/Z,* Barthes characterises rereading as an anti-establishment, anticonsumerist activity, 'which is tolerated only in certain marginal categories of readers (children, old people, and professors)'.[58] In contrast to the 'the commercial and ideological habits of our society, which would have us 'throw away' the story once it has been consumed ('devoured'), so that we can then move on to another story, buy another book', rereaders play with texts rather than consume them; multiple readings discover 'not the real text, but a plural text: the same and new'. (*ibid.*) Furthermore, Barthes argues that rereading 'saves the text from repetition (those who fail to reread are obliged to read the same story everywhere), multiplies it in its variety and its plurality: rereading draws the text out of its internal chronology ('this happens before or after that') and recaptures a mythic time (without before or after)', an argument advanced by Lewis himself. Deborah Thacker also takes issue with Victor Nell's assumption that 'ludic reading', 'reading as a form of play' is based on need for security in child readers. She rightly objects that 're-reading can also be conceived of as an exercise in re-writing, or taking possession of a text in an active and open way'.[59] To Barthes's notion of the text as a space for play ('that play which is the return of the different' *S/Z,* 16), Thacker adds that children's rereading may also 'proceed from this notion of re-enacting the play of desire'.

So rather than polarising rereading into two opposing types (the type that 'dulls' consciousness as opposed to the one that 'heightens' it), I would argue that there is a continuum of experience linking the rereading of popular literature, children's literature, and adult, literary fiction. Likewise there is an overlap between children's and adults' motives for rereading; both may be looking for comfort and secure boundaries, as well as willing to challenge those boundaries. The most persuasive point that Appleyard makes in *Becoming a Reader* is that adults in the final phase of their development as readers characteristically read syncretically. That is, they incorporate all the characteristics of the previous phases. They read as children (repetitively, for security and mastery—according to his argument), as adolescents (looking for role models, or measures to 'judge the truth of experience'), as 'professional' readers (analysing the text for its aesthetic value), and as pragmatists ('comforting oneself with images of wisdom', 16–17). I would question the assumption of a unilinear development from phases one to five, but the concept of a pragmatic, syncretic reader (of any age) is a valid and useful one.

I would further argue that rereading intensifies this syncretism. Rereading childhood texts, we activate more of these 'phases' or types of reading at once than we would with other reading material. We saw an example of this above in Laura Baker's rereading of *The Lion, the Witch and the Wardrobe* ('I can see the devices that Lewis uses' and 'the adventure is still as exciting and enchanted for me now').

In rereading, our different temporal selves become synchronous for a while; the young and the old reader come together in the same room, so to speak. That composite identity can seem as though it is temporarily standing outside time, like the poet who looks through the Aleph in Borges's story of that name.[60] And the book itself goes through a similar metamorphosis when it is reread. As Galef, citing Barthes, puts it, 'the diachronic nature of the plot assumes a synchronicity, a conflation of events in the reader's mind'. Not only can the plot assume synchronicity, but characters can work free of their narrative circumstances, assuming forms and meanings that appear timeless. In 'On Stories', C.S. Lewis argues that 'in life and art . . . we are always trying to catch in our net of successive moments something that is not successive'. (20–21) For Lewis, the plot of a narrative acts as a net to catch 'what is not really a process at all'. (20) There is, of course, a strong vein of religious thinking in Lewis's concept of transcending time through narrative (just as there is in Paul Ricoeur's epic work on this topic[61]). The sense of synchronicity produced by rereading in particular is as Galef points out, 'as much an artistic stasis as a desired sempiternal aevum in religion'. (20)[62] Both Paradise and the reread text promise to free the reader 'from the suspense of unanticipated events, in a sense from chronology itself'. (*ibid.*) It is thus not surprising that C.S. Lewis was a great defender of rereading: 'not till the curiosity, the sheer narrative lust, has been given its sop and laid asleep, are we at leisure to savour the real beauties'. Only once you are free 'from the shock of actual surprise' can you attend to the text's 'intrinsic surprisingness'. This is how a plot might be read by someone who has stepped outside Plato's cave, who is able to grasp its '*quality* of unexpectedness', without needing to have their nerves fluttered by actually being surprised. ('On Stories,' 17) For Lewis, too, children's rereading demonstrates their instinctive neo-Platonic wisdom, their ability to step outside the cave of diachronicity.[63]

Except that we never do step entirely outside time while reading. Not only does the text seem different every time you read it, but you as a reader are different. And as you change, your perception of the characters, events, and the entire atmosphere and mood of the text will be subject to change as well. But the composite temporal perspective that rereading produces seems to me in any case much more appealing than the idea of being able to transcend time altogether. Wolfgang Iser describes these shifting temporal perspectives in this way: 'during the process of reading, there is an active interweaving of anticipation and retrospection, which on a second reading may turn into a kind of advance retrospection'.[64] Advance retrospection can feel like synchronicity, but its more complex texture weaves together the human experience of temporality: looking back, anticipation, being surprised, recognising the familiar, and so on. Moreover, once we come to know a text very well, once it has become thoroughly internalised, we then begin to alter and misremember it, until gradually it assumes a new shape, a virtually independent life, in our minds.[65] So even those elements of the text that have broken free of particular narrative circumstances never cease to change.

But there is another sense in which the experience of rereading fiction is open-ended, and that is, that fiction rarely provides us with answers or portable wisdoms. This is the central idea of Proust's 'On Reading', where he takes issue with Ruskin's idea that reading is 'a conversation with men much wiser and more interesting than those around us'. (112) But, replies Proust, reading is never as utilitarian as this, even if we might sometimes long for it to be. Taking childhood reading as the example that best illustrates his point (113), Proust remembers finding two or three beautiful sentences in Théophile Gautier's *Le Capitaine Fracasse*. These phrases provoked him to wish that Gautier 'could tell me exactly what I was to think of Shakespeare, Saintine, Sophocles', but of these things beyond *Le Captaine,* Gautier could tell him nothing. Thus, Proust concludes, it is one of the 'great and marvelous features of beautiful books' that 'our wisdom begins where that of the author ends' and although 'we would like to have him give us answers, . . . all he can do is give us desires'. (114)[66] Unlike Ruskin, and indeed many contemporary literary critics, Proust does not attribute to literature the power of making us good or wise. 'Reading is at the threshold of spiritual life', he argues. 'It can introduce us to it; it does not constitute it'. ('On Reading,' 116)

C.S. Lewis on Rereading Fairy Tales

Like Proust, C.S. Lewis sees the longing for something more, as an integral part of the reading experience. Creating this longing is, for him, what books are best designed to do; such a longing would then become the foundation for a reader's religious faith. But even before his conversion to Christianity, he took exception to utilitarian forms of reading in which, he said, the text was merely used as a 'trigger . . . for certain imaginative and emotional activities of your own'.[67] By contrast, repeated readings could help you as a reader to 'get yourself out of the way' and 'concentrate intensely on the work itself'.[68] Proust might appear guilty in Lewis's eyes of using others' writing as a trigger for his 'own imaginative activities', but both view the text as a threshold to spiritual discovery, rather than constituting the discovery itself. One thing that reading fiction does (or is supposed to do) is make us long for more understanding, beyond the text and beyond ourselves.

In a sense, then, what reading should provoke is not the instinct to pick up another book, but rather to set forth into the world and find our own adventures (to interpret Proust rather crassly). This notion of reading-up-to-the-threshold has much in common with Renaissance concepts of the imagination as a *nuncius* or mediator between Reason and the Will, or between rational thought and action. Thus Sidney says in *A Defence of Poetry* (1595) that dispensing ready-made wisdom is not the poet's function; rather, the poet's business is to inspire a reader to *want* to know, or to act on the knowledge they have: 'to be moved to do that which we know, or to be moved with desire to know, *hoc opus, hic labor est*'.[69] Francis Bacon expounds the theory more comprehensively in *The Advancement of Learning* (1605):

> The knowledge which respecteth the Faculties of the Mind of man is of two kinds; the one respecting his Understanding and Reason, and the other his Will, Appetite, and Affection; whereof the former produceth Position or Decree, the later Action or Execution. It is true that the Imagination is an agent or *nuncius* in both provinces, both the judicial and the ministerial. For Sense sendeth over to Imagination before Reason have judged: and Reason sendeth over to Imagination before the Decree can be acted; for Imagination ever precedeth Voluntary Motion: saving that this Janus of Imagination hath differing faces; for the face towards Reason hath the print of Truth, but the face towards Action hath the print of Good; which nevertheless are faces, *quales decet esse sororum* [with a likeness one would expect to find in sisters].[70]

In general, Bacon takes a rather low view of the imagination and the arts, so it is somewhat surprising to discover that it has such a crucial role to play in his study of science and learning. Bacon even goes on to stipulate that the relation of Reason (clearly, the highest human attribute) to Imagination is not that of lord to bondman, but rather—a huge concession, from this arch-rationalist—one of magistrate to free citizen (283–84). In fact, Reason turns out to be rather helpless, without the power of the Imagination to turn its insights into substantial action; just as worldly experience is in itself quite futile, unless the Imagination presents that experience to Reason in an engaging manner.

For these Renaissance thinkers, the imagination is a kind of Janus, god of thresholds, mediating between one type of perception and another. Its particular strength lies in stirring the emotions, which then drive the Will either to know more, or to act upon knowledge. I have quoted Bacon *in extenso*, because his argument seems closely related to Lewis's ideas about reading and rereading, particularly as he dramatises these ideas in *The Silver Chair*. First, it is worth mentioning Lewis's own theories of the imagination, as they are developed in *Surprised by Joy*.[71] As Peter Schakel has shown, Lewis wrote of three types of imagination: imagination as wish fulfilment, as invention, and as inspiration.[72] The role of inspiration, the highest form of imagination, is to convey intense feelings and impressions, and its presence can be measured by its affective impact on an audience. Schakel argues the early Lewis was much influenced by Coleridge's Romantic concept of the imagination.[73] While this is undoubtedly true, I think he is also as much interested in early Renaissance (or as he would say, late medieval) concepts of the imagination as a mediator. Lewis would certainly not be critical of Bacon's high estimation of rational thinking (think of Professor Kirk, complaining that logic was no longer taught at school, in *The Lion, the Witch and the Wardrobe*, 49). But with Bacon and Sidney, he believes that a rational being still needs to be 'be moved with desire to know' or 'to do that which we know'. Or in Lewis's own terms, a reader needs to be 'enchanted'.

All the child focalisers of *The Chronicles of Narnia* begin in a state of disenchantment, even *The Lion, the Witch and the Wardrobe*, which after the opening chapters, is largely focalised through Edmund rather than Lucy. Max Weber's idea that the modern world is 'disenchanted' is one that recurs in a very wide range of writers and contexts, but for C.S. Lewis 'disenchantment' refers to a state of spiritual depletion which, interestingly, could not be met directly by religious education or conversion.[74] Something had to alter in the depleted psyche *prior* to such a conversion, because, he asserted, 'religion can be rightly understood only by people who live in a world that is at least to some degree *enchanted*'.[75] In a letter that clearly intimates the need for an imaginary country like Narnia that could mediate between real and ideal worlds, Lewis wonders 'whether we shall not have to re-convert men to real Paganism as a preliminary to converting them to Christianity'.[76] Thus Lewis's Christianity was of the accommodating sort that might be rejected by sterner Protestant writers. In 'Ode on the Morning of Christ's Nativity' (1629), Milton banishes from the world all pagan gods and goddesses, and dwells languorously over their necessary departure:

> From haunted spring and dale
> Edged with poplar pale,
> The parting genius is with sighing sent,
> With flower-inwoven tresses torn
> The nymphs in twilight shade of tangled thickets mourn. (XX.184–88)[77]

Lewis's instincts were exactly the opposite: 'In emptying out the dryads and the gods . . . we appear to have thrown out the whole universe, ourselves included. We must go back and begin over again'.[78]

Lewis attributed to fairy tales and fantasy the power to re-enchant the disenchanted world by instilling a longing in the reader for a better world.[79] Thus,

> Fairy land arouses a longing for [the child] knows not what. It stirs and troubles him (to his life-long enrichment) with the dim sense of something beyond his reach and, far from dulling or emptying the actual world, gives it a new dimension of depth. He does not despise real

woods because he has read of enchanted woods: the reading makes all woods a little enchanted. This is a special kind of longing.[80]

Such longing leads to what Lewis referred to as 'joy' and Tolkien called 'evangelium': in Schakel's gloss, an 'intense, even painful, but desired, longing, which, after his conversion, [Lewis] came to believe was a desire for unity with the divine'.[81] Even if one accepts neither Lewis's Christian framework, nor his neo-Platonism, these ideas about fantasy and the fairy tale are, I believe, both compelling and relevant to our contemporary context. If postmodern capitalism is a socioeconomic system driven to unsustainable excess by the endless circulation of fantasy, perhaps some readers are turning to Lewis's form of fantasy as a kind of homeopathic medicine, curing by application of concentrated doses of the same (or a similar) disease.

If the fairy tale could move, or enchant, a reader to desire something beyond the threshold of the text, this power increases exponentially with a *remembered* fairy tale. 'All joy reminds', Lewis declared, somewhat sweepingly.[82] What this means for narrative is that rereading can produce a more intense form of longing, because the object of desire is now doubly elsewhere: 'a remembered experience triggers a longing not for the past but for something of which a past experience is a symbol'. (*Surprised by Joy*, 166) It could be argued that fairy tales always remind, since according to Jung, they liberate archetypes which dwell in the collective unconscious.[83] But in rereading fairy tales we remember being reminded, which triggers an even more potent form of longing. *The Chronicles of Narnia* are fairy tales by Lewis's own definition, but they also include within their realistic narrative, fairy tales recounted by various characters in more traditionally stylised forms. Thus in *The Silver Chair* the present narrative serves to remind the reader of another more remote tale. The fantasy points to an earlier fantasy in which is embedded a longing for something beyond itself. Yet this dynamic is not all backward looking or transcendent. We also see how the embedded fairy tale exerts an influence on the realistic narrative, as characters are inspired by, and act upon, what they long for and remember.[84]

The fairy tale moves by impressing on the reader's imagination a series of resonant images, visual scenes which carry a high emotional impact (whether because of their content, or because of associations triggered in the reader's own memory). Lewis frequently noted that the Narnian Chronicles were evolved from detailed visual images (a faun carrying parcels through a snowy wood, for example), rather than from the desire to impart an explicitly religious message.[85] Once again, Lewis seems to be drawing on Renaissance theories of the imagination, and its Janus-faced role in moving both Reason and the Will. In *A Defence of Poetry,* Sidney described literature as the art of creating 'speaking pictures', which, unlike philosophy or history, has the power to move a reader to true wisdom and virtuous action; the 'learned definitions' of the philosopher 'lie dark before the imaginative and judging power, if they be not illuminated or figured forth by the speaking picture of poesy'.[86] Similarly, Edmund Spenser, whose 'generall end' in *The Faerie Queene* (1596) was 'to fashion a gentleman or noble person in vertuous and gentle discipline', sought to achieve this end via the devious route of engaging the reader's imagination with startlingly vivid images, whose meanings were 'cloudily enwrapped' and could only be deciphered retrospectively.[87] As Peter Herman argues, Spenser's prefatory *Letter to Ralegh* is a plea to readers to take up *The Faerie Queene* again, withholding the stroke of judgement until they have 'made further trial' of the poem.[88]

Lewis's fourth Chronicle, *The Silver Chair*, is richly indebted to *The Faerie Queene*, and particularly to its first book, which critics have long praised for the vividness of its imagery and its 'fairy-tale-like' atmosphere.[89] As Harry Berger notes, 'Spenser's devices keep the fairytale world firmly before us: the fabulous narrative is to be taken seriously, not evaporated into ideological correlatives; *but it is to be taken seriously as play*'.[90] The scene in which Prince Rilian decapitates the serpent derives from one of Spenser's potent 'speaking pictures'.[91] Redcrosse Knight enters a cave which turns out to be a serpent's lair. The serpent springs at him from a dark corner, coils herself around him (it is female in Spenser as well), and attempts to crush him to death:

> And all attonce her beastly body raizd
> With doubled forces high aboue the ground:
> Tho wrapping vp her wrethed sterne arownd,
> Lept fierce vpon his shield, and her huge traine
> All suddenly about his body wound,
> That hand or foot to stirre he stroue in vaine:
> God helpe the man so wrapt in *Errours* endlesse traine. (I.i.18)

Spenser holds back the theological explanation until the final alexandrine line, allowing the dramatic visual image to create its impact on the reader first. It is only once the knight is wrapped in the serpent's coils, and we, as it were, are cloudily enwrapped in the vehicle of the allegory, that Spenser makes his meaning plain: the serpent represents 'Error', deviance from the true, Protestant religion, which is embodied in Redcrosse's neglected Lady, Una. Rereading this passage, we would no longer be surprised by the final line. In Lewis's terms, we would be able to attend to the intrinsic 'quality of unexpectedness' which it conveys: the suddenness with which disaster strikes, the fact that Redcrosse is helplessly enmeshed, before he is even aware of himself in danger. However, the knight saves himself by keeping his head, and his sword arm, free; he grabs the serpent by the throat, chokes her and eventually hacks off her head (I.i.19).

Rereading in *The Silver Chair*

Lewis reproduces this Spenserian picture in Chapter Twelve of *The Silver Chair* ('The Queen of Underland'), and has Pauline Baynes further heighten its impact on the reader, with a dramatic illustration of the verbal text. The Witch, assuming her serpent shape, ignores the children and Marsh-wiggle, and throws three coils round the prince's body:

> But the Prince was just in time. He raised his arms and got them clear: the living knot closed only round his chest—ready to crack his ribs like firewood when it drew tight.
>
> The Prince caught the creature's neck in his left hand, trying to squeeze it till it choked. This held its face (if you could call it a face) about five inches from his own. The forked tongue flickered horribly in and out, but could not reach him. With his right hand he drew back his sword for the strongest blow he could give. (183–84)

Lewis has a different way of inducing the reader to think 'God help the man so wrapped in error' but his aim is similarly, I think, to frame the moment, to get the reader to feel the full impact of this speaking picture. On the children's book reviewing Web site Kids' Review, two children (eight and ten years old) cited this as their favourite passage in the novel; it made a similar impression on me as a child.[92] The added descriptive details of forked tongue and inhuman face serve to heighten the nightmarish quality of the scene. And lest we forget, this monstrous flickering thing, until moments before, had been the exceptionally beautiful face of the Lady of the Green Kirtle. Baynes's illustration captures exactly this moment of entrapment, so that the scene lingers longer in the reader's mind than it might otherwise do. The description is also sure to activate in the reader any number of collective or personal, unconscious or conscious memories of mythic, folkloric and literary images (such as Spenser's, or his classical sources) of serpents and worms and superficially beautiful temptresses (sin being traditionally represented as woman to the waist, and serpent below), green or otherwise.[93] The image can be gender specific, embodying male fears of femininity, but it can equally conjure more universal fears of entrapment and engulfment, and the need to break free, to preserve one's distinct, human identity. For me, the image of the prince entangled with the snake is one of the novel's major 'speaking pictures', embodying a longing to break free, and at the same time to recover a sense of lost purpose or desire. I call it a 'speaking picture', in Sidney's sense, because it is one of the novel's many images that seems to press at the threshold between text and life, inviting an active response from the reader.

Other scenes in the novel echo and amplify this image of breaking free of false enchantment. The three travellers' descent into Underland is hellish in several senses, one of which is that it disorients them (literally, orientates them towards Dis, or Hell) psychologically and emotionally. Lewis brilliantly paces the narrative of their escape from Harfang, the giants' city. Their crashing haste across acres of rubble, pursued by baying hounds, culminates in a long, painful fall and then sudden, complete silence as they wake into total darkness:

The darkness was so complete that it made no difference at all whether you had your eyes open or shut. There was no noise . . . Long, long afterwards, without the slightest warning, an utterly strange voice spoke. They knew at once that it was not the one voice in the whole world for which each had secretly been hoping; the voice of Aslan. (155–56)

Lewis stalls the narrative, especially in the paragraph break between 'so tired' and 'long, long afterwards' so that the reader has time to assimilate their sense of abandonment beyond hope. As Bettelheim writes, 'there is no greater threat in life than that we will be deserted'.[94] For Jill, who suffers from claustrophobia, the terror is especially acute. In lingering over the travellers' despair, when they have (they think) reached rock bottom, Lewis allows the emotion to surface from the flow of plot, from the tyranny of 'what happens next'.

As noted above, Lewis's aim in the Chronicles is to induce a reader's longing for a truth or reality beyond the material world, or indeed the letter printed on the page. Here, the travellers are made sharply aware of such a longing for the first time: 'they knew at once that it was not the one voice in the whole world for which each had secretly been hoping'. As is often said of infernal journeys, one glimpses the face of God at the very bottom of Hell, when everything else is lost. Lewis gestures to this tradition when he has his travellers long for the voice of Aslan to fill the void of Underland. The fulfilment of such a longing will be the consolation offered at the end of the fairy tale, and indeed all seven of Lewis's fairy tales, but for the moment, desire is deferred, when an earthman or gnome appears instead of Aslan.

Once they have been captured by the earthmen, the Witch's slaves, they are ferried across a vast, Lethean lake, during which they lose their temporal bearings and sense of identity. Lewis describes them waking, sleeping and eating in an undifferentiated period of time, and concludes this speaking picture with a direct address to the reader: 'and the worst thing about it was that you began to feel as if you had always lived on that ship, in that darkness'. (166) The effect of the address is, I think, to bring readers of different ages into the same temporal frame, so that young or old, we feel aged by the journey. In this infernal eternity, the three travellers drift away from any contact with material reality. So by the time they arrive in the Witch's underworld kingdom, they have, in a sense, experienced as prolonged and profound a (dis)enchantment as the lost prince. To free him, they have also to remember their former selves.

In sending the children on an underworld journey in *The Silver Chair*, Lewis is drawing on the tradition of *katabatic* narrative, in which a hero undergoes a descent to Hell (or Hades) to recover lost love, wisdom or power.[95] In the classical tradition, the descent into the underworld is also about recovering buried memory. Virgil's Cumaean sibyl says to Aeneas, '*facilis descensus Averno . . . sed revocare gradum . . . hoc opus, hic labor est*' ('the descent to Avernus [the underworld] is easy, but to retrace your steps, this is the task, this the difficulty', *Aeneid* 6.126–29). She means primarily that it is difficult to get out of Hades once you've got down there, but as 'revocare' can also mean 'to recall',[96] a secondary meaning of the line is that it is difficult to remember and relate a journey through the underworld. In this sense, the labour consists of the difficulty of remembering, of drawing images up from the lost past. Sidney's allusion to this line in *A Defence of Poetry* highlights a third possible meaning. Arguing that the poet's task, unlike the philosopher or historian's, is to move the Reason and Will to understand and act upon knowledge, he concludes with the sibyl's words, 'hoc opus, hic labor est'. If the descent to the underworld is about acquiring wisdom or recovering lost desire, then the difficult return is to bring that desire to the surface, as the legendary Orpheus attempted to bring back Eurydice, or to put that other-worldly wisdom into practice in everyday reality, as was the heroic task of Odysseus and Aeneas. In *The Silver Chair,* when the three travellers wake up after their fall into Underland, they are greeted by the sibylline Warden of the Marches, who gloomily intones: 'many fall down, and few return to the sun-lit lands'. (140) At the end of the novel, the children prove their heroism by completing the rare return. Accompanied briefly by Caspian, they walk back through a magic doorway into their own world to face and overcome their demons, the school bullies at Experiment House. It is in Underland that their reawakened memories become longing, and longing becomes the impetus to change their own world.

Many readers cite the underworld temptation scene as the most memo-rable passage in *The Silver Chair,* in which the Witch attempts to persuade all four protagonists to forget their pasts and deny the existence of Narnia.[97] Jill, Eustace and Puddleglum have just cut the prince free from the enchant-ing chair, when the Witch appears unexpectedly in the doorway. She crosses quickly to the fire, throws magic powder on the flames, and addresses them in a charming, hypnotic voice. In addition to these antirational manoeuvres, she advances reasoned arguments as to why they should doubt the existence of any other world besides her own. Lewis gives the devil some very good lines here, putting in the Witch's mouth several strong objections to his own aes-thetic and moral philosophy. As a materialist, the Witch objects to the prince's attempt to prove the existence of unobservable phenomena. For example, he tries to prove the sun exists by comparing it to the lamp in the cave. But the Witch mocks his reasoning, and gently points to the material evidence before their eyes: 'the lamp is the real thing; the *sun* is but a tale, a children's story'. (178) She is particularly derisive about the apparently childlike credulity on which their reasoning is based. And her rebuke is particularly targeted at older, second time readers who ought to know better:

'tis a pretty make-believe, though, to say truth, it would suit you all bet-ter if you were younger. As for you, my lord Prince, that art a man full grown, fie upon you! Are you not ashamed of such toys?' (199)

She sounds very like a modern day critic of 'kiddult' readers. Narnia is not only a foolish concept because its existence is not materially provable; it is also a foolishly young story for older readers to engage with. Clearly these criticisms are meant to resonate beyond their immediate context to challenge Lewis's own readers. After all, *within* the diegesis, the Witch's arguments are false, even from a materialist perspective. As Eustace points out, they have already encountered the Lady and the prince in Narnia, so obviously she knows that Narnia is as materially real as Underland. But for the reader, of course, Narnia *is* an imaginary country, and it *is* 'merely' a children's story.

Puddleglum's response, which has inspired so many readers, defends both the instinct to believe in other worlds, and the pleasures of reading children's fiction.[98] As William Gray points out, this episode echoes Plato's famous description of the cave in which people cannot 'see anything of themselves or their fellows except the shadows thrown by the fire on the wall of the cave'.[99] The person who could step outside the cave (that is, material existence) would perceive the true nature of reality (Plato's ideal world of forms) but returning to the cave, would find it difficult to convince others of this visionary insight. However, unlike Plato's Socrates, Puddleglum doesn't attempt to persuade the others that Narnia actually exists (rightly, because it doesn't!). But he defends the idea of belief in a better world, regardless of whether it physically exists or not. And, moreover, the terms he chooses suggest that we can find such better worlds in children's literature:

'Suppose this black pit of a kingdom of yours *is* the only world. Well, it strikes me as a pretty poor one . . . But four babies playing a game can make a play-world which licks your real world hollow . . . That's why I'm going to stand by the play-world. I'm on Aslan's side even if there isn't any Aslan to lead it'. (201–02)

As Gray points out, Puddleglum's defence of Narnia closely echoes Lewis's later views on Christian faith. In 'They Asked for a Paper', he argues that if belief in God were just a delusion 'then we would have to say that the universe had produced no real thing of comparable value and that all explanations of the delusion seemed somehow less important than the thing explained'.[100] But this position is far from an orthodox believer's insistence on the *truth* of their religious conviction. Puddleglum (and Lewis) defend the need for faith on emotional grounds, an approach that would never convince a Richard Dawkins.[101]

Not coincidentally, Puddleglum's is also a perfect response for readers wishing to defend a postcredulous, postsuspense-driven reading of the Narnian Chronicles. In other words, Puddleglum defends the rereader's faith in Narnia, which is not so much a reasoned position as an emotional response based on memory. As Puddleglum stubbornly maintains, 'you won't make me forget Narnia . . . I know I was there once. I've seen the sky full of stars. I've seen the sun coming up out of the sea of a morning and sinking behind the mountains at night'. (196)

Unlike the reader, Puddleglum really can remember the Narnia of his earlier life, but he makes it easy for us to identify with him by choosing to remember things that are equally real to us (sun, sea and mountains). What Puddleglum articulates for the reader is the emotional memory of a formerly imagined paradise. Since we haven't actually seen much of this Narnia in *The Silver Chair,* it belongs to memories of former readings, or readings of earlier books in the series, as well as to remembered experiences of our own past. Puddleglum's resistance furthermore illustrates the power of the imagination as the mediator, between reason and action, in line with the Renaissance theories of imagination outlined above. He draws on a bank of emotionally weighted memories to conjure a speaking picture of Narnia by sun- and starlight, and this picture stirs him to action (he stamps out the Witch's fire), which then leads to a recovery of reason and rational choice.

Still, despite Lewis's technique of creating analogues between real and magic worlds, there is a fundamental difference between Puddleglum remembering his own, biographical history, and the reader remembering previous readings of a fantasy world. How can our 'memories' of Narnia function as speaking pictures, images so compelling that we will choose them over reality, and is it even desirable that we should be so moved by the memory of a mere fairy tale? In the Narnian Chronicles, Lewis creates a sense of retrospective longing in order to shape a reader's prospective desire to be changed. One of the narrative techniques he uses to pursue this aim is to weave together memory and fantasy, remembered and imaginary worlds, so that the one blends into the other in the reader's mind. Puddleglum's resistance to the Witch might be taken too, as a defence of this particular method of fairy-tale telling. The Witch derides the travellers' attempts to describe Narnia's suns and lions by analogy with her own lamps and cats ('look how you can put nothing into your make-believe without copying it from the real world of mine' [199]), but this is precisely how Lewis creates the impression of material reality in his magic worlds. One finds surprisingly few irreducibly magic elements in the Narnian Chronicles, but what supernatural elements there are, Lewis painstakingly visualises by analogy with natural phenomena a reader would recognise. Thus the brightness of the chasm leading down to Bism is compared to a stained glass window illuminated by a tropical, midday sun (225), and the height of Aslan's paradise is measured out in real-world mountains stacked on top of each other: 'imagine yourself at the top of the very highest cliff you know . . . And then imagine that the precipice goes on below that, as far again . . . ' (15) Lewis's use of the second person in such analogies invites the reader to identify with the character focalising the scene (in the latter case, Jill, standing on the edge of a cliff). He activates the reader's imagination by drawing on what he or she has already experienced and can easily visualise ('the highest cliff you know'), then extends this familiar image into new territory through repetition and amplification. Thus the Witch's mocking critique might very well serve as a description of Lewis's own narrative method; he puts 'nothing into [his] make-believe without copying it from the real world'. What seems important for Lewis is that the reader should begin the process from her own memories. The idea of such an image leading the reader into a more vivid existence is dramatised at the beginning of *The Voyage of the Dawn Treader*, when Edmund and Lucy are looking at the painting of a Narnian ship and wishing it were real, only to find themselves drawn into the frame and pitched into a tumultuous sea (10). The physical pull these characters feel is a materialisation of longing as retrospective anticipation, the blend of temporal perspectives arising from a mixture of memory (in *Voyage*, having been in Narnia before) and desire (wanting to return).

In *The Silver Chair*, however, the novel's main focaliser Jill Pole has only been told stories about Narnia by her friend Eustace. Like the reader, she has no actual memories to draw upon. This is the case with other child protagonists in the Narnia series, of course, but what Lewis explores here is the importance of becoming a *re*reader of Narnia, getting beyond the first, exciting encounter to feel the greater impact of a familiar return, in which the text and its images may strike us as remembered truths. We first meet Jill Pole sprawled on the grass, crying, on a 'dull autumn day on the damp little path which runs between the back of the gym and the shrubbery', a drear, in-between place which reflects her own depression (4). Unlike other child-focalisers in the series, she does not have any particularly strong character defect that needs to be purged through trial in Narnia; she seems rather to be a good example of a modern, disenchanted subject. A little forgetful and lazy, she falls asleep during the Parliament of Owls, forgets Aslan's instructions, and would rather have a good night's sleep in a luxurious castle than pursue a noble quest through physical hardship (and she is, of course, all the more likeable for these traits). Unlike Lewis's other young protagonists, she arrives in Narnia via Aslan's Country and a direct encounter with the Lion himself. So she has all the abstract knowledge of a second time visitor to Narnia, but none of the lived experience. If her quest as the novel's protagonist is to rescue a lost fairy-tale prince, her task as a rereader is to learn to feel the fairy tale as a liveable narrative, or, to put it another way, to allow the tale to assume a reality in her own life.

Two experiences in Aslan's Country provide her with the emotional ground for this psychological transformation to take place. First, she is indirectly responsible for Eustace falling from a precipice (as she admits to Aslan, she was boasting about having a good head for heights when Eustace tried to drag her back from the edge and fell himself). And secondly she receives instructions or 'signs' from Aslan himself about how to find the lost prince. The first experience is narrated in fragmented images, conveying both Jill's

initial shock and a retrospective sense of the experience as an imbedded, traumatic memory:

> two things she remembered as long as she lived (they often came
> back to her in dreams). One was that she had wrenched herself free
> of Scrubb's clutches; the other was that, at the same moment, Eustace
> himself, with a terrified scream, had lost his balance and gone hurtling
> to the depths. (25)

Here Jill's perspective on the fall of Eustace is temporally doubled so that we
are looking at once through a young, and an older, character's eyes. The slip-
page from calling Eustace by his surname ('Scrubb') to his Christian name
underlines this temporal shift, since the former mode of address was typically used between children at Experiment House. The horror she experiences
here becomes a traumatic memory which continues to motivate Jill's actions
throughout the story. Aslan intervenes to reverse the boy's fall, but Jill never
loses the feeling that she owes something to Eustace; remembering his terror of heights, for instance, she will force herself to master her fear of underground spaces. More generally, she arrives in Narnia with a belated sense of
being given a second chance to put things right. The experience gives Jill a
reserve of emotional memory on which to draw, like a second time reader for
whom a text has already begun to blend with the memory of lived events.

Her other experience, meeting Aslan and receiving the 'signs', could be
(and has been) interpreted as a straightforward, religious allegory. According
to this reading, Jill is the disciple receiving God's ten (or in this case, four)
commandments, which must be followed in order to re-enter Paradise. In such
allegorical terms, *The Silver Chair* is much more explicitly about the necessity
for Christian obedience than the other Chronicles. Unlike his relationship
with Lucy in *The Lion, the Witch and the Wardrobe*, Aslan's intervention here
is explicit and prescriptive; he spells out four signs by which he will guide
their quest (34). But these signs are tailored to test Jill's powers of memory and
develop her skills of rereading, rather than to inculcate a set of fixed beliefs.
Like Redcrosse Knight in *The Faerie Queene*, Jill knows in the abstract what
she is meant to believe. But she doesn't yet know how to recognise this truth
(Aslan's will) in reality. Still more, she lacks the *desire* to recognise it. As Sidney says, 'hoc opus, hic labor est'; the challenge is to awaken the desire to act
on what we already know to be true.[102] Jill is given a text to memorise and
then recognise in unfamiliar contexts. Like Redcrosse, she embarks on a pattern of misreading and correcting earlier readings. At first she forgets Aslan's
text completely, then (like a first time reader), she is too close to the text to
understand it properly. She actually falls into a letter of the third sign: a giant
rune cut into rock spelling the words 'Under me'. (*Silver Chair*, 98–101) But
gradually, once she has internalised the text she comes to read it more clearly;
she realises her earlier misrecognition when she makes out the words 'Under

me' from the height of the castle window (118). And finally the text becomes a latent presence that returns to her without her conscious attempt to recall it.

Inside the Witch's cave, the travellers come upon the fourth and final sign, which requires them to do whatever is asked of them by someone invoking Aslan's name. The prince has been bound in his silver chair, and they are told he will change into a deadly serpent if he is released. When bound, and apparently enchanted (though actually sane for the first time), the prince, invoking Aslan, demands to be released:

'It's the sign', said Puddleglum.
'It was the *words* of the sign', said Scrubb more cautiously. (185)

If Scrubb still concerns himself with the letter of the text, Jill feels its import more deeply and wonders, not whether to believe in it, but how to react to it. It is not knowledge itself that is at stake ('"Oh, if only we knew!" said Jill. "I think we do know", said Puddleglum'.(186)), but how to act on what they know. Aslan's instructions would indicate that they should free the prince, but this will put their own lives at risk. At this moment, the fairy tale assumes a terrible reality; they can choose either to accept it as real, and face the consequences, or leave it bound and unrealised, like the prince strapped to his magic chair. The impetus leading to the travellers' threshold crossing from understanding to action is nicely balanced between the novel's principle 're-readers': Puddleglum being the first to feel the truth, and Jill the first to act on her understanding (186). From the moment that they learn to 're-read' in this active way, things turn out magically right for them. The bound stranger turns out to be the very prince they are seeking. The fairy tale, quite literally, comes to life before their eyes.

In this way, one might interpret *The Silver Chair* as a novel about two rereaders, the adult Puddleglum, and the child Jill, bringing a half-forgotten fairy tale to life. But one might also take Prince Rilian as the novel's principle subject. Read in this light, it is the prince, buried in a Lethean underworld, who conjures three travellers from a fantasy world (or three worlds—Experiment House, Aslan's Country, and the Overland of Narnia) in order to release him from spiritual paralysis and amnesia. A biographical reading of *The Silver Chair* would suggest parallels between the prince's entrapment by the older enchantress and Lewis's own personal history. According to William Gray, Lewis was much affected by the slow, painful death of his mother, and later he became involved in a difficult relationship with an older woman (Mrs Moore), which eventually he broke off after ten years.[103] But one need not resort to biographical parallels to see Rilian as the protagonist-*manqué* of *The Silver Chair*. From the first, his absence is the blank space around which the narrative revolves, and through repeated retellings of his story he gradually emerges into view, like the underlayer of a palimpsest.[104] We first hear of him through Aslan, as he delivers the signs to Jill. By the time she and Eustace arrive in Narnia, however, the lost prince has become a taboo topic. By the king his father's decree, Narnians are now forbidden to search for him, and the burial of his memory seems to have infected the whole kingdom with an atmosphere of forgetfulness. The opening chapters of the novel relate a whole series of misrecognitions. Eustace fails to recognise his friend Caspian, who has become an old man since they last met (time passing at a different rate in Narnia). Grieving and forgetful of his kingly duties, the aged Caspian, like Tennyson's Ulysses, sets forth recklessly on a journey to the end of the world from which no one expects him to return. His regent, a now deaf and ancient dwarf Trumpkin, fails to recognise the two children and why they have been sent to Narnia. Only the Owls are vigilant and wakeful (55). They call a midnight parliament in a ruined tower, and there an old owl recounts the forbidden story of the Queen's death by snakebite, the prince's pursuit of her killer, and his ten-year enchantment by the Lady of the Green Kirtle. But even the Owls only think of the prince as a fairy tale; they are very quick to say they won't accompany the children on the quest to find him. When, much later, the children encounter the prince on the edge of the ruined city of giants, he is suited in unmarked black armour, with his visor down, and no image on his shield. He remains silent while his Lady speaks to them. And even when they meet him properly in Underland, he still seems slightly unreal. Baynes's illustration depicts him as a kind of tapestry figure, arms outstretched in a generic gesture of welcome, but with a blank look on his face. Jill thinks he looks like Hamlet and finds something odd about his voice. It is not just that he is enchanted; it is that his narrative lacks emotional depth so that it is difficult for a reader to care whether he is freed or not. In his enchantment, he finds the sound of his real name ridiculous ('Billian? Trillian?' 153). But the moment when the children and Puddleglum recognise the fourth sign is also the moment when the fairy-tale prince rises to the surface of the narrative diegesis. Just as the prince demands to be released from his imprisoning chair, so the fairy tale of his enchantment demands to be felt and lived as real, rather than remembered as a story read long ago in childhood.

As André Green suggested, every interpretive conversation we have with a text arises from something that has 'already happened between the text and the analyst'.[105] Although I hope it is persuasive on its own terms, the line of interpretation I have just advanced (which takes the prince as the subject of the novel) stems from a re-encounter with *The Silver Chair* which differs substantially from my earlier, childhood readings. Prior to this most recent rereading, I was in what Lewis would have described as a disenchanted state of mind. Like many readers, I had reread *The Chronicles of Narnia* many times but *The Silver Chair* was one I had not returned to in several years. It was in this period of mental paralysis that the image of the prince trapped in the serpent's coils returned to me forcibly and unannounced. I took the book off the shelf and reread the chapter closely and indeed obsessively. It seemed to hold me clamped to the chair, and I shook as the images materialised in my head, both familiar and shockingly new. Now that the image of Rilian had worked free of its immediate context, I suddenly felt the full force of his ten years underground: I felt him holding off the poisonous flickering tongue which was also the alluring face of his Lady (the most difficult devil being the kind you love, rather than hate), I felt the imperative to break free whatever the consequences, and I thought, 'I have to *do* something'.

Remembering Virginia Woolf's acerbic remark about books that leave you with a feeling you should 'join a society, or, more desperately, write a cheque', I should add that my sense of having to react to the text did not go so far as to dictate what I should actually do.[106] As Proust says, our favourite books cannot give us answers; 'all [they] can do is give us desires'. (114) Although in my case, the image of the prince compelled me to act, I don't know whether my response was necessarily the right one. I am not even sure how, finally, to judge the prince's action in the novel. We are not speaking of rereading as conversion to certainty, but rather, as Barthes put it, rereading which 'multiplies the text in its variety and its plurality'. (S/Z 16) After beheading the serpent, Rilian declares he is glad that the Witch took her serpent form, as 'it would not have suited well either with my heart or with my honour to have slain a woman'. (204) But does this sense of scruple entirely make for the prince's lack of gallantry in killing his lover of ten years? In Lewis's source text, *The Faerie Queene*, Redcrosse attacks the serpent without provocation, simply because it is a knight's function to seek out monsters and slay them: 'The youthfull knight could not for ought be staide,/ But forth vnto the darksome hole he went'. (I.i.14) Whether this was wisdom or not depends on how you choose to interpret the allegory. A 'speaking picture' isn't a substitute for rational choice; it is simply the vehicle that restores in you a desire to exercise your reason. The contention of this chapter has been that when such verbal images return to us through memory as well as a fresh encounter, they can move us in unexpected ways. In the above example, it wasn't the fact that Lewis's image of a prince slaying a serpent derives from a long line of distinctly misogynistic images that was important to me as I remembered the scene. It was the fresh and unlooked-for identification with the bound figure that prompted me into action.

Proust also wrote that familiar books made excellent friendships because you could leave them on the shelf until you chose to engage with them ('On Reading', 123). As a rule I would agree with this, but there are also times when those familiar books appear to take themselves off the shelf and present themselves into your hands. Like the very oldest friends, childhood books take liberties with their readers in a manner that can be both affirmative and deeply unsettling. In Primo Levi's *If This Is a Man,* there is an episode of incomparably greater resonance than the one I just described, in which Levi is suddenly struck by something Dante's Ulysses says to his companions on the eve of their final sea voyage.[107] Having memorised the lines of Canto 26 of *Inferno* as a schoolboy, Levi, then a prisoner in Auschwitz, was attempting to teach them to a French friend as they went to fetch the day's rations of soup. But to the starved and debased *häftling* that Levi had become, Dante's lines returned with astonishing force and clarity, 'like the blast of a trumpet . . . as if I also was hearing it for the first time. For a moment I forget who I am and where I am'. (*If This Is a Man*, 119) The switch to present tense underlines Levi's confusion and sense of disorientation. In a later work, *The Drowned and the Saved*, Levi comments that this incident 'made it possible for me to re-establish a link with the past, saving it from oblivion and reinforcing my identity'. (112) But as he narrates the episode in *If This Is a Man*, it is the text that remembers, indeed reassembles him, rather than the other way around. For Primo Levi, Dante's *Inferno* was childhood reading, and the passage he had memorised was internalised and became part of the architecture of his younger self. A text like this can return to you unbidden, and because it seems to arise from somewhere beyond the self, it can also speak to you with particular force, with a ghostly authority that passes unhindered across the threshold of the text, into your actual life.

Conclusion
Crossing Thresholds of Time

Why did so many adult readers turn to reading children's fiction over the millennial decade in the UK? The reasons I have suggested are many and various, because the rise of crossover fiction and cross-reading cannot be reduced to an explanation for the popularity of any particular author or literary genre, as I hope to have demonstrated here. While Rowling's phenomenal success with Harry Potter provided an important catalyst, the expansion of children's fiction into adult markets finally proved to be a much more heterogeneous and inclusive development in contemporary literature. It was not only fantasy, but realist fiction, as well as many hybrid works inventively combining different genres, which found popularity with an extensive, mixed age readership.

While crossover fiction was certainly helped by increasingly sophisticated marketing techniques, we must look to broader changes in our social fabric to explain why children's fiction found, and is still finding, such an enthusiastic audience amongst adults. Advancements in science and technology have contributed to a pervasive sense of the fluidity of biological age groups, and we can no longer clearly distinguish the aspirations of the middle-aged from those of teenagers or younger children. In some respects, cross-reading may be understood as an extension of 'kiddultery', a broad based celebration of youth culture in a socio-economic sphere which places a premium on speed, flexibility and rapid capital turnover. In other respects, though, it may be understood as capitalism's antithesis: the expression of a desire for roots, for more stable and communally shared faiths and verities. One result of the destabilisation of traditional age categories seems to have been that adults and children sought out fresh encounters with the temporal edges of human subjectivity: memories of birth, anticipation of death, and the experience of adolescence. Meanwhile, adolescence itself came to signify a fundamental psychic metamorphosis at any biological stage of life.

In the novels considered in this study, I have traced the emergence of a more flexible, often doubled or Janus-faced sense of subjectivity. The celebration of lightness in J.K. Rowling's Harry Potter series deepens into a sense of connectivity, and a need for a social form of redemption in the face of mortal limit. Philip Pullman's *His Dark Materials* reaffirms the importance of life transitions, explicitly for children to 'come of age' in the classic sense expressed in the nineteenth-century bildungsroman, but also implicitly, for adults to regain the 'childly' capacity to exercise a fluid and imaginative empathy towards others. The perspective of a curious child, in Mark Haddon's *The Curious Incident of the Dog in the Night-time*, becomes the means for the development of a triple relation to otherness: to feel empathy for the estranged other, to see the world afresh through the other's eyes, and to see oneself as a stranger. In Geraldine McCaughrean's *The White Darkness,* the experience of psychic abjection reveals the fragility of identity, and the need for fantasy and love of the other. David Almond's *Clay* digs deep to reveal the doubleness of origins, how we are at once both creatures and creators in our relation to 'earliest things'. And C.S. Lewis's *The Silver Chair* provides a portrait of the rereader, enmeshed in the coils of an unenchanted existence, who by means of a much loved text unexpectedly finds a way to break free.

For the reader inclined to venture across, there are also many bridges interconnecting these different texts. One finds an encounter with the deathly providing a spectacle of 'true theatre' in *The White Darkness* and the later Harry Potter novels, There is the discovery of the extraordinary in the ordinary in *Clay* and *The Curious Incident of the Dog in the Night-time.* In *His Dark Materials* and *Clay*, the Biblical Fall from Eden is reimagined as an awakening of moral commitment to a social utopia, a 'Republic of Heaven' to be built in the here and now. Both these works also explore the idea of human life as a cycle emerging from and returning to dust or clay, the elemental matter of our natural world. *Clay* and *The Silver Chair* offer us ways of bridging the increasing divide between secular and faith communities, in their exploration of the psyche's fundamental spiritual instincts. And *The Silver Chair* and *The White Darkness* both make an impassioned case for the role of the imagination in preserving a sense of identity when reality threatens to overwhelm or extinguish it. In all, we have found affirmed the possibility of some kind of redemption through self-knowledge and empathy.

An adult reader of children's fiction is backward looking but not necessarily nostalgic. When director Andrew Adamson screened the iconic episode in Lewis's *The Lion, the Witch and the Wardrobe*, when Lucy first enters the wardrobe in the spare room, he depicted her edging backwards through fur coats and fir tree branches, turning at last to find herself deep in a lamplit, snowy forest. In one sense, this variation on the text (in which she enters face forward) shows the need for our generation to reimagine Narnia through fresh eyes. Having Lucy walk backwards increases the sense of suspense, and lends to the familiar scene an impression of (as if) first-time-ness, as she turns slowly round to take in the view. In another sense, though, she represents the way that both adults and children edge forward into the future, while seeing the past take shape before us. The ancient Greeks had a word for 'hereafter', οπισω, which also meant 'backwards,' because they regarded the future as something to be walked into backwards.[1] οπισω-βαμων, or walking backwards, into a text can therefore connote prospection as well as retrospection in a reader. Adamson's portrayal of Lucy (and the other Pevensies, since they enter Narnia in the same fashion, in the film) also provides a figure for the cross-reader who is ready to be surprised anew by a children's book, who is prepared to cross the threshold as if for the first time.

Reading children's fiction can help us to work out new ways of living in the present, when the major transitions of life are no longer as clearly distinguishable as they once were. Cross-reading will not produce a blandly universal literature, which would reduce our differences to a tyranny of sameness; on the contrary, it will heighten our consciousness of inhabiting a manifold time, in which the present is instinct with a sense of past and future. So to Calvino's six memos on how to thrive in the new millennium, we could, then, add a seventh: *note to (adult) self, read more children's fiction.*

Notes

Introduction

1   Joel Rickett, 'Liverpool Heads for *Holes* in One,' *The Bookseller* (6 September 2004).

2   Mikhail Bakhtin, *Speech Genres and Other Late Essays,* tr. Vern W McGee (Austin, TX: University of Texas Press, 1986). See especially 'The *Bildungsroman* and Its Significance in the History of Realism (Toward a Historical Typology of the Novel)', in *Speech Genres*, 10–59 (29), where he argues that a character's psychic emergence 'reflects the historical emergence of the world itself'.

3   David Rudd, 'Shirley, the Bathwater, and Definitions of Children's Literature,' *Papers: Explorations into Children's Literature* 5: 2&3 (1994): 95.

4   See Maria Nikolajeva, *Children's Literature Comes of Age: Toward a New Aesthetic* (London: Garland, 1996).

5   Steven Barfield, 'Of Young Magicians and Growing Up: J.K. Rowling, Her Critics, and the "Cultural Infantilism" Debate.' In Hallett, ed., *Scholarly Studies in Harry Potter*: 175–98.

6   Aaronovitch, 'What's so smart about being childish?' *The Independent* (6 June 2001). The article contains some valid points, though Nabokov is an odd choice of 'mature' author to cite, since presumably these stereotypical 'kiddults' would love *Lolita*. Aaronovitch goes on to voice his fears about infantilised adults preying sexually on children, and again, Nabokov's Humbert isn't exactly a wholesome counter-example.

7   Bayard, *Comment* ('How to Talk About Books One Has Never Read,' Paris: Minuit, 2007).

8   Jacobson, one of a panel of guests discussing, 'Why Are Adults Reading Children's Literature?' *Lebrecht Live*, BBC Radio 3 (27 January 2005).

9   Anon., *Times Literary Supplement*, 2005 (5330): 12–14.

10   Zipes, *Sticks and Stones* (New York: Routledge, 2002), 48 Suzy Jenvey, editor of Faber's children's literature list, argues, 'books are dropping into a popular cultural mainstream way of life in a way they haven't before. That's not infantilisation; it's a change in popular culture.' *The Daily Telegraph* (15 November 2003).

11   Pullman, Carnegie Medal speech (1996), quoted by Angelique Chrisafis, 'Fiction Becoming Trivial and Worthless, Says Top Author,' *The Guardian* (12 August 2002). In the same vein, S.F. Said opines that in contrast to postmodern, 'high literature' ('dull at best, meaningless at worst'), 'golden age children's literature offered vivid, bold storytelling of a profundity and scope that dwarfed any Booker Prize winner's'. Said, 'The Grown-up World of Kidult Books,' *The Daily Telegraph* (11 January 2003).

12   Pullman's publisher, David Fickling, agrees: '[against] the modernist and postmodernist rejection of narrative, what you're seeing now is a reassertion of the fundamental human desire for story'. *The Daily Telegraph* (15 November 2003)

13   Pullman quoted by Nigel Reynolds, 'Writers are losing the plot, says prize-winner', *The Daily Telegraph* (18 July 1996).

14   Musil, *The Man Without Qualities,* tr. Sophie Wilkins (New York: Knopf, 1995), 708.

15   Pullman, in Reynolds, 'Writers are losing the plot'.

16   *ibid.*

17   Pullman, 'Writing Fantasy Realistically', Sea of Faith National Conference (2002). Available online at: http://sofn.org.uk/conferences/pullman2002.html [accessed 8 November 2007].

18   'Why Are Adults Reading Children's Literature?' *Lebrecht Live*, BBC Radio 3 (27 January 2005). Mark Lawson argues similarly, 'as entertainment for adults tends to become bleaker and more distressing—which reflects the lives of many people—there is also a comfort-blanket hunger for lost innocence. Only this could explain the adult audience for Harry Potter'. 'Peter Pan Refills the Piggy Bank', *The Guardian* (17 June 2000).

19   Jacobson, in 'Why Adults are Reading Children's Literature,' *Lebrecht Live.*

20   Karen Coats, *Looking Glasses and Neverlands* (Iowa City: University of Iowa Press, 2004), 162.

21   Maria Nikolajeva, *Children's Literature Comes of Age* (London: Garland Publishing, 1996), 119. See also Nikolajeva's article, 'Exit Children's Literature?' *The Lion and the Unicorn,* 22: 2 (April 1998): 221–236.

22   Eccleshare, 'Review: Guardian Children's Fiction Prize', *The Guardian* (3 June 2006).

23   Sandra Beckett is preparing a volume in this series on international cross-over literature that is projected for publication in 2008.

24   'I always thought that [building] bridges is the best job there is . . . because roads go over bridges, and without roads we'd still be savages. In short, bridges are the opposite of borders, and borders are where wars start'. Primo Levi, *The Wrench* (*La chiave a stella*), tr. William Weaver (London: Abacus, 1986). See Mirna Cicioni, *Primo Levi: Bridges of Knowledge* (Oxford: Berg, 1995).

25   Julia Kristeva, *Strangers to Ourselves*, tr. Leon S. Roudiez (London: Harvester Wheatsheaf, 1991).

26   Jacqueline Rose, *The Case of Peter Pan: or, the Impossibility of Children's Fiction* (Basingstoke: Macmillan, 1984), 137.

27   Harold Bloom, 'Can 35 Million Readers Be Wrong? Yes'. *The Wall Street Journal* (11 July 2000): 16.

Chapter 1

1   See Robert Rosenblum, *The Romantic Child from Runge to Sendak* (London: Thames and Hudson, 1988).

2   Brian Alderson describes the 'quality of visionary wonder and otherworldliness' in MacDonald's prose, in F.J. Harvey Darton and Brian Alderson, *Children's Books in England: Five Centuries of Social Life*, ed. Brian Alderson, 3rd edition (London: The British Library and Oak Knoll Press, 1999), 265.

3   Alderson, *Children's Books in England*, 276.

4   Lewis Carroll, *Alice's Adventures in Wonderland*, ed. Richard Kelly (Letchworth, Hertfordshire: Broadview Press, 2000), 50.

5   Reviews reprinted in Carroll, *Alice's Adventures*, ed. Kelly, 270–75.

6   Jacqueline Rose, *The Case of Peter Pan: The Impossibility of Children's Fiction* (Basingstoke: Macmillan, 1984). See also Alderson, *Children's Books in England*, 310.

7   S.F. Said, 'The Godfather of Harry Potter,' *The Daily Telegraph* (15 October 2002).

8   Anon., 'Harry Potter Finale Sales Hit 11m,' BBC News 24 (23 July 2007). *http://news.bbc.co.uk/1/hi/entertainment/6912529.stm* [accessed 7 October 2007].

9   'Harry Potter Finale Sales Hit 11m,' BBC News 24 (23 July 2007).

10   Charlie Griffiths, director of the National Literacy Association, said: 'We cannot sing the praises of Rowling high enough . . . . Anyone who can persuade children to read should be treasured and what she's given us in Harry Potter is little short of miraculous.' Quoted in Stephen McGinty, 'The Legacy of Harry: The J.K. Rowling Story, Part III,' *The New Scotsman* (18 June 2003).

11   Nigel Reynolds, 'Adult Fans Taking Over Harry Potter,' *The Daily Telegraph* (22 June 2007). *http://www.telegraph.co.uk/arts/main.jhtml?xml=/arts/2007/06/22/nosplit/booldharry12.xml* [accessed 2 November 2007].

12   See, for example, Simon Taylor, ed., *Children's Publishing—Market Assessment* (Keynote, 2005).

13   Sam Leith, 'Diary of the Literary Year', *The Daily Telegraph* (4 December 2004); Cosima Marriner, 'Harry Potter Casts Spell on Publishing', *The Guardian* (9 July, 2005); and Jim White, 'Sign Here to Book Your Money-Back Guarantee', *The Daily Telegraph* (4 October 2004).

14   Amanda Craig, 'No More Mr Big Bad!' *The Times* (26 August 2006).

15   White, 'Sign Here', *The Daily Telegraph* (4 October 2004).

16   Marriner, 'Harry Potter Casts Spell', *The Guardian* (9 July 2005).

17   Tom Holman and Joel Rickett, 'Busy Bologna Targets Fiction', *The Bookseller* (18 April 2002).

18   Holman and Rickett, 'Busy Bologna', *Bookseller* (18 April 2002).

19   Caroline Horn, 'Publishers Get Strategic', *The Bookseller* (20 May 2004).

20   Francesca Dow, quoted by Caroline Horn in 'Publishers Get Strategic.'

21   Kenshole quoted in Shannon Maughan and Diane Roback, 'Seeing Stars', *Publishers Weekly* (5 September 2005).

22   The idea of gatekeepers maintaining the distinction between 'high' and 'low' culture, particularly between literature and 'sub-literature' is developed by Pierre Bourdieu in his *Distinction: A Social Critique of the Judgement of Taste*, tr. Richard Nice (Cambridge, MA: Harvard University Press, 1984).

23   See the Costa Award web-site. *http://www.costabookawards.com/awards/index.aspx* [accessed 30 October 2007].

24   Tonkin, 'Whitbread: An Inevitable Victory for a Dark and Complex Fable', *The Independent* (23 January 2002).

25   The Costa Awards Web site: *http://www.costabookawards.com* [accessed 19 January 2008].

26   See the Man Booker Prize Web site. *www.themanbookerprize.com* [accessed 19 October 2007].

27   For the Guardian Children's Book Prize, see *http://books.guardian.co.uk* [accessed 19 October 2007].

28   See the Carnegie Greenaway Medal Web site. *www.carnegiegreenaway.org.uk* [accessed 19 October 2007].

29   Brabazon, press release, quoted on the Carnegie Greenway Medal Web site. *http://www.cilip.org.uk/aboutcilip/newsandpressreleases/archive2004/news040430.htm* [accessed 19 October 2007]. See also Boyd Tonkin, who

interviews Brabazon in 'A Week in Books: Join the Generation-Jumping Party', *The Independent* (7 May 2004).

30 Press release, 9 July 2004, quoted on Carnegie web-site. *http://www. carnegiegreenaway.org.uk/pressdesk/press.php?release=pres_carnegie_ win_04.htm* [accessed 30 October 2007]. Jennifer Donnelly, *A Gathering Light* (the original US title was *A Northern Light*, London: Bloomsbury, 2003).

31 Adèle Geras, 'Hotel du lac,' *The Guardian* (7 June 2003). *http://books. guardian.co.uk/review/story/0,,971928,00.html* [accessed 2 November 2007].

32 Interview with Jennifer Donnelly, 'Carnegie Winner Offers Message for Teens', *The Bookseller* (16 July 2004): 30.

33 Jennifer Donnelly, 'Paperback Writer', *The Guardian* (10 July 2004).

34 Review by a pupil at St Joseph's Academy, posted on *Book Brother: Vote to Evict*: *http://www.4ureaders.net/attitudev2/page.asp?idno=932&text only=0* [accessed 11 April 2007].

35 Falconer, unpublished telephone interview with Colin Brabazon, 10 August 2005.

36 Descriptions from the Richard and Judy Book Club Web site. See: *www.channel4.com/entertainment/tv/microsites/R/richardandjudy/ keep4archive/summer_read_vote* [accessed 11 April 2007].

37 The paratext is any supporting material, such as cover, title-page, publisher's blurb, etc., that helps present the text to a reader. On this concept, see Gérard Genette, *Paratexts: Thresholds of Interpretation*, tr. Jane Lewin (Cambridge: Cambridge University Press, 2007).

38 Sales figures provided to the author by Richard Knight of Nielsen Book-Scan, July 2006 and April 2007.

39 Waterstone's and Channel 4 carried out a survey of more than 50,000 readers in 1997 of Britons' top one hundred most loved books, in which *The Lord of the Rings* came first.

40 Proust disagrees with Ruskin that reading should be considered a 'conversation' for reading, 'contrary to conversation, consists for each of us in receiving the communication of another thought, but while we remain all alone, that is to say, while continuing to enjoy the intellectual power we have in solitude'. See Marcel Proust, 'On Reading', in *On Reading Ruskin: Prefaces to* La Bible d'Amiens *and* Sésame et les Lys, tr. and ed. Jean Autret, William Burford and Phillip J. Wolfe (New Haven, NJ: Yale University Press, 1987), 99–129 (112). On Proust's essay, see also Chapter Seven of this study.

41 Lian Hearn, *Tales of the Otori* series, comprising *Across the Nightingale Floor* (Sydney: Hodder, c2002; London: Macmillan, 2002; Picador, 2003;

Young Picador, 2004); *Grass for His Pillow* (London: Macmillan, c2003; Young Picador, 2004); *Brilliance of the Moon* (London: Macmillan, c2004; Young Picador, 2004; Picador, 2006); *The Harsh Cry of the Heron* (London: Macmillan, c2006); and a prequel to the series, *Heaven's Net is Wide* (London: Macmillan, c2007).

42 For a full list of the different editions of Hearn's *Tales of the Otori,* see Pan Macmillan's web-site. *http://www.panmacmillan.com* [accessed 28 October 2007].

43 Elliott quoted by Holman and Rickett, 'Busy Bologna.'

44 Falconer, unpublished telephone interview with Rebecca McNally (24 August 2006).

45 Bedell, 'Suddenly Last Summer', *The Observer* (25 July 2004).

46 See also Boyd Tonkin's useful, broad-ranging review of successful cross-over novels, 'Once Upon a Time in the Marketing Department', *The Independent* (6 November 2002).

47 Maria Nikolajeva, *Children's Literature Comes of Age: Toward a New Aesthetic* (London: Garland Publishing, 1996).

48 Cf. Mark Haddon, when asked to define the difference between children's and adult's fiction: 'It's not a difference between one book and another, or between one reader and another. It's a difference between ways of writing and ways of reading'. 'B Is for Bestseller', *The Observer* (11 April 2004).

49 David Rudd, 'Shirley, the Bathwater, and Definitions of Children's Literature', *Papers: Explorations into Children's Literature* 5: 2–3 (1994): 88–103 (90).

50 Barbara Wall, *The Narrator's Voice: The Dilemma of Children's Fiction* (Basingstoke: Macmillan, 1991), 20–36.

51 For an online discussion forum of *His Dark Materials*, including child and adult contributors, see *http://bridgetothestars.net/forum/* [accessed 7 November 2007].

52 Similarly, Rudd argues that Wall's notion of dual address is monologic because it describes a communication channel that flows only one way. 'Shirley, the Bathwater, and Definitions', 92.

53 See Hans Vaihinger, *The Philosophy of 'As If',* trans. C.K. Ogden (London: Kegan Paul, 1924).

54 Janice Alberghene, 'Childhood's End?' *Children's Literature* 13 (1985): 188–93.

55 This is implicit in the otherwise excellent studies, Nikolajeva's *Children's Literature Comes of Age* and Sandra Beckett's edited collection, *Transcending Boundaries: Writing for a Dual Audience of Children and Adults* (New York: Garland, 1999), which includes essays entitled 'Children's, Adult, Human . . . ?', 'Fiction for All Ages?' and '"Ages: All"'. The idea of

an end of children's literature is also mooted in S.F. Said's 'The Grown-up World of Kidult Books', *The Daily Telegraph* (11 January 2003); Bel Mooney's 'Writing Through Ages', *The Times* Books (28 August 2002); and S. Moss's 'Let's Forget about "Children's Writing"', *The Guardian* (23 January 2002). Contrastingly, the children's writer Anne Fine expresses her reservations about literature for 'all ages' in Dalya Alberge's article, 'Children's Tale Works Magic on Whitbread,' *The Times* News (23 January 2002): 3.

56 Philip Pullman, 'What! No Soap?' *Notes from the Royal Society of Literature* 20 (2002): 44.

57 Similarly, Jack Zipes argues that if we do not find ways to engage with children, their culture and their literature, they will continue to bear the burden of sorting out 'the contradictions that are inevitable and intolerable in our society', and our vested interests will 'drive them forward into hysteria, violence, and bewilderment'. See Zipes, *Sticks and Stones: The Troublesome Success of Children's Literature from Slovenly Peter to Harry Potter* (London: Routledge, 2002), xi.

58 Jonathan Myerson, 'Harry Potter and the Sad Grown-ups', *The Independent* (14 November 2001).

59 And as Philip Pullman puts it, 'I was once a child, and so were all the other adults who produce children's literature; and those who read it, the children, will one day be adults . . . there must be some kind of continuum'. ('What! No Soap?' 43)

60 See, for example, Zohar Shavit, who criticises 'a new genre of writing for children, one which addresses the parents, very often at the expense of their children'. 'The Double Attribution of Texts for Children and How It Affects Writing for Children,' in Beckett, ed. *Transcending Boundaries*, 83–98 (90).

61 Exploring some different angles of the 'predatory' argument are Neil Postman's *The Disappearance of Childhood*, Dorothy Suransky's *The Erosion of Childhood* (1982), John Sommerville's *The Rise and Fall of Childhood* (1982), Michael and Diane Medved's *Saving Childhood* (1998) and Joseph Zornado's *Inventing the Child: Culture, Ideology and the Story of Childhood* (2001).

62 Deborah Thacker, 'Disdain or Ignorance? Literary Theory and the Absence of Children's Literature', *The Lion and the Unicorn* 24.1 (January 2000): 1–17.

63 On crossover fiction heralding a new Golden Age, see, for example: Angela Lambert, 'A Golden Age for the Kids?' in *Prospect Magazine* 72 (March 2002), *http://www.prospect-magazine.co.uk* [accessed 1 November 2007]; and Dina Rabinovitch, 'The Greatest Stories Ever Told', *The Guardian* (31 March, 2005), who describes the present era as 'truly extraordinary'. In 2001, a *Guardian* leader article claimed, we are

'a golden age for children's fiction' and 'at best a bronze age for literary fiction, with the behemoths of yesteryear (Rushdie, Amis, Barnes) stuck in repetitive middle age'. (anon., 'Literary Expansion: Children's Books Break Through the Barrier', *The Guardian* (18 August 2001)). On the first 'Golden Age', so-termed, see Humphrey Carpenter, *Secret Gardens: a Study of the Golden Age of Children's Literature* (Boston, MA: Houghton Mifflin Company, 1991).

64   Catherine Bennett remarks, a striking move 'even for an administration which has always been eager to ingratiate itself with the under-16s'. See Bennett, 'Peter, Po and Pokémon', *The Guardian* (2 November 2000).

65   Peter Martin, 'Coming Soon: TV's New Boy Network', *The New York Times* (11 August 1985).

66   Ben Summerskill, 'Playtime as Kidults Grow Up at Last', *The Observer* (23 July 2000).

67   Summerskill, 'Playtime as Kidults Grow Up at Last'.

68   See Jess Cartner-Morley, 'Real Life Suspended: Frocks for Grown-up Fairies', *The Guardian* (13 September 2002).

69   See *The Guardian* Weekend, Fashion (8 September 2001). Photos by Rob Fuller, Clothes by Dolce & Gabbana, Nicole Fahri, Jasper Conran Collection, Paul Smith et al.

70   Hensher, 'When Adults Want to Become Children Again', *The Independent* (16 July 2002).

71   Will Self, *Feeding Frenzy* (London: Penguin, 2001).

72   McLean, 'Don't Look Back in Anger', *The Guardian* TV and Radio (5 April 2001).

73   Melissa Katsalis, 'Hot Tots Are So Cool', *The Times* (14 November 2002): 8–9.

74   Bennett, 'Peter, Po and Pokémon: On Mandelson's New Kidology', *The Guardian* (2 November 2000).

75   Timothy Garton Ash, *The Guardian* (7 February 2002).

76   *http://news.bbc.co.uk/1/hi/health/4971930.stm* [accessed 4 November 2007].

77   Chris Anderson, 'A Survey of the Young: Bright Young Things', *The Economist,* Know Future (23 December 2000): 4. Hereafter cited as 'Bright Young Things'.

78   Don Tapscott, *Growing Up Digital: The Rise of the Net Generation* (New York: McGraw-Hill, 1997). Cited by Anderson, 'Bright Young Things', 7.

79   Psydata Market-Research Institute, Frankfurt, quoted by Anderson, 'Bright Young Things'.

80   This transformation was discussed on 'In Business', BBC Radio 4 (10 May 2007).

81 Stephanie Calman, *Confessions of a Failed Grown-Up: Bad Motherhood and Beyond* (London: Pan Macmillan, 2006), 5. The passage continues, 'I should have been a grown-up by now. I'm just not. I'm sorry—OK?' Compare: Andrew Collins's *That's Me in the Corner: Adventures of an Ordinary Boy in a Celebrity World* (London: Time Out Group Ltd, 2007) where the 'boy' in the title refers to the 42-year-old author, reflecting on the 17 jobs he has held in the 17 years since leaving college. On a slightly more polished note, the Gallic Bernard Chapuis's *Vieux Garçon* 'est écrit avec un coeur d'adolescent parisien et un style de romancier britannique blanchi sous le crachin', according to a front page advertisement in *Le Monde* (2 February 2007).

82 Nick Cave interview on BBC Radio 4, *Loose Ends* (5 May 2007). Cave said he had in mind T S Eliot's 'J. Alfred Prufrock' when he wrote the song, but Cave's Grinderman is vertiginously free, unlike Eliot's convention-bound Prufrock.

83 A striking import was French Algerian teenager Faïza Guène's *Just Like Tomorrow* (*Kiffe kiffe demain*), about life in a Parisian *banlieu* (London: Definitions, 2006).

84 See *http://www.shutupkidproductions.com* [accessed 7 November 2007].

85 See Gareth McLean, 'Thank Heavens for Little Girls', *The Guardian* (30 March 2001). See also Mark Lawson, 'Peter Pan Fills the Piggy Bank', *The Guardian* (17 June 2000).

86 'The Commercialisation of Childhood', Compass Report, 2006, endorsed by Archbishop Rowan Williams. Available at *www.compassonline.org.uk/publications* [accessed 7 July 2007].

87 Palmer, *Toxic Childhood* (London: Orion, 2006), 13.

88 Jack Zipes, *Sticks and Stones: The Troublesome Success of Children's Literature from Slovenly Peter to Harry Potter* (London: Routledge, 2002).

89 See *http://england.shelter.org.uk* [accessed 13 April 2007].

90 The findings were drawn from a survey of twenty-one nations analyzed on six criteria: material well-being, health and safety, education, peer and family relationships, behaviours and risks, and young people's own subjective sense of well-being. See 'Child Poverty in Perspective: An Overview of Child Well-Being in rich Countries', *Unicef*, Innocenti Research Centre, Report Card no. 7 (14 February 2007), *http://www.unicef-icdc.org* [accessed 13 April 2007].

91 'Community Soundings. The Primary Review Witness Sessions', *The Primary Review—Children, Their World, Their Education*, Interim Reports (Cambridge: University of Cambridge, October 2007). *http://news.bbc.co.uk/1/shared/bsp/hi/pdfs/12_10_2007primary.pdf* [accessed 13 October

2007]. Reported on BBC Radio 4, *http://news.bbc.co.uk/1/hi/uk/7041265. stm* [accessed 13 October 2007].

92   Mary Riddle cites Marina Warner's *Managing Monsters: Six Myths of Our Time* (London: Vintage, 1994), who analyses historical instances in which adults become punitive and callous to children, when the latter are seen to betray an abstract myth of innocence. See Riddle, 'Childhood', in J. Lotherington, ed., *The Seven Ages of Life* (London: The Centre for Reform, 2002), 35–56.

93   Coleman, 'Into Adulthood', in *The Seven Ages of Life*: 57–80 (76).

94   BBC Radio 4 (10 May 2007).

95   Bogdan Costea, Norman Crump and John Holm, 'Dionysus at Work? The Ethos of Play and the Ethos of Management', *Culture and Organization* 11:2 (June 2005): 139–51 (140). Hereafter referred to as 'Dionysus at Work?'

96   See also Lewis Pinault, *The Play Zone: Unlock your Creative Genius and Connect with Consumers* (London: Collins, 2004), 5.

97   See also Pascal Bruckner, *The Temptation of Innocence: Living in the Age of Entitlement* (New York: Algora Publishing, 2000) and *L'euphorie perpétuelle: essai sur le devoir de bonheur* (Paris: Livres de Poche, 2002).

98   Charles Taylor, *Sources of the Self: the Making of the Modern Identity* (Cambridge, MA: Harvard University Press, 1989), cited by Costea, Crump and Holm, 145.

99   'When it becomes form [the signifier in a myth-system], the meaning leaves its contingency behind; it empties itself, it becomes impoverished, history evaporates, only the letter remains'. Roland Barthes, *Mythologies*, tr. Annette Lavers (London: Granada, 1973), 117.

100   Two examples of the winds of cultural change: On the occasion of the release of his film, *Lions for Lambs*, Robert Redford talked to Mark Lawson about the need for films to be more engaged with political and environmental issues (BBC Radio 4, Front Row [30 October 2007]); Paula Wagner, Tom Cruise's co-producer on the film *Valkyrie,* calls for 'an end to apathy' on the part of American audiences (BBC Radio 4, The Film Programme [2 November 2007]).

Chapter 2

1.   A.S. Byatt, 'Harry Potter and the Childish Adult', *New York Times* (11 July 2003).

2   Frank Furedi, 'The Children Who Won't Grow Up,' *Spiked* (9 July 2003). *http://www.spiked-online.com/Articles/00000006DE8D.htm* [accessed 20 June 2007].

3   J.K. Rowling, *Harry Potter and the Philosopher's Stone* (1997), *Harry Potter and the Chamber of Secrets* (1998), *Harry Potter and the Prisoner of*

Azkaban (1999), *Harry Potter and the Goblet of Fire* (2000), *Harry Potter and the Order of the Phoenix* (2003), *Harry Potter and the Half-Blood Prince* (2005), *Harry Potter and the Deathly Hallows* (2007), London: Bloomsbury. Hereafter cited respectively as *Stone, Chamber, Prisoner, Goblet, Phoenix, Half-Blood* and *Hallows*.

4   For a fuller discussion of the hostile critical response to Harry Potter, see Steven Barfield, 'Of Young Magicians and Growing Up: J.K. Rowling, Her Critics, and the "Cultural Infantilism" Debate', in Cynthia Hallett, ed. *Scholarly Studies in Harry Potter* (Lampeter: Edwin Mellen Press, 2005), 175–98.

5   John Pennington, 'From Elfland to Hogwarts, or the Aesthetic Trouble with Harry Potter,' *The Lion and the Unicorn* 26:1 (2002): 78–89 (79).

6   Suman Gupta, *Re-reading Harry Potter* (Basingstoke: Palgrave Macmillan, 2003), 85.

7   On the generic eclecticism of *Harry Potter*, see Steven Barfield, 'Of Young Magicians,' 182–92; and Julia Eccleshare, *A Guide to the Harry Potter Novels* (London: Continuum, 2002), 32–46.

8   'Contrary to the general view that Harry Potter was made by media hype, these awards [Children's Book Award, Young Telegraph Paperback of the Year, Birmingham Cable Children's Book Award, Sheffield Children's Book Award] confirm the reality: the origins of its success in the UK lay in children's wholehearted and enthusiastic adoption of it as a book to read and enjoy,' Julia Eccleshare, *A Guide to the Harry Potter Novels* (London: Continuum, 2002), 13.

9   Suman Gupta, *Re-reading*, 133–40.

10   Nadine Gordimer, 'The Flash of Fireflies,' in Charles May, ed., *The New Short Story Theories* (Athens, OH: Ohio University Press, 1994), 263–67 (263).

11   See Ursula Heise, *Chronoschisms: Time, Narrative and Postmodernism* (Cambridge: Cambridge University Press, 1997), 6; and Rachel Falconer, 'Telescoping Timescapes: Short Fiction and the Contemporary Sense of Time,' in Wim Tigges, ed., *Moments of Moment: Aspects of the Literary Epiphany* (Amsterdam: Rodopi, 1999), 445–66.

12   Brad Silberling directed *Lemony Snicket's A Series of Unfortunate Events* for Paramount Pictures (2004). See: *http://www.unfortunateeventsmovie. com/intro.html* [accessed 25 January 2008].

13   See: *http://www.billyelliotthemusical.com/* [accessed 17 November 2007]

14   Mikhail Bakhtin, 'The Problem of Speech Genres,' in *Speech Genres and Other Late Essays,* eds. Emerson and Holquist, tr. Vern McGee (Austin: University of Texas Press, 1986), 99.

15 Gupta observes that while in our world, advertising makes magical claims for products which turn out to be false, in Rowling's magic world, magical advertisements are declarative statements of fact (*Rereading*, 139).

16 Italo Calvino, *Six Memos for the Next Millennium: the Charles Eliot Norton Lectures* 1985–86, tr. Patrick Creagh (London: Vintage, 1996), 7.

17 William Wordsworth, 'The World is Too Much with Us' (1807), in M.H. Abrams and S. Greenblatt, eds., *The Norton Anthology of English Literature* (London: Norton, 2000), Vol. 2, 297.

18 Giovanni Boccaccio, *The Decameron* (wr. 1353), VI.9, tr. G. H. McWilliam (London: Penguin, 2003), quoted by Calvino, *Six Memos*, 11–12.

19 See *Italian Folktales*, selected and retold by Italo Calvino, tr. G. Martin (London: Penguin, 1982).

20 Jerry Griswold, *Feeling Like a Kid: Childhood and Children's Literature*. Baltimore: Johns Hopkins University Press, 2006.

21 Debbie Mynot writes that 'the novels offer both simplicity and complexity', in Cynthia Hallett, ed., *Scholarly Studies in Harry Potter* (Lampeter: Edwin Mellen Press, 2005), ix. Likewise, Cynthia Hallett maintains that they 'offer the magic of imagination: both the creativity of child's play and that of complex literary trope and allusion.' Hallett, *Scholarly Studies*, 4.

22 Wall, *The Narrator's Voice*, 20–36.

23 For a list of spells cast in the Harry Potter series, see *http://en.wikipedia. org/wiki/Spells_in_Harry_Potter* [accessed 25 January 2008].

24 According to Ron Cooley, this anti-institutional heroism is one reason for Harry's appeal to American readers since in the US, 'there is a longstanding tradition of civil disobedience, particularly in the culture of the United States'. See 'Harry Potter and the Temporal Prime Directive', in Hallett, ed., *Scholarly Studies*, 29–42 (32).

25 Sarah Maier, 'Educating Harry Potter: a Muggle's Perspective on Magic and Knowledge in the Wizard World of J.K. Rowling,' in *Scholarly* Studies, ed. Hallett, 7–28 (15).

26 James Ziegler, 'Primitive, Newtonian and Einsteinian Fantasies: Three Worldviews', in *The Scope of the Fantastic: Theory, Technique, Major Authors*, eds. R. Collins and H. Pearce (London: Greenwood Press, 1985), 66.

27 Christopher Lydon, 'Interview with J.K. Rowling,' *The Connection*, WBUR Radio (12 October, 1999). See: *http://www.accio-quote.org/ articles/1999/1099-connectiontransc2.htm* [accessed 21 December 2007].

28 William Wandless, 'Hogwarts vs. "The 'Values' Wasteland": *Harry Potter and the Formation of Character*', in *Scholarly Studies*, ed. Hallett, 217–40 (234).

29 Geordie Greig, '"There would be so much to tell her". Interview with J.K. Rowling', *Tatler* (10 January 2006).

30 See Dorota Guttfeld, 'Coping with Mortality: Lewis, LeGuin and Rowling on the Inhumanness of Immortality', in *Towards or Back to Human Values?: Spiritual and Moral Dimensions of Contemporary Fantasy*, eds. J. Deszcz-Tryhubczak and M. Oziewicz (Newcastle: Cambridge Scholars Press, 2006), 198–208.

31 See Rachel Falconer, 'Tolkien, Dante, and Crossover Epic', in Pat Pinsent, ed., *Books and Their Boundaries: Writers and Their Audiences* (Pied Piper Publishing: Staffordshire, 2004), 98–113.

32 Cf. William Wordsworth, 'My Heart Leaps Up', and Chapter Six of this study.

33 For an alternative reading of this scene as the culmination of Harry's education in 'misapprehension and correction', see Cooley, 'Temporal Prime Directive', 37.

34 In doing so, they reverse one of the novel's major transgressions of the genre of magic story: that is, the murder of a child's animal companion. When C.S. Lewis has the unicorn and other Talking Beasts slaughtered in *The Last Battle*, he commits a similar generic violation of the magic story and animal fable (147–48).

35 Ernelle Fife, 'Reading J.K. Rowling Magically: Creating C.S. Lewis's "Good Reader"', in Hallett, ed., *Scholarly Studies in Harry Potter*, 137–58 (145).

36 Cooley, 'Temporal Prime Directive', 40.

37 See *http://www.mugglenet.com* and *http://www.hpfgu.org.uk* [accessed 25 January 2008].

38 See Wolfgang Iser, *The Implied Reader: Patterns of Communication in Prose Fiction from Bunyan to Beckett* (London: Johns Hopkins University Press, 1974) and *The Act of Reading* (London: Routledge, 1978).

39 The 'chronotope' in Bakhtin's coinage signifies the representation of 'time space' in a text; more generally, it is a term which highlights 'the intrinsic connectedness of temporal and spatial relationships.' (Bakhtin, 'Forms of Time and of the Chronotope', *The Dialogic Imagination*, p. 86) Hence a 'chronotopic image' is a motif or image which epitomises the sense of time-space of a particular work; the road is an obvious chronotopic image of the road movie, or in Bakhtin's analysis, the adventure novel ('Forms of Time,' 243–45).

40 Cooley compares the reader of *Harry Potter* to the Miltonic reader characterised by Stanley Fish, in *Surprised by Sin: the Reader in* Paradise

Lost (London: Macmillan, 1967). In Fish's reading, Milton constantly tempts the reader to adopt the devil's perspective, only to be corrected and enlightened later on. Cf. Cooley, 'Temporal Prime Directive,' 41.

41 Daniela Teo, 'The Riddle of the Seven Tasks: a 7 x 7 Matrix—an Editorial by Daniela Teo,' posted on Mugglenet.com. See: *www.mugglenet.com/editorials/editorials/edit-teomea05.shtml* [accessed 15 June 2007].

42 The children's responses to Harry Potter, argues Gupta, 'express little apart from enthusiasm and the ubiquity of these sorts of adult mediation'. But it has to be said, he also dismissed many adult readers' responses: 'a large number of ecstatic reviews have attested to the pleasure that adults have derived from reading these books: though this is often justified by such sentimental and ultimately meaningless notions as making up for lost childhood or rediscovering the child in oneself'. (*Re-reading*, 11) I will address this theme of 'rediscovering the child' in one's 'lost' childhood books in the final chapter.

43 Hermione Dawson, email to Falconer (31 July 2005).

44 Tim Parks, in a review of Salman Rushdie's *The Ground Beneath Her Feet*, 'Gods and Monsters', *The New York Review* (6 May 1999): 12–16 (12–13).

45 Peter Brooks, *Reading for the Plot: Design and Intention in Narrative* (Oxford: Clarendon Press, 1984).

46 Kermode writes 'our scepticism, our changed principles of reality, force us to discard the fictions that are too fully explanatory, too consoling'. *The Sense of an Ending: Studies in the Theory of Fiction* (Oxford: Oxford University Press, 1979), 161.

47 Contrastingly, John Mullan writes of *Hallows*, 'now there is little time for psychologising. Narrative drive has taken over—and a good thing too'. 'A Shapely Plot and No Loose Ends', *The Guardian* (21 July 2007).

48 Suman Gupta has an excellent discussion of the importance of blood in the Potter series (*Re-reading*, 99–110).

49 *The Libation Bearers*, 466–75, in *Aeschylus I: Oresteia*, tr. R. Lattimore (London: Chicago University Press, 1953).

50 In ancient Greek, *miaros* means 'defiled with blood, polluted, abominable, foul, brutal, coarse or disgusting'. (H.G. Liddell and R. Scott, eds., *Liddell and Scott Greek-English Lexicon* (Oxford: Clarendon Press, 1996, ninth edition). Sophocles uses the term, for example, in *Oedipus at Colonnus* (1374) and *Antigone* (172), as does Euripides in *Iphigenia in Taurus* (1229) and *Hippolytus* (316–318).

51 Michael Gilleland offers a more literal translation of Rowling's epigraph: 'it is for the house [to apply the] absorbent remedy for these [wounds],

not from others outside, but from themselves, through savage blood-stained strife'. To this he adds, 'Garvie has a good note on the adjective ἔμμοτον, which I translated as 'absorbent': μοτοί are plugs of lint for dressing festering wounds, or, more precisely, for keeping them open until they suppurate and can heal from within . . . .This is one of the most certain cases of a borrowing by Aeschylus from medical terminology'. See Gilleland, 'Harry Potter and Aeschylus', *http://laudatortemporisacti.blogspot.com/2007/07/harry-potter-and-aeschylus.html* [accessed 9 November 2007].

52   Shawn Adler, 'Harry Potter Author J.K. Rowling Opens Up About Books,' MTV News (17 October 2007). See: *http://www.mtv.com/news/articles/1572107/20071017/index.jhtml* [accessed 9 November 2007].

53   Voldemort mocks Harry as 'the boy who survived by accident' but the resurrected Harry confidently retorts, 'Accident, when I decided to fight . . . ? Accident, that I didn't defend myself tonight, and still survived, and returned to fight again?' (*Hallows*, 591)

54   Bakhtin's theory of carnival is developed mainly in *Rabelais and His World*, tr. Hélène Iswolsky (Bloomington, IN: Indiana University Press, 1984), while his concept of polyphony is most fully explored in *Problems of Dostoevsky's Poetics*, ed. and tr. Caryl Emerson (London: University of Minnesota Press, 1984).

55   Cf. Gary Saul Morson, *Narrative and Freedom: the Shadows of Time* (New Haven: Yale University Press, 1996).

56   Jean-Paul Sartre, *Sketch for a Theory of the Emotions* (1939), tr. Philip Mairet (London: Methuen, 1962), 63, quoted by Kermode, *The Sense of an Ending*, 135.

57   A very similar dynamic operates in the crossover television series, Joss Whedon's *Buffy the Vampire Slayer*, when Buffy dies for her sister but is resurrected.

58   'Nam Sibyllam quidem Cumis ego ipse oculis meis vidi in ampulla pendere, et cum illi pueri dicerent: Sibylla ti theleis; respondebat illa: apothanein thelo'. Petronius, *Satyricon*, with an English translation by M. Heseltine (London: Heinemann, 1975).

Chapter 3

1.   See: *http://www.goldencompassmovie.com* [accessed 25 January 2008]. Chris Weitz directed the film *The Golden Compass* for New Line Cinema in 2007. The Tolkien reference is to the film trilogy directed by Peter Jackson, *The Lord of the Rings* (New Line Cinema, 2001–2003).

2   Philip Pullman, *His Dark Materials* trilogy, comprising: *Northern Lights* (London: Scholastic, 1995; US title: *The Golden Compass*), *The Subtle*

Knife (London: Scholastic, 1997), *The Amber Spyglass* (London: Scholastic, 2000). Hereafter cited in the text as *Northern Lights, Subtle Knife* and *Amber Spyglass.*

3   Laura Miller, 'Religious Furor over *The Golden Compass*', *Los Angeles Times* (2 December 2007). See http://www.latimes.com/features/books/la-bk-miller2dec02,0,1352215.story?coll=la-books-headlines [accessed 2 December 2007].

4   These figures, supplied by Nielson BookScan, refer to the two children's editions of *Northern Lights* (Scholastic Point, 1995 and 1998), ISBNs 0590139614 and 0590660543); also *The Subtle Knife* (Scholastic Point, 1998), ISBN 0590112899; *The Amber Spyglass* (Scholastic Point, 2001), ISBN 043999358X.

5   Figures refer to the adult editions of *Northern Lights, The Subtle Knife* and *The Amber Spyglass* (Scholastic Press, 2001), ISBNs 0439994128, 0439994136 and 0439994144.

6   Achuka, 'Interview with Philip Pullman'. See: *http://www.achuka.co.uk/archive/interviews/ppint.php* [accessed 1 December 2007].

7   Achuka, 'Interview with Philip Pullman'.

8   See Andrea Gayle Holm Allingham, 'Defending the Imagination: Charles Dickens, Children's Literature, and the Fairy Tale Wars', *The Victorian Web* (2000). http://www.victorianweb.org/authors/dickens/pva/pva25.html [accessed 20 January 2008].

9   Philip Pullman, 'Miss Goddard's Grave', University of East Anglia Lecture. See: *http://www.philip-pullman.com/pages/content/index.asp?PageID=113* [accessed 1 December 2007].

10   Philip Pullman, 'Writing Fantasy Realistically', Sea of Faith National Conference (2002). See: *http://sofn.org.uk/conferences/pullman2002.html* [accessed 1 December 2007]. Hereafter referred to in the text as 'Writing Fantasy'.

11   In Chapter 7, we will find a similar point being made by C.S. Lewis in his criticism of a film adaptation of Rider Haggard's *King Solomon's Mines.*

12   *http://www.goldencompassmovie.com* [accessed 25 January 2008].

13   Pullman, 'Writing Fantasy'. His idea of 'self-possession' is comparable to the Blake's representation of the wisdom that arises out of the marriage of innocence and experience. See Blake, *Songs of Innocence and of Experience: Shewing the Two Contrary States of the Human Soul* (1789) and *The Marriage of Heaven and Hell* (1790). For further discussion of children's fiction and Romanticism, see Chapter 6.

14   Eric Hobsbawm distinguishes between *heim,* the remembered home of infancy, and *heimat,* the collective sense of a 'patria' or homeland. See Hobsbawm, 'Introduction', *Social Research* 58:1 (Spring, 1991): 65–68.

15 John Durham Peters, 'Exile, Nomadism, and Diaspora: the Stakes of Mobility in the Western Canon', in Hamid Naficy, *Home, Exile, Homeland: Film, Media, and the Politics of Place* (Routledge: London, 1999): 17–44 (37).

16 William Shakespeare, *As You Like It*, II.7.143–66, in *As You Like It*, ed. Cynthia Marshall (Cambridge: Cambridge University Press, 2004).

17 For informal glosses on these and other neologisms which have evolved from the concept of the 'kid(d)ult', see *http://www.wordspy.com/* [accessed 1 January 2008].

18 Watterson, *Calvin and Hobbes Tenth Anniversary* (Andrews McMeel Publishing; 1995), 21. For a discussion of this passage in the context of Romanticism, see James McGavran, *Romanticism and Children's Literature in Nineteenth-Century England* (Athens: University of Georgia Press, 1991), 7.

19 Erik Erikson, *Identity: Youth and Crisis* (New York: Norton, 1968): 135–41; and Erikson, *The Life Cycle Completed: A Review* (New York: Norton, 1982): 61–72. See also Erikson's *Adulthood* (New York: Norton, 1978).

20 J.A. Appleyard, *Becoming a Reader: The Experience of Fiction from Childhood to Adulthood* (Cambridge: Cambridge University Press, 1991): 160–61.

21 Klaus Riegel, 'Adult Life Crises: A Dialectical Interpretation of Development', in *Life-Span Developmental Psychology: Normative Life Crises*, eds. Nancy Datan and Leon H. Gindberg (New York: Academic Press, 1975), 76. See also Riegel, 'The Dialectics of Human Development', *American Psychologist* 31, 10 (1976): 689–700, and Appleyard, *Becoming a Reader*, 161.

22 Philip Pullman, 'There Has to Be a Lot of Ignorance In Me When I Start a Story', *The Guardian* (18 February 2002).

23 Philip Pullman, 'Introduction', *John Milton's* Paradise Lost (Oxford: Oxford University Press, 2005), 10.

24 In *The Case of Peter Pan*, Jacqueline Rose explores the specifically adult investment in concepts of a timeless child paradise ('suppose . . . that Peter Pan is a little boy who does not grow up, not because he doesn't want to, but because someone else prefers that he shouldn't'. (3)

25 Rushdie asks, 'How does it come about, at the close of this radical and enabling film, . . . that we are given this conservative little homily? . . . Are we to believe that Dorothy has learned no more on her journey than that she didn't need to make such a journey in the first place? . . ."*Is that right?*" Well, excuse *me*, Glinda, but is it hell.' *The Wonderful Wizard of Oz* (London: BFI Publishing, 1992), 56–57.

26   A misquotation of John Keats's description of the Romantic imagination, which Keats compares to Adam's imagination in Milton's *Paradise Lost*. Keats says, 'he awoke and found it true', although strictly speaking, he didn't, because at first sight, Eve ran away from him and had to be persuaded to turn back. Keats, 'Letter to Benjamin Bailey' (22 November 1817), in H.E. Rollings, ed., *The Letters of John Keats*, 2 vols. (Cambridge, MA: Harvard University Press, 1958), Vol. 1, 185.

27   Leonardo da Vinci, 'Lady with an Ermine' (Czartoryskich Museum, Krakov). For the influence on Pullman, see MoreIntelligentLife.com, 'An Interview with Philip Pullman', 3 December 2007: *http://www.moreintelligentlife.com/node/697* [accessed 28 January 2008].

28   Gilles Deleuze and Félix Guattari, *Nomadology: the War Machine*, tr. Brian Massumi (New York: Semiotexte, 1986). See also Rosi Braidotti, *Nomadic Subjects: Embodiment and Sexual Difference in Contemporary Feminist Theory* (New York: Columbia University Press, 1994).

29   Stephan Elliott, dir., *The Adventures of Priscilla, Queen of the Desert* (Australian Film Finance Corporation, 1994).

30   The 'addressivity' [*obrashchennost*] of an utterance is its 'quality of turning to someone', M.M. Bakhtin, 'The Problem of Speech Genres', in *Speech Genres and Other Late Essays*, eds. Emerson and Holquist, tr. Vern McGee (Austin: University of Texas Press, 1986), 99. The subject feels 'responsibility' [*otvetstvennost*] at the moment 'where the ought-to-be (obligation) in principle confronts me within myself as another world'. Bakhtin, 'Author and Hero in Aesthetic Activity', in M. Holquist, ed., *Art and Answerability: Early Philosophical Essays* (Austin: University of Texas Press, 1981), 119.

31   Dave Weich, 'Interview with Philip Pullman', Powells Interviews with Authors, (31 August 2000). See http://www.powells.com/authors/pullman.html [accessed 12 December 2007].

32   Morson and Emerson argue persuasively that in Bakhtin's theory of carnival, 'there is no longer a self, there is only the carnival mask; other people can accomplish what "I" can if they adopt my festive clothes. Carnival as a whole appears to offer a perfect "alibi for being"'. G.S. Morson and C. Emerson, *Mikhail Bakhtin: Creation of a Prosaics* (Stanford, CA: Stanford University Press, 1990), 95.

33   Cf. Virgil, *Aeneid* 6 (19BC), in H. Rushton Fairclough, tr., *Virgil* (London: William Heinemann Ltd.), Vol. 1, 508–72.

34   Cf. Angela Carter, 'I am all for putting new wine in old bottles, especially if the pressure of the new wine makes the bottles explode'. Carter, 'Notes from the Front Line,' in *Shaking a Leg: Collected Journalism and Writings* (London: Vintage, 1998), 37.

35 For a discussion of these and other descent narratives written by contemporary women writers, see Rachel Falconer, 'Engendering Dissent in the Underworld', in Falconer, *Hell in Contemporary Literature: Western Descent Narratives Since 1945* (Edinburgh: Edinburgh Press, 2005), 144–71.

36 Maria Nikolajeva, *Children's Literature Comes of Age* (London: Garland Publishing, 1996), 99–100.

37 M.M. Bakhtin, *Problems of Dostoevsky's Poetics*, ed. and tr. Caryl Emerson (London: University of Minnesota Press, 1984), 74. Bakhtin actually writes 'author' rather than 'narrator', but he rarely makes a distinction between the two.

38 M.M. Bakhtin, 'Discourse in the Novel', in *The Dialogic Imagination: Four Essays,* ed. Michael Holquist, trs. Caryl Emerson and Michael Holquist (Austin, TX: University of Texas Press, 1984), 334.

39 Bakhtin, 'Discourse in the Novel', 332 and *passim*.

40 Philip Pullman, email posting to *children-literature-uk*, an academic online discussion forum (19 May 2004). See: *http://www.jiscmail.ac.uk/lists/children-literature-uk.html* [accessed 20 December 2007]. This discussion was taken up again in 2007, when Pullman expanded further on his concept of 'sprite fiction' (12 March 2007). Many thanks to Philip Pullman for permission to quote these postings.

41 Marina Warner writes persuasively that Pullman's concept of daemons may be read as an instance of Pythagorian, Ovidian metamorphic identity. However, she does not consider the idea that the narrator's voice in *His Dark Materials* may be metamorphic in the same way. Nor does she address Pullman's assertion that adults have settled, rather than metamorphic daemons, which would appear to contradict her reading of the trilogy. See Warner, *Fantastic Metamorphoses, Other Worlds: Ways of Telling the Self* (Oxford: Oxford University Press, 2002), 206–08.

42 'Mike in the Middle', Amazon.com review [accessed 12 July 2007].

43 Salman Rushdie, *Shame* (London: Jonathan Cape, 1983), 29.

44 Cf. Philip Pullman's later publication, *Lyra's Oxford* (New York: Knopf, 2003).

45 Barnes & Noble.com, 'The Man Behind the Magic: An Interview with Philip Pullman.' See: *http://search.barnesandnoble.com/booksearch/isbninquiry.asp?ean=9780440238133&displayonly=ITV&z=y* [accessed 12 December 2007].

46 Philip Pullman, 'Prize Winning Lecture at the Swedish Royal Library' (awarded jointly to Pullman and Ryôji Arai in 2005). See the Astrid Lindgren Memorial Award site: http://www.alma.se/default_a.aspx?i

d=247&epslanguage=EN and for the text of Philip Pullman's speech: http://www.alma.se/templates/KR_Page.aspx?id=3131&epslanguage=EN [accessed 21 December 2007].

47 A fifteen-year-old from Cumbria, Amazon.co review [accessed 12 July 2007].

48 Child's review posted on *Kids' Review* [accessed 12 July 2007]. Thanks to Martin Hill for permission to quote from this site.

49 An adult reader from Iowa, posted on Amazon.com [accessed 12 July 2007].

50 Bakhtin, 'Author and Hero in Aesthetic Activity', in *Art and Answerability*, 119.

51 Julia Kristeva, *Strangers to Ourselves*, tr. Leon S. Roudiez. London: Harvester Wheatsheaf, 1991.

52 Citations of *Paradise Lost* are from *Milton: Paradise Lost* (c1667), ed. A. Fowler. Harlow: Longman, 1998, 2nd edition. Hereafter cited in the text as *Paradise Lost*.

Chapter 4

1. Dave Weich, 'Interview with Mark Haddon', Powells Interviews with Authors. *http://www.powells.com/authors/haddon.html* [accessed 10 December 2007].

2   Haddon, 'B is for Bestseller', *The Observer* (11 April 2004). *http://books.guardian.co.uk/departments/childrenandteens/story/0,6000,1189538,00.html* [accessed 9 July 2007]. Mark Haddon, *The Curious Incident of the Dog in the Night-time* (London: Jonathan Cape, and Oxford: Definitions (David Fickling Books), 2003). Hereafter cited in the text as *Curious Incident*.

3   Bill Greenwell notes a number of novels published about this condition at the time of Haddon's; he compares the 'authenticity' of the various representations in 'The Curious Incident of Novels about Asperger's Syndrome,' *Children's Literature in Education* 35:3 (September 2004): 271–84.

4   For example, Dean Powell reports 'the insatiable hunger for children's fantasy' in 'Harry Potter: Potty about Potter (etc.)—however old you are', in *The Western Mail* (9 November 2002), while Boyd Tonkin's review of crossover fiction lists and discusses only children's fantasy novels, in 'Once Upon a Time in the Marketing Department', *The Independent* (6 November 2002). Bel Mooney reviews the 'new clutch of books in the "crossover genre"' as 'a move away from über-realism' and opines that 'it is no accident that all the "crossover" titles involve magical quests'. 'Is it for kids? Is it for grownups?' *The Times* (28 August 2002). Meanwhile, in the 2002 BAFTA awards, screen adaptations of children's fantasy dominated nearly

all the top nominations (see Maev Kennedy, 'Hobbits Run Rings Round Potter', *The Guardian* (29 January 2002).

5   Examples of the media response to this triumvirate of crossovers include: John Walsh, 'Mark Haddon: This Year's Big Read', *The Independent* (22 January 2004) and 'The Curious Case of the Dog that Did Bark', *The Bookseller* (30 Jan 2004).

6   Rachel Falconer, unpublished interview with David Fickling (Oxford, 10 August 2006).

7   Weich, 'Interview with Mark Haddon', Powells.com.

8   Falconer, interview with Fickling.

9   Kate Kellaway, 'Interview with Mark Haddon', *The Observer* (April 27, 2003). Sales figures provided by Nielsen BookScan (25 April 2007).

10 Jasper Rees, 'We're All Reading Children's Books,' *The Daily Telegraph* (15 November 2003).

11 Germaine Greer, 'it's a book for children. It's a book for adults. It's a book for me, who spent 65 years with someone I couldn't understand [Greer's mother, who may have had Asperger's]'. http://news.bbc.co.uk/1/hi/programmes/newsnight/review/2941558.stm [accessed 18 April 2007]. Cf. Julia Eccleshare's comment on Haddon's novel: 'it is one of the few titles for which the ubiquitous claim of "crossover" is not a gimmick. It genuinely has equal, though different, appeal to all readers—15-year-old Christopher Boone's narrative voice is at once childlike in its observations, and adult in its profundity'. Eccleshare, 'The Guardian's Children Fiction Prize', *The Guardian* (4 October 2003).

12 Nigel Reynolds, 'Prize Double Will Help to settle author's debts', *The Daily Telegraph* (13 November 2003): 10.

13 Figures supplied by Nielsen BookScan.

14 In a sample week, 4–10 April 2004, the adult Vintage edition sold 68,164 copies, while the children's Red Fox edition sold 21,275 copies. Figures supplied by Nielsen BookScan.

15 On Christopher Boone as an inadequate narrator, see John Mullan, 'Through Innocent Eyes,' *The Guardian* (24 April 2004), and Mullan, *How Novels Work* (Oxford: Oxford University Press, 2006), 50–52.

16 Hanks, 'The Curious Success of Mark Haddon,' *The Independent* (25 August 2006): *http://arts.independent.co.uk/books/features/article1221478.ece* [accessed 10 December 2007].

17 Review posted on Kids' Review: *http://www.kidsreview.org.uk/* [accessed 2 June 2007].

18 Falconer, interview with Fickling.

19 Christopher Marlowe, *The Jew of Malta*, I.1.37. *Complete Plays and Poems*, eds. E.D. Pendry and J.C. Maxwell (London: Dent, 1976).

20   Bachelard compares the botanist to P. de Boissy's description of a gar-
      den 'où les enfants regardent grand'. (de Boissy, *Main première*, 21;
      Gaston Bachelard, *The Poetics of Space*, tr. Maria Jolasp [Boston: Bea-
      con Press, 1969]), 155. In a post-lecture discussion, Joanny Moulin
      suggested that Bachelard may be playing with the phrase *voir grand*, to
      aggrandise what you see, in a megalomaniacal way. Falconer, unpub-
      lished lecture, 'Mark Haddon's *Curious Incident*', Aix-en-Provence (16
      June 2007).

21   See Susan Hancock, 'Miniature Worlds', in K. Reynolds, ed., *Childhood
      Remembered* (London: Roehampton Institute, 1998): 114–26.

22   Griswold, 'Smallness', in *Feeling like a Kid*, 51–74.

23   See Christine Wilkie, 'The Garden, the Wolf and the Dream of Child-
      hood', in Reynolds, ed., *Childhood Remembered*: 91–105.

24   See Christopher Williams, 'Ian McEwan's *The Cement Garden* and the
      Tradition of the Child/Adolescent as "I-Narrator", *Biblioteca della Ric-
      erca Diretta da Giovanni Dotoli*, Cultura Straniera 66 (Brindisi, 4–16
      October 1993).

25   See Augustine, *Confessions* 11:20:21, tr. F.J. Sheed (Cambridge: Hackett,
      2006); and Paul Ricoeur, *Time and Narrative*, Vol 1, Part 1, Chapters
      1–3. On Augustine and Ricoeur, see M.B. Pranger, 'Time and Narrative
      in Augustine's *Confessions*', *Journal of Religion* 81:3 (July 2001).

26   Other unusually observant and curious children can be found in McE-
      wan's fiction for children (e.g., *The Daydreamer*) and for adults (e.g.,
      Atonement and *The Cement Garden*).

27   Arthur Conan Doyle, 'Adventures of Sherlock Homes: The Adventure
      of Silver Blaze', *Strand Magazine*, Vol. IV (December, 1892): 291–306.

28   For an exploration of interpretations of Alice in recent adult fiction,
      see Cris Hollingsworth, ed., *Spaces of Wonderland* (Iowa City: Univer-
      sity of Iowa Press, forthcoming, 2009).

29   Milton is quoting Virgil's line from Eclogues, 'to compare great things
      with small'. On the ubiquity of this phrase and concept in classi-
      cal literature, see J.S. Coolidge, *Comparative Literature* 17:1 (1965):
      1–23.

30   Cf. Wall, *The Narrator's Voice*, 20–36. One finds the idea of the
      restricted/spacious view being explored, too, in adult fiction and
      film. In Jonze's *Being John Malkovich* (1999), the (adult) protagonist is
      filmed crawling through a cupboard door in a spare room to find him-
      self staring through the eyes of another person who has access to an
      altered reality. But what he sees in his out-of-body experience remains
      framed throughout in a heavy black border, reminding the viewer of
      his restricted eyeline while inhabiting this foreign body.

31   See Rachel Cameron, 'Watching Alice: The Child as Narrative Lens in *Alice's Adventures in Wonderland'*, in *Papers: Explorations into Children's Literature* 9:3 (December 1999): 23–29.

32   Victor Shklovsky, 'Art as Technique', collected in David Lodge, ed., *Modern Criticism and Theory* (London: Longmans, 1988): 16–30.

33   Rose, *The Case of Peter Pan*, 2–3.

34   Jacques Lacan, *The Four Fundamental Concepts of Psycho-analysis: The Seminar of Jacques Lacan, Book XI*, ed. Jacques-Alain Miller, tr. Alan Sheridan (New York: W W Norton, 1998), 95. The episode is discussed by Jean-Michel Rabaté, in 'Lacan's Turn to Freud', *The Cambridge Companion to Lacan*, ed., Rabaté (Cambridge: Cambridge University Press, 2007).

35   Craig Raine, 'A Martian Sends a Postcard Home' (c1979); Kurt Vonnegut, *Slaughterhouse-Five, or the Children's Crusade: a Duty Dance with Death* (c1969), (London: Vintage, 2003).

36   Guillermo del Toro, *Pan's Labyrinth* (*El Laberinto del Fauno*), tr. Guillermo del Toro. Warner Bros., 2006. See: *http://www.panslabyrinth. com* [accessed 27 January 2007].

37   'Children's fiction ... secures, places and frames the child' by setting up a world in which 'the adult comes first (author, maker, giver) and the child comes after (reader, product, receiver) but where neither of them enter the space in between'. Rose, *The Case of Peter Pan*, 2.

38   Bakhtin, *Problems of Dostoevsky's Poetics*, ed. and tr., Caryl Emerson (London: University of Minnesota Press, 1984), 73.

39   Christopher enumerates a list of his 'behavioural problems', identified by medical experts, 59–60.

40   Crossover Literature seminar, University of Sheffield (March, 2005).

41   Bethany Whittingham, Crossover Literature seminar (March, 2005).

42   'The implied author ... includes, in short, the intuited apprehension of a completed artistic whole' (73); it is the 'implicit picture of an author who stands behind the scenes, whether as a stage manager, as puppeteer, or as an indifferent God, silently paring his fingernails'. Wayne Booth, *The Rhetoric of Fiction* (London: University of Chicago Press, 1983), 151.

43   Haddon comments, 'if Christopher were real he couldn't/wouldn't have written the novel. So, in one sense, it would have been more "authentic" to have written it in the third person, but what was overwhelmingly more important from my point of view was to treat his worldview with complete respect and that meant handing him the reins'. See his article, 'I'm Flattered, Amazed, Deeply Moved and Sometimes a Little Dizzy', (*The Guardian*, 2 February 2004).

44 Eugène Ionesco, *Rhinocéros* (1959), tr. Derek Prouse (London: Samuel French, 1960).

45 In a similar way, Alasdair Gray sardonically describes the isolationist fantasies of the artist Duncan Thaw in his dystopic novel, *Lanark: A Life in Four Books* (London: Pan Books, 1994), 338.

Chapter 5

1. Mark Haddon, 'B Is for Bestseller', *The Observer* (11 April 2004).

2 Boyd Tonkin, 'A Week in Books', *The Independent* (2 September 2005).

3 Charles Dickens, *Dombey and Son*, ed. Andrew Saunders (London: Penguin Classics, 2002). The novel was adapted for radio by producers Jeremy Mortimer and Jessica Dromgoole, and broadcast on BBC Radio 4 Woman's Hour Drama, 19–23 November 2007. This particular passage, about the dismemberment of Carker, was adapted almost verbatim, and narrated with particular gusto.

4 Haruki Murakami, *The Wind-Up Bird Chronicle* (London: Vintage, 2003), 158–60.

5 Meg Rosoff, *How I Live Now* (London: Puffin, 2004). Lian Hearn [Gillian Rubenstein], *Tales of the Otori: Heaven's Net is Wide* (2007), *Across the Nightingale Floor* (2002), *Grass for His Pillow* (2003), *Brilliance of the Moon* (2004), *The Harsh Cry of the Heron* (2006), published by Pan Macmillan in several editions, in children's and adults' imprints (Macmillan, Macmillan Children's Books and Picador).

6 Julia Kristeva, *Powers of Horror: an Essay on Abjection,* tr. Leon Roudiez (New York: Columbia University Press, 1982), 3. Hereafter cited in the text as *Powers*.

7 Jacques Lacan, *The Four Fundamental Concepts of Psycho-analysis,* ed. Jacques-Alain Miller, tr. Alan Sheridan (New York: W.W. Norton, 1998). For an introduction to Lacan's three 'orders' of the psyche (the Symbolic, the Imaginary and the Real), see Dylan Evans, *An Introductory Dictionary of Lacanian Psychoanalysis* (London: Routledge, 1996), 82, 131–32, 159, 202. Evans defines the Symbolic as: a set of differentiated and differentiating signifiers governed by the Law (of the Phallus/the Father) which determines subjectivity, while the Real is that which is outside language and unassimilable to symbolisation (for example, death, horror, bliss, the primary mother-child dyad).

8 Giles Deleuze and Félix Guattari, *Anti-Oedipus: Capitalism and Schizophrenia* (London: Athlone Press, 1984). See also Sharla Hutchison, Chiara Briganti and Robert Con Davis-Undiano, 'Psychoanalytic Criticism

3: The Post-Lacanians,' in *The Johns Hopkins Guide to Literary Theory and Criticism,* eds. Groden, Kreiswirth and Szeman (London: Johns Hopkins University Press, 2nd edition, 2005).

9   Slavoj Žižek, 'Welcome to the Desert of the Real', in *Welcome to the Desert of the Real, Five Essays on September 11 and Related Dates* (London: Verso, 2002). The essay is accessible online at: *http://www.theglobalsite. ac.uk/times/109zizek.htm* [accessed 12 April 2006]. For comparable psychoanalytic interpretations of 9/11 as abjecting for the West, see Susan Sontag, 'First Reactions', *The New Yorker* (24 September 2001) and Chalmers Johnson, *Blowback, the Costs and Consequences of American Empire* (London: Time Warner, 2002).

10   For a Marxist psychoanalytic approach to tragedy, see Terry Eagleton, *Sweet Violence: The Idea of the Tragic* (Oxford: Blackwell, 2003).

11   *Peripateia* (reversal of fortune) and *anagnorisis* (discovery, recognition) are two of the stages of tragedy discussed by Aristotle in *Poetics*. See *Aristotle: Poetics,* tr. Malcolm Heath (Harmondsworth: Penguin, 1996).

12   Prospero of Caliban, in Shakespeare's *The Tempest* V.1.275–76, in *The Tempest,* ed. Rex Gibson (Cambridge: Cambridge University Press, 2005).

13   On the notion of 'viral evil,' see Jean Baudrillard, *The Transparency of Evil,* tr. James Benedict (London: Verso, 2002), 81.

14   Karen Coats, *Looking Glasses and Neverlands* (Iowa City: University of Iowa Press, 2007), 138. Hereafter cited in the text as *Looking Glasses*.

15   Boyd Tonkin, 'A Week in Books', *The Independent* (2 September 2005).

16   The theatre production of Blackman's *Noughts and Crosses* was reviewed by Kirsty Lang on Front Row, BBC Radio 4 (7 December 2007).

17   Meg Rosoff's *How I Live Now* was adapted for radio by Elizabeth Burke (December 2007). See: *http://www.bbc.co.uk/radio4/womanshour/drama/* [accessed 17 December 2007].

18   For reviews of the theatre production of Morpurgo's *Private Peaceful,* see: *http://www.theatre-wales.co.uk/news/newsdetail.asp?newsID=2333* [7 Dec 2007]. Two other notable examples of adolescent fiction containing vivid and explicit descriptions of extreme violence which also crossed to adult readerships are Stuart Hill's *The Cry of the Icemark* and Peter Dickinson's *The Cup of the World*.

19   Sue Vice explores this point in *Children Writing the Holocaust* (Basingstoke: Palgrave Macmillan, 2004).

20   Karín Lesnik-Oberstein, *Children's Literature: New Approaches* (Basingstoke: Palgrave Macmillan, 2004), 205.

21   Julia Kristeva, 'The Adolescent Novel', in *New Maladies of the Soul*, tr. Ross Guberman (New York: Columbia University Press, 1990), 135–53 (136).

22   In 'the Imaginary' order, the subject's ego is formed by identifying with fantastic projections of the self onto others. See Dylan Evans, *An Introductory Dictionary of Lacanian Psychoanalysis* (London: Routledge, 1996), 131–32.

23   See also Nicholas Tucker, 'Depressive Stories for Children', *Children's Literature in Education* 37:3 (September 2006).

24   Kristeva, *Powers of Horror*, 9.

25   Geraldine MCaughrean, *The White Darkness* (Oxford: Oxford University Press, 2005). Hereafter cited in the text as *White Darkness*.

26   Quotations from, respectively, Boyd Tonkin, 'A Week in Books', *The Independent* (4 December 2005); Nicholas Tucker, email to Falconer (31 January 2007), Adèle Geras, 'Snow Fun', *The Guardian* (10 September 2005). See also Kate Kellaway, 'Can You Trust a Man Who Makes His Own Teabags?' *The Observer* (18 September 2005), and Nicholas Tucker, www.oup.com/uk/catalogue/?ci=9780192726186&view=oxed [accessed 13 December 2007].

27   McCaughrean, *A Pack of Lies: Twelve Stories in One* (Oxford: Oxford University Press, 1988), awarded the Carnegie Medal in 1988. McCaughrean's *Not the End of the World* (Oxford: Oxford University Press, 2004) won the Whitbread (now Costa) Children's Book Award in 2004 (to date, McCaughrean is the only author to have won the award three times). *Not the End of the World* attracted a substantial adult readership and was reviewed on BBC Radio 4's *Woman's Hour* (29 November 2004).

28   Peter Bramwell, 'Review of McCaughrean's *The White Darkness*,' *Write Away*. See *http://improbability.ultralab.net/writeaway/whitedarkness.htm* [accessed 10 December 2007]. For some writers and critics, the constraints of the adolescent narratorial voice are precisely the problem with first-person young adult fiction. As John Stephens writes, 'the illusion of realism requires a child-narrator who lacks the verbal sophistication of an adult' and the result of employing such narrators is to create 'extremely solipsistic subject positions for character-narrators, which are then replicated by readers'. Stephens, *Language and Ideology in Children's Fiction* (London: Longman, 1992), 252.

29   Nicholas Tucker, 'Geraldine McCaughrean: Surfing the Sea of Stories', *The Independent* (15 December 2007).

30   For example, *Golden Myths and Legends of the World* (London: Orion, 1998). See McCaughrean's Web-site for a complete listing of her

adaptations of myths and legends: *http://www.geraldine-mccaughrean. co.uk/main.html* [accessed 30 January 2008].

31 Brontë, *The Glass Town Saga 1826–1832*, in *An Edition of the Early Writings of Charlotte Brontë*, ed. Christine Alexander. (Oxford: Blackwell, 1987, Vol.1).

32 Jules Verne, *Journey to the Centre of the Earth* (*Voyage au centre de la terre* (c1864), tr. William Butcher (Oxford: Oxford World's Classics, 1992). Sym recalls her father's excitement over a trip to Snæfells (120 kilometres from Reykjavík), the entrance to the underworld for Lidenbrock and his nephew Axel (*White Darkness*, 150).

33 'Dis' being another name for Hades, the Greek underworld.

34 John Milton, *Paradise Lost* I.254–55; quoted in the epigraph to *White Darkness*.

35 Dante Alighieri, *Inferno* 34.25, in *The Divine Comedy: Inferno,* vol 1: *Text,* tr. Charles Singleton (Princeton, NJ: Princeton University Press, 1989). For a discussion of this passage, and parallels in contemporary fiction, see Falconer, *Hell in Contemporary Literature* (Edinburgh: Edinburgh University Press, 2005).

36 Roland Barthes, *The Pleasure of the Text* (*Le plaisir du texte,* 1973), tr. Richard Miller (Toronto: HarperCollins Canada, 1975), 14. For an analysis of Barthes's concepts of *plaisir* versus *jouissance*, see Robert Miklitsch, 'Difference: Roland Barthes's Pleasure of the Text, Text of Pleasure', *boundary* 2, Vol. 12: 1 (Autumn, 1983): 101–114.

37 Letter from Franz Kafka to Oskar Pollak (27 January 1904), quoted in *White Darkness*, 263.

38 Sym is quoting lines 121–22 of 'The Rime of the Ancient Mariner'. See *Coleridge, Poems and Prose*, ed. K. Raine (London: Penguin, 1957), p. 41.

39 Joseph Conrad, *Heart of Darkness*, ed. R. Kimbrough (London: Norton, 1988), 85.

40 T.S. Eliot, *The Waste Land,* 360–64, in *The Waste Land,* ed. Michael North (London: Norton, 2004).

Chapter 6

1 David Almond, *Clay* (London: Hodder Children's, 2005).

2 As Almond has said in interview, 'there's something very basic and fundamental about working with the earth, making stuff from it . . . Once I started working with the idea in the story, it drew in so many links: Frankenstein obviously, and the Jewish myth of the golem, and Christian creation where God creates man from the clay of the

earth and breathes life into him. Setting the book in Felling was a way of grounding those stories and making them mine'. (Benedicte Page, 'Frankenstein Goes to Tyneside', *The Independent on Sunday*, 6 November 2005) Elsewhere he notes his sources in more detail: 'Years back, I saw an opera in Newcastle called *The Golem* . . . When I first finished the book, there was a part when one of the characters told the golem legend. I thought that I would have to take that out, because it was too obvious'. He also cites the influence of David Wisniewski's picture book of the golem legend. (Lindsey Fraser, 'Interview with David Almond', Edinburgh International Book Festival, 17 August 2005). www.edbookfest.co.uk/downloads/ 05_08_17_david_almond.doc [accessed 22 July 2007].

3   Mary Shelley, *Frankenstein, or The Modern Prometheus* (c1818), ed. Marilyn Butler (Oxford: Oxford Paperbacks, 1998).

4   See Percy Bysshe Shelley, *Prometheus Unbound* (c1820, Black Box Press, 2007).

5   See, for example, Paul Wegener and Carl Boese's expressionist film, *Der Golem* (1920). For another recent retelling in crossover fiction, cf. Michael Chabon's *The Amazing Adventures of Kavalier and Clay* (London: Picador, 2001).

6   This is the third of five constituent features of magic realist texts, as outlined by Wendy Faris, 'Scheherazade's Children: Magical Realism and Postmodern Fiction', in Zamora and Faris, eds., *Magical Realism: Theory, History, Community* (London: Duke University Press, 1995), 163–90. The aesthetic of creating a 'hesitation in the reader' between two contradictory understandings of events, one naturalistic (or 'realist') and the other marvellous (or 'magic'), was a central theme of Tvetan Todorov's *The Fantastic: A Structural Approach to a Literary Genre*. Imogen Stubbs's review of *Clay* demonstrates Almond's success in producing this structural hesitation: 'the reader is never entirely sure what's real and what isn't . . . there's this constant crossover between reality and imagination, good and evil, beauty and darkness, everyday ordinariness and magical extraordinariness'. Christopher Middleton, 'Interview with Imogen Stubbs', *The Daily Telegraph* (3 June 2006). For further discussion of faith and magic realism, see Christopher Warnes, 'Naturalizing the Supernatural: Faith, Irreverence and Magical Realism,' in *Literature Compass* 2:1 (January 2005). *http://www.blackwellsynergy.com* [accessed 20 December 2007].

7   Quoted in Page, 'Frankenstein Goes to Tyneside'.

8   Quoted in Page, 'Frankenstein Goes to Tyneside'.

9   According to author Julie Bertagna, writers of adult fiction are often 'embarrassed to tell a straight story . . . without that knowing, ironic eye'.

(Gillian Bowditch, 'Interview with Julie Bertagna: It's Not a Kid's Game Anymore', *Sunday Times* [24 November 2002]). On 'literary knowingness', see also Philip Pullman, quoted by Nigel Reynolds, 'Writers Are Losing the Plot, Says Prize-winner', *The Daily Telegraph* (18 July 1996), and the Introduction and Chapter 3 of the present study.

10   Stroud quoted in Jasper Rees, 'We're All Reading Children's Books', *The Daily Telegraph* 15 November 2003). The Bartimaeus trilogy comprises: *The Amulet of Samarkand* (London: Corgi Children's, 2003), *Golem's Eye* (London: Doubleday, 2004); and *Ptolemy's Gate* (Doubleday Children's, 2005). In the attack on 'hifalutin' adult fiction, specific authors are rarely named, and it is perhaps invidious for me to do so here. But in the interests of clarity, some names and titles might be cited. In *A Poetics of Postmodernism*, Linda Hutcheon begins by mentioning the following: García Márquez's *One Hundred Years of Solitude*, Grass's *The Tin Drum*, Fowles's A *Maggot*, Doctorow's *Loon Lake*, Reed's *The Terrible Twos*, Kingston's *The Woman Warrior*, Findley's *Famous Last Words* and Rushdie's *Shame* (*A Poetics of Postmodernism* [London: Routledge, 1988]). In *Postmodern Fiction*, Brian McHale begins with Samuel Beckett, Alain Robbe-Grillet, Carlos Fuentes, Vladimir Nabokov, Robert Coover and Thomas Pynchon (*Postmodern Fiction* (London: Routledge, 1987)).

11   Musil, *The Man Without Qualities*, 708 (see the Introduction to this study).

12   Joanna Briscoe, 'So What's the Real Story?' *The Independent* (15 May 2003).

13   Nicholas Clee, 'Can the Magic Last Forever?' *The Independent* (15 September 2004). In a similar vein, Kate Kellaway cited Morpurgo, Philip Pullman and Jamila Gavin (author of successful crossover fictions such as *Coram Boy* and *Blood Stone*) as proponents of the view that the 'storytelling ability itself is key to the crossover book—adults enjoy clear narratives.' All three writers are 'great believer[s] in the oral tradition'. 'Pullman Class', *The Observer* (2 November 2003).

14   Falconer, unpublished interview with David Fickling. Maria Nikolajeva, *From Mythic to Linear: Time in Children's Literature* (Lanham, MD: Scarecrow Press, 1999).

15   S.F. Said, 'The Godfather of Harry Potter', *The Daily Telegraph* (15 October 2002).

16   Kevin Crossley-Holland's *Arthur* trilogy comprises: *The Seeing Stone*, *At the Crossing-Places*, *King of the Middle March* (London: Orion, 2001–03).

17   Claire Armistead, 'Saturday Review: Books: Arthur Reborn', (*The Guardian*, 29 September 2001).

18   Michelle Paver, quoted in Jonathan Brown, 'Record £3m Advance for Children's Author', *The Independent* (2 September 2002). Paver's *Chronicles* include: *Wolf Brother, Spirit Walker, Soul Eater* and *Outcast* (London: Corgi Children's).

19   Bel Mooney, 'Is It for Kids? Is It for Grown-ups?' *The Times* (28 August 2002).

20   Samuel Taylor Coleridge and William Wordsworth, *Lyrical Ballads, with a Few Other Poems* (c1798), ed. Michael Mason (London: Longman, 2007, second edition).

21   Boyne, *The Boy in the Striped Pyjamas* (Oxford: David Fickling Books, 2006). Shame Hegarty, 'Horror Through a Child's Eyes,' *Irish Times* (28 January 2006). Hegarty avers that Boyne's novel, though addressed to children, is 'a subtle, calculatedly simple and ultimately moving story. For any age'.

22   Anon., *Irish Times* (3 June 2006).

23   For example, Amanda Craig, 'Love and Revenge in a Tale Full of Eastern Promise', *The Times* (21 August 2002).

24   Philip Pullman, quoted in Claire Armistead, 'The *Holes* Phenomenon', *The Guardian* (17 October 2003).

25   Jan Mark, 'About a Boy', *The Guardian* (11 January 2003).

26   Julia Eccleshare, 'Review: Guardian Children's Fiction Prize', *The Guardian* (3 June 2006).

27   Wall, *The Narrator's Voice*, 20–36.

28   Boyd Tonkin, 'Once Upon a Time in the Marketing Department', *The Independent* (6 November 2002).

29   Salman Rushdie, *Haroun and the Sea of Stories* (Bath: Chivers, 1990), 146.

30   Rushdie, *The Ground Beneath Her Feet* (London: Jonathan Cape, 1999), 466.

31   Patrick Cave, discussion board posting, BBC Radio 4 *Lebrecht Live* programme, 'Why Are Adults Reading Children's literature?' (27 February 2005). *www.bbc.co.uk/radio3/lebrechtlive/pip/l3bqw/* [accessed 22 July 2007].

32   On the influence of Wordsworth's 'Immortality Ode' on nineteenth-century conceptions of childhood, see Richardson, 'Romanticism and the End of Childhood,' in James McGavran, ed., *Literature and the Child*, 23–44 (25), who also cites Barbara Garlitz, 'The Immortality Ode: Its Cultural Progeny,' *Studies in English Literature* 6 (1966): 639–49.

33   See Richardson, 'Romanticism and the End of Childhood', 25.

34   See, for example, James McGavran, *Romanticism and Children's Literature in Nineteenth-Century England* (Athens, OH: University of Georgia Press, 1991), 12.

35   Boswell quoted in Daniel Rosenthal, 'Child's Play', *The Times* (15 December 2003).

36   Adrian Mitchell, *With Great Pleasure*, BBC Radio 4 (10 February 2007). The quotation is from the last line of Plate 27 in Blake's *The Marriage of Heaven and Hell* (1790).

37   Nicholson quoted in Jasper Rees, 'We're All Reading Children's Books', *The Daily Telegraph* (15 November 2003).

38   Ted Hughes, 'Myth and Education', in Geoff Fox, ed., *Celebrating Children's Literature in Education* (London: Teachers' College Press, 1995), 3–18 (15).

39   Ted Hughes, 'Myth and Education', 16. Coleridge's celebrated Romantic definition of the imagination is as follows: 'The primary imagination I hold to be the living power and prime agent of all human perception, and as a repetition in the finite mind of the eternal act of creation in the infinite I AM. The secondary I consider as an echo of the former, coexisting with the conscious will, yet still as identical with the primary in the kind of its agency, and differing only in degree, and in the mode of its operation. It dissolves, diffuses, dissipates, in order to recreate; or where this process is rendered impossible, yet still, at all events, it struggles to idealize and to unify. It is essentially vital, even as all objects (*as* objects) are essentially fixed and dead'. *Biographia Literaria*, Chapter 13, in H.J. Jackson, ed., *Samuel Taylor Coleridge* (Oxford: Oxford University Press, 1985), 155–482 (313).

40   'The reason Milton wrote in fetters when he wrote of Angels & God, and at liberty when of Devils & Hell, is because he was a true Poet, and of the Devil's party without knowing it'. William Blake, *The Marriage of Heaven and Hell*, Plate 6. In Blake, *The Marriage of Heaven and Hell*, intro. G. Keynes (Oxford: Oxford Paperbacks, 1975), xvii. On Philip Pullman's endorsement of Blake's reading of Milton see, for example, 'I Am of the Devil's Party', *The Telegraph* (29 January 2002).

41   Rushdie, *The Jaguar Smile, a Nicaraguan Journey* (Oxford: ISIS, 1989), 12.

42   Gabriel García Márquez, 'A Very Old Man with Enormous Wings', in *Collected Stories* trans. Gregory Rabaassa and J. S. Bernstein (London: Penguin, 1991), 186–93.

43   On the child focaliser in adult magic realism, see Anne Hegerfeldt, *Lies That Tell the Truth: Magic Realism Seen Through Contemporary Fiction from Britain* (Amsterdam: Rodopi, 2005), 146–56. The term 'focaliser' is used in narrative theory to distinguish the point of view (who sees) from the narrator (who tells). See Gérard Genette, *Narrative Discourse*, tr. Jane Lewin (Oxford: Blackwell, 1986), Chapter 5.

44   For a comparison of the two novels, see Don Latham, 'Magical Realism and the Child Reader: The Case of David Almond's *Skellig*', in *Alice's Academy* (January 2006). *http://www.the-looking-glass.net/rabbit/v10i1/alice1.html* [accessed 22 July 2007].

45   Allende, *The City of the Beasts*, tr. M. Peden (London: Flamingo, 2002). And cf. Eva Ibbotson's *Journey to the River Sea* (London: Macmillan Children's Books, 2001). However, Philip Swanson makes a case for ambiguity in Allende's novel: 'Magic Realism and Children's Literature: Isabel Allende's *La Ciudad de las Bestias*' in Stephen Hart and Wen-chin Ouyang, eds., *A Companion to Magical Realism* (Woodbridge: Támesis, 2005), 168–80. See also Swanson, 'Latin Lessons for Young Americans: Isabel Allende's Fiction for Children', in *Revista de Estudios Hispánicos* 41 (2007): 173–89.

46   On revisions of Piaget, see J.A. Appleyard, *Becoming a Reader: The Experience of Fiction from Childhood to Adulthood* (Cambridge: Cambridge University Press, 1990), 175.

47   Carol Birch, 'Deep in the Forest', *The Guardian* (30 November 2002).

48   'Mary Shelley . . . suggests through *Frankenstein* that the fantasy, now becoming a reality, of artificially creating life out of dead matter is rooted in the same masculinist desires for autonomy and depreciation of the body and the feminine that feminist critics have located within canonical Romanticism'. Richardson, 'Romanticism and the End of Childhood', 39.

49   John Milbank, 'Problematizing the Secular: The Post-postmodern Agenda', in Philippa Berry and Andrew Wernick, eds., *Shadow of Spirit: Postmodernism and Religion* (London: Routledge, 1992), 30–44 (30).

50   See Philippa Berry, *Shadow of Spirit: Postmodernism and Religion*, 3, 5, and 7 (notes 10 and 11); Edith Wyschogrod, *Saints and Postmodernism* (Chicago: Chicago University Press, 1990); Maurice Blanchot, 'The Limits of Experience: Nihilism', in *The New Nietzsche*, ed. David Allison (Cambridge MA: MIT Press, 1985): 121–28; Luce Irigaray, *Marine Lover: Of Friedrich Nietzsche*, tr. Gillian Gill (NY: Columbia U P, 1991); Jacques Derrida, 'Of an Apocalyptic Tone Recently Adopted in Philosophy', tr. John Leavey Jr., *Semeia* 23 (1982): 63–97; Derrida, 'Comment ne pas parler,' in *Psyché: inventions de l'autre* (Paris: Galiée, 1987): 535–96; Mark Taylor, *Erring: an A/Theology* (Chicago: Chicago University Press, 1984). For studies of religious mysticism and deconstruction, see Herman Rapaport, *Heidegger and Derrida: Reflections on Time and Language* (London: University of Nebraska Press, 1989); John Caputo, *The Mystical Element in Heidegger's Thought* (Athens OH: University of Ohio Press, 1978); Kevin Hart, *The Trespass*

of the Sign: Deconstruction, Theology and Philosophy (Cambridge: Cambridge University Press, 1990); Susan Handelman, *The Slayers of Moses: The Emergence of Rabbinic Interpretation in Modern Literary Theory* (Albany: State University of NY Press, 1982).

51 John McClure, 'Postmodern/Post-Secular: Contemporary Fiction and Spirituality', in *Modern Fiction Studies* 41.5 (1995): 141–63.

52 David Harvey, *The Condition of Postmodernity: An Inquiry into the Origins of Cultural Change* (Oxford: Blackwell, 1990), 302.

53 Quotations from Douglas Kennedy, 'Selling Rapture', *The Guardian* (9 July 2005).

54 Berry, *Shadow of Spirit*, 2.

55 Richard Dawkins, *The God Delusion* (London: Bantam Press, 2006). Other books in the genre include: Daniel C. Dennett, *Breaking the Spell: Religion as a Natural Phenomenon*; Sam Harris, *The End of Faith: Religion, Terror and the Future of Reason* and *Letter to a Christian Nation*; Christopher Hitchens, *God is Not Great: How Religion Poisons Everything*; David Mills, *Atheist Universe: The Thinking Person's Answer to Christian Fundamentalism*; and Victor J. Stenger, *God: The Failed Hypethesis. How Science Shows That God Does Not Exist.*

56 Claire Armistead, quoted on David Almond's Web page. See: *http://www.davidalmond.com/books/review.html* [accessed 20 January 2008]. Nicolette Jones, amongst others, noted the novel's crossover appeal: 'extraordinary storytelling, not beneath the attention of adult readers'. *The Sunday Times* (1 November 2005).

57 Mary Shelley likewise referred to her novel, *Frankenstein, or the Modern Prometheus,* as 'my hideous progeny'. See her preface to the revised edition (London: 1831).

58 Fraser, 'Interview with Almond'.

59 Satan curses himself in the second person, thus revealing a divided consciousness, in *Paradise Lost* IV.71. On his concept of the mirror stage, Lacan wrote, 'the mirror stage is a phenomenon to which I assign a twofold value. In the first place, it has historical value as it marks a decisive turning point in the mental development of the child. In the second place, it typifies an essential libidinal relationship with the body-image'. *Some Reflections on the Ego*; see also *La relation d'objet,* both in *Écrits,* tr. Bruce Fink (New York: Norton, 2006). The above quotation cited in Evans, *An Introductory Dictionary of Lacanian Psychoanalysis,* 115.

60 For literary applications of Freud's theory that a major symptom of trauma is the return of the past experienced as present, see Paul Antze and Michael Lambek, eds., *Tense Past: Cultural Essays in Trauma and Memory* (1996);

James Berger, *After the End: Representations of Post-Apocalypse* (1999); Cathy Caruth, *Unclaimed Experience: Trauma, Narrative History* (1996); Nicola King, *Memory, Narrative, Identity: Remembering the Self* (2000); Valerie Krips, *The Presence of the Past: Memory, Heritage, and Childhood in Postwar Britain* (2000); Dominick LaCapra, *Writing History, Writing Trauma* (2001); Sue Vice, *Children Writing the Holocaust* (2004); and Anne Whitehead, *Trauma Fiction* (2004).

61   Almond quoted in Page, 'Frankenstein Goes to Tyneside'.

62   Drawing on Alasdair MacIntyre's *After Virtue*, Charles Taylor argues that as no moral framework is shared by everyone in the modern period, modern identity is defined by its need to be constructed and affirmed. To be a modern self is to find oneself 'on a quest' for identity. See Taylor, *Sources of the Self: The Making of the Modern Identity* (Cambridge, MA: Harvard University Press, 1989), 17.

63   Yann Martel, *Life of Pi* (Toronto: Vintage, 2002), 352.

64   Quoted in Page, 'Frankenstein Goes to Tyneside'.

65   A Jungian emphasis is amongst the 'secondary' characteristics of magic realism according to Faris ('Scheherazade's Children,' 178) and of children's literature, according to Maria Nikolajeva, *From Mythic to Linear*.

66   Cf. the reviews of *Clay* which stressed its mesmerising effects on the reader: 'hypnotic story-telling' (*Look at a Book*); an 'atmospheric, weird, lyrical and completely engaging masterpiece', Graham Marks, *Publishing News*, 'Books of the Year'.

67   In Lewis Carroll's *Through the Looking-Glass and What Alice Found There*, Tweedledum and Tweedledee startle Alice by suggesting she only exists because the Red King is dreaming her: 'He's dreaming now', said Tweedledee: 'and what do you think he's dreaming about?' Alice said, 'Nobody can guess that'. 'Why, about YOU!" Tweedledee exclaimed, clapping his hands triumphantly. 'And if he left off dreaming about you, where do you suppose you'd be?' 'Where I am now, of course', said Alice. 'Not you!' Tweedledee retorted contemptuously. 'You'd be nowhere. Why, you're only a sort of thing in his dream!' 'If that there King was to wake', added Tweedledum, 'you'd go out—bang!—just like a candle!' *Alice's Adventures in Wonderland* (1865), in Carroll, *Alice in Wonderland* (London: W.W. Norton & Co., 1992): 144–45.

68   As in Dante's *Commedia*, *terza rime* proceeds in groups of three rhyming lines, linked in a chain: aba bcb cdc, etc. For an excellent discussion of the implications of Dante's rhyme scheme, and its connection to Augustine's concept of the threefold nature of time (anticipation, attention, memory), see John Freccero, *The Poetics of Conversion*, *The Poetics of Conversion*, ed. Rachel Jacoff (Cambridge, MA: Harvard University Press, 1986), 25.

For Augustine and the child's gaze, see Chapter 4 of the present study. I use the term 'chain of being' reservedly, since it is more commonly invoked in an earlier generation of Renaissance literature scholarship, where the 'chain' is social not temporal, and suggests a predetermined place in a hierarchy leading from God (at the top) down through a stratified society (see E.M.W. Tillyard, *The Elizabethan World Picture*, London: Vintage, 1959).

69 William Wordsworth, 'My Heart Leaps Up', in Harold Bloom and Lionel Trilling, eds., *Romantic Poetry and Prose* (London: Oxford University Press, 1972), 168.

70 'I was writing about somewhere that I'd left behind. It seemed like a different country but I'd actually been there, so I was like an explorer going back to that place'. (Fraser, 'Interview with Almond') 'The past is a country from which we have all emigrated . . . its loss is part of our common humanity'. Rushdie, *Imaginary Homelands: Essays and Criticism, 1981–1991*, London: Granta Books, 1992, 12.

71 As McGavran explains, 'the Romanticisms of Maria Edgeworth, Dorothy Wordsworth and Mary Shelley emphasised rationality, community and cooperation in contrast to their male counterparts (Blake and Wordsworth); their constructions of childhood were correspondingly different', *Romanticism and Children's Literature*, 9.

72 Latham, 'Magical Realism and the Child Reader'. Cf. Julia Eccleshare's view (which Almond's *Clay* also challenges): 'the convention of offering a corner of hope . . . may come to be the defining characteristic [of children's fiction]'. Eccleshare, 'Review: Guardian Children's Fiction Prize', *The Guardian* (3 June 2006).

Chapter 7

1 Hodder Children's began republishing Enid Blyton in 1997, and ten years later, sealed a deal lasting until 2026, to publish the entire *Famous Five* and *Secret Seven* series (see Graham Marks, 'It's "rightsology"', Publishing News. http://www.publishingnews.co.uk [accessed 19 October 2007]. Other new editions of classics include George MacDonald's *At the Back of the North Wind* (Puffin Classics, 1994) and *The Princess and the Goblin* (Puffin Classics, 1996); S.E. Hinton's *The Outsiders* (Puffin Modern Classics, 2003; Penguin Classics, 2006); H. Rider Haggard's *King Solomon's Mines* (Oxford Paperbacks, 1998; Hodder Headline, 2007); Mary Norton's *The Borrowers* (Puffin Modern Classics, 1993); Charlotte M. Yonge's novels for girls (e.g., *The Heir of Redclyffe*, Oxford Paperbacks, 1997); and G. A. Henty's adventure novels for boys (all ninety-nine now available in hard and soft covers, and on CD from

Robinson Books). See the Bibliography of this study for more examples of re-edited children's classics.

2   For example, the new Hodder Headline edition of Rider Haggard's *King Solomon's Mines* (2007) came out with two different issues, one for adults, one for children, and bearing the tagline 'the most amazing book ever written!' The new edition made no excuses for the novel's dated representation of noble savages, and it was enthusiastically reviewed on BBC Radio 4, on 8 July 2007. In addition to these new editions from mainstream publishing houses, there are many small publishers that specialise in selling deluxe, collectible editions of children's classics. For an excellent example, see http://www.janenissenbooks.co.uk/ [accessed 15 August 2007].

3   Peter Jackson, dir., *The Lord of the Rings: the Fellowship of the Ring*; *The Two Towers; The Return of the King* (New Line Cinema, 2001– 03); Andrew Adamson, dir., *The Chronicles of Narnia: The Lion, the Witch and the Wardrobe* (Walt Disney Pictures and Walden Media, 2005).

4   Chris Noonan, dir., *Miss Potter* (Phoenix Pictures, 2006).

5   Tim Burton, dir., *Charlie and the Chocolate Factory* (Warner Bros., 2005); Mark Forster, Mark, dir., *Finding Neverland* (Miramax Films, 2004); Stephen Spielberg, dir., *Hook* (Amblin Entertainment, 1991).

6   http://news.bbc.co.uk/1/hi/england/beds/bucks/herts/4079704.stm [accessed 15 August 2007].

7   C.S. Lewis, *The Chronicles of Narnia*, including: *The Lion, the Witch and the Wardrobe* (c1950); *Prince Caspian* (c1951); *The Voyage of the Dawn Treader* (c1952); *The Silver Chair* (c1953); *The Horse and His Boy* (c1954); *The Magician's Nephew* (c1955); *The Last Battle* (c1956). London: Collins, 2001.

8   C.S. Lewis, *The Chronicles of Narnia* (Collins Film tie-in edition, 2005).

9   An adult cabby driver and his wife are allowed into Narnia on the day of its creation, in *The Magician's Nephew*, 95. They are, in a sense, reborn as humanity in its infancy, and they become the Adam and Eve of the new world.

10   C.S. Lewis, 'On Three Ways of Writing for Children' in *Of Other Worlds: Essays and Stories* (New York: Harcourt Brace Jovanovich, 1966), 22–34 (24). Cf. Matthew 18.3, discussed in Chapter Six.

11   On paratexts, see Gérard Genette, *Paratexts: Thresholds of Interpretation*, tr. Jane Lewin (Cambridge: Cambridge University Press, 2007).

12   Sue Batt discusses 'Crossover Books' on the Bootrusted Web site. See http://www.booktrusted.co.uk/articles/documents [accessed 24 July 2007].

13 E.g., C.S. Lewis, *The Chronicles of Narnia* (Collins Full-Colour Collector Edition, 2000; and Lewis, *The Complete Chronicles of Narnia Hardback Box Set*, illustrated by Pauline Baynes, 2006).

14 Results of the Tesco survey were reported in *The Telegraph* (21 February 2005). Another survey, conducted in 2002 by education publisher Kumon showed similarly that, according to Simon Davies, 'parents are introducing their children to the reading books that they enjoyed as youngsters, while at the same time reading children's books that have captured the imaginations of today's generation' (*The Guardian*, 23 September 2002). For these and other recent surveys of reading habits in the UK, see http://www.literacytrust.org.uk [accessed 25 July 2007].

15 For a report of the survey, see *The Times Higher Education Supplement* (12 September 2003): http://www.literacytrust.org.uk/Database/stats/popularearly.html#Top [accessed 25 July 2007].

16 Falconer, unpublished interview with Cordelia Dawson, Oxford (19 August 2007).

17 See http://www.bbc.co.uk/arts/bigread/ [accessed 20 September 2007].

18 Francis Spufford, *The Child That Books Built* (London: Faber and Faber, 2002). Hereafter cited as *The Child*.

19 Primo Levi, *The Search for Roots: a Personal Anthology,* tr. Peter Forbes (London: Allen Lane, Penguin, 2001).

20 Mark Lawson, 'Interview with Philip Roth', Front Row, BBC Radio 4 (2 October 2007).

21 See http://www.bbc.co.uk/radio4/nationaltreasures/ [accessed 5 August 2007].

22 Clifford Geertz, *Available Light: Anthropological Reflections on Philosophical Topics* (Princeton, NJ: Princeton University Press, 2001), 220.

23 Alice Hoffman in conversation with Kathryn Hughes, Open Book, BBC Radio 4 (14 January 2007). See http://www.bbc.co.uk/radio4/arts/openbook/openbook_20070114.shtml [accessed 20 September 2007].

24 Susan Sontag, 'Literature is Freedom,' in *At the Same Time: Essays and Speeches* (New York: Farrar, Straus and Giroux, 2007), 205–209 (209).

25 Marcel Proust, *Remembrance of Things Past*, Vol. 1, tr. C. K. Scott Moncrieff and Terence Kilmartin (New York: Vintage, 1982), 48–51.

26 Quotations are taken from student discussion board postings, on the Intranet of the University of Sheffield, Crossover Literature module (Lit 210), 2002–2007.

27 Marcel Proust, 'On Reading', in *On Reading Ruskin: Prefaces to* La Bible d'Amiens *and* Sésame et les lys, tr. and ed. Jean Autret, William Burford

and Phillip J. Wolfe (New Haven, NJ: Yale University Press, 1987), 99–129 (110). The essay, originally published as 'Sur la lecture' (1905), begins with a fine self-portrait of Proust as an obsessive young reader (99–110). Hereafter cited in the text as 'On Reading'.

28 Elisabeth Ladenson, 'Rereading Proust: Perversion and Prolepsis in *A la recherché du temps perdu*', in David Galef, ed., *Second Thoughts: A Focus on Rereading* (Detroit, MI: Wayne State University Press, 1998), 249–65 (264). She continues, 'Proust's novel bridges Barthes's categories of *texte de plaisir and texte de jouissance,* offering us a textual pleasure that lead to endless consummation in the act of rereading'. (264).

29 Jack Zipes, *Happily Ever After: Fairy Tales, Children, and the Culture Industry* (London: Routledge, 1997), 1. See the Bibliography for Zipes's extensive writing on fairy tales.

30 Jack Zipes, *Fairy Tale as Myth; Myth as Fairy Tale* (Lexington, KY: University Press of Kentucky, 1994), 7.

31 http://disney.go.com/disneypictures/narnia/ [accessed 24 September 2007].

32 http://disney.go.com/disneypictures/narnia/fanclub/fanclub_winners. html [accessed 24 September 2007].

33 Quoted in Michael White, *C.S. Lewis:. The Boy Who Chronicled Narnia, a Biography* (London: Abacus, 2005), 216.

34 Quoted in White, *C.S. Lewis,* 216–17.

35 C.S. Lewis, 'On Stories', in *Of Other Worlds: Essays and Stories,* 1–21. Hereafter cited in the text as 'On Stories'.

36 On Lewis defining the Chronicles as fairy tales, see Margaret and Michael Rustin, *Narratives of Love and Loss; Studies in Modern Children's Fiction* (London: Verso, 1987), 40–59 (40).

37 Philip Pullman, 'The Darkside of Narnia', *The Guardian* (1 October 1998), archived at: http://reports.guardian.co.uk/articles/1998/10/1/p-24747. html [accessed 24 September 2007]. All the quotations of Pullman about Lewis in the following two paragraphs are from this article. For a reply to Pullman, see Greg Easterbrook, 'In Defence of C.S. Lewis', *The Atlantic Online* (October 2001):http://www.theatlantic.com/ doc/prem/200110/easterbrook [accessed 24 September 2007]. For a response to the specific charges of misogyny and racism, see White, *C.S. Lewis,* 224.

38 Ironically, the same canonisation has occurred to Philip Pullman, which in turn is attracting an equally virulent critical backlash. See, for example, Peter Hitchens, 'A Labour of Loathing', *The Spectator* (18 January 2003): http://www.spectator.co.uk/archive/features/10760/a-labour-of-loathing.thtml [accessed 24 September 2007].

39 U.C. Knoepflemacher, 'The Critic as Former Child: A Personal Narrative', *Papers: Explorations into Children's Literature* 12:1 (April 2002): 5–9 (5). André Green, 'The Double and the Absent', in *On Private Madness* (Madison, CT: International Universities Press, 1986), 311–30.

40 Writing for a particular, living child can also be dialogic, as Lewis's account of the composition process suggests: 'the two participants modify each other. You would become slightly different because you were talking to a child and the child would become slightly different because it was being talked to be an adult. A community, a composite personality, is created and out of that the story grows'. ('On Three Ways', 22–34 (23)).

41 Green, 'The Double and the Absent', in *On Private Madness*, 311–330.

42 Sigmund Freud, *Beyond the Pleasure Principle. The Complete Psychological Works of Sigmund Freud*, vol. 18, tr. James Strachey (London: Vintage, 2001), 16–17, cited by Galef, who adds, 'these preferences are particularly notable in children, who love to have their favorite books reread to them, insisting no word be changed' (*Second Thoughts*, 26).

43 Freud, 'Beyond the Pleasure Principle', cited by Karen Odden in 'Retrieving Childhood Fantasies: A Psychoanalytic Look at Why We (Re)read Popular Literature', in *Second Thoughts*, ed. Galef, 126–51 (126).

44 Odden, 'Retrieving Childhood Fantasies', 129.

45 Victor Nell, *Lost in a Book: The Psychology of Reading for Pleasure* (New Haven, NJ: Yale University Press, 1988), 231.

46 J.A. Appleyard, *Becoming a Reader: The Experience of Fiction from Childhood to Adulthood* (Cambridge: Cambridge University Press, 1991).

47 Vladimir Nabokov, *Lectures on Literature*, ed. F. Bowers (New York: Harcourt Brace Jovanovich, 1980), 3.

48 Matei Calinescu, *Rereading* (London: Yale University Press, 1983).

49 A. J. Tamburri, *Semiotics of Re-Reading: Guido Gozzano, Aldo Palazzeschi, and Italo Calvino* (London: Associated University Presses, 2003), 20–31.

50 Italo Calvino, *Why Read the Classics?* tr. Martin Mclaughlin (London: Jonathan Cape, 1999).

51 J.R.R. Tolkien, 'On Fairy Stories' (1938), reprinted in *Tree and Leaf,* ed. J. R. R. Tolkien (London: Allen and Unwin, 1964).

52 Leavis, *Fiction and the Reading Public* (London: Chatto and Windus, [c1932] 1965).

53 Odden, 'Retrieving Childhood Fantasies', 126–51. See also Victor Watson, *Reading Series Fiction: From Arthur Ransome to Gene Kemp* (London: Routledge, 2000).

54   Peter Brooks, *Reading for the Plot* (Oxford: Clarendon Press, 1984).

55   Wolfgang Iser, *The Implied Reader: Patterns of Communication in Prose Fiction from Bunyan to Beckett* (London: Johns Hopkins University Press, 1974), 280.

56   Marianne Hirsch, 'Reading, Re-reading and Writing,' *PMLA* 119 (March 2004): http://www.phenomenologyonline.com/articles/hunsberger.html 2 [accessed 25 August 2007].

57   'By repeating [the fort-da game], unpleasurable though it was, as a game, he took on an *active* part'. Freud, 'Beyond the Pleasure Principle', 15–16.

58   Roland Barthes, 'How many readings?' in *S/Z*, tr. R. Miller (Oxford: Blackwell, 1990), 15–16.

59   Deborah Thacker, 'Disdain or Ignorance?' 5.

60   Jorge Luis Borges, 'The Aleph', in Borges, *Collected Fictions*, tr. Andrew Hurley (London: Penguin, 1988), 274–86.

61   Paul Ricoeur, *Time and Narrative*, trs. Kathleen McLaughlin and David Pellauer (Chicago: University of Chicago Press, 1984), 3 vols.

62   On modernist literature, Galef cites Joseph Frank, *The Idea of Spatial Form* (London: Rutgers University Press, 1991). And if modern literature is 'not a linear progression but a radial pattern linked by associations, then re-reading is the best access to it'. (Galef, *Second Thoughts*, 20) See also Juliet Dusinberre, *Alice to the Lighthouse* (London: St Martin's Press, 1987), for an excellent study of modernist writers and their childhood reading.

63   C.S. Lewis, 'The children understand this well when they ask for the same story over and over again, and in the same words'. ('On Stories,' 18)

64   Iser, *The Implied Reader* (London: Johns Hopkins University Press, 1974), 282.

65   Galef argues this point, too, in *Second Thoughts*, 23.

66   'The end of their wisdom appears to us but the beginning of ours', writes Proust, 'so that it is at the moment when they have told us all they could tell us that they create in us the feeling that they have told us nothing yet'. ('On Reading', 115)

67   C.S. Lewis, *An Experiment in Criticism* (Cambridge: Cambridge University Press, 1961), 16.

68   Lewis, *An Experiment in Criticism* (Cambridge: Cambridge University Press, 1961), 19.

69   Sir Philip Sidney, *A Defence of Poetry* (or, *An Apology for Poetry*, c1595), ed. J.A. Van Dorsten (Oxford: Oxford University Press, 1966), 95.

70   Sir Francis Bacon, *The Advancement of Learning* (c1605), in H. Dick, ed., *Selected Writings of Francis Bacon* ((New York: Random House, 1955), 283.

71   Lewis, *Surprised by Joy*. New York: Harcourt, 1956. Hereafter cited in the text.

72   See Peter Schakel, *Imagination and the Arts in C.S. Lewis* (London: University of Missouri Press, 2002), 7.

73   Schakel argues that prior to Lewis's conversion to theism in 1929, he was particularly influenced by Coleridge's Romantic concept of the imagination (*Imagination*, 9–10). On Coleridge's *Biographia Literaria,* and David Almond's reworking of the Romantic imagination, see Chapter 6 of the present study.

74   On Max Weber, see Anthony Cascardi, 'The Disenchantment of the World', in Cascardi, *The Subject of Modernity* (Cambridge: Cambridge University Press, 1992), 16–71. On C.S. Lewis and 're-enchantment', see Wesley Kort, *C.S. Lewis. Then and Now* (Oxford: Oxford University Press, 2001), 33–52.

75   Lewis, quoted by Kort, *C.S. Lewis*, 32.

76   C.S. Lewis, *Present Concerns,* ed. W. Hooper (London: Harcourt Brace Jovanovich 1986), 66.

77   Milton, 'On the Morning of Christ's Nativity', in *Milton: Complete Shorter Poems*, ed. J. Carey. Harlow: Longman, 1997, 2nd edition, 101–116 (112).

78   Lewis, *Present Concerns,* ed. W. Hooper (London: Harcourt Brace Jovanovich, 1986), 85.

79   Lewis distinguished between dangerous fantasy, that was 'always superficially realistic' from fantasy that could not be mistaken for reality, that produced longing for a better world. The latter is 'an *askesis,* a spiritual exercise' while the former is 'a disease'. ('In Three Ways', 30)

80   Lewis, 'On Three Ways of Writing for Children', in *Of Other Worlds: Essays and Stories* (New York: Harcourt Brace Jovanovich, 1966), 22–34 (29–30).

81   Schakel, *Imagination,* 8. Walter Hooper follows Lewis in averring, 'there is, I believe, a connection between our longing for Heaven and fairy tales such as those of Lewis's'. See Hooper's *Past Watchful Dragons* (New York: Collier Books, 1979), 33.

82   C.S. Lewis, *Surprised by Joy* (New York: Harcourt, 1956), 78. Cited by Schakel, *Imagination,* 8.

83   In 'Three Ways' Lewis writes, 'for Jung, fairy tales liberate the Archetypes which dwell in the collective unconscious'. (27) John Buchan's views are Jungian when he writes that fairy tales are 'close to the tap-root

of humanity', 'the delight of our childhood', 'part of our unconscious thought' and 'closer to mankind than any written word'. ('The Novel and the Fairy Tale', *The English Association* Pamphlet no. 79 (July 1931): 1–16 (16)).

84   John Buchan, in 'The Novel and the Fairy Tale', explores the inter-relation of these two genres in the Victorian period. Alison Lurie also touches on the subject of the hybridisation of fairy tale with realist narration in 'Fairy Tale Fiction', *Don't Tell the Grownups: Subversive Children's Literature* (Boston, MA: Little, 1990), 29–40.

85   In 'It All Began with a Picture', Lewis writes, 'All my seven Narnian books . . . began with seeing pictures in my head'. (*Of Other Worlds*, 4) In 'Sometimes Fairy Stories May Say Best What's to Be Said', he also briskly dismissed Christian allegorical interpretations of the Chronicles: 'Some people seem to think that I began by asking myself how I could say something about Christianity to children; then fixed on the fairy tale as an instrument . . . This is all pure moonshine . . . Everything began with images'. (*Of Other Worlds*, 36)

86   Sir Philip Sidney, *A Defence of Poetry*, 32–33.

87   Sir Edmund Spenser, 'A Letter of the Authors Expounding His Whole Intention . . . to Sir Walter Raleigh [sic]', *The Faerie Queene*, ed. Thomas P. Roche, Jr. (Penguin Books: Harmondsworth, 1984), 15.

88   See Peter Herman, "With-hold till further triall': Spenser's Letter to Ralegh and Modes of Rereading in the 1590 *Faerie Queene* in *Second Thoughts*, ed. Galef, 196–227 (207): 'the kind of rereading that Spenser regularly activates is a highly Protestant activity. Using Redcrosse as an antimodel, Spenser keeps urging the reader to go back over his poem . . . in exactly the same way that the Protestant tradition encouraged everyone to reread the Bible'.

89   C.S. Lewis, *The Silver Chair* (New York: Harper Collins, 2000 [c1953]). Hereafter cited as *Silver Chair*. Greenlaw, Osgood and Padelford, the editors of the Variorum edition of Spenser, comment on 'the unfaltering conviction' of Book 1, 'the indefiniteness of romance' in its opening stanza, of the hybrid monster Errour, that 'Romance delights in the exhibition of these heterogeneous personages'. (*The Works of Edmund Spenser, a Variorum Edition* (Baltimore: Johns Hopkins Press, 1932), 175, 182). Amongst other critics, John Cox notes Lewis's debt to Spenser's figure of Errour. See John Cox, 'Epistemological Release in *The Silver Chair*', in Peter Schakel, *The Longing for a Form: Essays on the Fiction of C.S. Lewis* (Kent, OH: Kent State University Press, 1977), 159–68 (161–62). In the following analysis, I take *The Silver Chair* to be the fourth volume in the seven *Chronicles of Narnia*, and not the sixth, as it appears in the recently reordered series.

The decision to reorder the Chronicles is based on very scanty evidence of authorial intention; Lewis received a letter from a boy who said he thought the Chronicles should proceed in chronological order; Lewis replied: 'I think I agree with your order for reading the books more than with your mother's ... [But] perhaps it does not matter very much in which order anyone reads them', cited in Schakel, *Imagination*, 44. Perhaps he just wanted to side with the child out of politeness? But anyway, if 'order does not matter', it follows that chronology should not be allowed to determine the shape and meaning of the series. Schakel agrees that the original order is the only defensible one; 'the only reason for putting *The Magician's Nephew* first [and the others in a new order] is to have the reader encounter events in chronological order, the order in which they happened, and that, as every storyteller knows, is quite unimportant as a reason'. (44) Gratifyingly, not a single Brain of Britain could answer a question relating to the reordered Chronicles (BBC Radio 4, 26 November 2007).

90   Berger, Harry, Jr. *Revisionary Play: Studies in the Spenserian Dynamics* (London: University of California Press, 1988), 60.

91   Spenser himself draws on a rich literary tradition including: Hesiod, *Theogony* 5.301; Ovid, *Metamorphoses* 1.422–33; Langland, *Piers Plowman* 18.335; *Revelations* 9.7–10 (Greenlaw, Osgood and Padelford, eds., *The Works of Edmund Spenser*, 182).

92   KidsReview, http://www.kidreview.org.uk [accessed 26 September 2007].

93   William Gray touches on a range of other literary sources for *The Silver Chair*, in addition to Book 1 of *The Faerie Queene*: Malory for the diction; Geraldine in Christina Rossetti's poem 'Goblin Market' and MacDonald's novel *Lilith* for the Witch/Lady of the Green Kirtle (to which one should certainly add John Keats's 'La Belle Dame Sans Merci'); MacDonald's *The Princess and the Goblin* for Underland; *The Faerie Queene* Book 2,7.51–3 for the silver chair. See Gray, *C.S. Lewis* (Plymouth: Northcote House, 1998), 77.

94   Bruno Bettelheim, *The Uses of Enchantment: the Meaning and Importance of Fairy Tales* (London: Penguin, 1991), 145.

95   See Rachel Falconer, *Hell in Contemporary Literature* (Edinburgh: Edinburgh University Press, 2005); David Pike, *Passage Through Hell: Modernist Descents, Medieval Underworlds* (London: Cornell University Press, 1997); Alan Bernstein, *The Formation of Hell: Death and Retribution in the Ancient and Early Christian Worlds* (London: Cornell University Press, 1993); and Raymond Clark, *Catabasis: Vergil and the Wisdom Tradition* (Amsterdam: B.R. Gruner, 1979).

Cf. McCaughrean's use of this tradition in *The White Darkness* (see Chapter 5 of this study).

96 'revocare', 13b, in *The Oxford Latin Dictionary*, ed. P.G.W. Glare (Oxford: Clarendon Press, 1983).

97 In an online discussion thread devoted to identifying passages from the Chronicles which they reread most frequently, several adult readers cited Puddleglum's response to the Witch as amongst their favourites (and all who chose *The Silver Chair* as their favourite Chronicle, singled out this speech as its most memorable passage). For example, one posting read, 'whenever I am home alone I pace up and down in our living room and read my favorite chapters out loud to myself . . . By now I have a good part of the first chapter in the Silver Chair memorised as well as the one just after they free Rilian. Something about dear old Puddleglum . . . saying 'I'm on Aslan's side, even if there isn't any Aslan to lead it. I'm going to live as like a Narnian as I can, even if there isn't any Narnia' is so dramatic and noble and I just love to read it over and over'. Aslans-Girl, Into the Wardrobe discussion board (Tuesday 21 September 2004): http://cslewis.drzeus.net/forums [accessed 16 Sept 2007].

98 'That passage about Puddleglum is the one I always turn back to. It's so moving. I just wish I felt like that about something!' Jillpole77 (Wednesday 1 June 2005): http://cslewis.drzeus.net/forums [accessed 16 Sept 2007].

99 Plato, *The Republic,* tr. Desmond Lee, (Harmondsworth: Penguin, 1974, second edition), 316–325 (317). For Lewis's use of Plato, see Gray, *C.S. Lewis,* 75–76.

100 C.S. Lewis, *They Asked for a Paper: Papers and Addresses* (London: Bles, 1962), 196. Quoted by Gray, *C.S. Lewis,* 78.

101 'Religion's power to console doesn't make it true', Richard Dawkins, *The God Delusion,* 394.

102 As Gray writes, 'the real theme is not so much the *getting* as the *keeping* of knowledge' and 'the role of the emotions in preserving the memory of the true and the real'. (*C.S. Lewis,* 75, 76)

103 Gray, *C.S. Lewis,* 78–79.

104 Cf. Gérard Genette, *Palimpsests: Literature in the Second Degree*, trs. Channa Newman and Claude Doubinsky (Lincoln, NE: University of Nebraska Press, 1997).

105 Green, 'The Double and the Absent', 311–330.

106 Virginia Woolf, 'Mr Bennett and Mrs Brown' (1923), reprinted in Virginia Woolf, *A Woman's Essays* (London: Penguin, 1992), 69–87 (77).

107 *If This is a Man* and *The Truce*, tr. Stuart Woolf (London: Abacus, 1995). The remembered lines from Dante's Ulysses are, 'Think of your breed; for brutish ignorance/Your mettle was not made; you were made men,/

To follow after knowledge and excellence'. (*If This is a Man*, 119; Dante, *Inferno* 26.118–20).

Conclusion

1   H.G. Liddell and R. Scott, eds., *Liddell and Scott Greek-English Lexicon* (Oxford: Clarendon Press, 1996, ninth edition), 1238–39.

Selected Bibliography

Primary Texts

Abrams, M.H. and S. Greenblatt, eds. *The Norton Anthology of English Literature*. London: Norton, 2000, 2 vols., 7th edition.

Adams, Douglas. *The Hitchhiker's Guide to the Galaxy*. London: Pan Books, c1979.

Adams, Richard. *Watership Down*. London: Rex Collings, c1972.

Aiken, Joan. *The Wolves of Willowby Chase* (c1962). London: Red Fox, 2004.

Alcott, Louisa May. *Little Women* (c1868). London: Signet Classics, 2004.

Alexander, Lloyd. *The First Chronicles of Prydain* [*The Book of Three* (c1964); *The Black Cauldron* (c1966); *The Castle of Llyr* (c1968)]. London: Fontana, 1986.

————— *The Second Chronicles of Prydain* [*Taran Wanderer* (c1979); *The High King* (c1979)]. London: Fontana, 1986.

Allende, Isabel. *The City of the Beasts* (*La Ciudad de las Bestias,* c2002), tr. Margaret Peden. London: Flamingo, 2002.

Almond, David. *Skellig* (c1998). London: Hodder Children's, 2002.

————— *The Fire-Eaters*. London: Hodder Children's, c2003.

————— *Clay*. London: Hodder Children's, c2005.

Amis, Martin. *Experience*. London: Jonathan Cape, c2000.

Aeschylus. *The Libation Bearers* (458BC). In *Aeschylus I: Oresteia,* tr. R. Lattimore. London: Chicago University Press, 1953.

Augustine, St. *Confessions* (wr. 397), tr. F.J. Sheed. Cambridge: Hackett, 2006.

Barrie, J. M. *Peter Pan in Kensington Gardens* (c1906); *Peter and Wendy* (c1904). Oxford: Oxford University Press, 1991.

Bawden, Nina. *Carrie's War* (c1973). London: Puffin, 2003.

Belloc, Hilaire. *The Bad Child's Book of Beasts* (c1896). London: Duckworth, 1973.

————— *Cautionary Tales for Children* (c1908). London: Duckworth, 1973.

Blackman, Malorie. The *Noughts and Crosses* trilogy [*Noughts and Crosses* (c2001); *Knife Edge* (c2004); *Checkmate* (c2005)]. London: Corgi Children's, 2006.

Blake, William. *Songs of Innocence and of Experience: Shewing the Two Contrary States of the Human Soul* (c1789). Oxford: Oxford Paperbacks, 1970.

————— *The Marriage of Heaven and Hell* (c1790), intro. by G. Keynes. Oxford: Oxford Paperbacks, 1975.

Bloom, Harold and Lionel Trilling, eds. *Romantic Poetry and Prose*. London: Oxford University Press, 1972.

Blyton, Enid. *The Famous Five* series (21 vols., c1942–1963). London: Hodder Children's, 2007 (6 vols.).

————— *The Secret Seven* series (15 vols., c1949–1963). London: Hodder Children's, 2007 (10 vols.).

Boccaccio, Giovanni. *The Decameron* (wr. 1353), tr. G. H. McWilliam. London: Penguin, 2003.

Borges, Jorge Luis. *Collected Fictions*, tr. Andrew Hurley. London: Penguin, 1988.

Boyce, Frank Cottrell. *Millions*. London: Macmillan's, 2004.

————— *Framed*. London: Macmillan's, 2005.

Boyne, John. *The Boy in the Striped Pyjamas*. Oxford: David Fickling Books, 2006.

Brontë, Charlotte. *The Glass Town Saga 1826–1832*. In *An Edition of the Early Writings of Charlotte Brontë*, ed. Christine Alexander. Oxford: Blackwell, 1987, 2 vols.

Bunyan, John. *The Pilgrim's Progress* (c1678). Oxford: Oxford World's Classics, 2004.

Burgess, Melvin. *Junk* (c1996). London: Penguin, 1997.

———— *Lady: My Life as a Bitch*. London: Andersen, c2001.

———— *Bloodsong*. London: Andersen, c2005.

Burnett, Frances Hodgson. *The Secret Garden* (c1911). London: Walker Books, 2007.

Calman, Stephanie. *Confessions of a Failed Grown-Up: Bad Motherhood and Beyond*. London: Pan Macmillan, 2006.

Calvino, Italo. *Italian Folktales* (1956), tr. G. Martin. London: Penguin, 1982.

Carroll, Lewis [Charles Dodgson]. *Alice in Wonderland* [including *Alice's Adventures in Wonderland* (c1865); *Through the Looking-Glass and What Alice Found There* (c1871); *The Hunting of the Snark* (c1876)]. London: Norton, 1992.

Carter, Angela. *Nights at the Circus* (c1984). London: Picador, 1985.

———— *Wise Children* (c1991). London: Vintage, 1992.

Chabon, Michael. *The Amazing Adventures of Kavalier and Clay* (c2000). London: Picador, 2001.

———— *Summerland*. London: Collins, c2002.

Chambers, Aidan. *Postcards from No Man's Land*. London: Bodley Head, c1999.

Clarke, Susanna. *Jonathan Strange & Mr Norrell*. London: Bloomsbury, 2004.

Coleridge, Samuel Taylor. 'The Rime of the Ancient Mariner' (c1789). In *Coleridge, Poems and Prose*, ed. K. Raine. London: Penguin, 1957.

Coleridge, Samuel Taylor, and William Wordsworth, *Lyrical Ballads, with a Few Other Poems* (c1798), ed. Michael Mason. London: Longman, 2007, 2nd edition.

Colfer, Eoin. The *Artemis Fowl* series [*Artemis Fowl* (2001); *Artemis Fowl: The Arctic Incident* (2002); *Artemis Fowl: The Eternity Code* (2003); *Artemis Fowl: The Opal Deception* (2005); *Artemis Fowl and the Lost Colony* (2006)]. London: Puffin.

Collins. Andrew. *That's Me in the Corner: Adventures of an Ordinary Boy in a Celebrity World*. London: Time Out Group Ltd, 2007.

Conrad, Joseph. *Heart of Darkness* (c1902), ed. R. Kimbrough. London: Norton, 1988.

Cooper, Susan. The *Dark is Rising* series [*Over Sea, Under Stone* (c1965); *The Dark Is Rising* (c1973); *Greenwitch* (c1974); *The Grey King* (c1975); *Silver on the Tree* (c1977)]. London: Puffin, 1984.

———— *Seaward*. Oxford: Bodley Head, c1983.

Corder, Zizou [Louisa Young and Isabel Adomakoh Young]. *Lion Boy*. London: Puffin, c2003.

Cormier, Robert. *The Chocolate War* (c1975). London: Puffin, 2001.

Crossley-Holland, Kevin. The *Arthur* trilogy [*The Seeing Stone*. c2000; *At the Crossing-Places* (c2001); *King of the Middle March* (c2003)]. London: Orion Children's Books.

Dahl, Roald. *James and the Giant Peach* (c1961). London: Puffin, 2007.

———— *Charlie and the Chocolate Factory* (c1964). London: Puffin, 2007.

———— *The BFG* (c1982). London: Puffin, 2007.

———— *Matilda* (c1988). London: Puffin, 2007.

Dante Alighieri. *The Divine Comedy* (wr.1308–21), tr. Charles Singleton. Princeton, NJ: Princeton University Press, 1989, 6 vols.

Dawood, N.J., tr. *Tales from the Thousand and One Nights* (first collected c. 800–900). Penguin: Harmondsworth, 1973.

Defoe, Daniel. *Robinson Crusoe* (c1719). Oxford: Oxford University Press, 2007.

Dick, Philip K. *The Man in the High Castle* (c1962). London: Penguin Classics, 2001.

———— *Do Androids Dream of Electric Sheep?* (c1968). London: Gollancz, 2007.

Dickens, Charles. *The Adventures of Oliver Twist* (c1837–39). Oxford: Oxford University Press, 1987.

———— *The Old Curiosity Shop: a Tale* (c1840–41). London: Penguin Classics, 2001.

———— *A Christmas Carol* (c1843). London: Penguin Classics, 2003.

———— *Dombey and Son* (c1848). Penguin Classics, 2002.

———— *David Copperfield* (c1849–50). London: Penguin Classics, 1994.

Dickinson, John. *The Cup of the World*. London: Corgi, c2005.

Dickinson, Peter. *The Kin* [*Suth's Story, Noli's Story, Po's Story*, and *Mana's Story*]. London: Macmillan Children's Books, 1998.

Donnelly, Jennifer. *A Gathering Light* (original US title, *A Northern Light*, c 2003). London: Bloomsbury, 2003.

Druitt, Tobias [Diane Purkiss and Michael Dowling]. *Corydon and the Island of Monsters*. London: Simon and Schuster, 2005.

Eliot, T.S. *The Waste Land* (c1922), ed. Michael North. London: Norton, 2004.

Ende, Michael. *The Neverending Story* (c1979). London: Penguin Books, 1984.

Fisher, Catherine. *Corbenic*. London: Red Fox Definitions, c2002.

Frayn, Michael. *Spies* (c2002). Oxford: Heinemann, 2005.

Funke, Cornelia. *The Thief Lord* (c2000), tr. Oliver Latsch. Frome: Chicken House, 2003.

——— The *Inkheart* trilogy [*Inkheart* (c2003); *Inkspell* (c2005) *Inkdeath* (c2008)]. Frome: Chicken House.

Gaiman, Neil. *Neverwhere* (c1996). London: Headline, 2000.

——— *Coraline*. London: Bloomsbury, c2002.

Garner, Alan. *The Weirdstone of Brisingamen* (c1960). London: CollinsVoyager, 2002.

——— *The Moon of Gomrath* (c1963). London: CollinsVoyager, 2002.

——— *Elidor* (c1965). London: CollinsVoyager, 2002.

——— *The Owl Service* (c1967). London: CollinsVoyager, 2002.

——— *Red Shift* (c1973). London: CollinsVoyager, 2002.

——— *The Stone Book Quartet* (c1979). London: Flamingo, 1999.

Gavin, Jamila. *Coram Boy*. London: Mammoth, c2000.

——— *The Blood Stone*. London: Egmont, c2003.

Golding, William. *Lord of the Flies* (c1954). London: Faber, 2002.

Grahame, Kenneth. *Wind in the Willows* (c1908). London: Egmont, 2006.

——— *Dream Days* (c1898).

Gray, Alasdair. *Lanark: a Life in Four Books*. London: Pan Books, 1994.

Guène, Faïza, *Just Like Tomorrow* (*Kiffe kiffe demain*, c2004), tr. Sarah Adams. London: Definitions, 2006.

Haddon, Mark. *The Curious Incident of the Dog in the Night-time*. Oxford: Definitions (David Fickling Books), 2003; London: Jonathan Cape, 2003.

Haggard, H. Rider. *King Solomon's Mines* (c1885). Oxford Paperbacks, 1998; London: Penguin Classics, 2007; Hodder Headline, 2007.

Hare, Bernard. *Urban Grimshaw and the Shed Crew*. London: Sceptre, c2005.

Hartnett, Sonya. *Thursday's Child* (c2000). London: Walker Books, 2002.

Hearn, Lian [Gillian Rubenstein]. *Tales of the Otori* series: *Across the Nightingale Floor* (Sydney: Hodder, c2002; London: Macmillan, 2002; Picador, 2003; Young Picador, 2004); *Grass for His Pillow* (London: Macmillan, c2003; Young Picador, 2004); *Brilliance of the Moon* (London: Macmillan, c2004; Young Picador, 2004; Picador, 2006); *The Harsh Cry of the Heron* (London: Macmillan, c2006); *Heaven's Net is Wide* (London: Macmillan, c2007).

Heinlein, Robert. *Starship Troopers* (c1959). London: Hodder & Stoughton, 2005.

——— *Stranger in a Strange Land* (c1961). London: Hodder, 2007.

Henty, George Alfred. 122 historical fiction novels, from *A Search for a Secret* (1867) to *By Conduct and Courage, A Story of Nelson's Days* (1905). See Project Gutenberg [http://www.gutenberg.org].

Hill, Stuart. *The Cry of the Icemark*. Frome: Chicken House, c2005.

Hill, Susan. *I'm the King of the Castle*. London: Hamilton, c1970.

Hinton, S.E. *The Outsiders* (c1967). London: Puffin Modern Classics, 2003; Penguin Classics, 2006.

Hoffman, Alice. *Indigo*. London: Scholastic, c2002.

Hoffman, Heinrich. *Der Struwwelpeter*, c1845. In *Struwwelpeter: Fearful Stories & Vile Pictures to Instruct Good Little Folks*, intro. by J. Zipes. Los Angeles: Feral House, 1999.

Hoffmann, E.T.A. *Nutcracker and Mouse King* (c1816). In *Alexandre Dumas and E.T.A. Hoffmann: Nutcracker and Mouse King and The Tale of the Nutcracker*, tr. Joachim Neugroschel. London: Penguin Classics, 2007.

Hornby, Nick. *About a Boy*. London: Gollancz, c1998.

Horowitz, Anthony. The *Alex Rider* books [*Stormbreaker* (c2001); *Point Blanc* (c2002), *Skeleton Key* (c2003), *Eagle Strike* (c2004) , *Scorpia* (c2005), *Ark Angel* (c2006)]. London: Puffin.

——— *The Power of Five* series [*Day of the Dragon* (c1989); *Raven's Gate* (c2005); *Evil Star* (c2006); *Nightrise* (c2007); *Necropolis* (c2008)]. London: Walker Books.

Hughes, Richard. *A High Wind in Jamaica* (c1929). London: Harvill, 1998.

Huxley, Aldous. *Brave New World* (c1932). London: Voyager Classics, 2001.

Ibbotson, Eva. *Journey to the River Sea*. London: Macmillan Children's Books, c2001.

Ionesco, Eugène. *Rhinocéros* (c1959), tr. Derek Prouse. London: Samuel French, 1960.

Ishiguro, Kazuo. *When We Were Orphans*. London: Faber, 2000.

——— *Never Let Me Go*. London: Faber, 2005.

Jacques, Brian. The *Redwall* series. London: Red Fox, c1991+.

Jansson, Tove. *Finn Family Moomintroll* (c1948), tr. Elizabeth Portch. London: A & C Black, 1986.

Kerr, P.B. *Children of the Lamp: The Akhenaten Adventure.* London: Scholastic, c2004.

King, Robert. *Apple of Doom.* Inverness: Aultbea Publishing, 2005.

Kingsley, Charles. *The Water Babies: A Fairy Tale for a Land-Baby* (c1863). London: Bloomsbury, 1993.

Kipling, Rudyard. *The Jungle Books* (c1894). London: Penguin, 1987.

———— *Stalky & Co.* (c1899). Thirsk: House of Stratus, 2002.

———— *Kim.* London (c1901).New York: Everyman's Library, 1995.

———— *Just So Stories* (c1902). London: Little, Brown, 1993.

Klein, Rachel. *The Moth Diaries.* London: Faber, c2004.

Laird, Elizabeth. *The Garbage King.* London: Macmillan, c2003.

Lear, Edward. *The Book of Nonsense* (c1846); *Nonsense Songs* (c1870). In *The Book of Nonsense and Nonsense Songs.* London: Godfrey Cave Associates, 1996.

Lee, Harper. *To Kill a Mockingbird* (c1960). New York: Fawcett Popular Library, 1962.

LeGuin, Ursula K. The *Earthsea* novels [*A Wizard of Earthsea* (c1968); *The Tombs of Atuan* (c1971); *The Farthest Shore* (c1972); *Tehanu: The Last Book of Earthsea* (c1990); *The Other Wind* (c2001)]. London: Puffin, 1993.

L'Engle, Madeline. Time Quartet [*A Wrinkle in Time* (c1962); *A Wind in the Door* (c1973); *A Swiftly Tilting Planet* (c1978); *Many Waters* (c1986)]. New York: Yearling, 2001.

Levi, Primo. *If This Is a Man* (*Se questo è un uomo,* c1958) and *The Truce* (*La Tregua,* c1963), tr. Stuart Woolf. London: Abacus, 1995.

———— *The Wrench* (*La chiave a stella,* c1978), tr. William Weaver. London: Abacus, 1986.

———— *The Search for Roots, a Personal Anthology,* tr. Peter Forbes. London: Allen Lane, Penguin, 2001.

Lewis, C.S. *The Chronicles of Narnia* [*The Lion, the Witch and the Wardrobe* (c1950); *Prince Caspian* (c1951); *The Voyage of the Dawn Treader* (c1952); *The Silver Chair* (c1953); *The Horse and His Boy* (c1954); *The Magician's Nephew* (c1955); *The Last Battle* (c1956)]. London: Collins, 2001; Collins Film Tie-in Ed., 2005.

———— *The Silver Chair.* New York: HarperCollins, 2000.

Lingren, Astrid. The *Pippi Longstocking* books (11 vols., c1945–2000), tr. Tony Ross. Oxford: Oxford University Press, 2000.

London, Jack. *The Call of the Wild* (c1903). In London, *The Call of the Wild, White Fang, and Other Stories.* Oxford: Oxford Paperbacks, 1998.

MacDonald, George. *Phantastes: a Faerie Romance* (c1858). London: Azure, 2002.

———— *The Light Princess* (c1864). New York: Farrar Straus Giroux, 1992.

———— *The Golden Key* (c1867). New York: Farrar Straus Giroux, 1992.

———— *At the Back of the North Wind* (c1871). London: Puffin, 1994.

———— *The Princess and the Goblin* (c1872). London: Puffin, 1996.

———— *The Lost Princess: a Double Story* (c1875). Leominster: Gracewing, 1992.

Márquez, Gabriel García. 'A Very Old Man With Enormous Wings'. In *Collected Stories,* trs. Gregory Rabaassa and J. S. Bernstein. London: Penguin, 1991: 186–93.

Martel, Yann. *Life of Pi* (c2001). Toronto: Vintage, 2002.

Maxwell, Gavin. *Ring of Bright Water* (c1960). London: Penguin, 2001.

McCaughrean, Geraldine. *Golden Myths and Legends of the World.* London: Orion, c1998.

———— *A Pack of Lies: Twelve Stories in One* (c1988). Oxford: Oxford University Press, 2002.

———— *Not the End of the World.* Oxford: Oxford University Press, c2004.

———— *The White Darkness.* Oxford: Oxford University Press, c2005.

———— *Peter Pan in Scarlet: The Official Sequel.* Oxford: Oxford University Press, c2006.

McEwan, Ian. *The Cement Garden* (c1978). London: Vintage, 2007.

———— *The Daydreamer* (c 1994). London: Faber, 1994; Red Fox, 1995.

———— *Atonement* (c2001). London: Vintage, 2002.

———— *The Child in Time* (c1987). London: Vintage, 1997.

Milne, A.A. *Winnie-the-Pooh* (c1926). London: Egmont, 2006.

Milton, John. *Milton: Paradise Lost* (c1667), ed. A. Fowler. Harlow: Longman, 1998, 2nd edition.

———— *Milton: Complete Shorter Poems,* ed. J. Carey. Harlow: Longman, 1997, 2nd edition.

Montgomery, L.M. *Anne of Green Gables* (c1908). London: Puffin, 1988.

Morpurgo, Michael. *Private Peaceful.* London: Collins, c2003.

Murakami, Haruki. *The Wind-Up Bird Chronicle.* London: Vintage, 2003.

Newberry, Linda. *Sisterland.* Oxford: David Fickling Books, c2003.

———— *Set in Stone.* Oxford: David Fickling Books, c2006.

Nicholson, William. The *Wind on Fire* trilogy [*The Wind Singer*. London: Mammoth, c2000; *Slaves of the Mastery*. London: Mammoth, c2001; *Firesong*. London: Egmont, c2002].

Nix, Garth. The *Old Kingdom* trilogy [*Sabriel* (c1995), *Liriel: Daughter of the Clayr* (c2001), *Abhorsen* (c2004)]. London: Collins, 2003, 2004.

Norton, Mary. *The Borrowers* (c1952). London: Puffin Modern Classics, 1993.

Oppel, Kenneth. The *Silverwing* series [*Silverwing* (c1997); *Sunwing* (c1999); *Firewing* (c.2002); *Darkwing* (c2007)]. Hodder Children's, 2007.

Orwell, George. *Animal Farm: A Fairy Story* (c1945). London: Penguin, 1998.

———— *Nineteen Eighty-Four* (c1949). London: Penguin, 2004.

Oyeyemi, Helen. *The Icarus Girl*. London: Bloomsbury, c2005.

Paolini, Christopher. The *Inheritance* cycle [*Eragon* (c2002); *Eldest* (c2005); *Brisingr* (c2008)]. London: Doubleday, 2004.

Patten, Brian. *The Story Giant*. London: HarperCollins, c2001.

Paver, Michelle. *Chronicles of Ancient Darkness* [*Wolf Brother* (c2004), *Spirit Walker* (c2005), *Soul Eater* (c2006), and *Outcast* (c2007)]. London: Orion.

Pearce, Philippa. *Tom's Midnight Garden* (c1958). London: Puffin, 2005.

Petronius Arbiter, *Satyricon* (*circa* 100AC), tr. M. Heseltine. London: Heinemann, 1975.

Pratchett, Terry. The *Discworld* novels (c1983+). London: Corgi Adult.

Price, Susan. *Sterkarm* [*The Sterkarm Handshake* (c1998). London: Scholastic Point, 2003; *A Sterkarm Kiss* (c2003). London: Scholastic Point, 2004].

Proust, Marcel. *Remembrance of Things Past*, tr. C. K. Scott Moncrieff and Terence Kilmartin. New York: Vintage, 1982.

Pullman, Philip. *His Dark Materials* trilogy, containing *Northern Lights* (c1995); *The Subtle Knife* (c1997); *The Amber Spyglass* (c2000), London: David Fickling Books for Scholastic.

———— *Lyra's Oxford*. New York: Knopf, 2003.

Rees, Celia. *Witch Child* (c2000). London: Bloomsbury, 2007.

Reeve, Philip. *Mortal Engines*. London: Scholastic, c2001.

Rosoff, Meg. *How I Live Now*. London: Penguin, c2004.

———— *Just In Case*. London: Penguin, c2006.

Rossetti, Christina. *Goblin Market* (c1862). San Francisco: Chronicle Books, 1997.

Rousseau, Jean-Jacques. *Oeuvres Complètes*, ed. B. Gagnebin and M. Raymond. Paris: Gallimard, 1956–69, 4 vols.

Rowling, J.K. The *Harry Potter* series [*Harry Potter and the Philosopher's Stone* (1997); *Harry Potter and the Chamber of Secrets* (1998); *Harry Potter and the Prisoner of Azkaban* (1999); *Harry Potter and the Goblet of Fire* (2000); *Harry Potter and the Order of the Phoenix* (2003); *Harry Potter and the Half-Blood Prince* (2005); *Harry Potter and the Deathly Hallows* (2007)]. London: Bloomsbury.

Rushdie, Salman. *The Jaguar Smile, a Nicaraguan Journey*. Oxford: ISIS, 1989.

———— *Haroun and the Sea of Stories*. Bath: Chivers, 1990.

———— *Shame*. London: Jonathan Cape, 1983.

———— *The Ground Beneath Her Feet*. London: Jonathan Cape, c1999.

Sachar, Louis. *Holes* (c1998). London: Bloomsbury, 2000.

Saint-Exupéry, Antoine de. *The Little Prince* (*Le Petit Prince*, c1943). London: Egmont, 1991.

Salinger, J.D. *The Catcher in the Rye* (c1951). London: Penguin, 1994.

Scieszka, Jon. *The Stinky Cheese Man and Other Fairly Stupid Tales* (c1992). London: Puffin, 1993.

Sendak, Maurice. *Where the Wild Things Are* (c1963). London: Red Fox, 2000.

———— *Higglety Pigglety Pop!: Or There Must be More to Life* (c1967). London: Bodley Head, 1969.

———— *In the Night Kitchen* (c1970). London: Red Fox, 2001.

———— *We Are All in the Dumps with Jack and Guy: Two Nursery Rhymes with Pictures* (c1983). London: HarperCollins, 1993.

Serraillier, Ian. *The Silver Sword* (c1956). London: Red Fox, 2003.

Shakespeare, William. *As You Like It* (c1623), ed. Cynthia Marshall. Cambridge: Cambridge University Press, 2004.

———— *The Tempest* (c1623), ed. Rex Gibson (Cambridge: Cambridge University Press, 2005).

Shelley, Mary. *Frankenstein: Or The Modern Prometheus* (c1818), ed. Marilyn Butler. Oxford: Oxford Paperbacks, 1998.

Shelley, Percy Bysshe. *Prometheus Unbound* (c1820). Black Box Press, 2007.

Shriver, Lionel. *We Need to Talk About Kevin* (c2003). London: Serpent's Tail, 2005.

Shulman, Polly. *Enthusiasm*. New York: Penguin, c2006.

Silverstein, Shel. *Where the Sidewalk Ends* (c1974). London: Marion Boyars Publishers Ltd, 2003.
Smith, Dodie. *I Capture the Castle* (c1949). London: Virago, 1996.
Snicket, Lemony [Daniel Handler]. *A Series of Unfortunate Events* [16 vols., from *The Bad Beginning* (c1999) to *The End* (c2006)]. London: Egmont.
Spenser, Edmund. *The Works of Edmund Spenser, a Variorum Edition,* eds. E. Greenlaw, C. G. Osgood and F. M. Padelford. Baltimore: the Johns Hopkins Press, 1932.
———— *The Faerie Queene* (c1596), ed. A. C. Hamilton. Harlow: Pearson Longman, 2007, 2nd edition.
Stevenson, Robert Louis. *Treasure Island* (c1882). Dorking: Templar Publishing, 2005.
———— *Kidnapped* (c1886), ed. Donald M. McFarlan. London: Penguin, 1994.
Stroud, Jonathan. The *Bartimaeus* trilogy [*The Amulet of Samarkand* (c2003); *The Golem's Eye* (c2004); *Ptolemy's Gate* (c2005)]. London: Doubleday Children's.
Sutcliff, Rosemary. The *Eagle of the Ninth* sequence [*The Eagle of the Ninth* (c1954); *The Silver Branch* (c1957); *The Lantern Bearers* (c1959); *Sword at Sunset* (c1963)]. Oxford: Oxford University Press, 2001+.
Swift, Jonathan. *Gulliver's Travels* (c1745). London: Vintage, 2007.
Taylor, G.P. *Shadowmancer*. London: Faber, c2003.
Thompson, Kate. *The New Policeman.* London: Bodley Head, c2005.
Tolkien, J.R.R. *The Lord of the Rings* [*The Fellowship of the Ring*; *The Two Towers*; *The Return of the King* (c1954–55)]. Toronto: Methuen, 1971.
Townsend, Sue. *The Secret Diary of Adrian Mole Aged 13 ¾.* London: Metheun, c1982.
Tracy, P.J. [P.J. Lambrecht and Traci Lambrecht]. *Live Bait.* London: Penguin, 2005.
———— *Snow Blind.* London: Penguin, 2007.
Twain, Mark. *The Adventures of Huckleberry Finn* (c1885). In *The Annotated Huckleberry Finn,* ed., Michael P. Hearn. London: Norton, 2001.
Urquhart, Emma Maree. *Dragon Tamers.* Inverness: Aultbea Publishing, 2004.
Verne, Jules. *Journey to the Centre of the Earth* [*Voyage au centre de la terre* (c1864)], tr. William Butcher. Oxford: Oxford World's Classics, 1992.
Virgil [P. Vergilius Maro]. *Aeneid* (c19BC). In *Opera,* ed. R.A.B. Mynors. Oxford: Clarendon, 1980.
———— *Virgil,* tr. H. Rushton Fairclough, 2 vols. London: William Heinemann Ltd., 1978.
Vonnegut, Kurt. *Slaughterhouse-Five: Or the Children's Crusade, a Duty Dance with Death* (c1969). London: Vintage, 2003.
Watterson, Bill. *Calvin and Hobbes* (c1985–95). Collected in *The Calvin and Hobbes Tenth Anniversary Book.* Kansas City: Andrews and McMeel, 1995.
Wells, H.G. *The War of the Worlds* (c1898). In *The War of the Worlds: A Critical Text of the 1898 London First Edition,* ed., Leon Stover. Jefferson, N.C.: McFarland, 2001.
White, E.B. *Charlotte's Web* (c1952), intro. by J. Eccleshare. London: Puffin, 2003.
White, T.H. *The Once and Future King* [*The Sword in the Stone* (c1938); *The Queen of Air and Darkness* (c.1939); *The Ill-Made Knight* (c1940); *The Candle in the Wind* (c1941)]. London: Collins, 1978.
Wilder, Laura Ingalls. *Little House on the Prairie* (c1935). London: Mammoth, 1992.
Williamson, Henry. *Tarka the Otter* (c1928). London: Bodley Head, 1982.
Wilson, Jacqueline. *The Story of Tracy Beaker.* London: Doubleday, c1991.
Wordsworth, William. *The Prelude: 1799, 1805, 1850.* Eds. Jonathan Wordsworth, M. H. Abrams, and Stephen Gill. New York: Norton, 1979.
Wyss, Johann David. *The Swiss Family Robinson* (*Schweizerische Robinson,* c1812), intro. by John Seeyle. London: Penguin, 2007.
Yonge, Charlotte M. *The Heir of Redclyffe* (c1854), ed. Barbara Dennis. Oxford: Oxford Paperbacks, 1997.
Zelazny, Roger. *The Chronicles of Amber* [*Nine Princes in Amber* (c1970); *The Guns of Avalon* (c1972); *Sign of the Unicorn* (c1975); *The Hand of Oberon* (c1976); *The Courts of Chaos* (c1978)]. London: Millennium, 2000.
Zusak, Markus, *The Book Thief* (c2005). London: Bodley Head, 2007.

Film and TV

Adamson, Andrew. *The Chronicles of Narnia* [*The Lion, the Witch and the Wardrobe* (2005); *Prince Caspian* (2008)]. Walt Disney Pictures and Walden Media.
Adamson, Andrew and Vicky Jenson. *Shrek* (2001), *Shrek 2* (2004). DreamWorks.

Boyle, Danny. *Millions*. Mission Pictures, 2004.
Burton, Tim. *Charlie and the Chocolate Factory*. Warner Bros., 2005.
Columbus, Chris. *Harry Potter and the Sorcerer's Stone*. 1492 Pictures, 2001.
———— *Harry Potter and the Chamber of Secrets*. 1492 Pictures, 2002.
Cuarón, Alfonso. *Harry Potter and the Prisoner of Azkaban*. Warner Bros., 2004.
Daldry, Stephen. *Billy Elliot*. Arts Council of England, 2000.
del Toro, Guillermo. *Pan's Labyrinth (El Laberinto del Fauno)*, tr. Giullermo del Toro. Warner Bros., 2006.
Docter, Pete and David Silverman. *Monsters, Inc*. Pixar Animation Studios, 2001.
Fangmeier, Stefen. *Eragon*. Fox 2000 Pictures, 2006.
Fleming, Victor. *The Wizard of Oz*. MGM, 1939.
Forster, Mark. *Finding Neverland*. Miramax Films, 2004.
Groening, Matt. *The Simpsons*. TV series. Twentieth Century Fox Television, 1989+.
Huda, Menhaj. *Kidulthood*. Stealth Films Ltd., 2006.
Jackson, Peter. *The Lord of the Rings* [*The Fellowship of the Ring* (2001); *The Two Towers* (2002); *The Return of the King* (2003)]. New Line Cinema.
Jonze, Spike. *Being John Malkovich*. Gramercy Pictures, 1999.
Kelly, Richard. *Donnie Darko*. Pandora Cinema, 2001.
Lasseter, John. *Toy Story*. Walt Disney Pictures, 1995.
Lasseter, John and Ash Brannon. *Toy Story 2*. Pixar Animation Studies, 1999.
Lord, John and Nick Park. *Chicken Run*. Aardman Animations, 2000.
Lucas, George. *Star Wars: Episodes I–VI*. Lucasfilm, 1977–2007.
Marshall, Penny. *Big*. Gracie Films, 1988.
Mendes, Sam. *American Beauty*. DreamWorks, 1999.
Miller, Chris and Raman Hui. *Shrek the Third*. DreamWorks, 2007.
Minkoff, Rob. *Stuart Little* (1999), *Stuart Little 2* (2002). Columbia Pictures Corporation.
Newell, Mike. *Harry Potter and the Goblet of Fire*. Warner Bros, 2005.
Newman, Sydney, C.E. Webber, Donald Wilson (creators). *Dr Who*. BBC TV, 1963–present.
Noonan, Chris. *Miss Potter*. Phoenix Pictures, 2006.
Park, Nick. *The Wrong Trousers*. Aardman Animations, 1993.
Sax, Geoffrey. *Stormbreaker*. Samuelson Productions, 2006.
Segal, Philip. *Doctor Who (The Enemy Within)*. Universal Television, BBC Television, BBC Worldwide, and Fox Network, 1996.
Silberling, Brad, *Lemony Snicket's A Series of Unfortunate Events*. Paramount Pictures, 2004.
Spielberg, Stephen. *E.T: the Extra-Terrestrial*. Amblin Entertainment, 1982.
———— *Raiders of the Lost Ark*. Lucasfilm, 1981.
———— *Indiana Jones and the Temple of Doom*. Lucasfilm, 1984.
———— *Hook*. Amblin Entertainment, 1991.
Stovall, Chaille Patrick. *Party Animals (Or How to Get to the White House in 5 Easy Steps)*. Shut Up Kid Productions, 2001.
Weitz, Chris. *The Golden Compass*. New Line Cinema, 2007.
Whedon, Joss. *Buffy the Vampire Slayer*. TV series. Twentieth Century Fox Television, 1997–2003.
Yates, David. *Harry Potter and the Order of the Phoenix*. Warner Bros., 2007.

Secondary Criticism

Abanes, Richard. *Harry Potter and the Bible: the Menace Behind the Magick*. Camp Hill, PA: Horizon, 2001.
Adorno, Theodor. *The Culture Industry: Selected Essays on Mass Culture*. London: Routledge, 1991.
Alberghene, Janice. 'Childhood's End?' *Children's Literature* 13 (1985): 188–93.
Almond, David. 'David Almond Talks to Benedict Page'. *Bookseller* 5198 (2005): 20.
Anatol, Giselle, ed. *Reading Harry Potter: Critical Essays*. Westport, CT: Praeger, 2003.
Ang, Susan. *The Widening World of Children's Literature*. Basingstoke: Macmillan, 2000.
Antze, Paul and Michael Lambek, eds. *Tense Past: Cultural Essays in Trauma and Memory*. London: Routledge, 1996.
Appleyard, J.A. *Becoming a Reader. The Experience of Fiction from Childhood to Adulthood*. Cambridge: Cambridge University Press, 1990.
Apseloff, M.F. *They Wrote for Children Too: An Annotated Bibliography of Children's Literature by Famous Writers for Adults*. Westport, CT: Greenwood Press, 1989.

Ariès, Philippe. *Centuries of Childhood: a Social History of Family Life,* tr. Robert Baldick. New York: Vintage, 1962.

Aristotle. *Poetics,* tr. Malcolm Heath. Harmondsworth: Penguin, 1996.

Armitt, Lucie. *Theorizing the Fantastic.* London: Arnold, 1996.

Armstrong, Karen. *The Battle for God.* London: Ballantine Books, 2001.

Bachelard, Gaston. *The Poetics of Space,* tr. Maria Jolasp. Boston: Beacon Press, 1969.

Bacon, Sir Francis. *The Advancement of Learning* (c1605), in H. Dick, ed., *Selected Writings of Francis Bacon.* (New York: Random House, 1955.

Bakhtin, Mikhail (M.M.). *The Dialogic Imagination: Four Essays,* tr. C. Emerson and M. Holquist, ed. M. Holquist. Minnesota: University of Texas Press, 1984.

———— *Rabelais and His World,* tr. Hélène Iswolsky. Bloomington, IN: Indiana University Press, 1984.

———— *Problems of Dostoevsky's Poetics,* ed. and tr. Caryl Emerson. London: University of Minnesota Press, 1984.

———— *Speech Genres and Other Late Essays,* eds. Caryl Emerson and Michael Holquist, tr. Vern W McGee. Austin, TX: University of Texas Press, 1986.

Barfield, Steven. 'The Resources of Unrepresentability: A Lacanian Glimpse of Beckett's *Three Dialogues'.* In *Samuel Beckett Today/Aujourd'hui* Vol. 13, *Three Dialogues Revisited,* ed. Marius Buning et al. Amsterdam & Atlanta: Rodopi, 2003: 15–27.

Barfield, Steven. 'Of Young Magicians and Growing Up: J.K. Rowling, Her Critics, and the "Cultural Infantilism" Debate'. In *Scholarly Studies in Harry Potter,* ed. Hallett: 175–98.

Barthes, Roland. *Mythologies,* tr. Annette Lavers. London: Granada, 1973.

———— *The Pleasure of the Text (Le plaisir du texte,* c1973), tr. Richard Miller (Toronto: HarperCollins Canada, 1975),, tr. Richard Miller. Toronto: HarperCollins Canada, 1975.

———— *S/Z,* tr. R. Miller. Oxford: Blackwell, 1990.

Baudrillard, Jean. *The Transparency of Evil,* tr. James Benedict. London: Verso, 2002.

Beckett, Sandra. *Transcending Boundaries: Writing for a Dual Audience of Children and Adults.* New York: Garland, 1999.

Berger, Harry, Jr. *Revisionary Play: Studies in the Spenserian Dynamics.* London: University of California Press, 1988.

Berger, James. *After the End: Representations of Post-Apocalypse.* Minneapolis: University of Minnesota Press, 1999.

Bernstein, Alan. *The Formation of Hell: Death and Retribution in the Ancient and Early Christian Worlds.* London: Cornell University Press, 1993.

Berry, Philippa and Andrew Wernick, eds. *Shadow of Spirit: Postmodernism and Religion.* London: Routledge, 1992.

Bettleheim, Bruno. *The Uses of Enchantment: The Meaning and Importance of Fairy Tales.* London: Penguin, 1991.

Blake, Andrew. *The Irresistible Rise of Harry Potter.* London: Verso, 2002.

Blanchot, Maurice. 'The Limits of Experience: Nihilism'. In *The New Nietzsche,* ed. David Allison. Cambridge MA: MIT Press, 1985: 121–28.

Bloom, Harold. 'Can 35 Million Readers Be Wrong? Yes'. *The Wall Street Journal* (11 July 2000): 16.

———— 'Dumbing Down American Readers'. *The Boston Globe* (24 September 2003).

Blum, Virginia. *Hide and Seek: The Child Between Psychoanalysis and Fiction.* Urbana: University of Illinois Press, 1995.

Booth, Wayne. *The Rhetoric of Fiction.* London: University of Chicago Press, 1983, 2nd edition.

Bourdieu, Pierre. *Distinction: A Social Critique of the Judgement of Taste,* tr. Richard Nice. Cambridge, MA: Harvard University Press, 1984.

Borges, J.L. 'Narrative Art and Magic'. In *The Total Library: Non-Fiction 1922–1986,* ed. Eliot Weinberger, tr. Esther Allen, Suzanne Levine and Eliot Weinberger. Harmondsworth: Penguin, 2000: 75–82.

Braidotti, Rosi. *Nomadic Subjects: Embodiment and Sexual Difference in Contemporary Feminist Theory.* New York: Columbia University Press, 1994.

Bramwell, Peter. 'Review of McCaughrean's *The White Darkness', Write Away. http://improbability.ultralab.net/writeaway/whitedarkness.htm*

Brennan, Geraldine. 'Painful Truths About a Violent Society'. *Times Educational Supplement* 2 (15 November 1996): 6.

Briggs, Melody and Richard S. Briggs. 'Stepping into the Gap: Contemporary Children's Fantasy Literature as a Doorway to Spirituality'. In *Towards or Back to Human Values,* eds. Deszcz-Tryhubczak and Oziewicz: 30–47.

Bristow, Jenny. 'Harry Potter and the Meaning of Life'. *Spiked* (19 June 2003).

Brooks, Peter. *Reading for the Plot: Design and Intention in Narrative*. Oxford: Clarendon Press, 1984.

Brown, Devin. 'Marvelous and Yet Not Strange: Tolkien's Sacramental Ordinary.' In *Towards or Back to Human Values*, eds. Deszcz-Tryhubczak and Oziewicz: 109–120.

Bruckner, Pascal. *The Temptation of Innocence: Living in the Age of Entitlement*. New York: Algora Publishing, 2000.

——— *L'euphorie perpétuelle: essai sur le devoir de bonheur*. Paris: Livres de Poche, 2002.

Buchan, John. 'The Novel and the Fairy Tale'. *The English Association* Pamphlet no. 79 (July 1931): 1–16.

Buckland, Corinne. 'Fantasy and the Recovery of the Numinous'. In *Towards or Back to Human Values*, eds. Deszcz-Tryhubczak and Oziewicz: 17–29.

——— 'Fantasy, the Moral Imagination and the Good'. In *Towards or Back to Human Values*, eds. Deszcz-Tryhubczak and Oziewicz: 97–108.

Byatt, A. S. 'Harry Potter and the Childish Adult'. *New York Times* (7 July 2003).

Calinescu, Matei. *Rereading*. London: Yale University Press, 1993.

Calvino, Italo. *Six Memos for the Next Millennium: the Charles Eliot Norton Lectures 1985–86*, tr. Patrick Creagh (London: Vintage, 1996).

——— *Why Read the Classics?* tr. Martin Mclaughlin. London: Jonathan Cape, 1999.

Cameron, Rachel. 'Watching Alice: the Child as Narrative Lens in *Alice's Adventures in Wonderland*'. In *Papers: Explorations into Children's Literature* 9:3 (December 1999): 23–29.

Campbell, Joseph. *The Hero With a Thousand Faces* (c1949). Princeton: Princeton University Press, 1972.

Caputo, John. *The Mystical Element in Heidegger's Thought*. Athens, OH: University of Ohio Press, 1978.

Carter, Angela. *Shaking a Leg: Collected Journalism and Writings*. London: Vintage, 1998.

Caruth, Cathy. *Unclaimed Experience: Trauma, Narrative and History*. London: Johns Hopkins University Press, 1996.

Cascardi, Anthony. *The Subject of Modernity*. Cambridge: Cambridge University Press, 1992.

Caselli, Daniela. 'Reading Intertextuality. The Natural and the Legitimate: Intertextuality in *Harry Potter*'. In *Children's Literature: New Approaches*, ed. Lesnik-Oberstein, Karín: 168–188.

Cirella-Urrutia, Anne. 'The "Childification" of Adulthood in Aurand Harris's *Punch and* Judy'. *Bookbird* 38,1 (2000): 42–44.

Clark, Raymond. *Catabasis: Vergil and the Wisdom Tradition*. Amsterdam: B.R. Gruner, 1979.

Coats, Karen. *Looking Glasses and Neverlands*. Iowa City: University of Iowa Press, 2004.

Cocks, Neil. 'The Implied Reader. Response and Responsibility: Theories of the Implied Reader in Children's Literature'. In *Children's Literature: New Approaches*, ed. Lesnik-Oberstein, Karín: 93–117.

Colbert, David. *The Magical Worlds of Harry Potter*. New York: Weatherhill, 2001.

Coleman, John. 'Into Adulthood'. In *The Seven Ages of Life*, ed. Lotherington: 57–80.

Coleridge, Samuel Taylor. *Biographia Literaria* (c1817). In *Samuel Taylor Coleridge*, ed. H.J. Jackson. Oxford: Oxford University Press, 1985: 155–482.

Collins, Robert and Howard Pearce, eds. *The Scope of the Fantastic: Theory, Technique, Major Authors*. London: Greenwood Press, 1985.

Connolly, Paula T. 'The Marketing of Romantic Childhood: Milne, Disney and a Very Popular Stuffed Bear'. In *Literature and the Child*, ed. McGavran:188–210.

Cooley, Ron. 'Harry Potter and the Temporal Prime Directive: Time Travel, Rule-breaking, and Misapprehension in *Harry Potter and the Prisoner of Azkaban*'. In *Scholarly Studies in Harry Potter*, ed. C. Hallett: 29–42.

Cox, John. 'Epistemological Release in *The Silver Chair*.' In *The Longing for a Form*, ed. P. Schakel: 159–68.

Curry, Patrick. *Defending Middle-Earth: Tolkien, Myth and Modernity*. London: Harper, 1997.

Darton, F.J. Harvey and Brian Alderson. *Children's Books in England: Five Centuries of Social Life*, ed. Brian Alderson. The British Library & Oak Knoll Press, 1999, 3rd edition.

Dawkins, Richard. *The God Delusion*. London: Bantam Press, 2006.

Deleuze, Gilles and Félix Guattari. *Anti-Oedipus: Capitalism and Schizophrenia*. London: Athlone Press, 1984.

——— *Nomadology: the War Machine*, tr. Brian Massumi. New York: Semiotexte, 1986.

Derrida, Jacques. 'Of an Apocalyptic Tone Recently Adopted in Philosophy', tr. John Leavey Jr. *Semeia* 23 (1982): 63–97.

———— 'Comment ne pas parler'. In *Psyché: inventions de l'autre*. Paris: Galiée, 1987: 535–96.

Deszcz-Tryhubczak, Justyna and Marek Oziewicz, eds. *Towards or Back to Human Values? Spiritual and Moral Dimensions of Contemporary Fantasy*. Newcastle: Cambridge Scholars Press, 2006.

D'Haen, Theo. 'Magic Realism and Postmodernism: Decentering Privileged Centers'. In *Magical Realism*, eds. Zamora and Faris, 191–208.

Dresang, Eliza. *Radical Change: Books for Youth in a Digital Age*. New York: H.W. Wilson, 1999.

Dusinberre, Juliet. *Alice to the Lighthouse: Children's Books and Radical Experiment in Art*. Basingstoke: Macmillan, 1999.

Eagleton, Terry. *Sweet Violence: the Idea of the Tragic*. Oxford: Blackwell, 2003.

Eccleshare, Julia, *A Guide to the Harry Potter Novels*. London: Continuum, 2002.

Egoff, Sheila and Judith Saltman. *The New Republic of Childhood*. Oxford: Oxford University Press, 1990.

Eliade, Mircea. *Myth and Reality (Aspectes du mythe*, c1963), tr. W. R. Trask . London: Allen & Unwin, 1964.

English, James F. *A Concise Companion to Contemporary Fiction*. Oxford: Blackwell, 2006.

Erikson, Erik H. *Identity: Youth and Crisis*. New York: Norton, 1968.

———— *Adulthood*. New York: Norton, 1978.

———— *The Life Cycle Completed: a Review*. New York: Norton, 1982.

Evans, Dylan. *An Introductory Dictionary of Lacanian Psychoanalysis*. London: Routledge, 1996.

Evans, R. J. W. and Alexander Marr. *Curiosity and Wonder from the Renaissance to the Enlightenment*. Aldershot: Ashgate, 2006.

Falconer, Rachel. 'Crossover Literature'. In *The International Companion Encyclopedia of Children's Literature*, ed. Peter Hunt, 2004, 2 vols., 2nd edition: Vol. I, 556–75.

———— 'Tolkien, Dante and Crossover Epic'. In *Books and Their Boundaries*, ed., P. Pinsent: 98–113.

———— *Hell in Contemporary Literature: Western Descent Narratives since 1945* (Edinburgh: Edinburgh University Press, 2005).

Faris, Wendy. 'Scheherazade's Children: Magical Realism and Postmodern Fiction'. In *Magical Realism: Theory, History, Community*, eds., Zamora and Faris: 163–90.

Fife, Ernelle. 'Reading J.K. Rowling Magically: Creating C.S. Lewis's "Good Reader"'. In *Scholarly Studies in Harry Potter*, ed. Hallett: 137–58.

Fish, Stanley. *Surprised By Sin: The Reader in* Paradise Lost. Berkeley: University of California, 1967.

Fisher, Margery. *The Bright Face of Danger*. London: Hodder and Stoughton, 1986.

Fletcher, J., and A. Benjamin, eds. *Abjection, Melancholia and Love: The Work of Julia Kristeva*. London: Routledge, 1990.

Freccero, John. *The Poetics of Conversion*, ed. R. Jacoff. Cambridge, MA: Harvard University Press, 1986.

Freud, Sigmund. *Beyond the Pleasure Principle. The Standard Edition of the Complete Psychological Works of Freud*. Vol. 18. Trans. and eds. J. Strachey and A. Freud. London: Hogarth Press and the Institute of Psycho-analysis, 1953–74: 1–64.

Galef, David. 'Crossing Over: Authors Who Write Both Children's and Adults' Fiction'. *Children's Literature Association Quarterly* 20, 1 (1995): 29–35.

Galef, David, ed. *Second Thoughts: A Focus on Rereading*. Detroit, MI: Wayne State University Press, 1998.

Garlitz, Barbara. 'The Immortality Ode: Its Cultural Progeny'. *Studies in English Literature* 6 (1966): 639–49.

Geertz, Clifford. *Available Light. Anthropological Reflections on Philosophical Topics*. Princeton, NJ: Princeton University Press, 2001.

Genette, Gérard. *Narrative Discourse*, tr. Jane Lewin. Oxford: 1986.

———— *Palimpsests: Literature in the Second Degree*, trs. Channa Newman and Claude Doubinsky. Lincoln, NE: University of Nebraska Press, 1997.

———— *Paratexts: Thresholds of Interpretation*, tr. Jane Lewin. Cambridge: Cambridge University Press, 2007.

Gibbons, Sarah. 'Death and Rebirth: *Harry Potter* and the Mythology of the Phoenix'. In *Scholarly Studies in Harry Potter*, ed. Hallett: 85–106.

Glare, P.G.W., ed. *The Oxford Latin Dictionary*. Oxford: Clarendon Press, 1983.

Godwin, William. *The Enquirer: Reflections on Education, Manners and Literature*. New York: Augustus M. Kelly, 1965.

Gordimer, Nadine. 'The Flash of Fireflies'. In *The New Short Story Theories*, ed. Charles May. Athens, OH: Ohio University Press, 1994: 263–67.

Granger, John. *The Hidden Key to Harry Potter: Understanding the Meaning, Genius and Popularity of Joanne Rowling's Harry Potter Novels*. Port Hadlock, WA: Zossima Press, 2002.

Gray, William. *C.S. Lewis*. Plymouth: Northcote House, 1998.

Green, André. *On Private Madness*. Madison, CT: International Universities Press, 1986.

Greenway, Betty, ed. *Twice-Told Children's Tales: The Influence of Childhood Reading on Writers for Adults*. London: Routledge, 2005.

Grenz, Dagmar. 'E.T.A. Hoffmann as an Author for Children and Adults, or the Child and the Adult Reader of Children's Literature'. *Phaedrus* 13 (1988): 91–96.

Grieve, Ann. 'Metafictional Play in Children's Fiction'. In *Papers: Explorations into Children's Literature* 8:3 (December 1998): 5–15.

Griswold, Jerry. *Feeling Like a Kid: Childhood and Children's Literature*. Baltimore: Johns Hopkins University Press, 2006.

Gupta, Suman. *Re-reading Harry Potter*. Basingstoke: Palgrave Macmillan, 2003.

Guroian, Vigen. *Rallying the Really Human Things: The Moral Imagination in Politics, Literature, and Everyday Life*. Wilmington, DE: Intercollegiate Studies Institute, 2005.

Guttfeld, Dorota. 'Coping with Mortality: Lewis, Le Guin and Rowling on the Inhumanness of Immortality'. In *Towards or Back to Human Values*, eds. Deszcz-Tryhubczak and Oziewicz: 198–208.

Hallett, Cynthia Whitney, ed. *Scholarly Studies in Harry Potter: Applying Academic Methods to a Popular Text*. Lampeter: Edwin Mellen Press, 2005.

Hancock, Susan. 'Miniature Worlds'. In *Childhood Remembered*, ed. Reynolds: 114–26.

Handelman, Susan. *The Slayers of Moses: The Emergence of Rabbinic Interpretation in Modern Literary Theory*. Albany: State University of NY Press, 1982.

Hannabuss, Stuart. 'Books Adopted by Children'. In *International Companion Encyclopedia of Children's Literature*, eds. P. Hunt and S. Ray. London: Routledge, 1996, 1st edition: 422–31.

Harris, Sam. *The End of Faith: Religion, Terror, and the Future of Reason*. New York: Norton, 2004.

Hart, Kevin. *The Trespass of the Sign: Deconstruction, Theology and Philosophy*. Cambridge: Cambridge University Press, 1990.

Harvey, David. *The Condition of Postmodernity: An Inquiry into the Origins of Cultural Change*. Oxford: Blackwell, 1990.

Hay, David and Rebecca Nye. *The Spirit of the Child*. London: Harper Collins, 1998.

Hegerfeldt, Anne. *Lies That Tell the Truth: Magic Realism Seen Through Contemporary Fiction in Britain*. Rodopi: Amsterdam, 2005.

Heilman, Elizabeth E. ed. *Harry Potter's World: Multidisciplinary Critical Perspectives (Pedagogy and Popular Culture)*. London: Routledge, 2003.

Heise, Ursula. *Chronoschisms: Time, Narrative and Postmodernism*. Cambridge: Cambridge University Press, 1997.

Higgins, James. *Beyond Words: Mystical Fantasy in Children's Literature*. New York: Teachers' College Press, 1970.

Hirsch, Marianne. 'Reading, Re-reading and Writing'. In *PMLA* 119 (March 2004). *http://www.phenomenologyonline.com/articles/hunsberger.html* [accessed 28 January 2008].

Hobsbawm, Eric. 'Introduction'. *Social Research* 58:1 (Spring, 1991): 65–68.

Hollindale, Peter with Rhiannon Howell and Jacqui Newby. 'Re-reading the Self: Children's Books and Undergraduate Readers'. *Signal* 79 (January 1996): 62–74.

Hollingsworth, Cris, ed. *Spaces of Wonderland*. Iowa City: University of Iowa Press, forthcoming, 2009.

Hooper, Walter. *Past Watchful Dragons: A Guide to C.S. Lewis's Chronicles of Narnia*. London: Fount Paperbacks, 1980.

Huey, Peggy. 'A Basilisk, a Phoenix, and a Philosopher's Stone: Harry Potter's Myths and Legends'. In *Scholarly Studies in Harry Potter*, ed. Hallett: 65–84.

Hughes, Ted. 'Myth and Education'. In *Celebrating Children's Literature in Education*, ed. Geoff Fox. London: Teachers' College Press, 1995: 3–18.

Hume, Kathryn. *Fantasy and Mimesis: Responses to Reality in Western Literature*. London: 1984.

Hunt, Peter and Millicent Lenz. *Alternative Worlds in Fantasy Fiction: Ursula Le Guin, Terry Pratchett, Philip Pullman and Others*. London: Continuum, 2001.

Hunt, Peter, ed., *The International Companion Encyclopedia of Children's Literature*, ed. Peter Hunt. London: Routledge, 2004, 2nd edition, 2 vols.

Hutcheon, Linda. *A Poetics of Postmodernism: History, Theory, Fiction.* London: Routledge, 1988.

Inglis, Fred. *The Promise of Happiness: Value and Meaning in Children's Literature.* Cambridge: Cambridge University Press, 1981.

Irigaray, Luce. *Marine Lover: Of Friedrich Nietzsche,* tr. Gillian Gill. NY: Columbia University Press, 1991.

IRSCL Conference (Eighth International. Cologne, 1987): 'Books for Children, Books for Adults and the Relationship Between Them'. *Fundevogel* 41–42 (1987).

Irvine, Erica. 'A Look at Young Adult/Crossover Novels'. *Magpie* 11:2 (May 1996): 49–50.

Iser, Wolfgang, *The Implied Reader: Patterns of Communication in Prose Fiction from Bunyan to Beckett.* London: Johns Hopkins University Press, 1974.

Iser, Wolfgang, *The Act of Reading: A Theory of Aesthetic Response.* London: Routledge, 1978.

Jackson, Rosemary. *Fantasy: The Literature of Subversion.* London: Routledge, 2003.

Jameson, Fredric. 'On Magic Realism in Film'. *Critical Inquiry* 12:2 (Winter 1986): 301–25.

Jung, C.G. 'The Stages of Life'. In *The Structure and Dynamics of the Psyche: The Collected Works of C.G. Jung, 8,* tr. R.F.C. Hull. Princeton, NJ: Princeton University Press, 1959, 2nd edition.

Kanfer, Stefan. 'A Lovely, Profitable World of Kid Lit'. *Time* (29 December 1980): 38–41.

Kermode, Frank. *The Sense of an Ending: Studies in the Theory of Fiction.* Oxford: Oxford University Press, 1979.

King, Nicola. *Memory, Narrative, Identity: Remembering the Self.* Edinburgh: Edinburgh University Press, 2000.

Koehnecke, Diane. '*Smoky Night* and *Crack*: Controversial Subjects in Current Children's Stories'. *Children's Literature in Education* 32:1 (March 2001): 17–30.

Knoepflemacher, U.C. and M. Myers, guest eds. 'Cross Writing Child and Adult'. Special issue of *Children's Literature Association Papers* 25. New Haven, NJ: Yale University Press, 1997.

Knoepflemacher, U.C. 'The Critic as Former Child: A Personal Narrative'. In *Papers: Explorations into Children's Literature* 12:1 (April 2002): 5–9.

Knowles, Murray and Kirsten Malmkjaer, *Language and Control in Children's Literature.* New York: Routledge, 1995.

Kort, Wesley A. *C.S. Lewis: Then and Now.* Oxford: Oxford University Press, 2001.

Krips, Valerie. *The Presence of the Past: Memory, Heritage, and Childhood in Postwar Britain.* London: Garland, 2000.

Kristeva, Julia. *Powers of Horror: an Essay on Abjection* (*Pouvoirs de l'horreur,* c1980), tr. Leon Roudiez. New York: Columbia University Press, 1982.

——— 'The Adolescent Novel'. In *New Maladies of the Soul,* tr. Ross Guberman. New York: Columbia University Press, 1990: 135–53.

——— *Strangers to Ourselves,* tr. Leon S. Roudiez. London: Harvester Wheatsheaf, 1991.

Lacan, Jacques. *On Feminine Sexuality, the Limits of Love and Knowledge: The Seminar of Jacques Lacan, Book XX, Encore 1972–1973,* ed. Jacques-Alain Miller, tr. Bruce Fink. New York: Norton, 1998.

——— *The Four Fundamental Concepts of Psycho-analysis: The Seminar of Jacques Lacan, Book XI,* ed. Jacques-Alain Miller, tr. Alan Sheridan. New York: Norton, 1998.

——— *Écrits,* tr. Bruce Fink. New York: Norton, 2006.

LaCapra, Dominick. *Writing History, Writing Trauma.* London: John Hopkins University Press, 2001.

Ladenson, Elisabeth. 'Rereading Proust: Perversion and Prolepsis in *A la recherche du temps perdu*'. In *Second Thoughts,* ed. Galef: 249–65.

Latham, Don. 'Childhood in the Books of Lois Lowry'. In *The Lion and the Unicorn* 26:1 (January 2002): 1–15.

——— 'Magical Realism and the Child Reader: The Case of David Almond's *Skellig*'. *Alice's Academy* (January 2006). http://www.the-looking-glass.net/rabbit/v10i1/alice1.html [accessed 28 January 2008].

——— 'The Cultural Work of Magical Realism in Three Young Adult Novels'. *Children's Literature in Education* 38:1 (March 2007): 59–70.

Leavis, Q.D. *Fiction and the Reading Public* (c1932). London: Chatto and Windus, 1965.

Lenz, Millicent. *Nuclear-Age Literature for Youth: The Quest for a Life-Affirming Ethic.* Chicago, IL: American Library Association, 1990.

——— , ed. *His Dark Materials Illuminated: Critical Essays on Philip Pullman's Trilogy.* Detroit, MI: Wayne State University Press, 2005.

Lesnik-Oberstein, Karín. *Children's Literature: New Approaches.* Houndmills: Palgrave Macmillan, 2004.

Lewis, C S. *Surprised by Joy*. New York: Harcourt, 1956.
———— *An Experiment in Criticism*. Cambridge: Cambridge University Press, 1961.
———— *They Asked for a Paper: Papers and Addresses*. London: Bles, 1962.
———— 'On Three Ways of Writing for Children'. *Horn Book Magazine* 38 (October 1963): 459–69. Rpt. in *Of Other Worlds: Essays and Stories*. New York: Harcourt Brace Jovanovich, 1966: 22–34.
———— 'On Stories'. In *Essays Presented to Charles Williams*, ed. C.S. Lewis. Grand Rapids, MI: Eerdmans, 1966. Rpt. in *Of Other Worlds: Essays and Stories*. New York: Harcourt Brace Jovanovich, 1966: 1–21.
———— *Present Concerns*, ed. W. Hooper. London: Harcourt Brace Jovanovich, 1986.
Liddell, H.G. and R. Scott, eds., *Liddell and Scott Greek-English Lexicon* (Oxford: Clarendon Press, 1996, 9th Edition.
Lotherington, John, ed. *The Seven Ages of Life*. The Centre for Reform, 2002.
Lurie, Alison. *Don't Tell the Grownups: Subversive Children's Literature*. Boston, MA: Little, 1990.
———— *Boys and Girls Forever: Reflections on Children's Classics*. London: Chatto & Windus, 2003.
Lyotard, Jean-Francois. *The Postmodern Condition: A Report on Knowledge*, tr. Geoff Bennington and Brian Massumi. Minneapolis: 1984.
Maier, Sarah. 'Educating Harry Potter: A Muggle's Perspective on Magic and Knowledge in the Wizard World of J.K. Rowling'. In *Scholarly Studies in Harry Potter*, ed. C. Hallett: 7–28.
Manlove, C.N. *Modern Fantasy: Five Studies*. Cambridge: Cambridge University Press, 1975.
McCallum, Robyn. *Ideologies of Identity in Adolescent Fiction: The Dialogic Construction of Subjectivity*. London: Routledge, 1999.
McClure, John. 'Postmodern/Post-Secular: Contemporary Fiction and Spirituality'. *Modern Fiction Studies* 41.5 (1995): 141–63.
McDowell, Myles. 'Fiction for Children and Adults: Some Essential Differences'. In *Children's Literature in Education* (1972) and collected in *Writers, Critics and Children*, eds. Fox et al. London: Heinemann Educational, 1976.
McFarland, Thomas. *Romanticism and the Heritage of Rousseau*. Clarendon Press: Oxford, 1995.
McGann, Jerome. *The Romantic Ideology: A Critical Investigation*. Chicago: University of Chicago Press, 1983.
McGavran, James H., ed. *Romanticism and Children's Literature in Nineteenth-Century England*. Athens: University of Georgia Press, 1991.
———— , ed. *Literature and the Child: Romantic Continuations, Postmodern Contestations*. Iowa City: University of Iowa Press, 1999.
———— 'Romantic Continuations, Postmodern Contestations, or, "It's a Magical World, Hobbes, Ol' Buddy" . . . Crash!' In *Literature and the Child*, ed. McGavran: 1–22.
McGillis, Roderick. *The Nimble Reader: Literary Theory and Children's Literature*. New York: Twayne, 1996.
———— *Voices of the Other: Children's Literature and the Postcolonial Context*. London: Garland, 2000.
McHale, Brian. *Postmodern Fiction*. London: Routledge, 1987.
McMaster, Juliet. '"Adults' Literature" By Children.' *The Lion and the Unicorn* 25:2 (April 2001): 277–99.
Medved, Michael and Diane. *Saving Childhood: Protecting Our Children from the National Assault on Innocence*. London: Harper Paperbacks, 1998.
Meek, Margaret and Victor Watson. *Coming of Age in Children's Literature*. London: Continuum, 2003.
Miklitsch, Robert. 'Difference: Roland Barthes's Pleasure of the Text, Text of Pleasure'. In *boundary* 2, Vol. 12: 1 (Autumn, 1983): 101–114.
Milbank, John. 'Problematizing the Secular: The Post-postmodern Agenda'. In *Shadow of Spirit: Postmodernism and Religion*, eds. Berry and Wernick: 30–44.
Milner, Joseph O'Beirne and Lucy F. M. Milner. *Webs and Wardrobes. Humanist and Religious World Views in Children's Literature*. Lanham, MD: University Press of America, 1987.
Moore, Sharon. *We Love Harry Potter*. New York: St Martin's Griffin, 1999.
Morson, Gary Saul and Caryl Emerson. *Mikhail Bakhtin: Creation of a Prosaics*. Stanford, CA: Stanford University Press, 1990.
Morson, Gary Saul. *Narrative and Freedom: The Shadows of Time*. New Haven: Yale University Press, 1996.

Mullan, John. *How Novels Work*. Oxford: Oxford University Press, 2006.

Myers, Mitzi. 'Reading Children and Homeopathic Romanticism: Paradigm Lost, Revisionary Gleam, or "Plus Ça Change, Plus C'est la Meme Chose"?' In *Literature and the Child*, ed. McGavran: 44–84.

Nabokov, Vladimir. *Lectures on Literature*, ed. F. Bowers. New York: Harcourt Brace Jovanovich, 1980.

Natov, Roni. 'Harry Potter and the Extraordinariness of the Ordinary'. *The Lion and the Unicorn* 25:2 (April, 2001): 310–27.

——— *The Poetics of Childhood*. New York: Routledge, 2002.

Nel, Philip. *J.K. Rowling's Harry Potter Novels: A Reader's Guide*. London: Continuum, 2001.

Nell, Victor. *Lost in a Book: The Psychology of Reading for Pleasure*. New Haven, NJ: Yale University Press, 1988.

Nikolajeva, Maria. *Children's Literature Comes of Age: Toward a New Aesthetic*. London: Garland Publishing, 1996.

——— 'Exit Children's Literature?' *The Lion and the Unicorn* 22: 2 (April 1998): 221–236.

——— *From Mythic to Linear: Time in Children's Literature*. Lanham, MD: Scarecrow Press, 2000.

Nodelman, Perry. *The Pleasures of Children's Literature*. New York: Longman, 1996.

Odden, Karen. 'Retrieving Childhood Fantasies: A Psychoanalytic Look at Why We (Re)read Popular Literature'. In *Second Thoughts*, ed. Galef: 126–51.

O'Keefe, Daniel. *Stolen Lightning: The Social Theory of Magic*. London: Continuum, 1982.

Olivier, Marc. 'Lessons for the Four-year-old Botanist: Rousseau's "Forgotten Science" of Childhood'. In *The Child in French and Francophone Literature*, ed. Buford Norman. New York: Rodopi, 2004: 161–70.

Owen, Hazel. 'Once Upon a Time … There Was a Children's Book'. *School Librarian* 44:2 (1996): 45–46.

Oziewicz, Marek. 'The "Towards" and "back to" Human Value Movements in Fantasy Fiction'. In *Towards or Back to Human Values*, eds. Deszcz-Tryhubczak and Oziewicz: 2–16.

——— 'Envisioning Spirituality in a New Paradigm: Madeline L'Engle's *Time Quartet* and the Hope for Humanity's Survival'. In *Towards or Back to Human Values*, eds. Deszcz-Tryhubczak and Oziewicz: 62–81.

Palmer, Sue. *Toxic Childhood: How the Modern World is Damaging Our Children and What We Can Do About It*. London: Orion, 2006.

Payne, Max. 'Science and Spirituality in Philip Pullman's *His Dark Materials*'. In *Towards or Back to Human Values*, eds. Deszcz-Tryhubczak and Oziewicz: 220–26.

Pennington, John. 'From Elfland to Hogwarts, or the Aesthetic Trouble with Harry Potter'. In *Children's Literature Association Papers* 25, eds. Knoepflemacher and M. Myers: 78–89.

Pharr, Mary. '*In Medias Res*: Harry Potter as Hero-in-Progress'. In *The Ivory Tower*, ed. Lana Whited: 53–66.

Piaget, Jean. *The Child's Conception of the World* (*La Représentation du Monde Chez l'Enfant*, c1926). In *Selected Works*, tr. Joan and Andrew Tomlinson. London: Routledge, 1997.

Pinsent, Pat, ed. *Books and Their Boundaries: Writers and Their Audiences*. Staffordshire: Pied Piper Publishing, 2004.

——— 'The Education of a Wizard: Harry Potter and His Predecessors'. In *The Ivory Tower*, ed. Whited: 27–50.

——— 'Revisioning Religion and Spirituality: Contemporary Fantasy for Young Readers'. In *Towards or Back to Human Values*, eds. Deszcz-Tryhubczak and Oziewicz: 48–61.

Pike, David. *Passage Through Hell: Modernist Descents, Medieval Underworlds*. London: Cornell University Press, 1997.

Plato. *The Republic* (*circa* 360BC), tr. Desmond Lee. Harmondsworth: Penguin, 1974, 2nd edition.

Postman, Neil. *The Disappearance of Childhood*. London: W.H. Allen, 1983.

Propp, Vladimir. *Morphology of the Folktale*, trans. Laurence Scott. London: University of Texas Press, 1968.

Proust, Marcel. *On Reading Ruskin: Prefaces to* La Bible d'Amiens *and* Sésame et les Lys, ed. and tr. Jean Autret, William Burford and Phillip J. Wolfe. New Haven: Yale University Press, 1987.

Pullman, Philip. 'What! No Soap?' In *Notes from the Royal Society of Literature* 20 (2002): 42–52.

——— 'Writing Fantasy Realistically'. Sea of Faith National Conference (2002). *http://sofn.org.uk/conferences/pullman2002.html* [accessed 28 January 2008].

———— 'Miss Goddard's Grave'. University of East Anglia Lecture. *http://www.philip-pullman. com/pages/content/index.asp?PageID=113* [accessed 28 January 2008].

———— His Dark Materials*: The Definitive Guide.* London: Scholastic, 2007.

———— 'Introduction'. In *John Milton's* Paradise Lost. Oxford: Oxford University Press, 2005, 1–15.

Rabaté, Jean-Michel, ed. *The Cambridge Companion to Lacan.* Cambridge: Cambridge University Press, 2007.

Rapaport, Herman. *Heidegger and Derrida: Reflections on Time and Language.* London: University of Nebraska Press, 1989.

Reynolds, Kimberley, ed. *Childhood Remembered: Proceedings from the 4th Annual IBBY/MA Children's Literature Conference at Roehampton Institute, London. NCRCL Papers 3.* London: Roehampton Institute, 1998.

Richardson, Alan. 'Romanticism and the End of Childhood'. In *Literature and the Child,* ed. McGavran: 23–44.

Ricoeur, Paul. *Time and Narrative,* trs. Kathleen McLaughlin and David Pellauer. Chicago: University of Chicago Press, 1984, 3 vols.

Riddle, Mary. 'Childhood'. In *The Seven Ages of Life,* ed. Lotherington: 35–56.

Riegel, Klaus. 'Adult Life Crises: a Dialectical Interpretation of Development'. In *Life-Span Developmental Psychology: Normative Life Crises,* eds. Nancy Datan and Leon H. Gindberg. New York: Academic Press, 1975.

———— 'The Dialectics of Human Development'. *American Psychologist* 31, 10 (1976): 689–700.

Rose, Jacqueline. *The Case of Peter Pan: or the Impossibility of Children's Fiction.* Basingstoke: Macmillan, 1984.

Rosen, J. 'Breaking the Age Barrier'. *Publishers Weekly* (9 August 1997). *http://publishersweekly. reviewsnews.com* [Accessed 11 November 2002].

Rosenberg, Teya. 'Magical Realism and Children's Literature: Diane Wynne Jones's *Black Maria* and Salman Rushdie's *Midnight's Children* as a Test Case'. In *Papers: Explorations into Children's Literature* 11:1 (April 2001): 14–25.

Rosenblum, Robert. *The Romantic Child from Runge to Sendak.* Thames and Hudson, 1988.

Routledge, Christopher. 'Harry Potter and the Mystery of Ordinary Life'. In *Mystery in Children's Literature: From the Rational to the Supernatural,* eds. A. Gavin and C. Routledge. Houndmills: Palgrave, 2001: 202–08.

Rudd, David. 'Shirley, the Bathwater, and Definitions of Children's Literature'. *Papers: Explorations into Children's Literature* 5: 2–3 (1994): 88–103.

Ruddick, Nicholas, ed. *State of the Fantastic: Studies in the Theory and Practice of Fantastic Literature and Film.* Greenwich, CT: Greenwood Press, 1992.

Rushdie, Salman. *The Wizard of Oz.* London: BFI Publishing, 1992.

———— *Imaginary Homelands: Essays and Criticism, 1981–1991.* London: Granta Books, 1992.

Russell, David. 'Young Adult Fairy Tales for the New Age: Francesca Lia Block's *The Rose and the Beast'. Children's Literature in Education* 33:2 (June 2002): 107–115.

Rustin, Margaret and Michael Rustin. *Narratives of Love and Loss. Studies in Modern Children's Fiction.* London: Verso, 1987.

Sartre, Jean-Paul. *Sketch for a Theory of the Emotions* (c1939), tr. Philip Mairet. London: Methuen, 1962.

Schafer, Elizabeth. *Exploring Harry Potter.* London: Ebury, 2000.

Schakel, Peter. *The Longing for a Form: Essays on the Fiction of C.S. Lewis.* Kent, OH: Kent State University Press, 1977.

———— *Imagination and the Arts in C.S. Lewis: Journeying to Narnia and Other Worlds.* London: University of Missouri Press, 2002.

Sennett, Richard. *The Corrosion of Character. The Personal Consequences of Work in the New Capitalism.* 1999.

Shapiro, Marc. *J.K. Rowling: The Wizard Behind Harry Potter.* New York: Griffin, 2000.

Shavit, Zohar. *Poetics of Children's Literature.* Athens, GA: University of Georgia Press, 1986.

———— 'The Double Attribution of Texts for Children and How It Affects Writing for Children'. In *Transcending Boundaries,* ed. Beckett, 83–98.

Shklovsky, Victor. 'Art as Technique' (c1917), trs. Lee Lemon and Marion Reis. In *Modern Criticism and Theory: a Reader,* ed., David Lodge. London: Longmans, 1988: 16–30.

Sidney, Sir Philip. *A Defence of Poetry* (or, *An Apology for Poetry,* c1595), ed. J.A. Van Dorsten. Oxford: Oxford University Press, 1966.

Skubala, Piotr and Marek Oziewicz. 'Do We Live on the Symbiotic Planet? Ecological Principles of Life on Earth and Their Literary Implications'. In *Towards or Back to Human Values*, eds. Deszcz-Tryhubczak and Oziewicz: 150–60.

Sommerville, John. *The Rise and Fall of Childhood*. Beverly Hills: Sage Publications, 1982.

Sontag, Susan. *At the Same Time: Essays and Speeches*. New York: Farrar, Straus and Giroux, 2007.

Spretnak, Charlene. *States of Grace: Recovery of Meaning in the Postmodern Age*. London: HarperCollins, 1991.

Spufford, Francis. *The Child That Books Built. A Memoir of Childhood and Reading*. London: Faber & Faber, 2002.

Squires, Claire. *Philip Pullman, Master Storyteller: A Guide to the Worlds of His Dark Materials*. London: Continuum, 2007.

Stephens, John. *Language and Ideology in Children's Fiction*. London: Longman, 1992.

———— 'Children's Literature, Text and Theory: What Are We Interested in Now?' In *Papers: Explorations into Children's Literature* 10:2 (August 2000): 12–21.

Stone, Lawrence. *The Family, Sex and Marriage in England, 1500–1800*. London: 1977.

Suransky, Dorothy. *The Erosion of Childhood*.(1982), Chicago: University of Chicago Press, 1982.

Swanson, Philip. 'Magic Realism and Children's Literature: Isabel Allende's *La Ciudad de las Bestias*'. In *A Companion to Magical Realism*, eds. Stephen Hart and Wen-chin Ouyang. Woodbridge: Támesis, 2005: 168–80.

———— 'Latin Lessons for Young Americans: Isabel Allende's Fiction for Children'. *Revista de Estudios Hispánicos* 41 (2007): 173–89.

Swinfen, Ann. *In Defence of Fantasy: A Study of the Genre in English and American Literature since 1945*. London: Routledge, 1984.

Sylvester, Louise. 'A Knock at the Door: Reading Judith Kerr's Picture Books in the Context of Her Holocaust Fiction'. *The Lion and the Unicorn* 26:1 (January 2002): 16–30.

Tamburri, A.J. *Semiotics of Re-Reading: Guido Gozzano, Aldo Palazzeschi, and Italo Calvino*. London: Associated University Presses, 2003.

Tandello, Emmanuela, 'Semiotics of Re-reading'. *Modern Language Review* 102: 2 (April 2007): 536–37.

Taylor, Charles. *Sources of the Self: The Making of the Modern Identity*. Cambridge, MA: Harvard University Press, 1989.

Taylor, Mark. *Erring: A Postmodern A/theology*. Chicago: Chicago University Press, 1984.

Taylor, Simon, ed. *Children's Publishing—Market Assessment*. Keynote, 2005.

Teare, Elizabeth. 'Harry Potter and the Technology of Magic'. In *The Ivory Tower*, ed. Lana Whited: 329–42.

Thacker, Deborah. 'Disdain or Ignorance? Literary Theory and the Absence of Children's Literature'. *The Lion and the Unicorn* 24.1 (January 2000): 1–17.

Thorne, Brian. *Infinitely Beloved: The Challenge of Divine Intimacy*. London: Darton, Longman & Todd Ltd, 2003.

Tucker, Nicholas. 'The Rise and Rise of Harry Potter'. *Children's Literature in Education* 30, 4 (December 1999): 221–34.

———— *Darkness Visible: Inside the World of Philip Pullman*. Thriplow, Cambridge: Wizard Books, 2003.

———— 'Depressive Stories for Children'. *Children's Literature in Education* 37:3 (September 2006): 199–210.

Todorov, Tzvetan. *The Fantastic: a Structural Approach to a Literary Genre*, tr. Richard Howard. Cleveland, OH: Case Western Reserve University Press, 1973.

Tolkien, J R R. *Tree and Leaf*, ed. J.R.R. Tolkien. London: Allen and Unwin, 1964.

Vaihinger, Hans. *The Philosophy of 'As If'*, tr. C.K. Ogden. London: Kegan Paul, 1924.

Van der Walt, Thomas, ed. *Change and Renewal in Children's Literature*. London: Praeger, 2004.

Vice, Sue. *Children Writing the Holocaust*. Basingstoke: Palgrave Macmillan, 2004.

Wall, Barbara. *The Narrator's Voice: the Dilemma of Children's Fiction*. Basingstoke: Macmillan, 1991.

Wandless, William. 'Hogwarts vs. "The 'Values' Wasteland": Harry Potter and the Formation of Character'. In *Scholarly Studies in Harry Potter*, ed. Hallett: 217–40.

Warner, Marina. *From the Beast to the Blonde: On Fairytales and Their Tellers*. London: Chatto & Windus, 1994.

———— *Managing Monsters: Six Myths of Our Time*. London: Vintage, 1994.

—— *Fantastic Metamorphoses, Other Worlds: Ways of Telling the Self*. Oxford: Oxford University Press, 2002.

—— 'Did Harry Have to Grow Up?' *The Observer* (29 June 2003).

Warnes, Christopher. 'Naturalizing the Supernatural: Faith, Irreverence and Magical Realism'. *Literature Compass* 2:1 (January 2005). *http://www.blackwell-synergy.com* [accessed 28 January 2008].

Watson, Victor. *Reading Series Fiction: From Arthur Ransome to Gene Kemp*. London: Routledge, 2000.

Webb, Jean. 'Beyond the Knowing: the Frontier of the Real and the Imaginary in David Almond's *Skellig* and *The Fire-Eaters*'. In *Towards or Back to Human Values*, eds. Deszcz-Tryhubczak and Oziewicz: 242–51.

White, Michael. *C.S. Lewis. The Boy Who Chronicled Narnia, a Biography*. London: Abacus, 2005.

Whited, Lana A., ed. *The Ivory Tower and Harry Potter: Perspectives on a Literary Phenomenon*. Columbia, MO: University of Missouri Press, 2003.

Whitehead, Anne. *Trauma Fiction*. Edinburgh: Edinburgh University Press, 2004.

Wilkie, Christine. 'The Garden, the Wolf and the Dream of Childhood: From Philippa Pearce to Gillian Cross'. In *Childhood Remembered*, ed. Reynolds: 91–105.

Williams, Raymond. 'Advertising: the Magic System'. In *Problems in Materialism and Culture*. London: Verso, 1980.

Wojcik-Andrews, Ian. *Children's Films: History, Ideology, Pedagogy, Theory*. London: Garland, 2002.

Woolf, Virginia. 'Mr Bennett and Mrs Brown' (c1923). In Virginia Woolf, *A Woman's Essays*. London: Penguin, 1992: 69–87.

Wyschogrod, Edith. *Saints and Postmodernism*. Chicago: Chicago University Press, 1990.

Zamora, Lois Parkinson and Wendy B. Faris, eds. *Magical Realism: Theory, History and Community*. London: Duke University Press, 1995.

Ziegler, James D. 'Primitive, Newtonian and Einsteinian Fantasies: Three Worldviews'. In *The Scope of the Fantastic: Theory, Technique, Major Authors*, eds. Collins and Pearce, 1985: 69–75.

Zipes, Jack. *Breaking the Magic Spell: Radical Theories of Folk and Fairy Tales*. Lexington, KY: the University Press of Kentucky, 2002.

—— 'The Liberating Potential of the Fantastic Projection in Fairy Tales for Children'. In *The Scope of the Fantastic*, eds. Collins and Pearce, 1985: 309–25.

—— *Fairy Tale as Myth; Myth as Fairy Tale*. Lexington, KY: The University Press of Kentucky, 1994.

—— *Fairy Tales and the Art of Subversion: The Classical Genre for Children and the Process of Civilization*. London: Routledge, 1995.

—— *Happily Ever After: Fairy Tales, Children, and the Culture Industry*. New York: Routledge, 1997.

—— *When Dreams Came True: Classical Fairy Tales and their Tradition*. London: Routledge, 1998.

—— *Sticks and Stones: The Troublesome Success of Children's Literature from Slovenly Peter to Harry Potter*. London: Routledge, 2002.

Žižek, Slavoj. *The Sublime Object of Ideology*. London: Verso, 1989.

—— *Looking Awry: An Introduction to Jacques Lacan through Popular Culture*. Cambridge, MA: MIT Press, 1991.

—— *Welcome to the Desert of the Real: Five Essays on September 11 and Related Dates*. London: Verso, 2002.

Zornado, Joseph. *Inventing the Child: Culture, Ideology and the Story of Childhood*. London: Garland Publishing, 2001.

Index